EDMUND CLARENCE STEDMAN

Photogravure after a photograph from life

COMMITTEE OF SELECTION

EDWARD EVERETT HALE, Author of "The Man Without a Country."

JOHN B. GORDON, Former United States Senator.

NATHAN HASKELL DOLE, Associate Editor "International Library of Famous Literature."

JAMES B. POND, Manager Lecture Bureau; Author of "Eccentricities of Genius.'

GEORGE MCLEAN HARPER, Professor of English Literature, Princeton University.

LORENZO SEARS, Professor of English Literature, Brown University.

EDWIN M. BACON, Former Editor "Boston Advertiser" and "Boston Post."

J. WALKER MCSPADDEN, Managing Editor "Édition Royale" of Balzac's Works.

F. CUNLIFFE OWEN, Member Editorial Staff "New York Tribune."

TRUMAN A. DEWEESE, Member Editorial Staff "Chicago Times-Herald."

CHAMP CLARK, Member of Congress from Missouri.

MARCUS BENJAMIN, Editor, National Museum, Washington, D. C.

CLARK HOWELL, Editor "Atlanta Constitution."

INTRODUCTIONS AND SPECIAL ARTICLES BY

THOMAS B. REED,   HAMILTON WRIGHT MABIE,
LORENZO SEARS,   JONATHAN P. DOLLIVER,
CHAMP CLARK,   EDWARD EVERETT HALE,
          ALBERT ELLERY BERGH.

NOTE.—A large number of the most distinguished speakers of this country and Great Britain have selected their own best speeches for this Library. These speakers include Whitelaw Reid, William Jennings Bryan, Henry van Dyke, Henry M. Stanley, Newell Dwight Hillis, Joseph Jefferson, Sir Henry Irving, Arthur T. Hadley, John D. Long, David Starr Jordan, and many others of equal note.

CONTENTS

VOLUME IX

CONTENTS

ILLUSTRATIONS

VOLUME IX

HAMILTON WRIGHT MABIE

POE'S PLACE IN AMERICAN LITERATURE

[Address by Hamilton Wright Mabie, editor, essayist, lecturer (born in Cold Spring, N. Y., December 13, 1845; ———), delivered at the University of Virginia, Charlottesville, on the occasion of the unveiling of the Zolney bust of Edgar Allan Poe, October 7, 1899, the fiftieth anniversary of Poe's death.]

One fact about our literature has not received adequate attention—the fact that it had no childhood. In its beginnings it was the record of a people who had long passed the age of play and dreams, and were given over to pressing and exacting work. We are a young nation, but an old people; and our books, as distinguished from English books, are the products of a mature people in a new world. The world in which books are written has much to do with their quality, their themes, and their form; but the substance of the books of power is the deposit of experience in the hearts and minds of a race. In American literature we have a fresh field and an old race; we have new conditions, and an experience which antedates them. We were educated in the Old World, and a man carries his education with him. He cannot escape it, and would lose incalculably if he could.

The kind of originality which inheres in a new race and runs into novel forms we do not and shall not possess; the kind of originality which issues out of direct and hand-to-hand dealing with nature and life we may hope to develop on the scale of the Greeks or the English. A great literature must be waited for, and while we are waiting it is wise to be hopeful of the future; for expectation is often a kind of prophecy, and to believe in the possibility of

815

doing the best things in the best way is in itself a kind of preparation. To say that literature in this country, to the close of this century, is the product of an old race is not to charge it with lack of first-hand insight and force, but to explain some of its characteristics.

Goethe speaks of his mother's joyousness and love of stories. Her temperament was the gift which irradiated the pedantic father's bequest of order, industry, and method to the author of Faust. Art is the constant assertion that man has a right to live as well as to work; that the value of work depends largely upon spontaneity; and that the springs which gush from the soil have the greatest power of assuaging the thirst of the soul. This element of the uncalculated, the spontaneous, the uncontrolled, or at least undirected play of human energy finds full and free expression in the literature of the youth of races, and is the special and prime quality of literature at that stage of development. As the man is born first in the boy's temper and spirit and ideals, and born again in the struggles of experience, so the creative imagination of a race is shaped, colored, and formed largely in the earliest contacts of that race with nature and with life; with the order about it, and the inward and outward happenings of its life. Work and play, the conscious putting forth of energy and the unconscious responsiveness to all manner of impressions, must be kept in equilibrium, if there is to be continuous and rich productiveness. But the pressure of suffering and toil is so great upon the mature race, as upon the mature man, that it can be met only by a great accumulation in youth of idealism and joy. In the popular epics and in the early ballads there is a freshness, a vitality, an uncalculated and captivating charm, which make the reader of a more sophisticated age feel that in reading or hearing them he is near the springs of literature.

That there are close and vital ties between all the arts of expression and the life behind them; that the poem and the story reflect in interior and elusive but very real ways the quality of the race which fashioned them; that genius itself, although in a sense independent of character, is conditioned, for its full, free, and highest expression, upon character, the large majority of students of literature are

HAMILTON WRIGHT MABIE
Photogravure after a photograph from life

agreed.   But these structural laws are never obvious in
the great works of art; they are obeyed, not because they
have been arbitrarily imposed by an authority from without, but because they are at one with the deepest artistic
impulses and necessities.   Shakespeare does not need to
remind himself that he is an Englishman in order to write
like one; he has but to follow the line of least resistance in
expression, and his work will be English to the core.

Literature may be said to approach perfection in the
degree in which it reveals the life behind it, and at the
same time conceals all trace of intention, contrivance, or
method in making its revelation.   In the highest work of
all kinds obedience is spontaneous and apparently unconscious; for it is of the very essence of art that all traces of
the workman should be effaced.   A great poem has the
volume, the flow, the deep and silent fulness, of a river;
one cannot calculate the force of the springs which feed it;
one gets from it only a continuous impression of exhaustless and effortless power.   One has but to glance at the
Rhone to feel that the Alps are feeding it.   In the literature of races in their youth there may be no greater power
than in the literature of the same races at maturity, but
there is likely to be more buoyancy, confident ease, overflowing vitality, than at a later period; and these earlier
works enrich all later work by the qualities they bring into
the race consciousness.   There was something in Homer
which the dramatists could not reproduce, but which prof-
ited them much; there was a joy, a delight in life, a fragrance of the morning, in Chaucer which, reappearing in
Shakespeare, make the weight of tragedy bearable.   It is
well for a race, as for a man, that it has childhood behind it,
and that in those first outpourings of energy in play the
beauty of the new day and the young world sinks into its
heart and becomes part of its deepest consciousness; for it
is out of these memories and dreams that the visions of art
issue.   The artist is always a child in freshness of feeling;
in unworldly delight in the things which do not add to
one's estate, but which make for inward joy and peace; in
that easy possession of the world which brings with it the
sense of freedom, the right to be happy, and the faith that
life is greater than its works, and a man more important
than his toil.   A race, like an individual, must get this con-

sciousness of possession before the work of the day becomes imperative and absorbing. The man who has not
learned to play in childhood is not likely to learn to play
in maturity; and without the spirit of play—the putting forth of energy as an end in itself, and for the sake
of the joy which lies in pure activity—there can be no
art. For work becomes art only when it is transformed
into play.

Our race has had its youth, its dreams and visions; but
that youth was lived on another continent; so far as the
record of experience in our literature is concerned, we
have always been mature people at hard work. The beginnings of our art are to be found, therefore, not in epics,
ballads, songs, and stories, but in records of exploration,
reports of pioneers, chronicles and histories; in Captain
John Smith's "True Relation of Such Occurrences and
Accidents of Note as Hath Happened in Virginia"; in
William Bradford's "History of Plymouth"; in John
Winthrop's "History of New England," a narrative not
without touches of youth—"We had now fair sunshine
weather, and so pleasant a sweet air as did much
refresh us, and there came a smell off the shore like the
smell of a garden"; in Cotton Mather's "Magnalia"; in
"Poor Richard's Almanac"; in Mrs. Bradstreet's rhymed
history of "The Four Monarchies"; in Michael Wiggles-
worth's "Day of Doom," of which Lowell said that it became "the solace of every fireside, the flicker of the pine
knots by which it was conned perhaps adding a livelier
relish to its premonitions of eternal combustion." There
are touches of beauty in Jonathan Edwards at his best;
there is a spiritual charm in John Woolman's Journal; the
directness and simplicity of genuine literature are in
Franklin's Autobiography; in Freneau and Hopkinson
there are strains which, in a more fortunate time, might
easily have turned to melody; there were great notes
struck by the writers and orators of the Revolutionary
period—by Jefferson, Madison, Hamilton, Henry. But
in all this early expression of the English race in the New
World there is a clear, definite purpose, an ulterior aim,
a subordination of the art to the religious or political intention, which stamp the writing of the time as essentially
secondary.

Art involves forgetfulness of immediate ends; complete surrender to the inward impulse to give form to the beautiful idea or image or truth because it is beautiful. Of the naïveté of the old ballad, the careless rapture of Chaucer when the lark sings and the meadows grow sweet with the breath of May, the free and joyous play of imagination in Shakespeare, there is no trace in early writing on this continent. That writing was serious and weighty, often touching the heights of eloquence in noble argument for the inviolability of those rights which are the heritage of the English race; but the spontaneity, the freedom, the joyousness, of creative art were not in it. They could not be in it; the men who wrote our early chronicles and histories, who took part in the great debates which preceded the Revolution, and made the speeches which were heard from Williamsburg to Boston, had other work to do.

In Charles Brockden Brown a new note is heard—a note of mystery and tragedy; as if into the working world of the new continent the old elements of fate had come, to give experience a deeper tinge, and to make men aware that in the fresh as in the long-tilled soil the seeds of conflict and sorrow are sown. There is none of the joyousness of youth in Brown's romances; but there is the sense of power, the play of the imagination, the passion for expression for its own sake, which are the certain signs of literature. There is, above all, the dæmonic element, that elusive, incalculable, mysterious element in the soul of the artist, which is present in all art; and which, when it dominates the artist, forms those fascinating, mysterious personalities, from Aristophanes to Poe, who make us feel the futility of all easy endeavors to formulate the laws of art, or to explain with assurance the relations of genius to inheritance, environment, education, and temperament. In art, as in all products of the creative force, there is a mystery which we cannot dispel. If we could analyze genius, we should destroy it. To the time of the publication of Wieland, or the Transformation, it is easy to explain the written expression of American life, to show how it was directed and shaped by conditions in the New World; but with the publication of Wieland the inexplicable appears, the creative spirit begins to reveal itself.

Charles Brockden Brown did not master his material and organize it, and his work falls short of that harmony of spirit and form which is the evidence of a true birth of beauty; but there are flashes of insight in it, touches of careless felicity, which witness the possession of a real gift.

The prophecy which the discerning reader finds in Brown's sombre romances was fulfilled in the work of Poe and Hawthorne. It is conceivable that a student of the Puritan mind might have foreseen the coming of Hawthorne; for the great romancer, who was to search the Puritan conscience as with a lighted candle, was rooted and grounded historically in the world behind him. There was that in Hawthorne, however, which could not have been predicted: there was the mysterious coworking of temperament, insight, individual consciousness, and personality which constitutes what we call genius. On one side of Hawthorne's work there are lines of historical descent which may be clearly traced; on the other there is the inexplicable miracle, the miracle of art, the creation of the new and beautiful form. It is the first and perhaps the most obvious distinction of Edgar Allan Poe that his creative work baffles all attempts to relate it historically to antecedent conditions; that it detached itself almost completely from the time and place in which it made its appearance, and sprang suddenly and mysteriously from a soil which had never borne its like before.

There was nothing in the America of the third decade of the century which seemed to predict "The City in the Sea," "Israfel," and the lines "To Helen." It is true, work of genuine literary quality had been produced, and a notable group of writers of gift and quality had appeared. Irving had brought back the old joyousness and delight in life for its own sake in "Knickerbocker's History of New York" and in the "Sketch Book"; Cooper had uncovered the romantic element in our history in "The Spy"; "Thanatopsis" had betrayed an unexpected touch of maturity; Emerson was meditating at Concord that thin volume on "Nature," so full of his penetrating insight into the spiritual symbolism of nature phenomena and processes; Longfellow had returned from that first year of foreign residence which had enriched his fancy, and through the sympathetic quality of his mind was to make him the interpreter of the Old World to the New.   Hawthorne, born five years earlier than Poe—so like him in certain aspects of his genius, so unlike him in temperament and character—destined to divide with him the highest honors of American authorship, was hidden in that fortunate obscurity in which his delicate and sensitive genius found perhaps the best conditions for its ripening.   The "Twice-Told Tales" did not appear until 1837.   Lowell was a schoolboy, a college student, and a reluctant follower of the law; the "Biglow Papers," his most original and distinctive contribution to our literature, being still a full decade in the future.   Oliver Wendell Holmes, born in the same year with Poe—that *annus mirabilis* which gave the world Poe, Holmes, Tennyson, Lincoln, Gladstone, Darwin, Mendelssohn, and Chopin—had touched the imagination of the country by the ringing protest against the destruction of the Constitution in "Old Ironsides," and in the same decade revealed his true lyric gift in "The Last Leaf."   Whittier was a young Quaker, of gentle nature but intense convictions, who was speaking to hostile audiences and braving the perils of mob violence in his advocacy of the anti-slavery cause.

These names suggest the purity and aspiration, the high idealism and the tender domestic piety, which were soon to give early American literature its distinctive notes. To these earlier poets, romancers, and essayists were, later, to be added the name of Sidney Lanier, whose affluent nature needed another decade for its complete unfolding and coördination; and of Walt Whitman, who was so rich in the elemental qualities of imagination, and so rarely master of them.   There was something distinctive in each of these writers—something which had no place in literature before they came, and is not likely to be repeated; and yet, from Bryant to Whitman, there were certain obvious relationships, both spiritual and historical, between each writer and his environment.   Each was representative of some deep impulse finding its way to action; of some rising passion which leaped into speech before it turned to the irrevocable deed.

To the men who were young between 1830 and 1840, there was something in the air which broke up the deeps of feeling and set free the torpid imagination. For the first time in the New World it became easy and natural for men to sing. Hitherto the imagination had been invoked to give wings and fire to high argument for the rights of men; now the imagination began to speak, by virtue of its own inward impulse, of the things of its own life. In religion, in the social consciousness, in public life, there were stirrings of conscience which revealed a deepening life of the spirit among the new people. The age of provincialism, of submission to the judgment and acceptance of the taste of older and more cultivated communities, was coming to an end. Dr. Holmes called the address delivered before the Phi Beta Kappa Society at Harvard College in August, 1837, " our declaration of intellectual independence." That independence was already partially achieved when Emerson spoke those memorable words:—

" Perhaps the time is already come . . . when the sluggard intellect of this continent will look from under its iron lids and fulfill the postponed expectation of the world with something better than the exertions of mechanical skill. Our day of dependence, our long apprenticeship to the learning of other lands, draws to a close. The millions that around us are rushing into life cannot always be fed on the sere remains of foreign harvests. Events, actions, arise that must be sung, that will sing themselves. Who can doubt that poetry will revive and lead in a new age, as the star in the contellation Harp, which now flames in our zenith, astronomers announce, shall one day be the pole-star for a thousand years? "

This striving of the spirit, breaking away from the old forms and feeling after new ways of speech, was shared by all the New England writers. Beneath his apparent detachment from the agitations of his time, Dr. Holmes was as much a breaker of old images as Lowell or Whittier; and Hawthorne, artist that he was to the last touch of his pen, is still the product of Puritanism. The breath of the new time was soft and fecundating on the old soil, and the flowers that were soon afield had the hue of the sky and the shy and delicate fragrance of the New England climate in them.

Poe stood alone among his contemporaries by reason of the fact that, while his imagination was fertilized by the movement of the time, his work was not, in theme or sympathy, representative of the forces behind it.   The group of gifted men, with whom he had for the most part only casual connections, reflected the age behind them or the time in which they lived; Poe shared with them the creative impulse without sharing the specific interests and devotions of the period.   He was primarily and distinctively the artist of his time; the man who cared for his art, not for what he could say through it, but for what it had to say through him.   Emerson, Lowell, Holmes, Whittier, Bryant, Irving, and, in certain aspects of his genius, Hawthorne might have been predicted; reading our early history in the light of our later development, their coming seems to have been foreordained by the conditions of life on the new continent; and, later, Whitman and Lanier stand for and are bound up in the fortunes of the New World, and its new order of political and social life.   Poe alone, among men of his eminence, could not have been foreseen.

This fact suggests his limitations, but it also brings into clear view the unique individuality of his genius and the originality of his work.   His contemporaries are explicable; Poe is inexplicable.   He remains the most sharply defined personality in our literary history.   His verse and his imaginative prose stand out in bold relief against a background which neither suggests nor interprets them.   One may go further, and affirm that both verse and prose have a place by themselves in the literature of the world. There are, it is true, evidences of Poe's sensitiveness to the English landscape, and to certain English philosophical and literary influences.   The five years spent in the Manor House school in the suburbs of the London of the early part of the century gave the future writer of "William Wilson" and "The Fall of the House of Usher" a store of reminiscences and impressions of landscape and architecture which touched some of his later work with atmospheric effects of the most striking kind, and gave that work a sombre and significant background of immense artistic value.   It is not difficult to find in his earlier verse, as Mr. Stedman has suggested, the influence of Byron and Moore, whose songs were in the heart of that romantic generation.   It is easy also to lay bare Poe's indebtedness to Coleridge. This is only saying, however, that no man of imagination ever grows up in isolation; every sensitive spirit shares in the impulses of its time, and receives its education for its own work at the hands of older teachers. When all is said, however, Poe remains a man of singularly individual genius, owing little to his immediate or even to his remoter environment; an artist who felt keenly the spirit of his art as it has found refuge in beautiful forms, but who detached himself with consistent insistence from the influence of other artists.

Until Poe began his brief and pathetic career, the genius of Virginia and of the South had found expression chiefly in the molding of national institutions and the shaping of national affairs; and it may be said without exaggeration that rarely in the history of the world has public life been enriched by so many men of commanding intellect and natural aptitude for great affairs. The high intelligence, the wide grasp of principles, and the keen practical sense of the earlier Southern statesmen gave the stirring and formative periods of our early history epic dignity. In such a society Bacon might have found food for those organ-toned essays on the greatness of states and the splendor of national fortunes and responsibilities. It was due largely to the Virginians that the earlier public discussions and the later public papers so often partook of the quality of literature. In Poe, however, the genius of the South seemed to pass abruptly from great affairs of state into the regions of pure imagination. In "The City in the Sea," "Israfel," and the verses "To Helen"—to recall three of Poe's earliest and most representative poems—there is complete detachment from the earlier interests and occupations, and complete escape into the world of ideality. It is part of the charm of these perfect creations that they are free from all trace of time and toil. Out of the new world of work and strife magical doors were flung wide into the fairyland of pure song; out of the soil tilled with heroic labor and courage a fountain suddenly gushed from unsuspected springs.

In this disclosure of the unforeseen in our literary development, in the possession of the dæmonic element in art, Poe stands alone in our literature, unrelated to his environment and detached from his time; the most dis-

tinctive and individual writer who has yet appeared in this
country.

Among the elements which go to the making of the true
work of art, the dæmonic holds a first place. It is the
essential and peculiar quality of genius—the quality which
lies beyond the reach of the most exacting and intelligent
work, as it lies beyond the search of analysis. A trained
man may learn the secrets of form; he may become an
adept in the skill of his craft; but the final felicity of touch,
the ultimate grace of effortless power, elude and baffle
him. Shakespeare is never so wonderful as in those perfect lines, those exquisite images and similes, those
fragrant sentences akin with the flowers in their freshness,
and in their purity with waters which carry the stars in
their depths, which light comedy and tragedy and history
as with a light beyond the sun. Other aspects of his work
may be explained; but the careless rapture of such phrases
as—

> "And those eyes, the break of day,
>   Lights that do mislead the morn";

> "Daffodils,
> That come before the swallow dares, and take
> The winds of March with beauty; violets dim,
> But sweeter than the lids of Juno's eyes,"

leaves us wondering and baffled. We have no key to
them. This natural magic, this divine ease in doing the
most difficult things, is the exclusive property of the man
of genius, and is his only in his most fortunate hours. No
man can command this consummate bloom on human
speech; it lies on his work as it lies on the fields, because
the creative spirit has passed that way. It came again and
again to Wordsworth during fifteen marvelous years; and
when it passed it left him cold and mechanical. It is the
pure spirit of art moving like the wind where it listeth,
and, like the wind, dying into silence again. This magic
was in Poe, and its record remains, and will remain, one of
our most precious literary possessions. The bulk of the
work upon which it rests is not great; its ethical significance is not always evident; it is not representative
after the manner of the great masters of poetry; but its
quality is perfect. The importance of half a dozen perfect

poems is not to be discovered in their mass; it lies in the revelation of the imagination which shines in and from them.   Among a practical people, dealing with the external relations of men, and largely absorbed in the work of the hands, the sudden flashing of the " light that never was on sea or land" was a spiritual event of high significance.   That men do not live by bread alone is the common message of religion and of art.   That message was delivered by Poe with marvelous distinctness of speech.   That he knew what he wanted to say, and that he deliberately and patiently sought the best way of saying it, is clear enough; it neither adds to nor detracts from the artistic value of what he did that he knew what he wanted to do.   The essential fact about him and his work is, that he was possessed by the passion for beauty for its own sake, and that at his best he had access to the region of pure ideality.

The spiritual value of art lies not only in its power to impart ideas, but also in its power to clear the vision, to broaden the range of human interests, and to liberate the imagination.   Poe's work attests again the presence of an element in the life of man and in the work of his hand which cannot be foreseen, calculated, or controlled; a quality not dissociated in its perfect expression from historic or material conditions, but in its origin independent of them.   It is the witness, in other words, of something divine and imperishable in the mind of man—something which allies him with the creative energy, and permits him to share it.   The fact that he is sometimes unworthy of this high disclosure of the ultimate beauty, and sometimes recreant to his faith and his gift, diminishes the significance and value of his work no more than a kindred infidelity nullifies the word of prophets of another order. In the mysterious spiritual economy of the universe there are coördinations of gift and character, relations of spirit and environment, which elude all efforts to formulate them; not because they lie outside the realm of law, but because the mind of man has not yet been able to explore that realm.   And in this very incompleteness of the philosophy of art lies that inexhaustible spiritual suggestiveness which is at once the inspiration of art and its burden. Poe is distinctively and in a unique sense the artist in our literature—the man to whom beauty was a constant and sufficient justification of itself.

Such a faith is not without its perils; but in a new and working world, whose idealism had run mainly along lines of action, it was essential and it was of high importance. This single-mindedness of Poe in the pursuit of perfection in phrase and form was not a matter of mere workmanship; it was the passion to match the word with the thought, the melody with the feeling, so vitally and completely that the ultimate harmony, in which all men believe and for which all men crave, might become once more a reality amid the dissonances of a struggling and imperfect society. It is the function of the prophet to declare the inexorable will of righteousness amid a moral disorder which makes that will, at times, almost incredible; it is the office of the artist to discern and reveal the ultimate beauty in a time when all things are in the making, and the dust and uproar of the workshop conceal even the faint prophecies of perfection.

In the vast workshop of the new society, noisily and turbulently coördinating itself, Poe's work has been often misunderstood and undervalued. Its lack of strenuousness, its detachment from workaday interests, its severance from ethical agitations, its remoteness from the common toils and experiences, have given it to many an unreal and spectral aspect; there has seemed to be in it a lack of seriousness which has robbed it of spiritual significance. Its limitations in several directions are evident enough; but all our poetry has disclosed marked limitations. The difficulty in estimating Poe's work at its true value has lain in the fact that his seriousness was expressed in devotion to objects not yet included in our range of keen and quick sympathies and interests. Poe was a pioneer in a region not yet adequately represented on our spiritual charts. To men engrossed in the work of making homes for themselves the creation of a Venus of Melos might seem a very unimportant affair; its perfection of pose and molding might not wholly escape them, but the emotion which swept Heine out of himself when he first stood before it would seem to such men hysterical and unreal. When the homes were built, however, and men were housed in them, they would begin to crave completeness of life, and then the imagination would begin to discern the priceless value of the statue which has survived the days when gods appeared on the earth. The turmoil of the struggle for existence in Greece has long since died into the all-devouring silence, but that broken figure remains to thrill and inspire a world which has forgotten the name of the man who breathed the breath of life into it.   It is a visible symbol not only of the passion for perfection, but of the sublime inference of that passion—the immortality of the spirit which conceived, and of the race among which the perfect work was born.

This passion, which is always striving to realize its own imperishableness in the perfection of its work, and to continue unbroken the record of creative activity among men, possessed Poe in his best moments, and bore fruit in his imaginative work.   He was far in advance of the civilization in which he lived, in his discernment of the value of beauty to men struggling for their lives in a world full of ugliness because full of all manner of imperfection; he is still in advance of any general development of the ability to feel as he felt the inward necessity of finding harmony, and giving it reality to the mind, the eye, and the ear.   In older communities, looking at our life outside the circle of its immediate needs and tasks, he has found a recognition often denied him among his own people.   If Poe has failed to touch us in certain places where we live most deeply and passionately, we have failed to meet him where he lived deeply and passionately.   Matthew Arnold held that contemporary foreign opinion of a writer is probably the nearest approach which can be made to the judgment of posterity.   The judgment of English, French, and German critics has been, as a whole, unanimous in accepting Poe at a much higher valuation than has been placed upon him at home, where Lowell's touch-and-go reference in the "Fable for Critics" has too often been accepted as an authoritative and final opinion from the highest literary tribunal.

The men of Lowell's generation in New England could not have estimated adequately the quality of Poe's genius nor the value of his work.   Their conception of their art was high and their practice of it fruitful, but their temper of mind threw them out of sympathy with the view of art which Poe held, and which has been illustrated in much of the most enchanting poetry in the literature of the world. The masters of pure song, with whom Poe belongs, could hardly have drawn breath in the rarefied air of the New England of the first four decades. It was an atmosphere in which Emerson breathed freely, and the purity and insight of his work, like that of Hawthorne's, will remain an enduring evidence that intense moral conviction and deep moral feeling are consistent with a true and beautiful art. But Keats could not have lived in the air which Emerson found so full of inspiration; and Keats is one of the poets of the century. This is only saying that if you have one quality in a very high stage of development, you are likely to be defective in other qualities equally important.

A national literature must have many notes, and Poe struck some which in pure melodic quality had not been heard before. As literary interests broaden in this country, and the provincial point of view gives place to the national, the American estimate of Poe will approach more nearly the foreign estimate. That estimate was based mainly on a recognition of Poe's artistic quality and of the marked individuality of his work. Lowell and Longfellow continued the old literary traditions; Poe seemed to make a new tradition. The dæmonic element in him, the pure individual force, brought with it that sense of freshness and originality which men are always eager to feel, and to which they often respond with exaggerated cordiality. It is not surprising that those who are full of the passion to create, and rarely endowed with the power, sometimes go too far in rewarding the man who does what they long to do, but cannot. The artist always pushes back the boundaries a little, and opens a window here and there through which the imagination looks out upon the world of which it dreams so gloriously, but which it sees so rarely; and we are not prone to mete out with mathematical exactness our praise of those who set us free. If we lose our heads for a time when Kipling comes with his vital touch, his passionate interest in living things, the harm is not great. Poe may have been overvalued by some of his eager French and German disciples, but, after all deductions are made, their judgment was nearer the mark than ours has been; and it was nearer the mark because their conception of literature was more inclusive and adequate.

The nature of Poe's material has had something to do not only with foreign appreciation of his genius, but with the impression of distinct individuality which his work produces. Sprung from a people of naturally optimistic temper, with unbounded confidence in their ability to deal with the problems of life, Poe stands solitary among men of his class in fastening, as by instinct, upon the sombre and tragical aspects of experience. In the high light which rests upon the New World, the mysterious gloom which enshrouds "The Fall of the House of Usher," "The Lady Ligeia," and "Ulalume" is thrown into more impressive relief. Against the wide content and peaceful domesticity of this fruitful continent, the story of "Berenice," "The Assignation," and "The Masque of the Red Death" are projected with telling effectiveness. The very limitations of Poe's interests and insight contribute to the definiteness and striking individuality of his work. One finds in it no trace of that vague generalizing tendency which an English critic has recently called the "Alexandrine note" in American literature; on the contrary, every touch contributes to the sharp distinctness of the whole.

The severance between the writer and his surroundings, already noted, is constantly brought home to the reader by the subjects, the persons, and the landscapes which appear in Poe's work. Tragedy in Shakespeare's historical plays is felt to be unusual and exceptional; it belongs to a few periods, it is wrought out in the careers of small groups of persons; but it is in no sense abnormal; it readily relates itself to English character and society. The tragic element in Scott and Dickens has the same natural setting, the same normal relationship to obvious social or political conditions. The tragic element in Poe's work, on the other hand, lies deep in the recesses of individual temperament, and seems remote, unreal, and fantastic, unless we approach it sympathetically. Some of it is unreal and phantasmal; but the potentialities of Poe's tragedy are in most men. They are, however, essentially subjective; for the action in Poe's stories is really sym-

bolical; that which is significant and appalling lies behind
it.   At this point Poe and Hawthorne approach each
other, and it is the pure subjectivity of the tragedy which
gives its working out at the hands of both writers a touch
of remoteness, and in some cases an element of unreality.

Poe, like Hawthorne, gives expression to the ideality of
the American mind: an ideality disclosed in very different
ways by Emerson and Lowell and Whittier; an ideality
which has made our literature pure and high, but has
robbed it so far of a certain robustness and power shared
by all the great writers of our language beyond the sea.
American literature, as contrasted with other literature, is
touched throughout with aspiration, but lacks solidity and
passion.   These defects in Poe's works, which are often
regarded as peculiar to it, are found in the work of his
contemporaries.   It would seem as if, so far, the imagination of the country had not been adequate to the task of
penetrating and illuminating its immense practical energies; or as if its activities were too vast and varied to
admit of imaginative coördination at this early day in our
history.   Poe reacted so radically from the practical
ideals and work of his time that he took refuge in pure
ideality.

The refuge of the artist is always to be found in his art;
and to a nature so sensitive as Poe's, a mind so delicately
adjusted to its tools and its task, and so easily thrown out
of relation to them, there was perhaps no other resource.
Between the art of the author of "Israfel" and the life
about him there was a deep abyss, which the poet never
attempted to cross.   The material with which he constantly dealt becomes significant alike of the extraordinary
susceptibility of his genius, and of the lack of the forms of
life about him to satisfy and inspire him.   He expresses
the dissonance which has so far existed between the essentially ideal quality of the American mind and the intensely
practical character of the task which has fallen to Americans.   If he had been born a century later his verse and
prose might have come closer to the heart of his people,
without losing that exquisite fineness which reveals the
rare and beautiful quality of his genius.   It is hardly possible to miss the significance of the fact that two men of
such temper and gifts as Hawthorne and Poe were driven

by inward necessity to deal with the life of an earlier time, with life in an older and riper society, or with the life of the spirit in its most disturbed and abnormal experiences. Such a fact throws a penetrating light on the delicacy of the adjustments between a genius of great sensitiveness and its environment, and sets at naught the judgment, so often and so hastily reached, that the American mind is essentially materialistic. That judgment is impeached by the whole body of our literature, but Poe and Hawthorne made it absolutely untenable.

Poe's dæmonic force, his passion for perfection of form, his ideality, and the sensitiveness of his temperament are all subtly combined in the quality of distinction which characterizes his best work in prose and verse. His individuality is not only strongly marked, but it is expressed with the utmost refinement of feeling and of touch. In his prose and verse, Poe was preëminently a man who not only brought artistic integrity and capacity to his work, but suffused it with purity, dignity, and grace. In the disconnected product of his broken life there is not a line to be blotted out on the score of vulgarity, lack of reticence, or even commonplaceness. In his most careless imaginative writing the high quality of his mind is always apparent. So ingrained is this distinction of tone that, however he may waste his moral fortunes, his genius is never cheapened nor stained. In his worst estate the great traditions of art were safe in his hands.

The quality of distinction was of immense importance in a literature like our own, which is still in its formative stages. Poe's exquisite craftsmanship has made the acceptance of cheap and careless work impossible. Such work may secure an easy popularity from time to time, but it can find no lodgment in the memory of the race on this continent. To go so far as Poe went toward perfection of form is to exclude from the contest all save the fleetest and the strongest. It is to do more, for the service of the artist really begins when his work is completely finished, and separated from his own personality: it is to keep before a people tempted to take lower views of life the reality of individual superiority. In a society which holds all the doors open, and affirms in institution and structure that a man shall go where he can, there is always the danger of confusing opportunity with gift. The final justification of democracy lies in its ability to clear the way for superiority; but it is often interpreted as signifying equality of endowment and skill. If, in the long run, democracy lowers instead of advancing the standards of character and achievement, it will be the most disastrous of political failures. Equality of opportunity for the sake of preparing the way for the highest and finest individualities will bring us, perhaps, as near a perfect social order as we can hope to attain. Poe was such a personality; a man whose gifts were of the most individual kind, whose tastes were fastidious, whose genius was full of a distinction which involved and expressed remoteness from average standards, detachment from the rush and turmoil of practical tasks. A nation at work with grimed hands is a noble spectacle; but if such a people is to get anything out of life after it has secured comfortable conditions, it must not only make room for poets and scholars and thinkers, but it must reserve for them its highest rewards.

Without the presence of the superior man, the "paradise of the average man," as this country has been called, would become a purgatory to all those who care chiefly, not for success, but for freedom and power and beauty. One of the greatest privileges of the average man is to recognize and honor the superior man, because the superior man makes it worth while to belong to the race by giving life a dignity and splendor which constitute a common capital for all who live. The respect paid to men like Washington and Lincoln, Marshall and Lee, Poe and Hawthorne, affords a true measure of civilization in a community. Such men invest life for the average man with romance and beauty. Failure to recognize and honor superiority of character, gift, and achievement is the peculiar peril of democracies, which often confuse the aristocracy of the divine order in the world with the aristocracy of arbitrary and artificial origin. So long as the saints shine in their righteousness it will be idle to attempt to conceal their superiority; in the order of the spiritual life the best survive. Of these best was Poe; a man whose faults are sufficiently obvious, because they bore their fruit in his career, but the quality of whose genius and art was

of the finest, if not of the greatest. In expressing the
idealism of the American mind, this rare and subtle workman made images of such exquisite shape and molding
that by their very perfection they win us away from lesser
and meaner ways of work. By the fineness of his craftsmanship he revealed the artistic potentialities of the
American spirit.

Of a proud and sensitive nature, reared among a proud
and sensitive people, Poe found in the region of pure
ideality the material which expressed most clearly his
genius, and received most perfectly the impress of his
craftsmanship. In the themes with which he dealt, and
in the manner in which he treated them, he went far to
eradicate the provincialism of taste which was the bane
of his time and section—the bane, indeed, of the whole
country. Poe's very detachment in artistic interest from
the world about him was a positive gain for the emancipa-
tion of the imagination of the young country, so recently
a province of the Old World. His criticism was almost
entirely free from that narrow localism which values a
writer because he belongs to a section, and not because
his work belongs to literature. He brought into the field
of criticism large knowledge of the best that had been
done in literature, and clear perception of the principles
of the art of writing. His touch on his contemporaries
who won the easy successes which are always within reach
in untrained communities was often caustic, as it had need
to be; but the instinct which made him the enemy of inferior work gave him also the power of recognizing the
work of the artist, even when it came from unknown
hands. He discerned the reality of imagination in Hawthorne and Tennyson as clearly as he saw the vulgarity
and crudity of much of the popular writing of his time.

By critical intention, therefore, as well as by virtue of
the possession of genius, which is never provincial, Poe
emancipated himself, and went far to emancipate American literature, from the narrow spirit, the partial judgment, and the inferior standards of a people not yet
familiar with the best that has been thought and said in the
world. To the claims of local pride he opposed the sovereign claims of art; against the practice of the half-
inspired and the wholly untrained he set the practice of

the masters.   When the intellectual history of the country is written, he will appear as one of its foremost liberators.

Poe's work holds a first place in our literature, not by reason of its mass, its reality, its range, its spiritual or ethical significance, but by reason of its complete and beautiful individuality, the distinction of its form and workmanship, the purity of its art.   With Hawthorne he shares the primacy among all who have enriched our literature with prose or verse; but, unlike his great contemporary, he has had to wait long for adequate and just recognition.   His time of waiting is not yet over; for while the ethical insight of Hawthorne finds quick response where his artistic power alone would fail to move, Poe must be content with the suffrages of those who know that the art which he practised with such magical effect is in itself a kind of righteousness.   "I could not afford to spare from my circle," wrote Emerson to a friend, "a poet, so long as he can offer so indisputable a token as a good poem of his relation to what is highest in Being." To those who understand that character is never perfect until it is harmonious, and truth never finally revealed until it is beautiful, Poe's significance is not obscured nor his work dimmed by the faults and misfortunes of his life. The obvious lessons of that pathetic career have been well learned; it is time to seek the deeper things for which this fatally endowed spirit stood; for the light is more than the medium through which it shines.

LORD MACAULAY

A SURVEY OF FOUR CENTURIES

[Address by Thomas Babington Macaulay, statesman, historian, essayist, poet (born in Rothley Temple, Leicestershire, October 25, 1800; died in Kensington, December 28, 1859), delivered before the University of Glasgow, March 21, 1849, in pursuance of his office as Lord Rector. The entry of March 22 in Macaulay's diary thus describes the event: "Another eventful and exciting day. I was much annoyed and anxious in consequence of hearing that there were great expectations of a fine oration from me at the Town Hall. I had broken rest, partly from the effect of the bustle which was over, and partly from the apprehension of the bustle which was to come. I turned over a few sentences in my head, but was ill-satisfied with them. Well or ill-satisfied, however, I was forced to be ready when the Lord Provost called for me. I felt like a man going to be hanged; and as such a man generally does, plucked up courage to behave with decency. We went to the City Hall, which is a fine room and was crowded as full as it could hold. Nothing but huzzaing and clapping of hands. The Provost presented me with a handsome box, silver gilt, containing the freedom of the city, and made a very fine speech on the occasion. I returned thanks with sincere emotion, and I hope with propriety. What I said was very well received and I was vehemently applauded at the close. At half past two I took flight for Edinburgh, and, on arriving, drove straight from the station to Craig Crook. I had a pleasant, painful half hour with Jeffrey; perhaps the last. He was in almost hysterical excitement. His kindness and praise were quite overwhelming. The tears were in the eyes of both of us."]

GENTLEMEN:—My first duty is to return you my thanks for the honor which you have conferred on me. You well know that it was wholly unsolicited; and I can assure you that it was wholly unexpected. I may add that, if I had been invited to become a candidate for your suffrages, I should respectfully have declined the invitation.

My predecessor, whom I am so happy as to be able to call my friend, declared from this place last year, in language which well became him, that he would not have come forward to displace so eminent a statesman as Lord John Russell. I can with equal truth affirm that I would not have come forward to displace so estimable a gentleman and so accomplished a scholar as Colonel Mure. But Colonel Mure felt last year that it was not for him, and I now feel that it is not for me, to question the propriety of your decision on a point of which, by the constitution of your body, you are the judges. I therefore gratefully accept the office to which I have been called, fully purposing to use whatever powers belong to it with a single view to the welfare and credit of your society.

I am not using a mere phrase of course, when I say that the feelings with which I bear a part in the ceremony of this day are such as I find it difficult to utter in words. I do not think it strange that, when that great master of eloquence, Edmund Burke, stood where I now stand, he faltered and remained mute. Doubtless the multitude of thoughts which rushed into his mind was such as even he could not easily arrange or express. In truth there are few spectacles more striking or affecting than that which a great historical place of education presents on a solemn public day. There is something strangely interesting in the contrast between the venerable antiquity of the body and the fresh and ardent youth of the great majority of the members. Recollections and hopes crowd upon us together. The past and the future are at once brought close to us. Our thoughts wander back to the time when the foundations of this ancient building were laid, and forward to the time when those whom it is our office to guide and to teach will be the guides and teachers of our posterity. On the present occasion we may, with peculiar propriety, give such thoughts their course. For it has chanced that my magistracy has fallen on a great secular epoch. This is the four hundredth year of the existence of your University. At such jubilees, jubilees of which no individual sees more than one, it is natural, and it is good, that a society like this, a society which survives all the transitory parts of which it is composed, a society which has a corporate existence and a perpetual succession, should review its annals, should retrace the stages of its growth from infancy to maturity, and should try to find, in the experience of generations which have passed away, lessons which may be profitable to generations yet unborn.

The retrospect is full of interest and instruction. Perhaps it may be doubted whether, since the Christian era, there has been any point of time more important to the highest interests of mankind than that at which the existence of your University commenced. It was at the moment of a great destruction and of a great creation. Your society was instituted just before the empire of the East perished; that strange empire which, dragging on a languid life through the great age of darkness, connected together the two great ages of light; that empire which, adding nothing to our stores of knowledge, and producing not one man great in letters, in science, or in art, yet preserved, in the midst of barbarism, those masterpieces of Attic genius which the highest minds still contemplate, and long will contemplate, with admiring despair. And at that very time, while the fanatical Moslems were plundering the churches and palaces of Constantinople, breaking in pieces Grecian sculptures, and giving to the flames piles of Grecian eloquence, a few humble German artisans, who little knew that they were calling into existence a power far mightier than that of the victorious Sultan, were busied in cutting and setting the first types. The University came into existence just in time to witness the disappearance of the last trace of the Roman empire, and to witness the publication of the earliest printed book.

At this conjuncture, a conjuncture of unrivaled interest in the history of letters, a man, never to be mentioned without reverence by every lover of letters, held the highest place in Europe. Our just attachment to that Protestant faith to which our country owes so much must not prevent us from paying the tribute which, on this occasion, and in this place, justice and gratitude demand, to the founder of the University of Glasgow, the greatest of the restorers of learning, Pope Nicholas the Fifth. He had sprung from the common people; but his abilities and his erudition had early attracted the notice of the great. He had studied much and traveled far. He had visited Britain, which, in wealth and refinement, was to his native

Tuscany what the back settlements of America now are to
Britain. He had lived with the merchant princes of Florence, those men who first ennobled trade by making trade
the ally of philosophy, of eloquence, and of taste. It was
he who, under the protection of the munificent and discerning Cosmo, arranged the first public library that modern Europe possessed. From privacy your founder rose
to a throne; but on the throne he never forgot the studies
which had been his delight in privacy. He was the center
of an illustrious group, composed partly of the last great
scholars of Greece, and partly of the first great scholars
of Italy, Theodore Gaza and George of Trebizond, Bes-
sarion and Filelfo, Marsilio Ficino and Poggio Bracciolini.
By him was founded the Vatican library, then and long
after the most precious and the most extensive collection
of books in the world. By him were carefully preserved
the most valuable intellectual treasures which had been
snatched from the wreck of the Byzantine empire. His
agents were to be found everywhere, in the bazaars of the
farthest East, in the monasteries of the farthest West,
purchasing or copying worm-eaten parchments, on which
were traced words worthy of immortality. Under his
patronage were prepared accurate Latin versions of many
precious remains of Greek poets and philosophers. But
no department of literature owes so much to him as history. By him were introduced to the knowledge of Western Europe two great and unrivaled models of historical
composition, the work of Herodotus and the work of
Thucydides. By him, too, our ancestors were first made
acquainted with the graceful and lucid simplicity of
Xenophon and with the manly good sense of Polybius.

It was while he was occupied with cares like these that
his attention was called to the intellectual wants of this
region, a region now swarming with population, rich with
culture, and resounding with the clang of machinery, a
region which now sends forth fleets laden with its admirable fabrics to the lands of which in his days no geographer had ever heard, then a wild, a poor, a half barbarous tract, lying on the utmost verge of the known
world. He gave his sanction to the plan of establishing
a University at Glasgow, and bestowed on the new seat of
learning all the privileges which belonged to the Univer-

sity of Bologna. I can conceive that a pitying smile passed over his face as he named Bologna and Glasgow together. At Bologna he had long studied. No spot in the world had been more favored by nature or by art. The surrounding country was a fruitful and sunny country, a country of cornfields and vineyards. In the city, the house of Bentivoglio bore rule, a house which vied with the house of Medici in taste and magnificence, which has left to posterity noble palaces and temples, and which gave a splendid patronage to arts and letters. Glasgow, your founder just knew to be a poor, a small, a rude town, a town, as he would have thought, not likely ever to be great and opulent; for the soil, compared with rich country at the foot of the Apennines, was barren, and the climate was such that an Italian shuddered at the thought of it. But it is not on the fertility of the soil, it is not on the mildness of the atmosphere, that the prosperity of nations chiefly depends. Slavery and superstition can make Campania a land of beggars, and can change the plain of Enna into a desert. Nor is it beyond the power of human intelligence and energy, developed by civil and spiritual freedom, to turn sterile rocks and pestilential marshes into cities and gardens. Enlightened as your founder was, he little knew that he was himself a chief agent in a great revolution, physical and moral, political and religious, in a revolution, destined to make the last first and the first last, in a revolution destined to invert the relative positions of Glasgow and Bologna. We cannot, I think, better employ a few minutes than in reviewing the stages of this great change in human affairs.

The review shall be short. Indeed I cannot do better than pass rapidly from century to century. Look at the world, then, a hundred years after the seal of Nicholas had been affixed to the instrument which called your college into existence. We find Europe, we find Scotland especially, in the agonies of that great revolution which we emphatically call the Reformation. The liberal patronage which Nicholas, and men like Nicholas, had given to learning, and of which the establishment of this seat of learning is not the least remarkable instance, had produced an effect which they had never contemplated. Ignorance was the talisman on which their power de-

pended; and that talisman they had themselves broken.
They had called in Knowledge as a handmaid to decorate
Superstition, and their error produced its natural effect.
I need not tell you what a part the votaries of classical
learning, and especially the votaries of Greek learning, the
Humanists, as they were then called, bore in the great
movement against spiritual tyranny. They formed, in
fact, the vanguard of that movement. Every one of the
chief Reformers—I do not at this moment remember a
single exception—was a Humanist. Almost every eminent Humanist in the north of Europe was, according to
the measure of his uprightness and courage, a Reformer.
In a Scottish University I need hardly mention the names
of Knox, of Buchanan, of Melville, of Secretary Mait-
land. In truth, minds daily nourished with the best literature of Greece and Rome necessarily grew too strong to
be trammeled by the cobwebs of the scholastic divinity;
and the influence of such minds was now rapidly felt by
the whole community; for the invention of printing had
brought books within the reach even of yeomen and of
artisans. From the Mediterranean to the Frozen Sea,
therefore, the public mind was everywhere in a ferment;
and nowhere was the ferment greater than in Scotland.
It was in the midst of martyrdoms and proscriptions, in
the midst of a war between power and truth, that the first
century of the existence of your University closed.

Pass another hundred years; and we are in the midst
of another revolution. The war between Popery and
Protestantism had, in this island, been terminated by the
victory of Protestantism. But from that war another war
had sprung, the war between Prelacy and Puritanism.
The hostile religious sects were allied, intermingled, confounded with hostile political parties. The monarchical
element of the constitution was an object of almost exclusive devotion to the Prelatist. The popular element of
the constitution was especially dear to the Puritan. At
length an appeal was made to the sword. Puritanism
triumphed; but Puritanism was already divided against
itself. Independency and Republicanism were on one
side, Presbyterianism and limited Monarchy on the other.
It was in the very darkest part of that dark time, it was
in the midst of battles, sieges, and executions, it was when

the whole world was still aghast at the awful spectacle of a
British King standing before a judgment-seat and laying
his neck on a block, it was when the mangled remains of
the Duke of Hamilton had just been laid in the tomb of
his house, it was when the head of the Marquess of Montrose had just been fixed on the Tolbooth of Edinburgh,
that your University completed her second century.

A hundred years more; and we have at length reached
the beginning of a happier period.   Our civil and religious
liberties had indeed been bought with a fearful price.
But they had been bought.   The price' had been paid.
The last battle had been fought on British ground.   The
last black scaffold had been set up on Tower Hill.   The
evil days were over.   A bright and tranquil century, a
century of religious toleration, of domestic peace, of temperate freedom, of equal justice, was beginning.   That
century is now closing.   When we compare it with any
equally long period in the history of any other great
society, we shall find abundant cause for thankfulness to
the Giver of all good.   Nor is there any place in the whole
kingdom better fitted to excite this feeling than the place
where we are now assembled.   For in the whole kingdom
we shall find no district in which the progress of trade, of
manufactures, of wealth, and of the arts of life, has been
more rapid than in Clydesdale.   Your University has partaken largely of the prosperity of this city and of the surrounding region.   The security, the tranquillity, the liberty, which have been propitious to the industry of the
merchant and of the manufacturer, have been also propitious to the industry of the scholar.   To the last century
belong most of the names of which you justly boast.   The
time would fail me if I attempted to do justice to the
memory of all the illustrious men who, during that period,
taught or learned wisdom within these ancient walls;
geometricians, anatomists, jurists, philologists, metaphy-
sicians, poets; Simpson and Hunter, Millar and Young,
Reid and Stewart; Campbell, whose coffin was lately
borne to a grave in that renowned transept which contains the dust of Chaucer, of Spenser, and of Dryden;
Black, whose discoveries form an era in the history of
chemical science; Adam Smith, the greatest of all the
masters of political science; James Watt, who, perhaps,

did more than any single man has done, since the " New Atlantis " of Bacon was written, to accomplish that gloriour prophecy. We now speak the language of humility when we say that the University of Glasgow need not fear a comparison with the University of Bologna.

A fifth secular period is about to commence. There is no lack of alarmists who will tell you that it is about to commence under evil auspices. But from me you must expect no such gloomy prognostications. I have heard them too long and too constantly to be scared by them. Ever since I began to make observations on the state of my country, I have been seeing nothing but growth, and hearing of nothing but decay. The more I contemplate our noble institutions, the more convinced I am that they are sound at heart, that they have nothing of age but its dignity, and that their strength is still the strength of youth. The hurricane, which has recently overthrown so much that was great and that seemed durable, has only proved their solidity. They still stand, august and immovable, while dynasties and churches are lying in heaps of ruin all around us. I see no reason to doubt that, by the blessing of God on a wise and temperate policy, on a policy of which the principle is to preserve what is good by reforming in time what is evil, our civil institutions may be preserved unimpaired to a late posterity, and that, under the shade of our civil institutions, our academical institutions may long continue to flourish.

I trust, therefore, that, when a hundred years more have run out, this ancient College will still continue to deserve well of our country and of mankind. I trust that the installation of 1949 will be attended by a still greater assembly of students than I have the happiness now to see before me. That assemblage, indeed, may not meet in the place where we have met. These venerable halls may have disappeared. My successor may speak to your successors in a more stately edifice, in an edifice which, even among the magnificent buildings of the future Glasgow, will still be admired as a fine specimen of the architecture which flourished in the days of the good Queen Victoria. But, though the site and the walls may be new, the spirit of the institution will, I hope, be still the same. My successor will, I hope, be able to boast that the fifth century of the University has even been more glorious than the fourth.   He will be able to vindicate that boast by citing a long list of eminent men, great masters of experimental science, of ancient learning, of our native eloquence, ornaments of the senate, the pulpit, and the bar. He will, I hope, mention with high honor some of my young friends who now hear me; and he will, I also hope, be able to add that their talents and learning were not wasted on selfish or ignoble objects, but were employed to promote the physical and moral good of their species, to extend the empire of man over the material world, to defend the cause of civil and religious liberty against tyrants and bigots, and to defend the cause of virtue and order against the enemies of all divine and human laws. I have now given utterance to a part, and to a part only, of the recollections and anticipations of which, on this solemn occasion, my mind is full.   I again thank you for the honor which you have bestowed on me; and I assure you that, while I live, I shall never cease to take a deep interest in the welfare and fame of the body with which, by your kindness, I have this day become connected.

WILLIAM McKINLEY

Photogravure after a photograph from life

WILLIAM McKINLEY

CHARACTERISTICS OF WASHINGTON

[Address by William McKinley, twenty-fourth President of the United States (born in Niles, O., January 29, 1843; died in Buffalo, N. Y., September 14, 1901), delivered at the unveiling of the Washington Statue, by the Society of Cincinnati, in Philadelphia, May 15, 1897.]

FELLOW CITIZENS:—There is a peculiar and tender sentiment connected with this memorial. It expresses not only the gratitude and reverence of the living, but is a testimonial of affection and homage from the dead.

The comrades of Washington projected this monument. Their love inspired it. Their contributions helped to build it. Past and present share in its completion, and future generations will profit by its lessons. To participate in the dedication of such a monument is a rare and precious privilege. Every monument to Washington is a tribute to patriotism. Every shaft and statue to his memory helps to inculcate love of country, encourage loyalty and establish a better citizenship. God bless every undertaking which revives patriotism and rebukes the indifferent and lawless! A critical study of Washington's career only enhances our estimation of his vast and varied abilities.

As Commander-in-Chief of the Colonial armies from the beginning of the war to the proclamation of peace, as president of the convention which framed the Constitution of the United States, and as the first President of the United States under that Constitution, Washington has a distinction differing from that of all other illustrious Americans. No other name bears or can bear such a relation to the Government. Not only by his military

genius—his patience, his sagacity, his courage, and his
skill—was our national independence won, but he helped
in largest measure to draft the chart by which the Nation
was guided; and he was the first chosen of the people to
put in motion the new Government. His was not the
boldness of martial display or the charm of captivating
oratory, but his calm and steady judgment won men's
support and commanded their confidence by appealing to
their best and noblest aspirations. And withal Washington was ever so modest that at no time in his career did
his personality seem in the least intrusive. He was above
the temptation of power. He spurned the suggested
crown. He would have no honor which the people did
not bestow.

An interesting fact—and one which I love to recall—is
that the only time Washington formally addressed the
Constitutional Convention during all its sessions over
which he presided in this city, he appealed for a larger
representation of the people in the National House of
Representatives, and his appeal was instantly heeded.
Thus was he ever keenly watchful of the rights of the people in whose hands was the destiny of our Government
then as now.

Masterful as were his military campaigns, his civil administration commands equal admiration. His foresight
was marvelous; his conception of the philosophy of government, his insistence upon the necessity of education,
morality, and enlightened citizenship to the progress and
permanence of the Republic cannot be contemplated even
at this period without filling us with astonishment at the
breadth of his comprehension and the sweep of his vision.
His was no narrow view of government. The immediate
present was not his sole concern, but our future good his
constant theme of study. He blazed the path of liberty.
He laid the foundation upon which we have grown from
weak and scattered Colonial governments to a united Republic whose domains and power as well as whose liberty
and freedom have become the admiration of the world.
Distance and time have not detracted from the fame and
force of his achievements or diminished the grandeur of
his life and work. Great deeds do not stop in their

growth, and those of Washington will expand in influence in all the centuries to follow.

The bequest Washington has made to civilization is rich beyond computation. The obligations under which he has placed mankind are sacred and commanding. The responsibility he has left for the American people to preserve and perfect what he accomplished is exacting and solemn. Let us rejoice in every new evidence that the people realize what they enjoy and cherish with affection the illustrious heroes of Revolutionary story whose valor and sacrifices made us a nation. They live in us, and their memory will help us keep the covenant entered into for the maintenance of the freest Government of earth.

The Nation and the name of Washington are inseparable. One is linked indissolubly with the other. Both are glorious, both triumphant. Washington lives and will live because what he did was for the exaltation of man, the enthronement of conscience, and the establishment of a Government which recognizes all the governed. And so, too, will the Nation live victorious over all obstacles, adhering to the immortal principles which Washington taught and Lincoln sustained.

AMERICAN PATRIOTISM

[Address by William McKinley, delivered at the dedication of the Cuyahoga County Soldiers' and Sailors' Monument at Cleveland, O., July 4, 1894. Mayor Robert Blee, Chairman of the Committee of Arrangements, introduced Mr. McKinley, then Governor of Ohio. Previous to the address, " Our Bonnie Flag " was sung by children who in singing the chorus beat the time of the music with flags.]

SOLDIERS AND SAILORS OF CUYAHOGA COUNTY, MY COMRADES AND FELLOW CITIZENS:—I wish the whole world might have witnessed the sight we have just seen and have heard the song we have just listened to from the school children of the City of Cleveland. With patriotism in our hearts and with the flag of our country in our hands, there is no danger of anarchy and there is no danger to the American Union. [Applause.]

The place, the day, and the occasion upon which we assemble, fill us with patriotic emotion. They are happily and appropriately united. This old Monumental Square is filled with hallowed memories. This day registers the birthday of the Declaration of Independence. And this Monument that we dedicate to-day attests that every promise of that declaration has been kept and performed. [Applause.] Standing in this presence, I am reminded that this Public Square has witnessed many interesting and memorable events. The first I recall was on the 10th day of September, 1860, when the monument to Commodore Perry was unveiled. It was a deeply interesting occasion. An immense crowd thronged this city as it throngs it to-day. Governor Sprague, of Rhode Island, with his staff and State officers, and the members of the Legislature of that State, and the Providence Light Infantry, participated in the interesting ceremony. Governor Dennison, the first war governor Ohio ever had, delivered the address of welcome. General J. W. Fitch, remembered by the older citizens of Cleveland, was the Grand Marshal of the day; and General Barnett, whose distinguished services in the war are yet fresh in the memory of the people, and who now participates in these ceremonies, was in command of the Cleveland Light Artillery Regiment. The great historian, George Bancroft, delivered the principal address of the day. It was probably, my fellow citizens, the greatest celebration that Cuyahoga County had seen up to that time. It was on this ground, too, that the Soldiers' and Sailors' Aid Society of Northern Ohio, aye, of the whole country, was organized, and some of the noble mothers who were at the birth of that organization are seated upon this platform to-day. These noble women gave unselfish devotion to the country, and money from all this section of the State poured into the coffers of that association for the relief of the men at the front, who were sustaining the flag. It was in this Square, too, that the remains of the martyred Lincoln, the great emancipator, rested as they journeyed to his Western home. It was on this very spot, almost where we stand to-day, that the whole population of Northern Ohio viewed for the last time him who had been captain of all our armies under the Constitution, and whose death was a sacrifice to the great cause of freedom and the Union. [Applause.]

Here, too, my fellow citizens, on this very spot, the remains of the immortal Garfield lay in state, attended by the Congress of the United States, by the supreme judiciary of the Nation, by the officers of the Army and the Navy of the United States, by the Governors and Legislators of all the surrounding States. The steady tread of a mourning State and Nation was uninterrupted through the entire night. It was here that the people looked upon his face for the last time forever.

Interesting, my fellow citizens, and patriotic as the scenes witnessed in the past have been, I venture to say that none of them has stirred so many memories or quickened such patriotic feeling as the services we perform to-day in the dedication of this beautiful structure to the memory of the loyal Soldiers and Sailors who contributed their lives to save the Government from dissolution. Cuyahoga County can well be proud of this great Memorial. It is a fitting tribute to the Soldiers living and the Soldiers dead. Cuyahoga's sons were represented in nearly every branch of the military service. Almost every Ohio regiment received some contribution from Cuyahoga County, whether in the infantry, cavalry, artillery, on land or on sea. Whether among white troops or colored troops Cuyahoga County's sons were to be found, they were always found at the post of greatest danger. [Applause.]

Nothing has so impressed me in the program to-day as the organization of the old Soldiers, carrying with them their tattered flags, which they bore a third of a century ago upon the fields of war. More than sixty of the old regimental flags will be carried by the survivors of their respective regiments, and the flag room at the capitol at Columbus could not supply the men of Cuyahoga County all the flags which they are entitled to bear. Is it any wonder that these old Soldiers love to carry the flags under which they fought and for which their brave comrades gave up their lives?

Is it any wonder that the old Soldier loves the flag under whose folds he fought and for which his comrades shed so much blood? He loves it for what it is and for what it represents. It embodies the purposes and history of the Government itself. It records the achievements of its defenders upon land and sea. It heralds the heroism and sacrifices of our Revolutionary fathers who planted free government on this continent and dedicated it to liberty forever. It attests the struggles of our army and the valor of our citizens in all the wars of the Republic. It has been sanctified by the blood of our best and our bravest. It records the achievements of Washington and the martyrdom of Lincoln. It has been bathed in the tears of a sorrowing people. It has been glorified in the hearts of a freedom-loving people, not only at home but in every part of the world. Our flag expresses more than any other flag; it means more than any other national emblem. It expresses the will of a free people and proclaims that they are supreme and that they acknowledge no earthly sovereign other than themselves. It never was assaulted that thousands did not rise up to smite the assailant. Glorious old banner!

When the Stars and Stripes were hauled down on Sumter, flags without number were raised above every fireside in the land and all the glorious achievements which that flag represented with all its hallowed memories glowed with burning fervor in the heart of every lover of liberty and the Union. The mad assault which was made upon the flag at that time aroused its defenders and kindled a patriotism which could not be quenched until it had extinguished the unholy cause which assaulted our holy banner.

What more beautiful conception than that which prompted Abra Kohn, of Chicago, in February, 1861, to send to Mr. Lincoln, on the eve of his starting to Washington to take the office of President, to which he had been elected, a flag of our country, bearing upon its silken folds these words from the fifth and ninth verses of the first chapter of Joshua: "Have I not commanded thee, be strong and of good courage? Be not afraid, neither be thou dismayed, for the Lord, our God, is with thee, whithersoever thou goest. There shall no man be able to stand before thee all the days of thy life. As I was with Moses, so shall I be with thee. I will not fail thee nor forsake thee."

Could anything have given Mr. Lincoln more cheer, or been better calculated to sustain his courage or strengthen his faith in the mighty work before him? Thus commanded, thus assured, Mr. Lincoln journeyed to the capital, where he took the oath of office and registered in heaven an oath to save the Union; and "the Lord, our God," was with him and did not fail nor forsake him until every obligation of oath and duty was sacredly kept and honored. Not any man was able to stand before him. Liberty was enthroned, the Union was saved and the flag which he carried floated in triumph and glory upon every flagstaff of the Republic.

What does this Monument mean? It means the immortal principle of patriotism. It means love of country. It means sacrifices for the country we love. It means not only love of country but love of liberty! This alone could have inspired over 2,800,000 Union soldiers to leave home and family and to offer to die if need be for our imperiled institutions. Love of country alone could have inspired 300,000 men to die for the Union. Nothing less sacred than this love of country could have sustained 175,000 brave men, who suffered and starved and died in rebel prisons. Nor could anything else have given comfort to the 500,000 maimed and diseased, who escaped immediate death in siege and battle to end in torment the remainder of their patriot lives. It is a noble patriotism and it impels you, my fellow countrymen, to erect this magnificent monument to their honor and memory. And similar love of country will inspire your remotest descendants to do homage to their valor and bravery forever.

This is what the monument means. The lesson it conveys to the present and all future generations. It means that the cause in which they died was a righteous one, and it means that the cause which triumphed through their valor shall be perpetuated for all time.

Charles Sumner said that President Lincoln was put to death by the enemies of the Declaration of Independence, but, said Sumner, though dead, he would always continue to guard that title-deed of the human race. So that it does seem to me that every time we erect a new monument to the memory of the Union Soldiers and Sailors, we are cementing the very foundations of the Government itself. We are doing that which will strengthen our devotion to free institutions and insure their permanency for the remotest posterity. We are not only rendering immortal the fame of the men who participated in the war by these magnificent structures, but we are doing better than that. We are making immortal the principles for which they contended and the union of free men for which they died. [Applause.]

Their erection may be a matter of comparatively little importance or concern to the Union Soldiers who are still living, but no one can accurately foretell the value and importance of their influence upon the young men and the young women from whom the Republic must draw her future defenders. Every time we erect a monument, every time we do honor to the Soldiers of the Republic, we reaffirm our devotion to the country, to the glorious flag, to the immortal principles of liberty, equality, and justice, which have made the United States unrivaled among the nations of the world. The union of these States must be perpetual. That is what our brave boys died for. That is what this monument must mean; and such monuments as this are evidences that the people intend to take care that the great decrees of the war shall be unquestioned and supreme. [Applause.]

The unity of the Republic is secure so long as we continue to honor the memory of the men who died by the tens of thousands to preserve it. The dissolution of the Union is impossible so long as we continue to inculcate lessons of fraternity, unity, and patriotism, and erect monuments to perpetuate these sentiments.

Such monuments as these have another meaning, which is one dear to the hearts of many who stand by me. It is, as Mr. Lincoln said at Gettysburg, that the dead shall not have died in vain; that the Nation's later birth of freedom and the people's gain of their own sovereignty shall not perish from the earth. That is what this monument means. That is the lesson of true patriotism; that what was won in war shall be worn in peace.

But we must not forget, my fellow countrymen, that the Union which these brave men preserved, and the liberties which they secured, places upon us, the living, the gravest responsibility. We are the freest Government on the face of the earth.   Our strength rests in our patriotism.   Anarchy flees before patriotism.   Peace and order and security and liberty are safe so long as love of country burns in the hearts of the people.   It should not be forgotten, however, that liberty does not mean lawlessness.   Liberty to make our own laws does not give us license to break them.   [Applause.]   Liberty to make our own laws commands a duty to observe them ourselves and enforce obedience among all others within their jurisdiction. Liberty, my fellow citizens, is responsibility, and responsibility is duty, and that duty is to preserve the exceptional liberty we enjoy within the law and for the law and by the law.

HENRY EDWARD, CARDINAL MANNING

PERSECUTION OF THE JEWS

[Address by Cardinal Manning, English Roman Catholic prelate and religious writer (born in Totteridge, Hertfordshire, July 15, 1808; died in London, January 14, 1892), delivered February 1, 1882, in the Egyptian Hall of the Mansion House, London, at a meeting convened by the Lord Mayor to give expression to the feeling excited in England by the then recently perpetrated atrocities upon the Jews in Russia.]

My Lord Mayor, Ladies and Gentlemen:—It has often fallen to my lot to move a resolution in meetings such as this, but never in my memory have I moved one with more perfect conviction of my reason or more entire concurrence of my heart. Before I use any further words, it will, perhaps, be better that I should read what that resolution is. It is, "That this meeting, while disclaiming any right or desire to interfere in the internal affairs of another country, and desiring that the most amicable relations between England and Russia should be preserved, feels it a duty to express its opinion that the laws of Russia relating to the Jews tend to degrade them in the eyes of the Christian population, and to expose Russian Jewish subjects to the outbreaks of fanatical ignorance."

I need not disclaim, for I accept the eloquent disclaimer of the noble lord, that we are not met here for a political purpose. If there were a suspicion of any party politics, I should not be standing here. It is because I believe that we are highly above all the tumults of party politics, that we are in the serene region of human sympathy and human justice, that I am here to-day. I can also declare that nothing can be further from my intention, as I am confident nothing can be further from yours, than to do that which would be a violation of the laws of mutual peace and order, and the respect which binds nations together, or to attempt to interfere or dictate in the domestic legislation of Russia. I am also bound to say that I share heartily in the words of veneration used by the noble earl [the Earl of Shaftesbury, who moved the first resolution: "That, in the opinion of this meeting, the persecution and the outrages which the Jews in many parts of the Russian dominion have for several months past suffered, are an offense to civilization to be deeply deplored."] towards his Imperial Majesty of Russia. No man can have watched the last year of the imperial family, no man can know the condition in which the Emperor stands now without a profound sympathy which would at once bind every disposition to use a single expression which would convey a wound to the mind of the Czar. Therefore, I disclaim absolutely and altogether that anything that passes from my lips—and I believe I can speak for all—should assume a character inconsistent with veneration for a person charged with a responsibility so great. Further, I may say that while we do not pretend to touch upon any question in the internal legislation of Russia, there are laws larger than any Russian legislation—the laws of humanity and of God, which are the foundation of all other laws, and if in any legislation they be violated, all the nations of Christian Europe, the whole commonwealth of civilized and Christian men would instantly acquire a right to speak out aloud.

And now I must touch upon one point, which I acknowledge has been very painful to me. We have all watched for the last twelve months the anti-Semitic movement in Germany. I look upon it with a twofold feeling—in the first place with horror as tending to disintegrate the foundations of social life, and, secondly, with great fear lest it may light up an animosity, which has already taken flame in Russia and may spread elsewhere. I have read with great regret an elaborate article, full, no doubt, of minute observations, written from Prussia and published in "The Nineteenth Century," giving a description of the class ani-

mosities, jealousies, and rivalries which are at present so
rife in that country. When I read that article, my first
feeling was one of infinite sorrow that the power and
energy of the Old Testament should be so much greater in
Brandenburg than those of the New. I am sorry to see
that a society penetrated with rationalism has not so much
Christian knowledge, Christian power, Christian character, and Christian virtue as to render it impossible that,
cultivated, refined, industrious, and energetic as they are,
they should endanger the Christian society of that great
kingdom. I have also read with pain accounts of the condition of the Russian Jews, bringing against them accusations which, if I touch upon them, I must ask my Jewish
friends near me to believe I reject with incredulity and
horror. Nevertheless, I have read that the cause of
what has happened in Russia is that the Jews have been
pliers of infamous trades—usurers, immoral, demorali-
zing, and I know not **what**. When I read these accusations, I ask, Will they **be cured** by crime, murder, outrage,
abominations of **every sort?** Are they not learning the
lesson from those who ought to teach a higher?

Again, if it be true, which I do not believe, that they are
in the condition described, are they not under penal laws?
Is there anything that can degrade men more than to
close against intelligence, energy, and industry all the honorable careers of public life? Is there anything that can
debase and irritate the soul of man more than to be told,
"You must not pass beyond that boundary; you must
not go within eighteen miles of that frontier; you must
not dwell in that town; you must live only in that province?" I do not know how any one can believe that the
whole population can fail to be affected in its inmost soul
by such laws; and if it be possible to make it worse, this
is the mode and the discipline to make it so.

They bring these accusations against the Russian Jews;
why do they not bring them against the Jews of Germany?
By the acknowledgment of the anti-Semitic movement,
the Jews in Germany rise head and shoulders above their
fellows. Why do they not bring these accusations against
the Jews of France? Is there any career of public utility,
any path of honor, civil or military, in which the Jews
have not stood side by side with their countrymen? If

the charge is brought against the Jews of Russia, who will bring it against the Jews of England? For uprightness, for refinement, for generosity, for charity, for all the graces and virtues that adorn humanity, where will be found examples brighter or more true of human excellence than in this Hebrew race? And when we are told that the accounts of those atrocities are not to be trusted, I ask if there were to appear in the newspapers long and minute narratives of murder, rapine, and other atrocities round about the Egyptian hall, in Old Jewry, in Houndsditch, in Shoreditch, if it were alleged that the Lord Mayor was looking on, that the metropolitan police did nothing, that the guards at the Tower were seen mingled with the mob, I believe you would thank any man who gave you an opportunity of exposing and contradicting the statement.

Well, then, I say we are rendering a public service to the public departments and Ministry of Russia by what we are doing now, and I believe it will carry consolation to the heart of the great prince who reigns over that vast empire. But let me suppose for a moment that these things are true—and I do not found my belief in their truth from what has appeared either in "The Times" newspaper or in the "Pall Mall Gazette," which has confirmed the statements. I hold the proofs in my own hand. And from whom do they come? From official documents, from the Minister of the Interior, General Ignatieff. The resolution speaks of the laws of Russia as regards its Jewish subjects. I do not assume to be an old jurist in English law, much less to say what the laws of Russia are in this respect. I should not know what to say on the resolution if I did not hold in my hand a rescript of much importance. I hope I shall not be told that, like the ukase, it is a forgery. These horrible atrocities had continued throughout May, June, and July, and in the month of August this document was issued. The first point in it is that it laments and deplores—what? The atrocities on the Jewish subjects of the Czar? By no means, but the sad condition of the Christian inhabitants of the southern provinces. The next point is that the main cause of these "movements and riots," as they are called, to which the Russian nation had been a stranger, is

but a commercial one.   The third point is that this conduct of the Jews has called forth " protests " on the part
of the people, as manifested by acts—of what do you
think?   Of violence and robbery.   Fourthly, we are told
by the Minister of the Interior that the country is subject
to malpractices, which were, it is known, the cause of the
agitation.

My Lord Mayor, if the logic of this document be calm,
the rhetoric and insinuation of it are most inflammatory,
and I can hardly conceive how, with that rescript in their
hands, the Russian population could not have felt that
they were encouraged to go on.   The document then
goes on to say, " We have appointed a Commission to inquire "—into what?   " First, what are the trades of the
Jews which are injurious to the inhabitants of the place;
and, secondly, what makes it impracticable to put into
force the already existing laws limiting the rights of the
Jews in the matter of buying and farming land and trading in intoxicants and usury.   Thirdly, how shall these
laws be altered so that the Jews can no longer evade them,
and what new laws may be passed to prevent their
evasion."

Besides answering the foregoing questions, the following additional information was sought—first, on usury;
secondly, on the number of public houses; thirdly, on the
number of persons in the service of the Jews; fourthly, on
the extent and acreage of the land; and, lastly, on the
number of Jewish agriculturists.   We have in our hands
the Russian laws affecting the Jewish subjects of the Empire.   I would ask what is the remedy for a population
in this state?   Is it more penal laws?   Is it to disqualify
them from holding land?   Is it to forbid them to send
their children to higher places of education?   No, my
Lord Mayor; I believe that the remedy for this state of
things is twofold—first, the vital supremacy of Christian
law in all its amplitude.   It was not by laws like these
that the Christians won the world and won the Imperial
power to execute justice among men.   It will not be by
laws other than these that the great Imperial power of
Russia will blend with the population of the Empire their
Jewish subjects.

The other remedy I believe to be this: a stern and merciful execution of justice upon evil-doers, coupled with a stern and rigorous concession of all that is right in the law of nature and of God to every man. All that is necessary for the protection of life and limb, and liberty and property—all that constitutes human freedom—this, and nothing less than this, will be the remedy for the evil of which the Minister of the Interior complains.

I look very hopefully to what may be the effect of this meeting. Do not let us overrate it. If we believe that this meeting will have done the work, and that we may cease to speak, its effect will not be what we desire. Let us not underrate it either. I believe that all through the United Kingdom there will be a response to this meeting. Manchester and Birmingham have begun; and wheresoever the English tongue is spoken throughout the world, that which your lordship has said so eloquently and so powerfully will be known. I believe at the very moment we are assembled here, a meeting of the same kind is assembled in New York; and what passes here will be translated into every language of Europe, and will pass even the frontiers of Russia. Like the light and the air, it cannot be excluded, and wheresoever there is human sympathy, the declarations that are made here and elsewhere will meet with a response that will tend to put an end to these horrible atrocities.

There is a book, my lord, which is common to the race of Israel and to us Christians. That book is a bond between us, and in that book I read that the people of Israel are the eldest people upon the earth. Russia, and Austria, and England are of yesterday compared with the imperishable people which, with an inextinguishable life and immutable traditions, and faith in God and in the laws of God, scattered as it is all over the world, passing through the fires unscathed, trampled into the dust, and yet never combining with the dust into which it is trampled, lives still a witness and a warning to us. We are in the bonds of brotherhood with it. The New Testament rests upon the Old. They believe in half of that for which we would give our lives. Let us then acknowledge that we unite in a common sympathy. I read in that book these words, "I am angry with a great anger with the wealthy nations that are at ease, because I was a little angry with Israel, and they helped forward the affliction." That is, my people were scattered; they suffered unknown and unimaginable sufferings, and the nations of the world that dwelt at ease and were wealthy, and had power in their hands, helped forward a very weighty affliction which was upon them all.

My lord, I only hope this—that not one man in England who calls himself a civilized or Christian man will have it in his heart to add by a single word to that which this great and ancient and noble people suffer; but that we shall do all we can by labor, by speech, and by prayer to lessen if it be possible, or at least to keep ourselves from sharing in sympathy with these atrocious deeds.

BRANDER MATTHEWS

AMERICAN LITERATURE

[Address by Brander Matthews, author, Professor of American literature in Columbia University, New York City (born in New Orleans, La., February 21, 1852; ——), delivered before the National Educational Association, July 8, 1896.]

The history of mankind is little more than the list of the civilizations that have arisen one on the ruin of the other, the Roman supplanting the Greek, as the Assyrian had been ousted by the Babylonian. The life of each of these successive civilizations was proportioned to the vitality of the ideas by which it was animated; and we cannot estimate it or even understand it except in so far as we are able to grasp these underlying principles. What the ideas were which dominated these vanished civilizations it is for us to discover for ourselves as best we may by a study of all the records they left behind them, and especially by a reverent examination of their laws, their arts, and their writings in so far as these have been preserved to us. Of all these relics of peoples now dead and gone, none is so instructive as literature, and none is so interesting; by its aid we are enabled to reconstruct the past, as we are also helped to understand the present.

Of the literatures which thus explain to us our fellow man as he was and as he is, three seem to me preëminent, standing out and above the others not only by reason of the greater number of me of genius who have illustrated them, but also by reason of their own more persistent strength and their own broader variety. These three literatures are the Greek, the French, and the English.

There are great names in the other modern languages,
no doubt—the names of Dante and of Cervantes and of
Goethe, than which, indeed, there are none greater. In
French literature, however, and in English there are not
wanting names as mighty as these. Fortunately, the possession of genius is not the privilege of any one language,
of any one country, or of any one century. Where French
literature and English can claim superiority over Italian,
Spanish, and German is rather in sustaining a higher average of excellence for a longer period of time. The literature of the Italian language, of the Spanish, and of the
German has no such bead-roll of writers of the first rank as
illustrates the literature of the French and of the English.
There is perhaps no more manly instrument of precision
than the Latin language, none which better repays the
struggle for its mastery; but Latin literature, if not second-
rate, when tried by the loftiest standards, is at least secondary, being transplanted from Greece, and lacking resolute
roots in its own soil. Nor is any dispute possible as to
the high value of Hebrew literature; as Coleridge declared, with characteristic insight, " sublimity is Hebrew
by birth"; but Hebrew literature has not the wide range
of the Greek, nor its impeccable beauty.

"Art is only form," said George Sand; and Goethe declared that the " highest operation of art is form-giving."
If we accept these sayings, there is no need to dwell on the
supreme distinction of Greek literature, for it is only in
Greek that we find the undying perfection of form. It is
there only that we have clear and deep thought always
beautifully embodied. Indeed, truth and beauty govern
Greek literature so absolutely that, old as it is, it seems to
us ever fresh and eternally young. After two thousand
years and more it strikes us to-day as startlingly modern.
Thoreau—whose own phrase was often Attic in its delicate precision—Thoreau asked: " What are the classics
but the noblest recorded thoughts of man? They are the
only oracles that are not decayed." Nevertheless, the
world has kept restlessly moving since the fall of Athens,
and mankind has developed needs that the Greeks knew
not. As Molière puts it, pithily, " The ancients are the
ancients, and we are the men of to-day." There are questions in America now, and not a few of them, undreamed

of in Sparta; and for the answers to these it is vain to go to Greek literature, modern as it may be in so many ways.

French literature has not a little of the moderation and of the charm of Greek literature. It is not violent; it is not boisterous, even; it is never freakish. It has balance and order and a broad sanity. It has an unfailing sense of style. It has lightness of touch, and it has also and always intellectual seriousness. The literature is like the language; and Voltaire declared that what was not clear was not French. And the language itself is the fit instrument of the people who use it and who have refined it for their needs—a people logical beyond all others, gifted in mathematics, devoid of hypocrisy, law-abiding, governed by the social instinct, inheritors of the Latin tradition and yet infused with the Celtic spirit.

To those of us who are controlled by the Anglo-Saxon ideals, whether or not we come of English stock, to those of us who adhere to Anglo-Saxon conventions, no other literature can serve as a better corrective of our inherited tendencies than the French. The chief characteristic of English literature is energy, power often ill-restrained, vigor often superabundant. From the earliest rude war-songs of the stalwart Saxon fighters who were beginning to make the English language, to the latest short story setting forth the strife of an American mining camp, there is never any lack of force in English literature. There is always the Teutonic boldness and rudeness—the Teutonic readiness to push forward and to shoulder the rest of the world out of the way—the Teutonic independence that leads every man to fight for his own hand, like the smith in Scott's story. What we do not discover in English literature, with all its overmastering vitality, is economy of effort, the French self-control, the Greek sense of form.

French literature and English literature have existed side by side for many centuries, each of them influencing the other now and again, and yet each of them preserving its own individuality, always and ever revealing the dominant characteristics of the people speaking its language. We need not attempt to weigh them one against the other, and to measure them with a foot rule, and to declare which is the greater. Equal they may be in the past and in the present; equal in the future they are not likely to be.   The qualities which make French literature what it is tend also to keep the French race from expansion; just as the qualities which make English literature what it is have sent the English-speaking stock forth to fill up the waste places of the earth, and to wrest new lands from hostile savages or from inhospitable nature.

French was the language of the courts of Europe when English was little better than a dialect of rough islanders. When Chaucer chose his native English as the vehicle of his verse he showed both courage and prescience—a courage and a prescience lacking in Bacon, who lived two hundred years later, and who did not feel himself insured against Time until his great work was safely entombed in Latin.   Even at the beginning of the Nineteenth century there were more men and women in the world speaking French than there were speaking English.   But now, at the end of the Nineteenth century, with the steady spread of our stock into the four quarters of the world, there are more than twice as many people using English as there are using French.   And the end is not yet; for while four-fifths of those who have French for their mother tongue abide in France or along its borders, not a third of those who have English for their mother tongue dwell in England.   Not only in England, Ireland, and Scotland is English spoken, and in all the many British colonies which encompass the globe about; it is also the native speech of the people of the United States.   English is the language of the stock which bids fair to prove itself the most masterful, hardy, and prolific, and which seems to possess a marvelous faculty for assimilating members of other allied stems, and of getting these newly received elements to accept its own hereditary ideals.

English literature is likely, therefore, to become in the future relatively more important and absolutely more influential.   As there has been no relaxing of energy among the peoples that now speak the English language, probably there will be no alteration of the chief characteristic of English literature, although in time the changes of environment must make more or less modification inevitable. It will be curious to see in a century how the ideals and the practices of the race will alter, after the race is no longer pent up in an island, after it has scattered itself over the world and assimilated other elements and adjusted itself to other social organizations. Here in America we can see already some of these results, for already is the American differentiated from the Englishman. We may not be able to declare clearly wherein the difference consists; but we all recognize it plainly enough. Colonel Higginson has suggested that the American has an added drop more of nervous fluid than the Englishman. It is perhaps apparent already that the American is swifter than the Englishman, slighter in build, springier in gait. Social changes are as evident as physical. Lowell remarked that if it was a good thing for an English duke that he had no social superior, it surely was not a bad thing for a Yankee farmer. Socially the American is less girt in by caste than the Englishman. These differences, obvious in life, are visible also in literature. We feel now, even if we do not care to define, the unlikeness of the writing of the British authors to the writing of the American authors. Neither man nor nature is the same in Great Britain as in the United States; and of necessity, therefore, there cannot be any identity between the points of view of the men of letters of the two countries.

In time, as there come to be more writers in Canada, we shall have a perspective from yet another point of view; and in due season others will be presented to us from Australia and from India. No doubt these future authors will cherish the tradition of English literature as loyally as we Americans cherish it here in the United States—as loyally as the British cherish it in the little group of islands which was once the home of the ancestors of us all. Race characteristics are inexorable, and it is very unlikely that there will ever be any irreconcilable divergence between these separate divisions of the English-speaking peoples. English literature will continue to flourish as sturdily as ever after the parent stem has parted into five branches. All of these branches will take the same pride in their descent from a common stock, and in their possession of a common literature and of a common language. A common language, I say, for the English language belongs to all those who use it, whether they live in London or in Chicago or in Melbourne.

It is not a little strange that it should now ever be

needful to say that the British have no more ownership
of the English language than we Americans have.   The
English language is the mother tongue of the inhabitants
of the British Isles, but so it is also the mother tongue of
the inhabitants of the United States.   It is not a loan to us,
which may be recalled; it is not a gift, which we have accepted; it is a heritage, which we derived from our forefathers.   We hold it by right of birth, and our title to it
is just as good as the title of our kin across the sea.   No
younger brother's portion is it that we claim in the English language, but a whole and undivided half.   It is an
American possession as it is a British possession, no more
and no less; and we hold it on the same terms that our
cousins do.   We have the rights of ownership, and the
responsibilities also, exactly as they have, and to exactly
the same extent.   The English language belongs to us
also; it is ours to use as we please, just as the common
law is ours, to modify according to our own needs; it is
ours for us to keep pure and healthy; and it is ours for
us to hand down to our children unimpaired in strength
and in subtlety.

   And as the language is a possession common to all the
English-speaking peoples, so also is the literature.   A
share in the fame of Chaucer and of Shakespeare, of Milton
and of Dryden, is part of the inheritance of every one of
us who has English for his master tongue, whatever his
fatherland.   If there be anywhere a great poet or novelist
or historian, it matters not where his birth or his residence
or what his nationality, if he makes use of the English
language he is contributing to English literature.   To
distinguish the younger divisions of English literature
from the older, we shall have to call that older division
British, meaning thereby that portion of our common
literature which is now produced by those who were left
behind in the old home when the rest of the family went
forth one by one to make their way in the world.   Thus
English literature, which was one and undivided till the
end of the Eighteenth century, has now in the Nineteenth
century two chief divisions—British and American; and
it bids fair in the Twentieth century to have three more—
Canadian, Australian, and Indian.

   Some such distinction between the several existing divisions of the English literature of our own time is needful, and it will be found useful. Absurd and very misleading is the antithesis sometimes made between American literature and English, since the American is but one of the divisions of the English literature of our time. Not long ago a pupil of one of the best private schools in New York maintained that American literature was just as important as English literature, producing in proof two companion manuals, of the same size externally, although of course, internally on a wholly different scale. Such a lack of proportion in the treatment of different parts of the literature of the English language is foolish and harmful. But a comparison of American literature with the merely British literature of to-day might be proper enough. What we need to grasp clearly is the fact that the stream of English literature had only one channel until the end of the last century, and that in this century it has two channels. The new mouth that this massive current has made for itself is American, and so we are compelled to call the old mouth British.

Through which of these channels the fuller stream shall flow in the next century no man can foretell to-day. It is a fact that the population of these United States is now nearly twice as large as the population of the British Isles, and not inferior in ability or in energy. But it is a fact also that in America a smaller proportion of the ability and the energy of the people seems to be devoted to the cause of letters. In a new country life itself offers the widest opportunities; and literature here has keener rivals and more of them than it can have in a land which has been cleared and tilled and tended since a time whereof the memory of man runneth not to the contrary. The earliest Americans had other duties than the writing of books; they had to lay deep the broad foundations of this mighty nation. It was more than two hundred years after the establishment of the first trading post on the island of Manhattan before Washington Irving published the " Sketch Book," the first work of American authorship to win a wide popularity beyond the borders of our own country—before Fenimore Cooper, a little later, published " The Spy," the first work of American authorship to win a wide popularity beyond the borders of our own language. We may say that American literature is now but little older than the threescore years and ten allotted as the span of a man's natural life. We had had authors, it is true, in the Eighteenth century, and at least two of these, Jonathan Edwards and Benjamin Franklin, hold high rank; but it was not until towards the end of the first quarter of the Nineteenth century that we began really to have a literature. It is scarcely an overstatement to say that there are men alive to-day who are as old as American literature is. But in the past three-quarters of a century American literature has taken root firmly, and blossomed forth abundantly, and spread itself abroad sturdily. Emerson followed Edwards and Franklin. Hawthorne and Poe followed Irving and Cooper. Bryant proved that Nature here in America was fit for the purposes of Art; and he was followed by Longfellow and Lowell, by Whittier and Holmes.

During these same threescore years and ten there were great writers in the other branch of the literature of our language, in British literature, perhaps greater writers than there were here in America, and of a certainty there were more of them. There is no need now to call the roll of the mighty men of letters alive in England at the middle of this century. But much as we admire these British authors, much as we respect them, I do not think that they are as close to us as the authors of our own country; we do not cherish them with the same affection. Just as the modern literatures are nearer to us than the ancient, because we ourselves are modern, just as English literature is nearer to us than French, because we ourselves speak English, so the American division of that literature is closer to us than the British. It helps us to understand one another, and it explains us to ourselves. If we accept the statement that, after all, literature is only a criticism of life, it is of value in proportion as its criticism of life is truthful. Surely it needs no argument to show that the life it is most needful for us Americans to have criticised truthfully is our own life. It is only in our own literature that we can hope to learn the truth about ourselves, and this, indeed, is what we must always insist upon in our literature—the truth, the whole truth, and nothing but the truth. Lowell reminded us that Goethe went to the root of the matter when he said that "people are always talking of the study of the ancients; yet what does this mean but apply yourself to the actual world and seek to express it, since this is what the ancients did when they were alive?"

As we consider the brief history of the American branch of English literature, we can see that the growth of a healthy feeling in regard to it has been hindered by two unfortunate failings—provincialism and colonialism. By provincialism I mean the spirit of Little Peddlington, the spirit that makes swans of all our geese. By colonialism I mean the attitude of looking humbly towards the old country for guidance and for counsel even about our own affairs.

Provincialism is local pride unduly inflated. It is the temper that is ready to hail as a Swan of Avon any local gosling who has taught himself to make an unnatural use of his own quills. It is always tempting us to stand on tiptoe to proclaim our own superiority. It prevents our seeing ourselves in proper proportion to the rest of the world. It leads to the preparation of school-manuals in which the threescore years and ten of American literature are made equal in importance to the thousand years of literature produced in Great Britain. It tends to render a modest writer, like Longfellow, ridiculous by comparing him implicitly with the half-dozen world-poets. In the final resort, no doubt, every people must be the judge of its own authors; but before that final judgment is rendered every people consults the precedents, and measures its own local favorites by the cosmopolitan and eternal standards.

Colonialism is shown in the timid deference towards foreign opinion about our own deeds and in the unquestioning acceptance of the foreign estimate upon our own writers. It might be defined almost as a willingness to be second-hand—a feeling which finds satisfaction in calling Irving the American Goldsmith; Cooper, the American Scott; Bryant, the American Wordsworth; and Whittier, the American Burns. Fifty years ago, when this silly trick was far more prevalent than it is now, Lowell satirized it in the "Fable for Critics":—

> "Why, there's scarcely a huddle of log-huts and shanties
> That has not brought forth its Miltons and Dantes;
> I myself know ten Byrons, one Coleridge, three Shelleys,
> Two Raphaels, six Titians (I think), one Apelles,
> Leonardos and Rubenses plenty as lichens,
> One (but that one is plenty) American Dickens,
> A whole flock of Lambs, any number of Tennysons;
> In short, if a man has the luck to have any sons,
> He may feel pretty certain that one out of twain
> Will be some very great person over again."

And elsewhere in the same poem Lowell protests against the literature that

> " . . . suits each whisper and motion
> To what will be thought of it over the ocean."

The corrective of colonialism is a manly self-respect, a wholesome self-reliance, a wish to stand firmly on our own feet, a resolve to survey life with our own eyes and not through any imported spectacles. The New World has already brought forth men of action—Washington, for example, and Lincoln—worthy of comparison with the best that the Old World has enrolled on her records. Has the New World produced any man of letters of corresponding rank? Matthew Arnold thought that there were only five world-classics—Homer, Dante, Shakespeare, Milton, and Goethe. This seems a list unduly scanted; but it would need to be five times larger before it included a single American name. What of it? Even if the American poets are no one of them to be inscribed among the two-score chief singers of the world, they are not the less interesting to us Americans, not the less inspiring. When an English author suggested to Sainte-Beuve that he did not think Lamartine an important poet, the great French critic suavely answered, "He is important to us." Without Lamartine there would be a blank in French literature. So we Americans may see clearly the defects of Bryant and of Whittier, and yet we may say that they are important to us, even though they, like Lamartine, are not among the foremost poets of their language or of their century.

Colonialism and provincialism, although they seem mutually destructive, still manage somehow to exist side by side in our criticism to-day. The best cure for them is a study of the two other great literatures, Greek and French. Too much attention to contemporary British literature is dangerous for us, since its chief characteristics are ours by inheritance. Matthew Arnold held that it was a work of supererogation for Carlyle to preach earnestness to the English, who already abounded in that sense. For us to follow the lead of the British in literature or in any other art is but saying ditto to ourselves. It is like the marriage of cousins—and for the same reasons to be deplored. But the study of Greek literature supplies us instantly with the eternal standards, the use of which cannot but be fatal to provincialism. And the study of French literature, which is as modern as our own and yet as different as may be in its ideals and its methods, is likely to serve as a certain antidote to colonialism.

The study of Greek literature, the greatest of the literatures of the past, and the study of French literature, the other great literature of the present, will lead us towards that American cosmopolitanism which is the antithesis of both provincialism and colonialism. An American cosmopolitanism, I said, for I agree with Coleridge in thinking that " the cosmopolitanism which does not spring out of, and blossom upon, the deep-rooted stem of nationality or patriotism, is a spurious and rotten growth." Stendhal, a Frenchman who did not care for France, and who found himself, at last, a man without a country, had for a motto, " I come from Cosmopolis." A fit motto for an American author might be " I go to Cosmopolis." I go to see the best the world has to offer, the best being none too good for American use; I go as a visitor, and I return always a loyal citizen to my own country.

As Plutarch tells us, " it is well to go for a light to another man's fire, but not to tarry by it, instead of kindling a torch of one's own." A torch of one's own!—that is a possession worth having, whether it be a flaming beacon on the hilltop or a tiny taper in the window. We cannot tell how far a little candle throws its beams, nor who is laying his course by its flickering light. The most that we can do—and it is also the least we should do—is to tend the flame carefully and to keep it steady.

DONALD GRANT MITCHELL

IRVING AS AUTHOR AND MAN

[Address by Donald G. Mitchell—" Ik Marvel "—(born in Norwich, Conn., April 12, 1822; ———), delivered at Tarrytown-on-Hudson, N. Y., April 3, 1883, at the commemoration of the one hundredth anniversary of the birth of Washington Irving. The exercises were held at the Second Reformed Church, under the auspices of the Washington Irving Association, and were presided over by Chief Justice Noah Davis, of the Supreme Court of New York.]

You are met to-night to pay tribute to the memory of a man we all loved—born a hundred years ago.

Yet, we who put voice to your tribute are brought to a pause at the very start. Who can say over again—in a way that shall make listeners—the praises of a balmy day in June?

Simply to recall him, however, is—I think—to honor him: for there is no memory of him however shadowy or vagrant which is not grateful to you—to me and to all the reading world.

It is now well-nigh upon thirty-five years since I first met Mr. Irving. It was in a sunny parlor in one of the houses of that Colonnade Row which stands opposite the Astor Library in Lafayette Place, New York. I can recall vividly the trepidation which I carried to that meeting—so eager to encounter the man whom all honored and admired—so apprehensive lest a chilling dignity might disturb my ideal. And when that smiling, quiet, well-preserved gentleman (I could hardly believe him sixty-five) left his romp with some of his little kinsfolk, to give me a hearty shake of the hand, and thereafter to run

on in lively, humorous chat—stealing all trepidation out of
me, by—I know not what—kindly magnetism of voice and
manner, it was as if some one were playing counterfeit—
as if the venerated author were yet to appear and displace
this beaming, winning personality, with some awful dignity that should put me again into worshipful tremor.

But no: this was indeed Mr. Irving—hard as it was to
adjust this gracious presence, so full of benignity, with
the author who had told the story of the Knickerbockers
and of Columbus.

Another puzzle to me was—how this easy-going gentleman, with his winning mildness and quiet deliberation—
as if he never *could*, and never *did*, and never *would*
knuckle down to hard task-work—should have reeled out
those hundreds—nay, thousands of pages of graceful,
well-ordered, sparkling English.

I could not understand how he did it. I do not think
we ever altogether understand how the birds sing and
sing; and yet, with feathers quite unruffled, and eyes always a-twinkle.

My next sight of Mr. Irving was hereabout, at his own
home. By his kind invitation I had come up to pass a
day with him at Sunnyside, and he had promised me a
drive through Sleepy Hollow. What a promise that was!
No boy ever went to his Christmas holidays more joyously,
I think, than I, to meet that engagement.

It was along this road, beside which we are assembled
to-night, that we drove. He all alert and brisk, with the
cool morning breeze blowing down upon us from the
Haverstraw heights and across the wide sweep of river.
He called attention to the spot of poor André's capture—
not forbearing that little touch of sympathy, which came
to firmer yet not disloyal expression, afterward, in his
story of Washington. A sweep of his whip-hand told me
the trees under which Paulding and the rest chanced to
be loitering on that memorable day.

We were whirling along the same road a short way
farther northward, when I ventured to query about the
memorable night-ride of Ichabod Crane and of the Head-
less Horseman.

Aye, it was thereabout that tragedy came off too.

"Down this bit of road the old horse 'Gunpowder'

came thundering: there away—Brom Bones with his Pumpkin—I tell you this in confidence," he said—"was in waiting; and along here they went clattering neck and neck—Ichabod holding a good seat till Van Ripper's saddle-girths gave way, and then bumping and jouncing from side to side as he clung to mane or neck (a little pantomime with the whip making it real), and so at last—away yonder—well, where you like, the poor pedagogue went sprawling to the ground—I hope in a soft place." And I think the rollicking humor of it was as much enjoyed by him that autumn morning, and that he felt in his bones just as relishy a smack of it all—as if Katrina Van Tassel had held her quilting frolic only on the yesternight.

Irving first came to know Tarrytown and Sleepy Hollow when a boy of fourteen or fifteen—he passing some holidays in these parts, I think, with his friend Paulding. To those days belong much of that idle sauntering along brook-sides hereabout, with fly-hooks and fish-rods, and memories of Walton, which get such delightful recognition in a certain paper of the "Sketch Book."

Then, too, he with his companions came to know the old Dutch farmers of the region, whose home interiors found their way afterward into his books.

I think he pointed out also, with a significant twinkle of the eye, which the dullest boy would have understood, some orchards, with which he had early acquaintance; and specially, too, upon some hilltop (which I think I could find now), a farmery, famous for its cider-mill and the good cider made there; he, with the rest, testing it over and over in the old slow way with straws, but provoked once on a time to a fuller test, by turning the hogshead, so they might sip from the open bung; and then (whether out of mischief or mishandling, he did not absolutely declare to me) the big barrel got the better of them, and set off upon a lazy roll down the hill—going faster and faster —they, more and more frightened, and scudding away slantwise over the fences—the yelling farmer appearing suddenly at the top of the slope, but too broad in the beam for any sharp race, and the hogshead between them plunging, and bounding, and giving out ghostly, guttural explosions of sound, and cider, at every turn. You may judge if Mr. Irving did not put a nice touch to that story!

After this memorable autumn drive amongst the hills, I
met with Mr. Irving frequently at his own home; and shall
I be thought impertinent and indiscreet if I say that at
times—rare times, it is true—I have seen this most amiable gentleman manifest a little of that restive choler
which sometimes flamed up in William the Testy—not
long-lived, not deliberate—but a little human blaze, of
impatience at something gone awry in the dressing of a
garden border, in the care of some stable pet—that was all
gone with the first blaze, but marked and indicated the
sources of that wrathy and pious zest (with which he is not
commonly credited) with which he loved to put a con-
temptuous thrust of his sharper language into the bloat
of upstart pride, and of conceit, and of insolent pretension.

The boy-mischief in him, which led him out from his
old home in William street, after hours, over the shed-
roof, lingered in him for a good while, I think, and lent not
a little point to some of the keener pictures of the Knickerbocker history; and, if I do not mistake, there was now
and then a quiet chuckle as he told me of the foolish indignation with which some descendants of the old Dutch
worthies had seen their ancestors put to a tender broil
over the playful blaze of his humor.

Indeed there was a spontaneity and heartiness about
that Knickerbocker history, which I think he carried a
strong liking for, all his life.

The "Sketch Book," written years later, and when necessity enforced writing, was done with a great audience
in his eye; and he won it, and keeps it bravely. I know
there is a disposition to speak of it rather patronizingly
and apologetically—as if it were reminiscent—Anglican—
conventional—as if he would have done better if he had
possessed our modern critical bias—or if he had been
born in Boston—or born a philosopher outright. Well,
perhaps so—perhaps so! But I love to think and believe
that our dear old Mr. Irving was born just where he should
have been born, and wrote in a way that it is hardly worth
our while to try and mend for him.

I understand that a great many promising young people, without the fear of the critics before their eyes, keep
on, persistently reading that old "Sketch Book," with its
"Broken Hearts," and "Wife" twining like a vine, and

"Spectre Bridegroom," and all the rest. And there are old people I know—one I am sure of—who never visit St. Paul's Churchyard without wanting to peep over Irving's shoulders into Mr. Newbury's shop, full of dear old toy-books;—who never go to Stratford-on-Avon but there is a hunt—first of all—for the Red Horse Tavern and the poker which was Irving's sceptre;—never sail on summer afternoons past the wall of the blue Catskills, but there is a longing lookout for the stray cloud-caps, and an eager listening for the rumbling of the balls which thundered in the ears of poor Rip Van Winkle.

What, pray, if the hero of " Bracebridge Hall " be own cousin to Sir Roger de Coverley? Is that a relationship to be discarded? And could any other than the writer we honor carry on more wisely the record of the cousin-ship, or with so sure a hand and so deft a touch declare and establish our inheritance in the rural beatitudes of England?

It may be true that as we read some of those earlier books of his we shall come upon some truisms which in these fast-paced times may chafe us—some rhetorical furbelows or broidery that belong to the wardrobes of the past—some tears that flow too easily,—but scarcely ever a page anywhere but, on a sudden, some shimmer of buoyant humor breaks through all the crevices of a sentence, a humor not born of rhetoric or measurable by critics' rules, but coming as the winds come, and playing up and down with a frolicsome, mischievous blaze, that warms, and piques, and delights us.

In the summer of 1852 I chanced to be quartered at the same hotel with him in Saratoga for a fortnight or more. He was then in his seventieth year, but still carrying himself easily up and down upon the corridors, and along the street, and through the grove at the spring. I recall vividly the tremulous pride with which, in those far-off days, I was permitted to join in many of these walks. He in his dark suit, of such cut and fit as to make one forget utterly its fashion and remember only the figure of the quiet gentleman, looking hardly middle-aged, with head thrown slightly to one side, and an eye always alert; not a fair young face dashing past us in its drapery of muslin but his eye drank in all its freshness and beauty

with the keen appetite and the grateful admiration of a
boy; not a dowager brushed us, bedizened with finery, but
he fastened the apparition in my memory with some pi-
quant remark, as the pin of an entomologist fastens a gaudy
fly. Other times there was a playful nudge of the elbow,
and a curious, meaning lift of the brow, to call attention
to something of droll aspect—perhaps some threatened
scrimmage amongst schoolboys—may be, only a passing
encounter between street dogs—for he had all the quick
responsiveness to canine language which belonged to the
author of "Rab and His Friends"; and I have known
him to stay his walk for five minutes together in a boyish,
eager intentness upon those premonitions of a dog encounter, watching the first inquisitive sniff—the reminiscent lift of the head—then the derogatory growl—the
growl apprehensive—the renewed sniff—the pauses for
reflection, then the milder and discursive growls—as if
either dog *could*, if he *would*—until one or the other, thinking more wisely of the matter, should turn tail, and trot
quietly away.

I trust I do not seem to vulgarize the occasion in bringing to view these little traits which set before us the man:
as I have already said, we cannot honor him more than by
recalling him in his full personality.

Over and over in his shrugs, in a twinkle of his eye, in
that arching of his brow, which was curiously full of meaning, did I see, as I thought, the germ of some new chapter,
such as crept into his sketch-books. Did I intimate as
much: "Ah," he would say, "that is game for young-
sters; we old fellows are not nimble enough to give chase
to sentiment."

He was engaged at that time upon his "Life of Washington," going out, as I remember, on one of these Saratoga days, for a careful inspection of the field of Burgoyne's surrender.

I asked after the system of his note-making for history.
"Ah," he said, "don't talk to me of system; I never had
any; you must go to Bancroft for that: I have, it is true,
my little budgets of notes—some tied one way, some another—and which, when I need, I think I come upon in
my pigeon-holes by a sort of instinct. That is all there
is of it."

There were some two or three beautiful dark-eyed women that summer at Saratoga, who were his special admiration, and of whose charm of feature he loved to discourse eloquently.   Those dark eyes led him back, doubtless, to the glad young days when he had known the beauties of Seville and Cordova.   Indeed, there was no episode in his life of which he was more prone to talk, than of that which carried him in his Spanish studies to the delightful regions which lie south of the Guadalquiver. Granada—the Alhambra—those names made the touchstone of his most gushing and eloquent talk.   Much as he loved and well as he painted the green fields of Warwickshire, and the hedges and the ivy-clad towers and the embowered lanes and the primroses and the hawthorn which set off the stories of ".Bracebridge Hall," yet, I think, he was never stirred by these memories so much as by the sunny valleys which lay in Andalusia, and by the tinkling fountains and rosy walls that caught the sunshine in the palace courts of Granada.

I should say that the crowning literary enthusiasms of his life were those which grouped themselves—first about those early Dutch foregatherings amongst the Van Twillers and the Stuyvesants and the Van Tassels—and next and stronger, those others which grouped about the great Moorish captains of Granada.

In the first—that is to say, his Knickerbocker studies— the historic sense was active but not dominant, and his humor in its first lusty wantonness went careering through the files of the old magnates, like a boy at play; and the memory of the play abode with him, and had its keen awakenings all through his life; there was never a year, I suspect, when the wooden leg of the doughty Peter Stuyvesant did not come clattering spunkily, and bringing its own boisterous welcome to his pleased recollection.

In the Spanish studies and amongst the Moors the historic sense was more dominant, the humor more in hand, and the magnificent ruins of this wrecked nation, which had brought its trail of light across Southern Europe from the far East, piqued all his sympathies, appealed to all his livelier fancies, and the splendors of court and camp lent a lustre to his pages which he greatly relished.   No English-speaking visitor can go to the Alhambra now, or henceforth ever will go thither, but the name of the author we honor to-night will come to his lip, and will lend, by some subtle magic, the master's silvery utterance to the dash of the fountains, to the soughing of the winds, to the chanting of the birds who sing in the ruinous courts of the Alhambra.

But I keep you too long [Cries of "No! no!—go on!"], and yet I have said no word of that quality in him which will, I think, most of all, make Centenary like this follow upon Centenary.

'Tis the kindness in him: 'Tis the simple good-heartedness of the man. Did he ever wrong a neighbor? Did he ever say an unkind thing of you, or me, or any one? Can you cull me a sneer that has hate in it anywhere in his books? Can you tell me of a thrust of either words or silence, which has malignity in it?

Fashions of books may change—do change; a studious realism may put in disorder the quaint dressing of his thought; an elegant philosophy of indifference may pluck out the bowels from his books. But the fashion of his heart and of his abiding good-will toward men will last— will last while the hills last.

And when you and I, sir, and all of us are beyond the reach of the centennial calls, I think that old Anthony Van Corlear's trumpet will still boom along the banks of the Hudson, heralding a man and a master, who to exquisite graces of speech added purity of life, and to the most buoyant and playful of humors added a love for all mankind.

CHARLES WHITLOCK MOORE

UNIVERSAL FRATERNITY OF MASONRY

[Address by Charles W. Moore, then R. W. Grand Secretary of the M. W. Grand Lodge of Massachusetts, delivered in Boston, November 29, 1856, at the celebration of the centennial anniversary of the Lodge of St. Andrew.]

WORSHIPFUL MASTER:—I suppose it to be entirely true, in view of the great accessions that have been made to its members within the last two or three years, that there are many persons present who entertain, at best, but a very general and indefinite idea of the antiquity, extent and magnitude of our Institution. And it is equally true that many even of our most intelligent and active young Brethren, not having their attention drawn to the subject, overlook its history and the extent of its influence, and naturally come to regard it in much the same light that they do the ordinary associations of the day; and this as naturally leads to indifference. Masonry, like every other science, whether moral or physical, to be rightly estimated, must be understood in all its relations and conditions. The intelligent Mason values it in the exact ratio that he has investigated its history and studied its philosophy.

But my immediate purpose is not to discuss the importance of the study of Masonry as a science, but to show its universality as a fraternity. This will necessarily involve to some extent the history of its rise and progress.

In the beginning of the Fifteenth century, Henry VI of England asked of our brethren of that day—"Where did Masonry begin?" And being told that it began in the East, his next inquiry was—"Who did bring it West-

erly?"—and he received for answer, that it was brought
Westerly by "the Phœnicians." These answers were
predicated, not on archæological investigations, for the
archæology of Masonry had not then been opened, but
on the traditions of the Order, as they had been transmitted from generation to generation, and from a period
running so far back along the stream of time that it had
been lost in the mists and obscurity of the mythological
ages. Recent investigations, guided by more certain
lights and more extensive and clearer developments of historical truth, have shown that these Brethren were not
misled by their traditions, and that their answers indicated, with remarkable precision, what the most learned
of our Brethren, in this country and in Europe, at the
present time believe to be the true origin of their Institution.

Freemasonry was originally a fraternity of practical
builders—architects and artificers. This is conceded by
all who are to any extent acquainted with its history or
its traditions. The Phœnicians, whose capital cities were
Tyre and Sidon, were the early patrons of that semi-
religious mystic fraternity or society of builders, known
in history as the "Dionysian Architects." That this fraternity were employed by the Tyrians and Sidonians in
the erection of costly temples to unknown Deities, in the
building of rich and gorgeous palaces, and in strengthening and beautifying their cities, is universally admitted.
That they were the "cunning workmen" sent by Hiram,
King of Tyre, to aid King Solomon in the erection of the
Temple on Mount Moriah, is scarcely less certain. Their
presence in that city at the time of the building of the
Temple, is the evidence of history; and Hiram, the widow's son, to whom Solomon intrusted the superintendence
of the workmen, as an inhabitant of Tyre, and as a skilled
architect and cunning and curious workman, was doubtless one of their number. Hence, we are scarcely claim-
ing too much for our Order, when we suppose that the
Dionysians were sent by Hiram, King of Tyre, to assist
King Solomon in the construction of the house he was
about to dedicate to Jehovah, and that they communicated
to their Jewish fellow-laborers a knowledge of the advantages of their fraternity, and invited them to a participa-

tion in its mysteries and privileges. The Jews were neither architects nor artificers. By Solomon's own admission, they were not even skilled enough in the art of building to cut and prepare the timber in the forests of Lebanon; and hence he was compelled to employ the Sidonians to do that work for him. "The Tyrians," says a learned foreign Brother, "were celebrated artists; Solomon, therefore, unable to find builders of superior skill, for the execution of his plans, in his own dominions, engaged Tyrians, who, with the assistance of the zealous Jews, who contented themselves in performing the inferior labor, finished that stupendous edifice." And we are told on the authority of Josephus that "the Temple at Jerusalem was built on the same plan, in the same style, and by the same architects, as the temples of Hercules and Astarte at Tyre." They were doubtless all three built by one of the companies of "Dionysian Architects," who at that time were numerous throughout Asia Minor, where they possessed the exclusive privilege of erecting temples, theatres, and other public buildings.

Dionysius arrived in Greece from Egypt about one thousand five hundred years before Christ, and there instituted, or introduced, the Dionysian mysteries. The Ionic migration occurred about three hundred years afterwards, or one thousand two hundred years B. C.—the emigrants carrying with them from Greece to Asia Minor the mysteries of Dionysius, before they had been corrupted by the Athenians. "In a short time," says Mr. Lawrie, "the Asiatic colonies surpassed the mother country in prosperity and science. Sculpture in marble, and the Doric and Ionic Orders were the result of their ingenuity." "We know," says a learned encyclopedist, "that the Dionysiacs of Ionia" (which place has, according to Herodotus, always been celebrated for the genius of its inhabitants), "were a great corporation of architects and engineers, who undertook, and even monopolized, the building of temples, stadiums, and theatres, precisely as the fraternity of Masons are known to have, in the Middle Ages, monopolized the building of cathedrals and conventual churches. Indeed, the Dionysiacs resembled the mystical fraternity, now called Freemasons, in many important particulars. They allowed no strangers to interfere in their employment; recognized each other by signs and tokens; they professed certain mysterious doctrines, under the tuition and tutelage of Bacchus; and they called all other men profane because not admitted to these mysteries."

The testimony of history is, that they supplied Ionia and the surrounding country, as far as the Hellespont, with theatrical apparatus, by contract. They also practised their art in Syria, Persia, and India; and about three hundred years before the birth of Christ, a considerable number of them were incorporated by command of the King of Pergamus, who assigned to them Teos as a settlement. It was this fraternity, whether called Greeks, Tyrians, or Phœnicians, who built the Temple at Jerusalem. That stupendous work, under God, was the result of their genius and scientific skill. And this being true, from them are we, as a fraternity, lineally descended, or our antiquity is a myth, and our traditions a fable. Hence the answer of our English Brethren of the Fifteenth century, to the enquiry of Henry VI, that Masonry was brought Westerly by the Phœnicians, indicated with great accuracy the probable origin of the Institution.

They might indeed have said to him that long anterior to the advent of Christianity, the mountains of Judea and the plains of Syria, the deserts of India and the valley of the Nile, were cheered by its presence and enlivened by its song;—that more than a thousand years before the coming of the "Son of Man," a little company of "cunning workmen," from the neighboring city of Tyre, were assembled on the pleasant Mount of Moriah, at the call of the wise King of Israel, and there erected out of their great skill a mighty edifice, whose splendid and unrivaled perfection, and whose grandeur and sublimity have been the admiration and theme of all succeeding ages. They might have said to him, that this was the craft-work of a fraternity to whose genius and discoveries, and to whose matchless skill and ability, the wisest of men in all ages have bowed with respect. They might have said to him that, having finished that great work, and filled all Judea with temples and palaces and walled cities, having enriched and beautified Azor, Gozarra, and Palmyra, with the results of their genius, these "cunning workmen" in after-times, passing through the Essenian associations, and finally issuing out of the mystic halls of the "Collegia Artificium" of Rome, burst upon the "dark ages" of the world like a bright star peering through a black cloud, and, under the patronage of the church, produced those splendid monuments of genius which set at defiance the highest attainments of modern art. And, if in addition to all this, they had said to him, that in the year A. D. 926, one of his predecessors on the throne of England had invited them from all parts of the continent, to meet him in general assembly at his royal city of York, the answer to his inquiry—"Who did bring it Westerly?"—would have been complete.

Henceforward, for eight centuries, Masonry continued an operative fraternity; producing both in England and on the Continent, those grand and unapproachable specimens of art which are the pride of Central Europe, and the admiration of the traveler. But it is no longer an operative association. We of this day, as Masons, set up no pretensions to extraordinary skill in the physical sciences. Very few of us—accomplished Masons as we may be—would willingly undertake to erect another Temple on Mount Moriah! Very certain we are that our own honored M. W. Grand Master,—*primus inter pares*, as all his Brethren acknowledge him to be, would hesitate a long time before consenting to assume the duties of architect for another Westminster Abbey, or a new St. Paul's. No. At the reorganization of the Craft and the establishment of the present Grand Lodge of England in 1717, we laid aside our operative character, and with it all pretensions to extraordinary skill in architectural science. We then became a purely moral and benevolent association, whose great aim is the development and cultivation of the moral sentiment, the social principle, and the benevolent affections, a higher reverence for God, and a warmer love for man. New laws and regulations, adapted to the changed condition of the Institution, were then made,—an entire revolution in its governmental policy took place, order and system obtained where neither had previously existed, and England became the great central point of Masonry for the whole world.

From this source have Lodges, Grand and Subordinate,

at various times, been established, and still exist and flourish—in France and Switzerland; in all the German States, save Austria (and there at different times, and for short seasons); all up and down the classic shores of the Rhine; in Prussia, Holland, Belgium, Saxony, Hanover, Sweden, Denmark, Russia, and even in fallen Poland; in Italy and Spain (under the cover of secrecy); in various parts of Asia; in Turkey; in Syria (as at Aleppo, where an English Lodge was established more than a century ago); in all the East India settlements, in Bengal, Bombay, Madras (in all of which lodges are numerous); in China, where there is a Provincial Grand Master and several Lodges; in various parts of Africa, as at the Cape of Good Hope and at Sierra Leone; on the Gambia and on the Nile; in all the larger islands of the Pacific and Indian oceans, as at Ceylon, Sumatra, St. Helena, Mauritius, Madagascar; the Sandwich group; in all the principal settlements of Australia, as at Adelaide, Melbourne, Parramatta, Sidney, New Zealand; in Greece, where there is a Grand Lodge; in Algeria, in Tunis, in the Empire of Morocco,—and wherever else in the Old World the genius of civilization has obtained a standpoint, or Christianity has erected the Banner of the Cross.

In all the West India islands, and in various parts of South America, as in Peru, Venezuela, New Granada, Guiana, Brazil, Chili, etc., Masonry is prospering as never before. In the latter Republic, the Grand Lodge of this Commonwealth has a flourishing subordinate, and the Grand Master has just authorized the establishment of another Lodge there.

On our own Continent the Order was never more widely diffused, or in a more healthy condition. In Mexico, even, respectable Lodges are maintained, in despite of the opposition of a bigoted Priesthood; and in all British America, from Newfoundland, through Nova Scotia and the Canadas to the icy regions of the North, Masonic Lodges and Masonic Brethren may be found, " to feed the hungry, clothe the naked and bind up the wounds of the afflicted."

On the condition of the Institution in our own country, I need not dwell. Every State and Territory—except the unorganized territory of Washington, including even

Kansas, has its Grand Lodge; and nearly every considerable town and village, its one or more subordinate Lodges. If we add to these, the large number of Chapters, Councils, Encampments, and other Masonic associations, which are spread all over the length and breadth of the land, we have the evidence of a prosperity unparalleled in the annals of any other human Institution, in any age of the world.

Masonry is indeed a universal Institution. History does not furnish its parallel. It exists where Christianity has not gone; and its claims will be respected even where the superior claims of religion would fail. It is never obscured by the darkness of night. The eye of day is always upon it. Its footprints are to be traced in the most distant regions and in the remotest ages of the earth. Among all civilized people, and in all Christianized lands, its existence is recognized. It came to our shores at an auspicious period; and it was here rocked in the Cradle of Liberty by a Washington, a Franklin, a Hancock, and a Warren. Unaffected by the tempests of war, the storms of persecution, or the denunciations of fanaticism, it still stands proudly erect in the sunshine and clear light of heaven, with not a marble fractured, not a pillar fallen. It still stands, like some patriarchal monarch of the forest, with its vigorous roots riveted to the soil, and its broad limbs spread in bold outline against the sky; and in generations yet to come, as in ages past, the sunlight of honor and renown will delight to linger and play amid its venerable branches. And if ever, in the Providence of God, lashed by the storm and riven by the lightning, it shall totter to its fall, around its trunk will the ivy of filial affection, that has so long clasped it, still cling, and mantle with greenness and verdure its ruin and decay.

GOUVERNEUR MORRIS

ORATION OVER ALEXANDER HAMILTON

[Funeral oration by Gouverneur Morris, statesman and man of affairs (born in Morrisania, N. Y., January 31, 1752; died there, November 6, 1816), pronounced before the porch of Trinity Church, New York City, over the body of Alexander Hamilton, just prior to the interment, July 14, 1804.]

If on this sad, this solemn occasion, I should endeavor to move your commiseration, it would be doing injustice to that sensibility which has been so generally and so justly manifested. Far from attempting to excite your emotions, I must try to repress my own; and yet, I fear, that, instead of the language of a public speaker, you will hear only the lamentations of a wailing friend. But I will struggle with my bursting heart, to portray that heroic spirit, which has flown to the mansions of bliss.

Students of Columbia—he was in the ardent pursuit of knowledge in your academic shades when the first sound of the American war called him to the field. A young and unprotected volunteer, such was his zeal, and so brilliant his service, that we heard his name before we knew his person. It seemed as if God had called him suddenly into existence, that he might assist to save a world! The penetrating eye of Washington soon perceived the manly spirit which animated his youthful bosom. By that excellent judge of men he was selected as an aid, and thus he became early acquainted with, and was a principal actor in the more important scenes of our revolution. At the siege of York he pertinaciously insisted on, and he obtained the command of a Forlorn Hope. He stormed the redoubt; but let it be recorded that not one single man of the enemy perished. His gallant troops, emulating the heroism of their chief, checked the uplifted arm, and spared a foe no longer resisting. Here closed his military career.

Shortly after the war, your favor—no, your discernment, called him to public office. You sent him to the convention at Philadelphia; he there assisted in forming that constitution which is now the bond of our union, the shield of our defence, and the source of our prosperity. In signing the compact, he expressed his apprehension that it did not contain sufficient means of strength for its own preservation; and that in consequence we should share the fate of many other republics, and pass through anarchy to despotism. We hoped better things. We confided in the good sense of the American people; and, above all, we trusted in the protecting providence of the Almighty. On this important subject he never concealed his opinion. He disdained concealment. Knowing the purity of his heart, he bore it as it were in his hand, exposing to every passenger its inmost recesses. This generous indiscretion subjected him to censure from misrepresentation. His speculative opinions were treated as deliberate designs; and yet you all know how strenuous, how unremitting were his efforts to establish and to preserve the constitution. If, then, his opinion was wrong, pardon, O pardon! that single error, in a life devoted to your service.

At the time when our government was organized, we were without funds, though not without resources. To call them into action, and establish order in the finances, Washington sought for splendid talents, for extensive information, and above all, he sought for sterling, incorruptible integrity. All these he found in Hamilton. The system then adopted, has been the subject of much animadversion. If it be not without a fault, let it be remembered that nothing human is perfect. Recollect the circumstances of the moment—recollect the conflict of opinion—and, above all, remember that a minister of a republic must bend to the will of the people. The administration which Washington formed was one of the most efficient, one of the best that any country was ever blessed with. And the result was a rapid advance in power and prosperity, of which there is no example in any other age or nation. The part which Hamilton bore is universally known.

His unsuspecting confidence in professions, which he believed to be sincere, led him to trust too much to the undeserving. This exposed him to misrepresentation. He felt himself obliged to resign. The care of a rising family, and the narrowness of his fortune, made it a duty to return to his profession for their support. But though he was compelled to abandon public life, never, no, never for a moment did he abandon the public service. He never lost sight of your interests. I declare to you, before that God, in whose presence we are now especially assembled, that in his most private and confidential conversations, the single objects of discussion and consideration were your freedom and happiness. You well remember the state of things which again called forth Washington from his retreat to lead your armies. You know that he asked for Hamilton to be his second in command. That venerable sage well knew the dangerous incidents of a military profession, and he felt the hand of time pinching life at its source. It was probable that he would soon be removed from the scene, and that his second would succeed to the command. He knew by experience the importance of that place—and he thought the sword of America might safely be confided to the hand which now lies cold in that coffin. Oh! my fellow citizens, remember this solemn testimonial that he was not ambitious. Yet he was charged with ambition, and, wounded by the imputation, when he laid down his command he declared, in the proud independence of his soul, that he never would accept of any office, unless in a foreign war he should be called on to expose his life in defence of his country. This determination was immovable. It was his fault that his opinions and his resolutions could not be changed. Knowing his own firm purpose, he was indignant at the charge that he sought for place or power. He was ambitious only for glory, but he was deeply solicitous for you. For himself he feared nothing; but he feared that bad men might, by false professions, acquire your confidence, and abuse it to your ruin.

Brethren of the Cincinnati—there lies our chief! Let

him still be our model. Like him, after long and faithful public services, let us cheerfully perform the social duties of private life. Oh! he was mild and gentle. In him there was no offence; no guile. His generous hand and heart were open to all.

Gentlemen of the bar—you have lost your brightest ornament. Cherish and imitate his example. While, like him, with justifiable and with laudable zeal, you pursue the interests of your clients, remember, like him, the eternal principle of justice.

Fellow citizens—you have long witnessed his professional conduct, and felt his unrivaled eloquence. You know how well he performed the duties of a citizen—you know that he never courted your favor by adulation or the sacrifice of his own judgment. You have seen him contending against you, and saving your dearest interests, as it were, in spite of yourselves. And you now feel and enjoy the benefits resulting from the firm energy of his conduct. Bear this testimony to the memory of my departed friend. I charge you to protect his fame. It is all he has left—all that these poor orphan children will inherit from their father. But, my countrymen, that fame may be a rich treasure to you also. Let it be the test by which to examine those who solicit your favor. Disregarding professions, view their conduct, and on a doubtful occasion ask, Would Hamilton have done this thing?

You all know how he perished. On this last scene I cannot, I must not dwell. It might excite emotions too strong for your better judgment. Suffer not your indignation to lead to any act which might again offend the insulted majesty of the laws. On his part, as from his lips, though with my voice—for his voice you will hear no more—let me entreat you to respect yourselves.

And now, ye ministers of the everlasting God, perform your holy office, and commit these ashes of our departed brother to the bosom of the grave.

WILLIAM MORRIS

ART AND THE BEAUTY OF THE EARTH

[Address by William Morris, poet, printer, and writer on socialism (born at Walthamstow, Essex, near London, March 24, 1834; died in Hammersmith, October 3, 1896), delivered at Burslem Town-Hall, October 13, 1881.]

We are here in the midst of a population busied about a craft which may be called the most ancient in the world, a craft which I look upon with the greatest interest, as I well may, since, except perhaps the noble craft of house-building, it is second to none other. And in the midst of this industrious population, engaged in making goods of such importance to our households, I am speaking to a School of Art, one of the bodies that were founded all over the country at a time when it was felt there was something wrong as between the two elements that go to make anything which can be correctly described as a work of industrial art, namely, the utilitarian and the artistic elements. I hope nothing I may say to-night will make you think that I undervalue the importance of these places of instruction; on the contrary, I believe them to be necessary to us, unless we are prepared to give up all attempt to unite these two elements of use and beauty.

Now, though no man can be more impressed with the importance of the art of pottery than I am, and though I have not, I hope, neglected the study of it from the artistic or historico-artistic side, I do not think myself bound to follow up the subject of your especial art; not so much because I know no more of the technical side of it than I have thought enough to enable me to understand it from the above said historico-artistic side; but rather because

I feel it almost impossible to dissociate one of the ornamental arts from the others, as things go now-a-days. Neither do I think I should interest you much, still less instruct you, if I were to recapitulate the general rules that ought to guide a designer for the industrial arts; at the very first foundation of these schools the instructors in them formulated those rules clearly and satisfactorily, and I think they have since been accepted generally, at least in theory. What I do really feel myself bound to do is to speak to you of certain things that are never absent from my thoughts, certain considerations on the condition and prospects of the arts in general, the neglect of which conditions would drive us in time into a strange state of things indeed; a state of things under which no potter would put any decoration on his pots, and indeed, if a man of strict logical mind, would never know of what shape to make a pot, unless the actual use it was to be put to drove him in one direction or another. What I have to say on these matters will not, I fear, be very new to you, and perhaps it may more or less offend you; but I will beg you to believe that I feel deeply the honor you have done me in asking me to address you. I cannot doubt you have asked me to do so that you might hear what I may chance to think on the subject of the arts, and it seems to me, therefore, that I should ill repay you for that honor, and be treating you unworthily, if I were to stand here and tell you at great length what I do not think. So I will ask your leave and license to speak plainly, as I promise I will not speak lightly.

Yet I would not have you think I underrate the difficulty of the art of plain speaking, an art as difficult, perhaps, as that of pottery, and not nearly so much of it done in the world; so what I will ask you to forgive me if I wound your feelings in any way will not be my downright meaning, my audacious and rash thought, but rather my clumsy way of expressing it; and in truth I expect to have your forgiveness, since in my heart I believe that a plain word spoken because it must be said, free from malice or self-seeking, can be no lasting offence to any one, whereas, what end is there to the wrong and damage that come of half-hearted speech, of words spoken in vagueness, hypocrisy, and cowardice?

You who in these parts make such hard, smooth, well-compacted, and enduring pottery understand well that you must give it other qualities besides those which make it fit for ordinary use. You must profess to make it beautiful as well as useful, and if you did not you would certainly lose your market. That has been the view the world has taken of your art, and of all the industrial arts since the beginning of history, and, as I said, is held to this day, whether from the force of habit or otherwise.

Nevertheless, so different is the position of art in our daily lives from what it used to be that it seems to me (and I am not alone in my thought), that the world is hesitating as to whether it shall take art home to it or cast it out.

I feel that I am bound to explain what may seem a very startling as it is assuredly a very serious statement. I will do so in as few words as I can. I do not know whether a sense of the great change which has befallen the arts in modern times has come home to most, or indeed to many, of you; a change which has only culminated in quite recent times within the lives of many of you present. It may seem to you that there has been no break in the chain of art, at all events since it began to struggle out of the confusion and barbarism of the early middle ages; you may think that there has been gradual change in it, growth, improvement (not always perhaps readily recognized at first, that latter), but that all this has taken place without violence or breakdown, and that the growth and improvement are still going on.

And this seems a very reasonable view to take of it, and is analogous beyond doubt to what has happened on other sides of human progress; nay, it is on this ground that your pleasure in art is founded, and your hopes for its future. That foundation for hope has failed some of us; on what our hopes are founded to-day I may be able to tell you partly this evening, but I will now give you a glimpse of the abyss into which our earlier hope tumbled.

Let us look back a little to the early middle ages, the days of barbarism and confusion. As you follow the pages of the keen-eyed, cool-headed Gibbon, you may well think that the genius of the great historian has been wasted over the mean squabbles, the bald self-seeking,

the ignoble superstition, the pomp and the cruelty of the
kings and scoundrels who are the chief persons named in
the story; yet also you cannot fail to know, when you
come to think of it, that the story has not been fully told;
nay scarce told at all, only a chance hint given, here and
there. The palace and the camp were but a small part of
their world surely; and outside them you may be sure that
faith and heroism and love were at work, or what birth
could there have been from those days? For the visible
tokens of that birth you must seek in the art that grew
up and flourished amid that barbarism and confusion, and
you know who wrought it. The tyrants, and pedants,
and bullies of the time paid dog's wages for it, and bribed
their gods with it, but they were too busy over other
things to make it; the nameless people wrought it; for no
names of its makers are left, not one. Their work only
is left, and all that came of it, and all that is to come of it.

What came of it first was the complete freedom of art in
the midst of a society that had at least begun to free itself
from religious and political fetters. Art was no longer
now, as in Egypt of olden time, kept rigidly within certain prescribed bounds that no fancy might play with, no
imagination overpass, lest the majesty of the beautiful
symbols might be clouded and the memory of the awful
mysteries they symbolized become dim in the hearts of
men. Nor was it any longer as in the Greece of Pericles,
wherein no thought might be expressed that could not
be expressed in perfect form. Art was free. Whatever
a man thought of, that he might bring to light by the
labor of his hands, to be praised and wondered at by his
fellows. Whatever man had thought in him of any kind,
and skill in him of any kind to express it, he was deemed
good enough to be used for his own pleasure and the
pleasure of his fellows; in this art nothing and nobody
was wasted; all people east of the Atlantic felt this art;
from Bokhara to Galway, from Iceland to Madras, all
the world glittered with its brightness and quivered with
its vigor. It cast down the partitions of race and religion
also. Christian and Mussulman were made joyful by
it; Kelt, Teuton, and Latin raised it up together; Per-
sian, Tartar, and Arab gave and took its gifts from one
another. Considering how old the world is it was not

too long-lived at its best. In the days when Norwegian, Dane, and Icelander stalked through the streets of Micklegarth, and hedged with their axes the throne of Kirialax the Greek king, it was alive and vigorous. When blind Dandolo was led from the Venetian galleys on to the conquered wall of Constantinople, it was near to its best and purest days. When Constantine Palæologus came back an old and careworn man from a peacefuller home in the Morea to his doom in the great city, and the last Cæsar got the muddle of his life solved, not ingloriously, by Turkish swords on the breached and battered walls of that same Constantinople, there were signs of sickness beginning to show in the art that sprang from there to cover East and West alike with its glory.

And all that time it was the art of free men. Whatever slavery still existed in the world (more than enough, as always) art had no share in it; and still it was only here and there that any great names rose above the host of those that wrought it. These names (and it was mainly in Italy only) came to the front when those branches of it that were the work of collective rather than individual genius, architecture especially, had quite reached their highest perfection. Men began to look round for something more startlingly new than the slow, gradual change of architecture and the attendant lesser arts could give them. This change they found in the glorious work of the painters, and they received it with an outspoken excitement and joy that seems strange indeed to us in these days when art is held so cheap.

All went better than well for a time; though in Italy architecture began to lose something of the perfection it had gained, yet it was scarcely to be noticed amidst the glory of the light that was increasing in painting and sculpture. In France and England meantime the change, as it was slower in growing to a head, so it had begun earlier, as witness the sculpture in the great French Churches, and the exquisite drawing of the illuminations of English books; while the Flemings, never very great in the art of building, towards the end of this period had found their true vocation as painters of a sweet and serious external naturalism, illuminated by color unsurpassed for purity and brightness.

So had the art of the middle ages climbed gradually to the top of the hill, doubtless not without carrying the seeds of the disease that was to end it, threatenings of great change which no doubt no one heeded at the time. Nor was there much to wonder at in their blindness, since still for centuries to come their art was full of life and splendor, and when at last its death drew near men could see in it nothing but the hope of a new life. For many years, a hundred years at least, before the change really showed itself, the expression of the greater thoughts that art can deal with was being made more difficult to men not specially learned. Without demanding the absolute perfection that was the rule in the days of Greece, people began to look for an intricacy of treatment that the Greeks had never dreamed of; men began to see hopes of realizing scenes of history and poetry in a far more complete way than the best of their forerunners had attempted. Yet for long the severance between artist and artisan (as our nicknames go) was not obvious, though doubtless things were leading up to it; it is, perhaps, noticeable chiefly in the difference between the work of nation and nation rather than among the individual workmen. I mean, for instance, that in the Thirteenth century England was going step by step with Italy as far as mere excellence is concerned, while in the middle of the Fifteenth England was rude, and Italy cultured; and even while the change was preparing, by one accident or another came a great access of discoveries of the art and literature of the ancient world, and, as it were, fate ran to meet the half-expressed longings of men.

Then, indeed, all hesitation was over, and suddenly, as it now seems to us, amidst a blaze of glory, the hoped-for new birth took place. Once, as I have said, the makers of beautiful things passed away nameless; but under the Renaissance there are more names of excellent craftsmen left to us than a good memory can well remember, and among those names are the greatest the world has ever known, or perhaps ever will know. No wonder men's exultation rose high; no wonder that their pride blinded them and that they did not know where they were; yet most pitiable and sad the story is. It was one of those strange times when men seem to themselves to have pierced through all the space which lies between longing and attainment.   They, it seems, and no others, have at last reached the spot where lie heaped together all the treasures of the world, vainly sought aforetime.   They, it seems, have everything, and no one of those that went before them had anything, nay, not even their fathers whose bones lie yet unrotted under the turf.

The men of the Renaissance looked at the thousand years behind them as a deedless blank, and at all that lay before them as a perpetual triumphal march.   We, taught so much by other people's failures, can see their position otherwise than that.   We can see that while up to that time, since art first began, it had always looked forward, now it was looking backward; that whereas once men were taught to look through the art at that which the art represented, they were now taught to deem the art an end in itself, and that it mattered nothing whether the story it told was believed or not.   Once its aim was to see, now its aim was to be seen only.   Once it was done to be understood, and to be helpful to all men: now the vulgar were beyond the pale, and the insults which the Greek slaveholders and the Roman tax-sweaters of old cast upon the people, upon all men but a chosen few, were brought forth and tricked up again in fantastic guise to adorn the day of boundless hope.

Not all this, indeed, came at once, but come it did, nor very slowly either, when men once began to look back. At the beginning of the Sixteenth century the new birth was in its heyday.   Before the Seventeenth had quite begun, what had become of its overweening hopes?   In Venice alone of all Italy was any art being done that was of any worth.   The conquered North had gained nothing from Italy save an imitation of its worst extravagance, and all that saved the art of England from nothingness was a tradition of the earlier days still lingering among a people rustic and narrow-minded indeed, but serious, truthful, and of simple habits.

I have just spoken somewhat of how this came about. But what was at the bottom of it, and what I wish you chiefly to note and remember is this, that the men of the Renaissance lent all their energies, consciously or unconsciously, to the severance of art from the daily lives of men, and that they brought it to pass, if not utterly in their own days, yet speedily and certainly. I must remind you, though I, and better men than I, have said it over and over again, that once every man that made anything made it a work of art besides a useful piece of goods, whereas now, only a very few things have even the most distant claim to be considered works of art. I beg you to consider that most carefully and seriously, and to try to think what it means. But first, lest any of you doubt it, let me ask you what forms the great mass of the objects that fill our museums, setting aside positive pictures and sculpture? Is it not just the common household goods of past time? True it is that some people may look upon them simply as curiosities, but you and I have been taught most properly to look upon them as priceless treasures that can teach us all sorts of things, and yet, I repeat, they are for the most part common household goods, wrought by "common fellows," as people say now, without any cultivation, men who thought the sun went round the earth, and that Jerusalem was exactly in the middle of the world.

Again, take another museum that we have still left us, our country churches. Take note of them, I say, to see how art ran through everything; for you must not let the name of "church" mislead you: in times of real art people built their churches in just the same style as their houses; "ecclesiastical art" is an invention of the last thirty years. Well, I myself am just fresh from an out-of-the-way part of the country near the end of the navigable Thames, where, within a radius of five miles, are some half-dozen tiny village churches, every one of which is a beautiful work of art, with its own individuality. These are the works of the Thames-side country bumpkins, as you would call us, nothing grander than that. If the same sort of people were to design and build them now (since within the last fifty years or so they have lost all the old traditions of building, though they clung to them longer than most people), they could not build anything better than the ordinary little plain Nonconformist chapels that one sees scattered about new neighborhoods. That is what they correspond with, not an architect-designed new Gothic church. The more you study archæology the more certain you will become that I am right in this, and that what we have left us of earlier art was made by the unhelped people. Neither will you fail to see that it was made intelligently and with pleasure.

That last word brings me to a point so important that at the risk of getting wearisome I must add it to my old sentence and repeat the whole. Time was when everybody that made anything made a work of art besides a useful piece of goods, and it gave them pleasure to make it. That is an assertion from which nothing can drive me; whatever I doubt, I have no doubt of that. And, sirs, if there is anything in the business of my life worth doing, if I have any worthy aspiration, it is the hope that I may help to bring about the day when we shall be able to say, So it was once, so it is now.

Do not misunderstand me; I am not a mere praiser of past times. I know that in those days of which I speak life was often rough and evil enough, beset by violence, superstition, ignorance, slavery; yet I cannot help thinking that sorely as poor folks needed a solace, they did not altogether lack one, and that solace was pleasure in their work. Ah, sirs, much as the world has won since then, I do not think it has won for all men such perfect happiness that we can afford to cast aside any solace that nature holds forth to us. Or must we forever be casting out one devil by another? Shall we never make a push to get rid of the whole pack of them at once?

I do not mean to say that all the work we do now is done without any pleasure, but I mean to say that the pleasure is rather that of conquering a good spell of work, a courageous and good feeling certainly, or of bearing up well under the burden, and seldom, very seldom, comes to the pitch of compelling the workman, out of the fulness of his heart, to impress on the work itself the tokens of his manly pleasure.

Nor will our system of organizing the work allow of it. In almost all cases there is no sympathy between the designer and the man who carries out the design; not unseldom the designer also is driven to work in a mechanical, down-hearted kind of way, and I don't wonder at it. I know by experience that the making of design after design, mere diagrams, mind you, without one's self executing them, is a great strain upon the mind. It is necessary, unless all workmen of all grades are to be permanently degraded into machines, that the hand should rest the mind as well as the mind the hand. And I say that this is the kind of work which the world has lost, supplying its place with the work which is the result of the division of labor. That work, whatever else it can do, cannot produce art, which must, as long as the present system lasts, be entirely confined to such works as are the work from beginning to end of one man: pictures, independent sculpture, and the like. As to these, on the one hand, they cannot fill the gap which the loss of popular art has made, nor can they, especially the more imaginative of them, receive the sympathy which should be their due. I must speak plainly and say that as things go it is impossible for any one who is not highly educated to understand the higher kind of pictures. Nay, I believe most people receive very little impression indeed from any pictures but those which represent the scenes with which they are thoroughly familiar. The aspect of this as regards people in general is to my mind much more important than that which has to do with the unlucky artist; but he also has some claim upon our consideration; and I am sure that this lack of the general sympathy of simple people weighs very heavily on him, and makes his work feverish and dreamy, or crabbed and perverse.

No, be sure if the people is sick its leaders also have need of healing. Art will not grow and flourish, nay, it will not long exist, unless it be shared by all people; and for my part I don't wish that it should.

Therefore it is that I stand before you to say that the world has in these days to choose whether she will have art or leave it, and that we also, each one of us, have to make up our minds which camp we will or can join, those that honestly accept art or those that honestly reject it.

Once more let me try to put into words what these two alternatives mean. If you accept it, it must be part of your daily lives, and the daily life of every man. It will be with us wherever we go, in the ancient city full of traditions of past time, in the newly-cleared farm in America or the colonies, where no man has dwelt for traditions to gather round him; in the quiet countryside as in the busy town, no place shall be without it. You will have it with you in your sorrow as in your joy, in your work-a-day hours as in your leisure. It shall be no respecter of persons, but be shared by gentle and simple, learned and unlearned, and be as a language that all can understand. It will not hinder any work that is necessary to the life of man at the best, but it will destroy all degrading toil, all enervating luxury, all foppish frivolity. It will be the deadly foe of ignorance, dishonesty, and tyranny, and will foster good-will, fair dealing, and confidence between man and man. It will teach you to respect the highest intellect with a manly reverence, but not to despise any man who does not pretend to be what he is not; and that which will be the instrument that it shall work with and the food that shall nourish it shall be man's pleasure in his daily labor, the kindest and best gift that the world has ever had.

Again I say, I am sure that this is what art means, no less; that if we attempt to keep art alive on other terms we are but bolstering up a sham, and that it would be far better for us to accept the other alternative, the frank rejection of art, as many people, and they not the worst of us, have already done. To these and not to me you must go if you want to have any clear idea of what is hoped for the future of the world when art is laid within her tomb. Yet I think I can in a measure judge from the present tendency of matters what is likely to happen to those things which we handicraftsmen have to deal with.

When men have given up the idea that the work of men's hands can ever be pleasurable to them they must, as good men and true, do their utmost to reduce the work of the world to a minimum; like us artists they must do all they can to simplify the life of man, to reduce his wants as much as possible; and doubtless in theory they will be able to reduce them more than we shall, for it is clear that the waste of tissue caused by a search after beauty will be forbidden: all ornament will cease from the work of men's hands, though still, wherever nature works there will be beauty. The garment shall be unadorned, though the moth that frets it is painted with silver and pearl. London shall be a desert of hideousness, though the blossom of the " London pride " be more daintily flecked than the minutest missal that ever monk painted. And when all is done there will yet be too much work, that is to say, too much pain in the world.

What then? Machines then. Truly we shall have a good stock to start with, but not near enough. Some men must press on to martyrdom, and toil to invent new ones, till at last pretty nearly everything that is necessary to men will be made by machines. I don't see why it should not be done. I myself have boundless faith in their capacity. I believe machines can do everything, except make works of art.

And yet again, what next? Supposing we shall be able to get martyrs enough (or say slaves) to make all the machines that will still be needed, and to work them, shall we still be able to get rid of all labor, of all that which we have found out is an unmitigated curse? And what will our consciences be like (since I started by supposing us all to be conscientious people), when we think we have done all that we can do, and must still be waited upon by groaning, discontented wretches? What shall we do, I say?

Well, I must say that my imagination will stretch no further than to suggest rebellion in general as a remedy, the end of which rebellion, if successful, must needs be to set up some form of art again as a necessary solace of mankind.

But to say the truth, this leads me to making another suggestion, a practical one I consider it. Suppose we start by rebelling at once; because when I spoke of the world having to choose between accepting and rejecting art, I did not suppose that its choice could be final if it chose to reject it. No, the rebellion will have to come and will be victorious, don't doubt that; only if we wait till the tyranny is firmly established our rebellion will have to be a Nihilistic one; every help would be gone save deadly anger and the hope that comes of despair; whereas if we begin now, the change and the counter-change will work together, and the new art will come upon us gradually, and we shall one day see it marching on steadily and victoriously, though its battle has raised no clamor, we, or our sons, or our sons' sons.

How shall our rebellion begin then? What is the remedy for the lack of due pleasure in their work which has befallen all craftsmen, and for the consequent **sickness** of art and degradation of civilization?

I am afraid whatever answer I may make to that question will disappoint you. I myself suffer so sorely from the lack above mentioned that I have little remedy in myself save that of fostering discontent. I have no infallible nostrum to cure an evil whose growth is centuries old. Any remedies I can think of are commonplace enough. In those old days of popular art, the world, in spite of all the ills that beset life, was struggling towards civilization and liberty, and it is in that way which we must also struggle, unless you think that we are civilized enough already, as I must confess I do not. Education on all sides is what we must look to. We may expect, if we do not learn much, to learn this at least, that we know but little, and that knowledge means aspiration or discontent, call it which you will.

I do not doubt that, as far as our schools of art go, education is bringing us to that point. I do not think any reasonable man can consider them a failure when the condition of the ornamental part of the individual arts is considered at the time of their foundation. True it is that those who established them were partly influenced by a delusive expectation that they would presently be able to supply directly a demand which was felt for trained and skilful designers of goods; but, though this hope failed them, they have no doubt influenced both that side of art and others also; among all that they have done not the least is that public recognition of the value of art in general which their very existence implies: or, to speak more correctly, their existence and the interest that is felt in them, is a token of people's uneasiness at the present disorganized state of the arts.

Perhaps you who study here and represent such a large body of people who must needs have some aspirations towards the progress of the arts, will excuse a word or two from me a little less general than the rest I have been saying. I think I have a right to look upon you as enrolled soldiers of that rebellion against blank ugliness that I have been preaching this evening. You, therefore, above all people are bound to be careful not to give cause to the enemy to blaspheme. You are bound to be specially careful to do solid, genuine work, and eschew all pretence and flashiness.

Be careful to eschew all vagueness. It is better to be caught out in going wrong when you have had a definite purpose, than to shuffle and slur so that people can't blame you because they don't know what you are at. Hold fast to distinct form in art. Don't think too much of style, but set yourself to get out of you what you think beautiful, and express it, as cautiously as you please, but, I repeat, quite distinctly and without vagueness. Always think your design out in your head before you begin to get it on the paper. Don't begin by slobbering and messing about in the hope that something may come out of it. You must see it before you can draw it, whether the design be of your own invention or nature's. Remember always, form before color, and outline, silhouette, before modeling; not because these latter are of less importance, but because they can't be right if the first are wrong. Now, upon all these points you may be as severe with yourselves as you will, and are not likely to be too severe.

Furthermore, those of you especially who are designing for goods, try to get the most out of your material, but always in such a way as honors it most. Not only should it be obvious what your material is, but something should be done with it which is specially natural to it, something that could not be done with any other. This is the very *raison d'etre* of decorative art: to make stone look like ironwork, or wood like silk, or pottery like stone is the last resource of the decrepitude of art. Set yourselves as much as possible against all machine work (this to all men). But if you have to design for machine work, at least let your design show clearly what it is. Make it mechanical with a vengeance, at the same time as simple as possible. Don't try, for instance, to make a printed plate look like a hand-painted one: make it something which no one would try to do if he were painting by hand, if your market drives you into printed plates: I don't see the use of them myself. To sum up, don't let yourselves be made machines, or it is all up with you as artists.

Though I don't much love the iron and brass machines, the flesh and blood ones are more terrible and hopeless to me; no man is so clumsy or base a workman that he is not fit for something better than that.

Well, I have said that education is the first remedy for the barbarism which has been bred by the hurry of civilization and competitive commerce. To know that men lived and worked mightily before you is an incentive for you to work faithfully now, that you may leave something to those who come after you.

What next is to be thought of after education? I must here admit that if you accept art and join the ranks of those who are to rise in rebellion against the Philistines, you will have a roughish time of it. "Nothing for nothing and not much for a dollar," says a Yankee somewhere, and I am sorry to say it is the rule of nature also. Those of us who have money will have to give of it to the cause, and all of us will have to give time, and thought, and trouble to it; and I must now consider a matter of the utmost importance to art and to the lives of all of us, which we can, if we please, deal with at once, but which emphatically claims of us time, thought, and money. Of all the things that is likely to give us back popular art in England, the cleaning of England is the first and the most necessary. Those who are to make beautiful things must live in a beautiful place. Some people may be inclined to say, and I have heard the argument put forward, that the very opposition between the serenity and purity of art and the turmoil and squalor of a great modern city stimulates the invention of artists, and produces special life in the art of to-day. I cannot believe it. It seems to me that at the best it but stimulates the feverish and dreamy qualities that throw some artists out of the general sympathy. But apart from that, these are men who are stuffed with memories of more romantic days and pleasanter lands, and it is on these memories they live, to my mind not altogether happily for their art; and you see it is only a very few men who could have even these doubtful advantages.

I abide by my statement that those who are to make beautiful things must live in beautiful places, but you must understand I do not mean to claim for all craftsmen a share of those gardens of the world, or of those sublime and awe-inspiring mountains and wastes that men make pilgrimages to see; that is to say, not a personal share. Most of us must be content with the tales of the poets and painters about these places, and learn to love the narrow spot that surrounds our daily life for what of beauty and sympathy there is in it.

For surely there is no square mile of earth's inhabitable surface that is not beautiful in its own way, if we men will only abstain from wilfully destroying that beauty; and it is this reasonable share in the beauty of the earth that I claim as the right of every man who will earn it by due labor; a decent house with decent surroundings for every honest and industrious family; that is the claim which I make of you in the name of art. Is it such an exorbitant claim to make of civilization? of a civilization that is too apt to boast in after-dinner speeches; too apt to thrust her blessings on far-off peoples at the cannon's mouth before she has improved the quality of those blessings so far that they are worth having at any price, even the smallest.

Well, I am afraid that claim is exorbitant. Both you as representatives of the manufacturing districts, and I as representing the metropolis, seem hitherto to have assumed that, at any rate; nor is there one family in a thousand that has established its claim to the right aforesaid. It is a pity though; for if the claim is to be considered inadmissable, then is it most certain that we have been simply filling windbags and weaving sand-ropes by all the trouble we have taken in founding schools of art, National Galleries, South Kensington Museums, and all the rest of it.

I have said education is good, is necessary, to all people; neither can you if you would withhold it; and yet to educate people with no hope, what do you expect to come of that? Perhaps you might learn what to expect in Russia.

Look you, as I sit at my work at home, which is at Hammersmith, close to the river, I often hear go past the window some of that ruffianism of which a good deal has been said in the papers of late, and has been said before at recurring periods. As I hear the yells and shrieks and all the degradation cast on the glorious tongue of Shakespeare and Milton, as I see the brutal reckless faces and figures go past me, it rouses the recklessness and brutality in me also, and fierce wrath takes possession of me, till I remember, as I hope I mostly do, that it was my good luck only of being born respectable and rich that has put me on this side of the window among delightful books and lovely works of art, and not on the other side, in the empty street, the drink-steeped liquor-shops, the foul and degraded lodgings. What words can say what all that means? Do not think, I beg of you, that I am speaking rhetorically in saying that when I think of all this, I feel that the one great thing I desire is that this great country should shake off from her all foreign and colonial entanglements, and turn that mighty force of her respectable people, the greatest power the world has ever seen, to giving the children of these poor folk the pleasures and the hopes of men. Is that really impossible? is there no hope of it? If so, I can only say that civilization is a delusion and a lie; there is no such thing and no hope of such a thing.

But since I wish to live, and even to be happy, I cannot believe it impossible. I know by my own feelings and desires what these men want, what would have saved them from this lowest depth of savagery: employment which would foster their self-respect and win the praise and sympathy of their fellows, and dwellings which they could come to with pleasure, surroundings which would soothe and elevate them; reasonable labor, reasonable rest. There is only one thing that can give them this, and that is art.

I have no doubt that you think this statement a ridiculous exaggeration, but it is my firm conviction nevertheless, and I can only ask you to remember that in my mind it means the properly organized labor of all men who make anything; that must at least be a mighty instrument in the raising of men's self-respect, in the adding of dignity to their lives. Once more, "Nothing for nothing and very little for a dollar." You can no more have art without paying for it than you can have anything else, and if you care about art, as you must when you come to know it, you will not shrink from the necessary sacrifice. After all, we are the descendants and countrymen of those who have well known how to give the lesser for the greater.

What you have to sacrifice is chiefly money, that is, force, and dirt; a serious sacrifice I know; but perhaps, as I have said, we have made greater in England aforetime; nay, I am far from sure that dirt will not in the long run cost us more in hard cash even than art will.

So which shall we have, art or dirt?

What is to be done, then, if we make the better choice? The land we live in is not very big either in actual acreage or in scale of fashion, but I think it is not our natural love for it only that makes us think it as fit as any land for the peaceful dwellings of serious men. Our fathers have shown us that, if it could otherwise be doubted. I say, without fear of contradiction, that no dwelling of men has ever been sweeter or pleasanter than an ancient English house; but our fathers treated our lovely land well, and we have treated it ill. Time was when it was beautiful from end to end, and now you have to pick your way carefully to avoid coming across blotches of hideousness which are a disgrace, I will not say to civilization, but to human nature. I have seen no statistics of the size of these blotches in relation to the unspoiled, or partially spoiled, country, but in some places they run together so as to cover a whole county, or even several counties, while they increase at a fearful rate, fearful in good earnest and literally. Now, while this goes on unchecked, nay, unlamented, it is really idle to talk about art. While we are doing this or letting it be done, we are really covertly rejecting art, and it would be honester and better for us if we did so openly. If we accept art we must atone for what we have done and pay the cost of it. We must turn this land from the grimy back-yard of a workshop into a garden. If that seems difficult, or rather impossible, to some of you, I cannot help it; I only know that it is necessary.

As to its being impossible, I do not believe it. The men of this generation even have accomplished matters that but a very little while ago would have been thought impossible. They conquered their difficulties because their faces were set in that direction; and what was done once can be done again. Why even the money and the science that we expend in devices for killing and maiming our enemies present and future would make a good nest-egg

towards the promotion of decency of life if we could make
up our minds to that tremendous sacrifice.

However, I am far from saying that mere money can
do much or indeed anything: it is our will that must do it.
Nor need I attempt to try to show how that will should
express itself in action. True I have, in common with
some others, ideas as to what steps would best help us
on our way, but those ideas would not be accepted by
you, and I feel sure that when you are thoroughly intent
on the goal you will find the means to reach it, and it is
of infinitesimal importance what those means may be.
When you have accepted the maxim that the external
aspect of the country belongs to the whole public, and
that whoever wilfully injures that property is a public
enemy, the cause will be on its way to victory.

Meantime it is encouraging to me to think there is one
thing that makes it possible for me to stand here, in a
district that makes as much smoke as pottery, and to say
what I have been saying on the subject of dirt, and that is
that quite lately there has been visible expression given
to a feeling on this subject, which has doubtless been long
growing. If I am a crazy dreamer, as may well be, yet
there are many members and supporters of such societies
as the Kyrle and the Commons Preservation Societies,
who have not time to dream, and whose craziness, if that
befel them, would be speedily felt throughout the country.

I pray your pardon for having tried your patience so
long. A very few words more, and I have done. Those
words are words of hope. Indeed, if I have said anything
that seemed to you hopeless, it has been, I think, owing to
that bitterness which will sometimes overtake an impatient man when he feels how little his own hands can do
towards helping the cause that he has at heart. I know
that cause will conquer in the end, for it is an article of
faith with me that the world cannot drop back into savagery, and that art must be its fellow on the forward
march. I know well it is not for me to prescribe the road
which that progress must take. I know that many things
that seem to me to-day clinging hindrances, nay, poisons
to that progress, may be furtherers of it, medicines to it,
though they be fated to bring terrible things to pass before
the visible good comes of them. But that very faith im-

pels me to speak according to my knowledge, feeble as it may be and rash as the words may sound; for every man who has a cause at heart is bound to act as if it depended on him alone, however well he may know his own unworthiness; and thus is action brought to birth from mere opinion.

And in all I have been saying I have had steadily in mind that you have asked me to speak to you as a friend, and that I could do no less than be quite open and fearless before my friends and fellow-craftsmen.

JOHN HENRY, CARDINAL NEWMAN

Photogravure after a photograph from life

JOHN HENRY, CARDINAL NEWMAN

KNOWLEDGE VIEWED IN RELATION TO LEARNING

[Address by Cardinal Newman, theologian, poet, Cardinal of the Catholic Church from 1879 (born in London, February 21, 1801; died in Birmingham, August 11, 1890), delivered to the Catholics of Dublin in 1852 and published with other discourses under the general title, "The Idea of a University." In these addresses Dr. Newman endeavored to win the sympathy of prelates and gentry to a plan for the higher education of Catholics, at the same time to lay down the lines of organization for the new institution and to define its aims and policy. Dr. Newman was Rector of the University until 1858.]

GENTLEMEN:—It were well if the English, like the Greek language, possessed some definite word to express, simply and generally, intellectual proficiency or perfection, such as "health," as used with reference to the animal frame, and "virtue," with reference to our moral nature. I am not able to find such a term;—talent, ability, genius, belong distinctly to the raw material, which is the subject-matter, not to that excellence which is the result of exercise and training. When we turn, indeed, to the particular kinds of intellectual perfection, words are forthcoming for our purpose, as, for instance, judgment, taste, and skill; yet even these belong, for the most part, to powers or habits bearing upon practice or upon art, and not to any perfect condition of the intellect, considered in itself. Wisdom, again, is certainly a more comprehensive word than any other, but it has a direct relation to conduct, and to human life. Knowledge, indeed, and Science express purely intellectual ideas, but still not a state or quality of the intellect; for knowledge, in its ordinary sense, is but one of its circumstances, denoting a possession or a habit; and science has been appropriated to the subject-matter of the intellect, instead of belonging in English, as it ought to do, to the intellect itself.   The consequence is that, on an occasion like this, many words are necessary, in order, first, to bring out and convey what surely is no difficult idea in itself,—that of the cultivation of the intellect as an end; next, in order to recommend what surely is no unreasonable object; and lastly, to describe and make the mind realize the particular perfection in which that object consists.   Every one knows practically what are the constituents of health or of virtue; and every one recognizes health and virtue as ends to be pursued; it is otherwise with intellectual excellence, and this must be my excuse, if I seem to any one to be bestowing a good deal of labor on a preliminary matter.

In default of a recognized term, I have called the perfection or virtue of the intellect by the name of philosophy, philosophical knowledge, enlargement of mind, or illumination; terms which are not uncommonly given to it by writers of this day: but, whatever name we bestow on it, it is, I believe, as a matter of history, the business of a University to make this intellectual culture its direct scope, or to employ itself in the education of the intellect, —just as the work of a Hospital lies in healing the sick or wounded, of a Riding or Fencing School, or of a Gymnasium, in exercising the limbs, of an Almshouse, in aiding and solacing the old, of an Orphanage, in protecting innocence, of a Penitentiary, in restoring the guilty.   I say, a University, taken in its bare idea, and before we view it as an instrument of the Church, has this object and this mission; it contemplates neither moral impression nor mechanical production; it professes to exercise the mind neither in art nor in duty; its function is intellectual culture; here it may leave its scholars, and it has done its work when it has done as much as this.   It educates the intellect to reason well in all matters, to reach out towards truth, and to grasp it.

This, I said in my foregoing discourse, was the object of a University, viewed in itself, and apart from the Catholic Church, or from the State, or from any other power which may use it; and I illustrated this in various ways. I said that the intellect must have an excellence of its own, for there was nothing which had not its specific good; that the word "educate" would not be used of intellectual culture, as it is used, had not the intellect had an end of its own; that, had it not such an end, there would be no meaning in calling certain intellectual exercises "liberal," in contrast with "useful," as is commonly done; that the very notion of a philosophical temper implied it, for it threw us back upon research and system as ends in themselves, distinct from effects and works of any kind; that a philosophical scheme of knowledge, or system of sciences, could not, from the nature of the case, issue in any one definite art or pursuit, as its end; and that, on the other hand, the discovery and contemplation of truth, to which research and systematizing led, were surely sufficient ends, though nothing beyond them were added, and that they had ever been accounted sufficient by mankind.

Here then I take up the subject; and, having determined that the cultivation of the intellect is an end distinct and sufficient in itself, and that, so far as words go, it is an enlargement or illumination, I proceed to inquire what this mental breadth, or power, or light, or philosophy consists in. A Hospital heals a broken limb or cures a fever: what does an Institution effect, which professes the health, not of the body, not of the soul, but of the intellect? What is this good, which in former times, as well as our own, has been found worth the notice, the appropriation, of the Catholic Church?

I have then to investigate, in the discourses which follow, those qualities and characteristics of the intellect in which its cultivation issues or rather consists; and, with a view of assisting myself in this undertaking, I shall recur to certain questions which have already been touched upon. These questions are three: the relation of intellectual culture, first, to mere knowledge; secondly, to professional knowledge; and thirdly, to religious knowledge. In other words, are acquirements and attainments the scope of a University Education? or expertness in particular arts and pursuits? or moral and religious proficiency? or something besides these three? These questions I shall examine in succession, with the purpose I have mentioned; and I hope to be excused, if, in this anxious undertaking, I am led to repeat what, either in these Discourses or elsewhere, I have already put upon paper. And first, of Mere Knowledge, or Learning, and its connection with intellectual illumination or Philosophy.

I suppose the *prima facie* view which the public at large would take of a University, considering it as a place of Education, is nothing more or less than a place for acquiring a great deal of knowledge on a great many subjects. Memory is one of the first developed of the mental faculties; a boy's business when he goes to school is to learn, that is, to store up things in his memory. For some years his intellect is little more than an instrument for taking in facts, or a receptacle for storing them; he welcomes them as fast as they come to him; he lives on what is without; he has his eyes ever about him; he has a lively susceptibility of impressions; he imbibes information of every kind; and little does he make his own in a true sense of the word, living rather upon his neighbors all around him. He has opinions, religious, political and literary, and, for a boy, is very positive in them and sure about them; but he gets them from his schoolfellows, or his masters, or his parents, as the case may be. Such as he is in his other relations, such also is he in his school exercises; his mind is observant, sharp, ready, retentive; he is almost passive in the acquisition of knowledge. I say this in no disparagement of the idea of a clever boy. Geography, chronology, history, language, natural history, he heaps up the matter of these studies as treasures for a future day. It is the seven years of plenty with him: he gathers in by handfuls, like the Egyptians, without counting; and though, as time goes on, there is exercise for his argumentative powers in the Elements of Mathematics, and for his taste in the Poets and Orators, still, while at school, or at least, till quite the last years of his time, he acquires, and little more; and when he is leaving for the University, he is mainly the creature of foreign influences and circumstances, and made up of accidents, homogeneous or not, as the case may be. Moreover, the moral habits, which are a boy's praise, encourage and assist this result; that is, diligence, assiduity, regularity, despatch, persevering application; for these are the direct conditions of acquisition, and naturally lead to it. Acquirements, again, are emphatically producible, and at a moment; they are a something to show, both for master and scholar; an audience, even though ignorant themselves of the subject of an examination, can comprehend when questions are answered and when they are not. Here again is a reason why mental culture is in the minds of men identified with the acquisition of knowledge.

The same notion possesses the public mind, when it passes on from the thought of a school to that of a University: and with the best of reasons so far as this, that there is no true culture without acquirements, and that philosophy presupposes knowledge. It requires a great deal of reading, or a wide range of information, to warrant us in putting forth our opinions on any serious subject; and without such learning the most original mind may be able indeed to dazzle, to amuse, to refute, to perplex, but not to come to any useful result or any trustworthy conclusion. There are indeed persons who profess a different view of the matter, and even act upon it. Every now and then you will find a person of vigorous or fertile mind, who relies upon his own resources, despises all former authors, and gives the world, with the utmost fearlessness, his views upon religion, or history, or any other popular subject. And his works may sell for a while; he may get a name in his day; but this will be all. His readers are sure to find on the long run that his doctrines are mere theories, and not the expression of facts, that they are chaff instead of bread, and then his popularity drops as suddenly as it rose.

Knowledge then is the indispensable condition of expansion of mind, and the instrument of attaining to it; this cannot be denied, it is ever to be insisted on; I begin with it as a first principle; however, the very truth of it carries men too far, and confirms to them the notion that it is the whole of the matter. A narrow mind is thought to be that which contains little knowledge; and an enlarged mind, that which holds a great deal; and what seems to put the matter beyond dispute is, the fact of the great number of studies which are pursued in a University, by its very profession. Lectures are given on every kind of subject; examinations are held; prizes awarded. There are moral, metaphysical, physical Professors; Professors of languages, of history, of mathematics, of experimental science. Lists of questions are published, wonderful for their range and depth, variety and difficulty; treaties are written, which carry upon their very face the evidence of extensive reading or multifarious information; what then is wanting for mental culture to a person of large reading and scientific attainments? what is grasp of mind but acquirement? where shall philosophical repose be found, but in the consciousness and enjoyment of large intellectual possessions?

And yet this notion is, I conceive, a mistake, and my present business is to show that it is one, and that the end of a Liberal Education is not mere knowledge, or knowledge considered in its matter; and I shall best attain my object, by actually setting down some cases, which will be generally granted to be instances of the process of enlightenment or enlargement of mind, and others which are not, and thus, by the comparison, you will be able to judge for yourselves, gentlemen, whether Knowledge, that is, acquirement, is after all the real principle of the enlargement, or whether that principle is not rather something beyond it.

For instance, let a person, whose experience has hitherto been confined to the more calm and unpretending scenery of these islands, whether here or in England, go for the first time into parts where physical nature puts on her wilder and more awful forms, whether at home or abroad, as into mountainous districts; or let one, who has ever lived in a quiet village, go for the first time to a great metropolis,—then I suppose he will have a sensation which perhaps he never had before. He has a feeling not in addition or increase of former feelings, but of something different in its nature. He will perhaps be borne forward, and find for a time that he has lost his bearings. He has made a certain progress, and he has a consciousness of mental enlargement; he does not stand where he did, he has a new center, and a range of thoughts to which he was before a stranger.

Again, the view of the heavens which the telescope opens upon us, if allowed to fill and possess the mind, may almost whirl it round and make it dizzy. It brings in a

flood of ideas, and is rightly called an intellectual enlargement, whatever is meant by the term.

And so again, the sight of beasts of prey and other foreign animals, their strangeness, the originality (if I may
use the term) of their forms and gestures and habits, and
their variety and independence of each other, throw us out
of ourselves into another creation, and as if under another
Creator, if I may so express the temptation which may
come on the mind. We seem to have new faculties, or a
new exercise for our faculties, by this addition to our
knowledge; like a prisoner, who, having been accustomed
to wear manacles or fetters, suddenly finds his arms and
legs free.

Hence Physical Science generally, in all its departments, as bringing before us the exuberant riches and
resources, yet the orderly course, of the Universe, elevates
and excites the student, and at first, I may say, almost
takes away his breath, while in time it exercises a tran-
quilizing influence upon him.

Again, the study of history is said to enlarge and enlighten the mind, and why? because, as I conceive, it gives
it a power of judging of passing events, and of all events,
and a conscious superiority over them, which before it
did not possess.

And in like manner, what is called seeing the world,
entering into active life, going into society, traveling,
gaining acquaintance with the various classes of the community, coming into contact with the principles and modes
of thought of various parties, interests, and races, their
views, aims, habits and manners, their religious creeds and
forms of worship,—gaining experience how various yet
how alike men are, how low-minded, how bad, how opposed, yet how confident in their opinions; all this exerts
a perceptible influence upon the mind, which it is impossible to mistake, be it good or be it bad, and is popularly
called its enlargement.

And then again, the first time the mind comes across
the arguments and speculations of unbelievers, and feels
what a novel light they cast upon what he has hitherto
accounted sacred; and still more, if it gives in to them
and embraces them, and throws off as so much prejudice
what it has hitherto held, and, as if waking from a dream,

begins to realize to its imagination that there is now no
such thing as law and the transgression of law, that sin
is a phantom, and punishment a bugbear, that it is free to
sin, free to enjoy the world and the flesh; and still further,
when it does enjoy them, and reflects that it may think and
hold just what it will, that "the world is all before it
where to choose," and what system to build up as its own
private persuasion; when this torrent of wilful thoughts
rushes over and inundates it, who will deny that the fruit
of the tree of knowledge, or what the mind takes for
knowledge, has made it one of the gods, with a sense of
expansion and elevation,—an intoxication in reality, still,
so far as the subjective state of the mind goes, an illumination?   Hence the fanaticism of individuals or nations, who
suddenly cast off their Maker.   Their eyes are opened;
and, like the judgment-stricken king in the Tragedy, they
see two suns, and a magic universe, out of which they
look back upon their former state of faith and innocence
with a sort of contempt and indignation, as if they were
then but fools, and the dupes of imposture.

On the other hand, Religion has its own enlargement,
and an enlargement, not of tumult, but of peace.   It is
often remarked of uneducated persons, who have hitherto
thought little of the unseen world, that, on their turning
to God, looking into themselves, regulating their hearts,
reforming their conduct, and meditating on death and
judgment, heaven and hell, they seem to become, in point
of intellect, different beings from what they were.   Before, they took things as they came, and thought no more
of one thing than another.   But now every event has a
meaning; they have their own estimate of whatever happens to them; they are mindful of times and seasons, and
compare the present with the past; and the world, no
longer dull, monotonous, unprofitable, and hopeless, is a
various and complicated drama, with parts and an object,
and an awful moral.

Now from these instances, to which many more might be
added, it is plain, first, that the communication of knowledge certainly is either a condition or the means of that
sense of enlargement, or enlightenment of which at this
day we hear so much in certain quarters: this cannot be
denied; but next, it is equally plain, that such communi-

cation is not the whole of the process. The enlargement
consists, not merely in the passive reception into the mind
of a number of ideas hitherto unknown to it, but in the
mind's energetic and simultaneous action upon and towards and among those new ideas, which are rushing in
upon it. It is the action of a formative power, reducing
to order and meaning the matter of our acquirements; it is
a making the objects of our knowledge subjectively our
own, or, to use a familiar word, it is a digestion of what
we receive, into the substance of our previous state of
thought; and without this no enlargement is said to follow. There is no enlargement, unless there be a comparison of ideas one with another, as they come before the
mind, and a systematizing of them. We feel our minds to
be growing and expanding *then*, when we not only learn,
but refer what we learn to what we know already. It is
not the mere addition to our knowledge that is the illumination; but the locomotion, the movement onwards, of
that mental center, to which both what we know, and what
we are learning, the accumulating mass of our acquirements, gravitates. And therefore a truly great intellect,
and recognized to be such by the common opinion of mankind, such as the intellect of Aristotle, or of St. Thomas,
or of Newton, or of Goethe (I purposely take instances
within and without the Catholic pale, when I would speak
of the intellect as such), is one which takes a connected
view of old and new, past and present, far and near, and
which has an insight into the influence of all these one on
another; without which there is no whole, and no center.
It possesses the knowledge, not only of things, but also of
their mutual and true relations; knowledge, not merely
considered as acquirement, but as philosophy.

Accordingly, when this analytical, distributive, harmo-
nizing process is away, the mind experiences no enlargement, and is not reckoned as enlightened or comprehensive, whatever it may add to its knowledge. For instance,
a great memory, as I have already said, does not make a
philosopher, any more than a dictionary can be called a
grammar. There are men who embrace in their minds a
vast multitude of ideas, but with little sensibility about
their real relations towards each other. These may be
antiquarians, annalists, naturalists; they may be learned

in the law; they may be versed in statistics; they are most
useful in their own place; I should shrink from speaking
disrespectfully of them; still, there is nothing in such attainments to guarantee the absence of narrowness of mind.
If they are nothing more than well-read men, or men of
information, they have not what specially deserves the
name of culture of mind, or fulfils the type of Liberal Education.

In like manner, we sometimes fall in with persons who
have seen much of the world, and of the men who, in
their day, have played a conspicuous part in it, but who
generalize nothing, and have no observation, in the true
sense of the word.   They abound in information in detail,
curious and entertaining, about men and things; and, having lived under the influence of no very clear or settled
principles, religious or political, they speak of every one
and every thing, only as so many phenomena, which are
complete in themselves, and lead to nothing, not discussing them, or teaching any truth, or instructing the hearer,
but simply talking.   No one would say that these persons,
well informed as they are, had attained to any great culture of intellect or to philosophy.

The case is the same still more strikingly where the
persons in question are beyond dispute men of inferior
powers and deficient education.   Perhaps they have been
much in foreign countries, and they receive, in a passive,
otiose, unfruitful way, the various facts which are forced
upon them there.   Seafaring men, for example, range
from one end of the earth to the other; but the multiplicity
of external objects, which they have encountered, forms
no symmetrical and consistent picture upon their imagination; they see the tapestry of human life, as it were on
the wrong side, and it tells no story.   They sleep, and
they rise up, and they find themselves, now in Europe, now
in Asia; they see visions of great cities and wild regions;
they are in the marts of commerce, or amid the islands of
the South; they gaze on Pompey's Pillar, or on the Andes;
and nothing which meets them carries them forward or
backward, to any idea beyond itself.   Nothing has a drift
or relation; nothing has a history or a promise.   Everything stands by itself, and comes and goes in its turn, like
the shifting scenes of a show, which leave the spectator

where he was. Perhaps you are near such a man on a particular occasion, and expect him to be shocked or perplexed at something which occurs; but one thing is much the same to him as another, or, if he is perplexed, it is as not knowing what to say, whether it is right to admire, or to ridicule, or to disapprove, while conscious that some expression of opinion is expected from him; for in fact he has no standard of judgment at all, and no landmarks to guide him to a conclusion. Such is mere acquisition, and, I repeat, no one would dream of calling it philosophy.

Instances, such as these, confirm, by the contrast, the conclusion I have already drawn from those which preceded them. That only is true enlargement of mind which is the power of viewing many things at once as one whole, of referring them severally to their true place in the universal system, of understanding their respective values, and determining their mutual dependence. Thus is that form of Universal Knowledge, of which I have on a former occasion spoken, set up in the individual intellect, and constitutes its perfection. Possessed of this real illumination, the mind never views any part of the extended subject-matter of Knowledge without recollecting that it is but a part, or without the associations which spring from this recollection. It makes everything in some sort lead to everything else; it would communicate the image of the whole to every separate portion, till that whole becomes in imagination like a spirit, everywhere pervading and penetrating its component parts, and giving them one definite meaning. Just as our bodily organs, when mentioned, recall their function in the body, as the word "creation" suggests the Creator, and "subjects" a sovereign, so, in the mind of the Philosopher, as we are abstractedly conceiving of him, the elements of the physical and moral world, sciences, arts, pursuits, ranks, offices, events, opinions, individualities, are all viewed as one, with correlative functions, and as gradually by successive combinations converging, one and all, to the true center.

To have even a portion of this illuminative reason and true philosophy is the highest state to which nature can aspire, in the way of intellect; it puts the mind above the influences of chance and necessity, above anxiety, suspense, unsettlement, and superstition, which is the lot of the many. Men, whose minds are possessed with some one object, take exaggerated views of its importance, are feverish in the pursuit of it, make it the measure of things which are utterly foreign to it, and are startled and despond if it happens to fail them. They are ever in alarm or in transport. Those on the other hand who have no object or principle whatever to hold by, lose their way every step they take. They are thrown out, and do not know what to think or say, at every fresh juncture; they have no view of persons, or occurrences, or facts, which come suddenly upon them, and they hang upon the opinion of others for want of internal resources. But the intellect which has been disciplined to the perfection of its powers, which knows, and thinks while it knows, which has learned to leaven the dense mass of facts and events with the elastic force of reason, such an intellect cannot be partial, cannot be exclusive, cannot be impetuous, cannot be at a loss, cannot but be patient, collected, and majestically calm, because it discerns the end in every beginning, the origin in every end, the law in every interruption, the limit in each delay; because it ever knows where it stands, and how its path lies from one point to another. It is the τετράγωνος of the Peripatetic, and has the " nil admirari " of the Stoic,—

> Felix qui potuit rerum cognoscere causas,
> Atque metus omnes, et inexorabile fatum
> Subjecit pedibus, strepitumque Acherontis avari.

There are men who, when in difficulties, originate at the moment vast ideas or dazzling projects; who, under the influence of excitement, are able to cast a light, almost as if from inspiration, on a subject or course of action which comes before them; who have a sudden presence of mind equal to any emergency, rising with the occasion, and an undaunted magnanimous bearing, and an energy and keenness which is but made intense by opposition. This is genius, this is heroism; it is the exhibition of a natural gift, which no culture can teach, at which no Institution can aim: here, on the contrary, we are concerned, not with mere nature, but with training and teaching. That perfection of the Intellect, which is the result of Education, and its *beau ideal*, to be imparted to individuals in their respective measures, is the clear, calm, accurate vision and comprehension of all things, as far as the finite mind can embrace them, each in its place, and with its own characteristics upon it. It is almost prophetic from its knowledge of history; it is almost heart-searching from its knowledge of human nature; it has almost supernatural charity from its freedom from littleness and prejudice; it has almost the repose of faith, because nothing can startle it; it has almost the beauty and harmony of heavenly contemplation, so intimate is it with the eternal order of things and the music of the spheres.

And now, if I may take for granted that the true and adequate end of intellectual training and of a University is not Learning or Acquirement, but rather, is Thought or Reason exercised upon Knowledge, or what may be called Philosophy, I shall be in a position to explain the various mistakes which at the present day beset the subject of University Education.

I say then, if we would improve the intellect, first of all, we must ascend; we cannot gain real knowledge on a level; we must generalize, we must reduce to method, we must have a grasp of principles, and group and shape our acquisitions by means of them. It matters not whether our field of operation be wide or limited; in every case, to command it, is to mount above it. Who has not felt the irritation of mind and impatience created by a deep, rich country, visited for the first time, with winding lanes, and high hedges, and green steeps, and tangled woods, and everything smiling indeed, but in a maze? The same feeling comes upon us in a strange city, when we have no map of its streets. Hence you hear of practised travelers, when they first come into a place, mounting some high hill or church tower, by way of reconnoitering its neighborhood. In like manner, you must be above your knowledge, not under it, or it will oppress you; and the more you have of it, the greater will be the load. The learning of a Salmasius, of a Burman, unless you are its master, will be your tyrant. "Imperat aut servit"; if you can wield it with a strong arm, it is a great weapon; otherwise,

Vis consili expers
Mole ruit sua.

You will be overwhelmed, like Tarpeia, by the heavy wealth which you have exacted from tributary generations.

Instances abound; there are authors who are as pointless as they are inexhaustible in their literary resources. They measure knowledge by bulk, as it lies in the rude block, without symmetry, without design. How many commentators are there on the Classics, how many on Holy Scripture, from whom we rise up, wondering at the learning which has passed before us, and wondering why it passed!

How many writers are there of Ecclesiastical History, such as Mosheim or Du Pin, who, breaking up their subject into details, destroy its life, and defraud us of the whole by their anxiety about the parts. The Sermons, again, of the English Divines in the Seventeenth century, how often are they mere repertories of miscellaneous and officious learning. Of course Catholics also may read without thinking; and in their case, equally as with Protestants, it holds good, that such knowledge is unworthy of the name, knowledge which they have not thought through, and thought out. Such readers are only possessed by their knowledge, not possessed of it; nay, in matter of fact they are often even carried away by it, without any volition of their own. Recollect, the Memory can tyrannize, as well as the Imagination. Derangement, I believe, has been considered as a loss of control over the sequence of ideas. The mind, once set in motion, is henceforth deprived of the power of initiation, and becomes the victim of a train of associations, one thought suggesting another in the way of cause and effect, as if by a mechanical process or some physical necessity. No one who has had experience of men of studious habits but must recognize the existence of a parallel phenomenon in the case of those who have over-stimulated the memory. In such persons Reason acts almost as feebly and as impotently as in the madman; once fairly started on any subject whatever they have no power of self-control; they passively endure the succession of impulses which are evolved out of the original exciting cause; they are passed on from one idea to another and go steadily forward, plodding along one line of thought in spite of the amplest concessions of the hearer, or wandering from it in endless digression in spite of his remonstrances. Now, if, as is very certain, no one would envy the madman the glow and originality of his conceptions, why must we extol the cultivation of that intellect, which is the prey, not indeed of barren fancies, but of barren facts, of random intrusions from without, though not of morbid imaginations from within? And in thus speaking I am not denying that a strong and ready memory is in itself a real treasure; I am not disparaging a well-stored mind, though it be nothing besides, provided it be sober, any more than I would despise a bookseller's shop: it is of great value to others, even when not so to the owner. Nor am I banishing, far from it, the possessors of deep and multifarious learning from my ideal University; they adorn it in the eyes of men; I do but say that they constitute no type of the results at which it aims; that it is no great gain to the intellect to have enlarged the memory at the expense of faculties which are indisputably higher.

Nor indeed am I supposing that there is any great danger, at least in this day, of over-education; the danger is on the other side. I will tell you, gentlemen, what has been the practical error of the last twenty years,—not to load the memory of the student with a mass of undigested knowledge, but to force upon him so much that he has rejected all. It has been the error of distracting and enfeebling the mind by an unmeaning profusion of subjects; of implying that a smattering in a dozen branches of study is not shallowness, which it really is, but enlargement, which it is not; of considering an acquaintance with the learned names of things and persons, and the possession of clever duodecimos, and attendance on eloquent lecturers, and membership with scientific institutions, and the sight of the experiments of a platform and the specimens of a museum, that all this was not dissipation of mind, but progress. All things now are to be learned at once, not first one thing, then another, not one well, but many badly. Learning is to be without exertion, without attention, without toil; without grounding, without advance, without finishing. There is to be nothing individual in it; and this, forsooth, is the wonder of the age. What the steam engine does with matter, the printing-press is to do with mind; it is to act mechanically, and the population is to be passively, almost unconsciously enlightened, by the mere multiplication and dissemination of volumes.   Whether it be the schoolboy, or the schoolgirl, or the youth at college, or the mechanic in the town, or the politician in the senate, all have been the victims in one way or other of this most preposterous and pernicious of delusions.   Wise men have lifted up their voices in vain; and at length, lest their own institutions should be outshone and should disappear in the folly of the hour, they have been obliged, as far as they could with a good conscience, to humor a spirit which they could not withstand, and make temporizing concessions at which they could not but inwardly smile.

It must not be supposed that, because I so speak, therefore I have some sort of fear of the education of the people: on the contrary, the more education they have, the better, so that it is really education.   Nor am I an enemy to the cheap publication of scientific and literary works, which is now in vogue; on the contrary, I consider it a great advantage, convenience, and gain; that is, to those to whom education has given a capacity for using them.   Further, I consider such innocent recreations as science and literature are able to furnish will be a very fit occupation of the thoughts and the leisure of young persons, and may be made the means of keeping them from bad employments and bad companions.   Moreover, as to that superficial acquaintance with chemistry, and geology, and astronomy and political economy, and modern history, and biography, and other branches of knowledge, which periodical literature and occasional lectures and scientific institutions diffuse through the community, —I think it is a graceful accomplishment, and a suitable, nay, in this day, a necessary accomplishment, in the case of educated men.   Nor, lastly, am I disparaging or discouraging the thorough acquisition of any one of these studies, or denying that, as far as it goes, such thorough acquisition is a real education of the mind.   All I say is, call things by their right names, and do not confuse together ideas which are essentially different.   A thorough knowledge of one science and a superficial acquaintance with many, are not the same thing; a smattering of a hundred things or a memory for detail, is not a philosophical or comprehensive view. Recreations are not education; accomplishments are not education. Do not say, the people must be educated, when, after all, you only mean amused, refreshed, soothed, put into good spirits and good humor, or kept from vicious excesses. I do not say that such amusements, such occupations of mind, are not a great gain; but they are not education. You may as well call drawing, and fencing education, as a general knowledge of botany or conchology. Stuffing birds or playing stringed instruments is an elegant pastime, and a resource to the idle, but it is not education; it does not form or cultivate the intellect.

Education is a high word; it is the preparation for knowledge, and it is the imparting of knowledge in proportion to that preparation. We require intellectual eyes to know withal, as bodily eyes for sight. We need both objects and organs intellectual; we cannot gain them, without setting about it; we cannot gain them in our sleep, or by haphazard. The best telescope does not dispense with eyes; the printing-press or the lecture-room will assist us greatly, but we must be true to ourselves, we must be parties in the work. A University is, according to the usual designation, an Alma Mater, knowing her children one by one, not a foundry, or a mint, or a treadmill.

I protest to you, gentlemen, that if I had to choose between a so-called University, which dispensed with residence and tutorial superintendence, and gave its degrees to any person who passed an examination in a wide range of subjects, and a University which had no professors or examinations at all, but merely brought a number of young men together for three or four years, and then sent them away as the University of Oxford is said to have done some sixty years since, if I were asked which of these two methods was the better discipline of the intellect,— mind, I do not say which is morally the better, for it is plain that compulsory study must be a good and idleness an intolerable mischief,—but if I must determine which of the two courses was the more successful in training, molding, enlarging the mind, which sent out men the more fitted for their secular duties, which produced better public men, men of the world, men whose names would descend to posterity, I have no hesitation in giving the preference to that University which did nothing, over that which exacted of its members an acquaintance with every science under the sun. And, paradox as this may seem, still if results be the test of systems, the influence of the public schools and colleges of England, in the course of the last century, at least will bear out one side of the contrast as I have drawn it. What would come, on the other hand, of the ideal systems of education which have fascinated the imagination of this age, could they ever take effect, and whether they would not produce a generation frivolous, narrow-minded, and resourceless, intellectually considered, is a fair subject for debate; but so far is certain, that the Universities and scholastic establishments, to which I refer, and which did little more than bring together first boys and then youths in large numbers, these institutions, with miserable deformities on the side of morals, with a hollow profession of Christianity, and a heathen code of ethics,—I say, at least they can boast of a succession of heroes and statesmen, of literary men and philosophers, of men conspicuous for great natural virtues, for habits of business, for knowledge of life, for practical judgment, for cultivated tastes, for accomplishments, who have made England what it is,—able to subdue the earth, able to domineer over Catholics.

How is this to be explained? I suppose as follows: When a multitude of young men, keen, open-hearted, sympathetic, and observant, as young men are, come together and freely mix with each other, they are sure to learn one from another, even if there be no one to teach them; the conversation of all is a series of lectures to each, and they gain for themselves new ideas and views, fresh matter of thought, and distinct principles for judging and acting, day by day. An infant has to learn the meaning of the information which its senses convey to it, and this seems to be its employment. It fancies all that the eye presents to it to be close to it, till it actually learns the contrary, and thus by practice does it ascertain the relations and uses of those first elements of knowledge which are necessary for its animal existence. A parallel teaching is necessary for our social being, and it is secured by a large school or a college; and this effect may be fairly called in its own department an enlargement of mind. It is seeing the world on a small field with little trouble; for the pupils or students come from very different places, and with widely different notions, and there is much to generalize, much to adjust, much to eliminate, there are inter-relations to be defined, and conventional rules to be established, in the process, by which the whole assemblage is molded together, and gains one tone and one character.

Let it be clearly understood, I repeat it, that I am not taking into account moral or religious considerations; I am but saying that that youthful community will constitute a whole, it will embody a specific idea, it will represent a doctrine, it will administer a code of conduct, and it will furnish principles of thought and action. It will give birth to a living teaching, which in course of time will take the shape of a self-perpetuating tradition, or a *genius loci,* as it is sometimes called; which haunts the home where it has been born, and which imbues and forms, more or less, and one by one, every individual who is successively brought under its shadow. Thus it is that, independent of direct instruction on the part of Superiors, there is a sort of self-education in the academic institutions of Protestant England; a characteristic tone of thought, a recognized standard of judgment is found in them, which as developed in the individual who is submitted to it, becomes a twofold source of strength to him, both from the distinct stamp it impresses on his mind, and from the bond of union which it creates between him and others,—effects which are shared by the authorities of the place, for they themselves have been educated in it, and at all times are exposed to the influence of its ethical atmosphere. Here then is a real teaching, whatever be its standards and principles, true or false; and it at least tends towards cultivation of the intellect; it at least recognizes that knowledge is something more than a sort of passive reception of scraps and details; it is a something, and it does a something, which never will issue from the most strenuous efforts of a set of teachers, with no mutual sympathies and no intercommunion, of a set of examiners with no opinions which they dare profess, and with no common principles, who are teaching or questioning a set of youths who do not know them, and do not know each other, on a large number of subjects, different in kind, and connected by no wide philosophy, three times a week, or three times a year, or once in three years, in chill lecture-rooms or on a pompous anniversary.

Nay, self-education in any shape, in the most restricted sense, is preferable to a system of teaching which, professing so much, really does so little for the mind. Shut your college gates against the votary of knowledge, throw him back upon the searchings and the efforts of his own mind; he will gain by being spared an entrance into your Babel. Few indeed there are who can dispense with the stimulus and support of instructors, or will do anything at all, if left to themselves. And fewer still (though such great minds are to be found), who will not, from such unassisted attempts, contract a self-reliance and a self-esteem, which are not only moral evils, but serious hindrances to the attainment of truth. And next to none, perhaps, or none, who will not be reminded from time to time of the disadvantage under which they lie, by their imperfect grounding, by the breaks, deficiencies, and irregularities of their knowledge, by the eccentricity of opinion and the confusion of principle which they exhibit. They will be too often ignorant of what every one knows and takes for granted, of that multitude of small truths which fall upon the mind like dust, impalpable and ever accumulating; they may be unable to converse, they may argue perversely, they may pride themselves on their worst paradoxes or their grossest truisms, they may be full of their own mode of viewing things, unwilling to be put out of their way, slow to enter into the minds of others;—but, with these and whatever other liabilities upon their heads, they are likely to have more thought, more mind, more philosophy, more true enlargement, than those earnest but ill-used persons, who are forced to load their minds with a score of subjects against an examination, who have too much on their hands to indulge themselves in thinking or investigation, who devour premise and conclusion together with indiscriminate greediness, who hold whole sciences on faith, and commit demonstrations to memory, and who too often, as might be expected, when their period of education is passed, throw up all they have learned in disgust, having gained nothing really by their anxious labors, except perhaps the habit of application.

Yet such is the better specimen of the fruit of that ambitious system which has of late years been making way among us: for its result on ordinary minds, and on the common run of students, is less satisfactory still; they leave their place of education simply dissipated and relaxed by the multiplicity of subjects, which they have never really mastered, and so shallow as not even to know their shallowness. How much better, I say, is it for the active and thoughtful intellect, where such is to be found, to eschew the College and the University altogether, than to submit to a drudgery so ignoble, a mockery so contumelious. How much more profitable for the independent mind, after the mere rudiments of education, to range through a library at random, taking down books as they meet him, and pursuing the trains of thought which his mother wit suggests. How much healthier to wander into the fields, and there with the exiled Prince to find "tongues in the trees, books in the running brooks." How much more genuine an education is that of the poor boy in the Poem [Crabbe's "Tales of the Halls"]—a Poem, whether in conception or in execution, one of the most touching in our language—who, not in the wide world, but ranging day by day around his widowed mother's home, "a dexterous gleaner" in a narrow field, and with only such slender outfit

> " .   .   .   as the village school and books a few
> Supplied,"

contrived from the beach, and the quay, and the fisher's boat, and the inn's fireside, and the tradesman's shop, and the shepherd's walk, and the smuggler's hut, and the mossy moor, and the screaming gulls, and the restless waves, to fashion for himself a philosophy and a poetry of his own!

RICHARD OLNEY

JOHN MARSHALL

[Address by Richard Olney, lawyer, statesman, Attorney-General and afterwards Secretary of State in the second cabinet of President Cleveland (born in Oxford, Mass., September 15, 1835; ———), delivered in Boston, Mass., before the Boston Bar Association, February 4, 1901, at the celebration of the centennial of the installation of the first Chief Justice of the Supreme Court of the United States. The occasion brought together a large and distinguished gathering of lawyers, representing the Bar Associations of Massachusetts.]

GENTLEMEN OF THE BAR:—I have felt much hesitation about taking even a small part in these exercises. The theme is too large for treatment in short space; it must suffer at the hands of whoever undertakes it without a command of time and leisure which but few favored mortals possess; it has been spoken to and written of by orators, historians, and statesmen for nearly seventy years, and it is to-day freshly and elaborately dealt with throughout the Union by many of its most eminent citizens. Indeed, for present purposes, what could be more intimidating than what has been just going on in this very community; than to know that the interesting utterances to which we have just listened [address of Henry St. George Tucker, of Virginia, special guest of the Association, whose remarks immediately preceded those of Mr. Olney] only supplement a morning of official and judicial eloquence at the Court-house and an afternoon of learned dissertation at Sanders Theater? In depressing circumstances like these, I can only hope for indulgence if you find me reiterating a thrice-told tale, and can promise nothing, except to make your ordeal tolerably brief.

I wish to remark upon but three things connected with the career of John Marshall. It is not obvious what most of us are born for, nor why almost any one might as well not have been born at all. Occasionally, however, it is plain that a man is sent into the world with a particular work to perform. If the man is commonly, though not always, unconscious of his mission, his contemporaries are as a rule equally blind, and it remains for after generations to discover that a man has lived and died for whom was set an appointed task, who has attempted and achieved it, and who has made the whole course of history different from what it would have been without him.

John Marshall had a mission of that sort to whose success intellect and learning of the highest order, as well as special legal ability and training, might well have proved inadequate. Yet—the mission being assumed—the first thing I wish to note, and the wonderful thing, is that to all human appearances Marshall was meant to be denied anything like a reasonable opportunity to prepare for it. For education generally, for instance, he was indebted principally to his father, a small planter, who could have snatched but little leisure from the daily demands of an exacting calling, and presumably could not have spent all that little on the eldest of his fifteen children. The parental tuition was supplemented only by the son's attendance for a short period at a country academy and by the efforts of a couple of Scotch clergymen, each of whom successively tutored him for about a year and in that time did something to initiate him into the mysteries of Latin.

Such, briefly put, was the entire Marshall curriculum in the way of general education. It was all over before he was eighteen, when the shadow of the revolutionary struggle began to project itself over the land, and Marshall joined the Virginia militia and became immersed in military affairs. As lieutenant of militia and lieutenant and captain in the Continental army he was in active service during almost the entire war, fought at Brandywine, Germantown, and Monmouth, was half-starved and half-frozen at Valley Forge, and during that terrible winter ate his share of the Dutch apple-pies, ever since historically famous for their capacity to be thrown across a room without damage to either inside or outside.

Marshall's opportunities as a student of law were on a
par with his educational opportunities generally. Though
he is said to have begun his legal studies when he was
eighteen, they were at once and continuously interrupted
by the military pursuits which occupied him until near the
close of the war. The only exception to be noted is that,
in an interval between the expiration of one military commission and the issuance of another, he attended a course
of law lectures by Chancellor Wythe of William and Mary
College.

Meagre as the knowledge and training thus acquired
would seem to be, they sufficed to procure him his license,
and in 1780 or 1781 he began to practise. In view of
what he subsequently became and achieved, it would be
a natural supposition that during the next twenty years he
must have been exclusively devoted to his profession and
by the incessant and uninterrupted study and application
of legal principles must have made up for the deprivations
of earlier years. Nothing could be further from the truth.
During those twenty years he was almost constantly in
public employment, and in public employment of an exciting and engrossing nature.

In this period arose and were settled the novel and
difficult questions following in the wake of the War of
Independence, questions of vital moment to each State
as well as to the country at large. Marshall was in the
thick of every discussion and every struggle. He was a
member of the Virginia Assembly; an Executive Coun-
cillor; general of militia; delegate to the State convention
which adopted the Federal Constitution; member of Congress; envoy to France; and when he was appointed Chief
Justice at the end of January, 1801, he was Secretary of
State in John Adams' cabinet and continued to act as
such until after Jefferson's inauguration. During this
entire period I doubt if there were any three consecutive
years during which Marshall was giving his entire time
and attention to the practice of his profession.

Contrast the poverty of this preparation with the greatness of the work before him. He probably did not appreciate it himself—it is certain, I think, that his fellow citizens and contemporaries were far from appreciating it.
To most of them the State was closer, dearer and vastly

more important than the nation—by all of them the significance of the place of the judiciary in the new Government was but dimly, if at all, perceived—while to the world at large the judiciary of a new nation of thirteen small States strung along the North Atlantic seaboard, comprising a population of some 4,000,000 souls, necessarily seemed a tribunal of the smallest possible account. Today the "American Empire," as Marshall himself was the first to call it, with its immense territory and its 75,000,000 of people, is a negligible factor nowhere on earth, and its national Supreme Court ranks as the most exalted and potent judicial tribunal that human skill has yet organized.

But the work Marshall was destined to undertake can be estimated only by considering its inherent character. All minor features being disregarded, there are two of capital importance. In the first place, here was a ship of state just launched which was to be run rigidly by chart—by sailing directions laid down in advance and not to be departed from, whatever the winds or the waves or the surprises or perils of the voyage—in accordance with grants and limitations of power set forth in writing and not to be violated or ignored except at the risk and cost of revolution and civil war. The experiment thus inaugurated was unique in the history of civilized peoples and believed to be of immense consequence both to the American people and to the human race. But there were also wheels within wheels, and the experiment of government according to a written text entailed yet another, namely, that of a judicial branch designed to keep all other branches within their prescribed spheres. To that end it was not enough to make the judicial branch independent of the legislative and executive branches. It was necessary to make it the final judge not only of the powers of those other departments, but of its own powers as well.

Thus the national judiciary became the keystone of the arch supporting the new political edifice and was invested with the most absolute and far-reaching authority. Since almost all legislative and executive action can in some way be put in issue in a suit, it is an authority often involving and controlling matters of high state policy external as well as internal. At this very moment is it not believed, indeed proclaimed in high quarters, that the question of Asiatic dependencies for the United States and incidentally of its foreign policy generally, practically hinges upon judgments of the national Supreme Court in cases requiring the exercise of its function as the final interpreter of the Constitution? What judicial tribunal in Christendom is or has ever been, directly or indirectly, the arbiter of issues of that character?

It was a national judiciary of this sort of which John Marshall became the head one hundred years ago. That he dominated his court on all constitutional questions is indubitable. That he exercised his mastery with marvelous sagacity and tact, that he manifested a profound comprehension of the principles of our constitutional government and declared them in terms unrivaled for their combination of simplicity and exactness, that he justified his judgments by reasoning impregnable in point of logic and irresistible in point of persuasiveness—has not all this been universally conceded for the two generations since his death and will it not be found to have been universally voiced to-day wherever throughout the land this centenary has been observed? "All wrong," said John Randolph of one of Marshall's opinions—"All wrong—but no man in the United States can tell why or wherein he is wrong."

If we consider the work to which he was devoted, it must be admitted to have been of as high a nature as any to which human faculties can be addressed. If we consider the manner in which the work was done, it must be admitted that anything better in the way of execution it is difficult to conceive. And if we consider both the greatness of the work and the excellence of its performance relatively to any opportunities of Marshall to duly equip himself for it, he must be admitted to be one of the exceptional characters of history seemingly foreordained to some grand achievement because fitted and adapted to it practically by natural genius alone.

If it be true—as it is, beyond cavil—that to Washington more than to any other man is due the birth of the American nation, it is equally true beyond cavil that to Marshall more than to any other man is it due that the nation has come safely through the trying ordeals of infantile weakness and youthful effervescence, and has triumphantly emerged into well-developed and lusty manhood. Had the Constitution at the outset been committed to other hands, it could have been, and probably would have been, construed in the direction of minimizing its scope and efficiency—of dwarfing and frittering away the powers conferred by it and of making the sovereignty of the nation but a petty thing as compared with the sovereignty of the state. Under Marshall's auspices, however, and his interpretation and exposition of the Constitution, the sentiment of nationality germinated and grew apace, a vigorous national life developed, and an indestructible union of indestructible States became a tangible and inspiring entity, appealing alike to the affections and the reason of men, and in which thus far at least they have seen both the ark of their safety and an ideal for which to willingly lay down their lives. I refer thus to the past because the past is assured and because there are those who look to the future with apprehension—who do not disguise their fear that the republic of Washington and Marshall is now suffering a mortal assault not from without but from within—not from "foreign levy," but from "malice domestic." Those who take this view include men of both the great political parties and men who deservedly command the highest respect and deference from their fellow countrymen.

Nevertheless, they must not be allowed to lessen our faith in the final triumph of the fundamental ideas which underlie our national life. The fathers did not build upon a quicksand but upon a rock—else the structure they reared could hardly have survived foreign aggression, a disputed succession, and a civil war the greatest and most sanguinary of modern times. But their work was by human hands for human use, and even their wisdom could not guard it against the follies and the sins of all future custodians.

That gross blunders have been committed, blunders unaccountable in their origin and as yet unfathomable in their consequences, may be admitted, is indeed sorrowfully admitted by many, if not a majority, of those who have nevertheless since contributed to keep their official authors in power. But blunders, however inexcusable or apparently injurious, must be deemed irretrievable only in the last resort, and heaven forbid any admission that the American republic can be wrecked by any one or even two administrations. The truth here, as almost always, lies between extremes—between ultra-conservatives and pessimists on the one hand and ultra-progressives and optimists on the other. The former would put back the hands of the clock a hundred years—would have us live and act as if the conditions of the Washington and Marshall era were still about us—in effect would have us tear up the railroad and sink the steamship and return the lightning to the heavens whence Franklin brought it down. The latter would have us believe that, to act well our part on the world-wide stage which alone limits the activities of modern civilized states, we must ape the fashionable international follies and vices of the period even to the point of warring upon, subjugating, and exploiting for trade purposes 8,000,000 of alien peoples in the Pacific seas, 7,000 miles from our own shores. Between these extremes lies the path of honor, of morality, of safety and of patriotism, and, notwithstanding present aberrations, the American people may be absolutely trusted sooner or later to find it and to walk in it. They will certainly not forget that this is the dawn of the Twentieth, not of the Nineteenth century. They will just as certainly determine that to be in touch with the best thought and temper of the time, to be the most truly progressive of all peoples, to do every duty and fulfil every function required by its high place in the world—they will certainly determine that to do and to be all this—neither means that the American nation must imitate the most questionable practices of other states nor requires any abandonment of American principles or American ideals. To believe or to hold otherwise is to despair of the Republic, and to despair of the Republic is to lose faith in humanity and in the future of the race.

The incalculable debt of the country to the two great Virginians, impossible of repayment, can never be too often or too emphatically recognized by the entire body of the American people. Upon the bar, however, devolves an especial duty, namely, to see to it that the merits of its incomparable chief are not obscured by the showier deeds of warriors and statesmen. The observance of this day, therefore, by the lawyers of the country generally is eminently appropriate, while we in this corner of the land are exceptionally favored in that Virginia has lent us for our celebration one of the foremost of her lawyers and citizens [Henry St. George Tucker]. In recognition of the honor of his presence and in appreciation of the immense services of his native State to the cause of a stable and coherent nationality, I propose that the company rise and drink to the ever-increasing prosperity of the Commonwealth of Virginia and to the good health and long life of her distinguished representative on this occasion.

WALTER PATER

RAPHAEL

[Address of Walter Pater, critic of art and literature (born in London, 1839; died in Oxford, July 30, 1894), delivered at Oxford, August 2, 1892, before the University Extension students.]

By his immense productiveness, by the even perfection of what he produced, its fitness to its own day, its hold on posterity, in the suavity of his life, some would add in the "opportunity" of his early death, Raphael may seem a signal instance of the luckiness, of the good fortune, of genius. Yet, if we follow the actual growth of his powers, within their proper framework, the age of the Renaissance —an age of which we may say, summarily, that it enjoyed itself, and found perhaps its chief enjoyment in the attitude of the scholar, in the enthusiastic acquisition of knowledge for its own sake:—if we thus view Raphael and his works in their environment we shall find even his seemingly mechanical good fortune hardly distinguishable from his own patient disposal of the means at hand. Facile master as he may seem, as indeed he is, he is also one of the world's typical scholars, with Plato, and Cicero, and Virgil, and Milton. The formula of his genius, if we must have one, is this: genius by accumulation; the transformation of meek scholarship into genius—triumphant power of genius.

Urbino, where this prince of the Renaissance was born in 1483, year also of the birth of Luther, leader of the other great movement of that age, the Reformation— Urbino, under its dukes of the house of Montefeltro, had wherewithal just then to make a boy of native artistic faculty from the first a willing learner. The gloomy old

940

fortress of the feudal masters of the town had been replaced, in those later years of the *Quattro-cento*, by a consummate monument of *Quattro-cento* taste, a museum of
ancient and modern art, the owners of which lived there,
gallantly at home, amid the choicer flowers of living humanity.   The ducal palace was, in fact, become nothing
less than a school of ambitious youth in all the accomplishments alike of war and peace.   Raphael's connection with
it seems to have become intimate, and from the first its
influence must have overflowed so small a place.   In the
case of the lucky Raphael, for once, the actual conditions
of early life had been suitable, propitious, accordant to
what one's imagination would have required for the childhood of the man.   He was born amid the art he was, not
to transform, but to perfect, by a thousand reverential
retouchings.   In no palace, however, but in a modest
abode, still shown, containing the workshop of his father,
Giovanni Santi.   But here, too, though in frugal form,
art, the arts, were present.   A store of artistic objects was,
or had recently been, made there, and now especially, for
fitting patrons, religious pictures in the old Umbrian manner.   In quiet nooks of the Apennines Giovanni's works
remain; and there is one of them, worth study, in spite of
what critics say of its crudity, in the National Gallery.
Concede its immaturity, at least, though an immaturity
visibly susceptible of a delicate grace, it wins you nevertheless to return again and again, and ponder, by a sincere
expression of sorrow, profound, yet resigned, be the cause
what it may, among all the many causes of sorrow inherent
in the ideal of maternity, human or divine.   But if you
keep in mind when looking at it the facts of Raphael's
childhood, you will recognize in his father's picture, not
the anticipated sorrow of the " Mater Dolorosa " over the
dead son, but the grief of a simple household over the
mother herself taken early from it.   That may have been
the first picture the eyes of the world's great painter of
Madonnas rested on; and if he stood diligently before it
to copy, and so copying, quite unconsciously, and with no
disloyalty to his original, refined, improved, substituted—
substituted himself, in fact, his finer self, he had already
struck the persistent note of his career.   As with his age,
it is his vocation, ardent worker as he is, to enjoy himself

—to enjoy himself amiably, and to find his chief enjoyment in the attitude of a scholar.   And one by one, one
after another, his masters, the very greatest of them, go
to school to him.

It was so especially with the artist of whom Raphael
first became certainly a learner—Perugino.   Giovanni
Santi had died in Raphael's childhood, too early to have
been in any direct sense his teacher.   The lad, however,
from one and another, had learned much, when, with his
share of the patrimony in hand, enough to keep him, but
not tempt him from scholarly ways, he came to Perugia,
hoping still further to improve himself.   He was in his
eighteenth year, and how he looked just then you may see
in a drawing of his own in the University galleries, of
somewhat stronger mold than less genuine likenesses
might lead you to expect.   There is something of a
fighter in the way in which the nose springs from the
brow between the wide-set, meditative eyes.   A strenuous lad! capable of plodding, if you dare apply that word
to labor so impassioned as his—to any labor whatever
done at Perugia, center of the dreamiest Apennine scenery.   Its various elements (one hardly knows whether one
is thinking of Italian nature or of Raphael's art in recount-
ing them), the richly-planted lowlands, the sensitive mountain lines in flight one beyond the other into clear distance,
the cool yet glowing atmosphere, the romantic morsels of
architecture, which lend to the entire scene I know not
what expression of reposeful antiquity, arrange themselves here as for set purpose of pictorial effect, and have
gone with little change into his painted backgrounds.   In
the midst of it, on titanic old Roman and Etruscan foundations, the later Gothic town had piled itself along the
lines of a gigantic land of rock, stretched out from the last
slope of the Apennines into the plain.   Between its fingers
steep dark lanes wind down into the olive-gardens; on the
finger-tips military and monastic builders had perched
their towns.   A place as fantastic in its attractiveness as
the human life which then surged up and down in it in
contrast to the peaceful scene around.   The Baglioni who
ruled there had brought certain tendencies of that age to a
typical completeness of expression, veiling crime—crime,
it might seem, for its own sake, a whole octave of fantastic

crime—not merely under brilliant fashions and comely
persons, but under fashions and persons, an outward pre-
sentment of life and of themselves, which had a kind of
immaculate grace and discretion about them, as if Raphael
himself had already brought his unerring gift of selection
to bear upon it all for motives of art.   With life in those
streets of Perugia, as with nature, with the work of his
masters, the mere exercises of his fellow-students, his
hand rearranges, refines, renews, as if by simple contact;
but was met here half-way in its renewing office by some
special aptitude for such grace in the subject itself.
Seemingly innocent, full of natural gaiety, eternally youthful, those seven and more deadly sins, embodied and
attired in just the jaunty dress then worn, enter now and
afterwards as spectators, or assistants, into many a sacred
foreground and background among the friends and kins-
men of the Holy Family, among the very angels, gazing,
conversing, standing firmly and unashamed.   During his
apprenticeship at Perugia Raphael visited and left his
work in more modest places round about, along those se-
ductive mountain or lowland roads, and copied for one of
them Perugino's " Marriage of the Virgin " significantly,
did it by many degrees better, with a very novel effect of
motion everywhere, and that grace which natural motion
evokes, and for a temple in the background a lovely bit of
his friend Bramante's sort of architecture, the true Renaissance or perfected *Quattro-cento* architecture.   He goes on
building a whole lordly new city of the like as he paints
to the end of his life.   That subject, we may note, as we
leave Perugia in Raphael's company, had been suggested
by the famous mystic treasure of its cathedral church, the
marriage ring of the Blessed Virgin herself.

Raphael's copy had been made for the little old Apennine town of Citta di Castello; and another place he visits
at this time is still more effective in the development of his
genius.   About his twentieth year he comes to Siena—
that other rocky Titan's hand, just lifted out of the surface
of the plain.   It is the most grandiose place he has yet
seen; has not forgotten that it was once the rival of
Florence; and here the patient scholar passes under an
influence of somewhat larger scope than Perugino's.
Perugino's pictures are for the most part religious con-

templations, painted and made visible, to accompany the action of divine service—a visible pattern to priests, attendants, worshippers, of what the course of their invisible thoughts should be at those holy functions. Learning in the workshop of Perugino to produce the like—such works as the Ansidei Madonna—to produce them very much better than his master, Raphael was already become a freeman of the most strictly religious school of Italian art, the so devout Umbrian soul finding there its purest expression, still untroubled by the naturalism, the intellectualism, the antique paganism, then astir in the artistic soul everywhere else in Italy. The lovely work of Perugino, very lovely, at its best, of the early Raphael also, is in fact "conservative," and at various points slightly behind its day, though not unpleasantly. In Perugino's allegoric frescoes of the *Cambio*, the Hall of the Money-changers, for instance, under the mystic rule of the Planets in person, pagan personages take their place indeed side by side with the figures of the New Testament, but are no Romans or Greeks, nor the Jews Jews, nor is any one of them, warrior, sage, king, precisely of Perugino's own time and place, but still contemplations only, after the manner of the personages in his church-work; or, say, dreams—monastic dreams—thin, do-nothing creatures, conjured from sky and cloud. Perugino clearly never broke through the meditative circle of the Middle Age.

Now Raphael, on the other hand, in his final period at Rome, exhibits a wonderful narrative power in painting; and the secret of that power—the power of developing a story in a picture, or series of pictures—may be traced back from him to Pinturicchio, as that painter worked on those vast, well-lighted walls of the cathedral library at Siena, at the great series of frescoes illustrative of the life of Pope Pius the Second. It had been a brilliant personal history, in contact now and again with certain remarkable public events—a career religious yet mundane, you scarcely know which, so natural is the blending of lights, of interest in it. How unlike that Peruginesque conception of life in its almost perverse other-worldliness, which Raphael now leaves behind him, but, like a true scholar, will not forget. Pinturicchio then had invited his remarkable young friend hither, "to assist him by his counsels," who, however, pupil-wise, after his habit also learns much as he thus assists. He stands depicted there in person in the scene of the canonization of Saint Catherine; and though his actual share in the work is not to be defined, connoisseurs have felt his intellectual presence, not at one place only, in touches at once finer and more forcible than were usual in the steady-going, somewhat Teutonic, Pinturicchio, Raphael's elder by thirty years. The meek scholar you see again, with his tentative sketches and suggestions, had more than learned his lesson; through all its changes that flexible intelligence loses nothing; does but add continually to its store. Henceforward Raphael will be able to tell a story in a picture, better, with a truer economy, with surer judgment, more naturally and easily than any one else.

And here at Siena, of all Italian towns perhaps most deeply impressed with mediæval character—an impress it still retains—grotesque, parti-colored—parti-colored, so to speak, in its genius—Satanic, yet devout of humor, as depicted in its old chronicles, and beautiful withal, dignified. It is here that Raphael becomes for the first time aware of that old pagan world, which had already come to be so much for the art-schools of Italy. There were points, as we saw, at which the school of Perugia was behind its day. Amid those intensely Gothic surroundings in the cathedral library where Pinturicchio worked, stood, as it remained till recently, unashamed there, a marble group of the three Graces—an average Roman work, in effect—the sort of thing we are used to. That, perhaps, is the only reason why for our part, except with an effort, we find it conventional or even tame. For the youthful Raphael, on the other hand, at that moment, antiquity, as with "the dew of herbs," seemed therein "to wake and sing" out of the dust in all its sincerity, its cheerfulness and natural charm. He turned it into a picture; has helped to make his original only too familiar, perhaps, placing the three sisters against his own favorite, so unclassic, Umbrian background indeed, but with no trace of the Peruginesque ascetic, Gothic meagreness in themselves; emphasizing rather, with a hearty acceptance, the nude, the flesh; made the limbs, in fact, a little heavy.

It was but one gleam he had caught just there in mediæval
Siena of that large pagan world he was, not so long afterwards, more completely than others to make his own.
And when somewhat later he painted the exquisite, still
Peruginesque, Apollo and Marsyas, semi-mediæval habits
again asserted themselves with delightfully-blent effects.
It might almost pass for a parable—that little picture in
the Louvre—of the contention between classic art and the
romantic, superseded in the person of Marsyas, a homely,
quaintly poetical young monk, surely! Only, Apollo himself also is clearly of the same brotherhood; has a touch,
in truth, of Heine's fancied Apollo " in exile," who, Christianity now triumphing, has served as a hired shepherd, or
hidden himself under the cowl in a cloister; and Raphael,
as if at work on choir-book or missal, still applies sym-
bolical gilding for natural sunlight. It is as if he wished
to proclaim amid newer lights—this scholar who never
forgot a lesson—his loyal pupilage to Perugino, and retains still something of mediæval stiffness, of the monastic
thoughts also, that were born and lingered in places like
Borgo San Sepolcro or Citta di Castello. *Chef-d'œuvre!*
you might exclaim, of the peculiar, tremulous, half-con-
vinced, monkish treatment of that after all damnable
pagan world. And our own generation certainly, with
kindred tastes, loving or wishing to love pagan art as sincerely as did the people of the Renaissance, and mediæval
art as well, would accept, of course, of work conceived in
that so seductively mixed manner, ten per cent. of even
Raphael's later, purely classical presentments.

   That picture was suggested by a fine old intaglio in the
Medicean collection at Florence, painted therefore after
Raphael's coming thither, and therefore also a survival
with him of a style limited, immature, literally provincial;
for in the phase on which he had now entered he is under
the influence of style in its most fully determined sense, of
what might be called the thorough-bass of the pictorial
art, of a fully realized intellectual system in regard to its
processes, well-tested by experiment, upon a survey of all
the conditions and various applications of it—of style as
understood by Da Vinci, then at work in Florence.
Raphael's sojourn there extends from his twenty-first to
his twenty-fifth year. He came with flattering recom-

mendations from the Court of Urbino; was admitted as an
equal by the masters of his craft, being already in demand
for work, then and ever since duly prized; was, in fact,
already famous, though he alone is unaware—is in his own
opinion still but a learner, and as a learner yields himself
meekly, systematically to influence; would learn from
Francia, whom he visits at Bologna; from the earlier
naturalistic works of Masolino and Masaccio; from the
solemn prophetic work of the venerable dominican, Bartolommeo, disciple of Savonarola. And he has already
habitually this strange effect, not only on the whole body
of his juniors, but on those whose manner had been long
since formed; they lose something of themselves by contact with him, as if they went to school again.

Bartolommeo, Da Vinci, were masters certainly of
what we call " the ideal " in art. Yet for Raphael, so loyal
hitherto to the traditions of Umbrian art, to its heavy
weight of hieratic tradition, dealing still somewhat con-
ventionally with a limited, non-natural matter—for
Raphael to come from Siena, Perugia, Urbino, to sharp-
witted, practical, masterful Florence was in immediate
effect a transition from reverie to realities—to a world of
facts. Those masters of the ideal were for him, in the
first instance, masters also of realism, as we say. Henceforth, to the end, he will be the analyst, the faithful re-
porter, in his work, of what he sees. He will realize the
function of style as exemplified in the practice of Da
Vinci, face to face with the world of nature and man as
they are; selecting from, asserting one's self in a transcript
of its veritable data; like drawing to like there, in obedience to the master's preference for the embodiment of the
creative form within him. Portrait-art had been nowhere
in the school of Perugino, but was the triumph of the
school of Florence. And here a faithful analyst of what
he sees, yet lifting it withal, unconsciously, inevitably, re-
composing, glorifying, Raphael too becomes, of course, a
painter of portraits. We may foresee them already in
masterly series, from Maddalena Doni, a kind of younger,
more virginal sister of La Gioconda, to cardinals and popes
—to that most sensitive of all portraits, the " Violin-
player," if it be really his. But then, on the other hand,
the influence of such portraiture will be felt also in his

inventive work, in a certain reality there, a certain con-
vincing loyalty to experience and observation. In his
most elevated religious work he will still keep, for security
at least, close to nature, and the truth of nature. His
modeling of the visible surface is lovely because he understands, can see the hidden causes of momentary action in
the face, the hands—how men and animals are really made
and kept alive. Set side by side, then, with that portrait
of Maddalena Doni, as forming together a measure of
what he has learned at Florence, the " Madonna del Gran
Duca," which still remains there. Call it on revision, and
without hesitation, the loveliest of his Madonnas, perhaps
of all Madonnas; and let it stand as representative of as
many as fifty or sixty types of that subject, onwards to
the Sixtine Madonna, in all the triumphancy of his later
days at Rome. Observe the veritable atmosphere about
it, the grand composition of the drapery, the magic relief,
the sweetness and dignity of the human hands and faces,
the noble tenderness of Mary's gesture, the unity of the
thing with itself, the faultless exclusion of all that does not
belong to its main purpose; it is like a single, simple axio-
matic thought. Note withal the novelty of its effect on
the mind, and you will see that this master of style (that's
a consummate example of what is meant by style) has been
still a willing scholar in the hands of Da Vinci. But, then,
with what ease, also, and simplicity, and a sort of natural
success not his!

It was in his twenty-fifth year that Raphael came to the
city of the popes, Michelangelo being already in high
favor there. For the remaining years of his life he paces
the same streets with that grim artist, who was so great
a contrast with himself, and for the first time his attitude
towards a gift different from his own is not that of a
scholar, but that of a rival. If he did not become the
scholar of Michelangelo it would be difficult, on the other
hand, to trace anywhere in Michelangelo's work the
counter influence usual with those who had influenced
him. It was as if he desired to add to the strength of
Michelangelo that sweetness which at first sight seems to
be wanting there. *Ex forti dulcedo:* and in the study of
Michelangelo certainly it is enjoyable to detect, if we may,
sweet savors amid the wonderful strength, the strange-

ness and potency of what he pours forth for us: with
Raphael, conversely, something of a relief to find in the
suavity of that so softly moving, tuneful existence, an
assertion of strength. There was the promise of it, as
you remember, in his very look as he saw himself at
eighteen; and you know that the lesson, the prophecy of
those holy women and children he has made his own, is
that "the meek shall possess." So, when we see him at
Rome at last, in that atmosphere of greatness, of the
strong, he too is found putting forth strength, adding that
element in due proportion to the mere sweetness and
charm of his genius; yet a sort of strength, after all, still
congruous with the line of development that genius has
hitherto taken, the special strength of the scholar and
his proper reward, a purely cerebral strength—the
strength, the power of an immense understanding.

Now the life of Raphael at Rome seems as we read of it
hasty and perplexed, full of undertakings, of vast works
not always to be completed, of almost impossible demands
on his industry, in a world of breathless competition, amid
a great company of spectators, for great rewards. You
seem to lose him, feel he may have lost himself, in the multiplicity of his engagements; might fancy that, wealthy,
variously decorated, a courtier, cardinal *in petto*, he was
"serving tables." But, you know, he was forcing into
this brief space of years (he died at thirty-seven) more
than the natural business of the larger part of a long life;
and one way of getting some kind of clearness into it, is to
distinguish the various divergent outlooks or applications,
and group the results of that immense intelligence, that
still untroubled, flawlessly operating, completely informed
understanding, that purely cerebral power, acting through
his executive, inventive or creative gifts, through the eye
and the hand with its command of visible color and form.
In that way you may follow him along many various roads
till brain and eye and hand suddenly fail in the very midst
of his work—along many various roads, but you can follow him along each of them distinctly.

At the end of one of them is the " Galatea," and in quite
a different form of industry, the data for the beginnings of
a great literary work of pure erudition. Coming to the
capital of Christendom, he comes also for the first time

under the full influence of the antique world, pagan art, pagan life, and is henceforth an enthusiastic archæologist. On his first coming to Rome a papal bull had authorized him to inspect all ancient marbles, inscriptions, and the like, with a view to their adaptation in new buildings then proposed. A consequent close acquaintance with antiquity, with the very touch of it, blossomed literally in his brain, and under his facile hand, in artistic creations, of which the Galatea is indeed the consummation. But the frescoes of the Farnese palace, with a hundred minor designs, find their places along that line of his artistic activity, and did not exhaust his knowledge of antiquity, his interest in and control of it. The mere fragments of it that still cling to his memory would have composed, had he lived longer, a monumental illustrated survey of the monuments of ancient Rome.

To revive something of the proportionable spirit at least of antique building in the architecture of the present, came naturally to Raphael as the son of his age; and at the end of another of those roads of diverse activity stands Saint Peter's, though unfinished. What a proof again of that immense intelligence, by which, as I said, the element of strength supplemented the element of mere sweetness and charm in his work, that at the age of thirty, known hitherto only as a painter, at the dying request of the venerable Bramante himself, he should have been chosen to succeed him as the director of that vast enterprise. And if little in the great church, as we see it, is directly due to him, yet we must not forget that his work in the Vatican also was partly that of an architect. In the Loggia, or open galleries of the Vatican, the last and most delicate effects of *Quattro-cento* taste come from his hand, in that peculiar arabesque decoration which goes by his name.

Saint Peter's, as you know, had an indirect connection with the Teutonic reformation. When Leo X pushed so far the sale of indulgences to the overthrow of Luther's Catholicism, it was done after all for the not entirely selfish purpose of providing funds to build the metropolitan church of Christendom with the assistance of Raphael; and yet, upon another of those diverse outways of his so versatile intelligence, at the close of which we behold his unfinished picture of the Transfiguration, what has been

called Raphael's Bible finds its place—that series of
biblical scenes in the Loggia of the Vatican. And here,
while he has shown that he could do something of Michelangelo's work a little more soothingly than he, this graceful Roman Catholic rivals also what is perhaps best in the
work of the rude German reformer—of Luther who came
to Rome about this very time, to find nothing admirable
there. Place, along with them, the Cartoons, and observe
that in this phase of his artistic labor, as Luther printed
his vernacular German version of the Scriptures, so
Raphael is popularizing them for an even larger world;
brings the simple, to their great delight, face to face with
the Bible as it is, in all its variety of incident, after they
had so long had to content themselves with but fragments
of it, as presented in the symbolism and in the brief lec-
tions of the Liturgy:—*Biblia Pauperum*, in a hundred
forms of reproduction, though designed for popes and
princes.

But then, for the wise, at the end of yet another of those
divergent ways, glows his painted philosophy in the Parnassus and the School of Athens, with their numerous
accessories. In the execution of those works, of course,
his antiquarian knowledge stood him in good stead; and
here, above all, is the pledge of his immense understanding, at work on its own natural ground on a purely intellectual deposit, the apprehension, the transmission to
others of complex and difficult ideas. We have here, in
fact, the sort of intelligence to be found in Lessing, in
Herder, in Hegel, in those who, by the instrumentality of
an organized philosophic system, have comprehended in
one view or vision what poetry has been, or what Greek
philosophy, as great complex dynamic facts in the world.
But then, with the artist of the sixteenth century, this
synoptic intellectual power worked in perfect identity with
the pictorial imagination and a magic hand. By him
large theoretic conceptions are addressed, so to speak, to
the intelligence of the eye. There had been efforts at
such abstract or theoretic painting before, or say, rather,
leagues behind him. Modern efforts, again, we know,
and not in Germany alone, to do the like for that larger
survey of such matters which belongs to the philosophy of
our own century, but for one or many reasons they have

seemed only to prove the incapacity of philosophy to be
expressed in terms of art.   They have seemed, in short,
so far, not fit to be seen literally—those ideas of culture,
religion, and the like.   Yet Plato, as you know, supposed
a kind of visible loveliness about ideas.   Well! in Raphael,
painted ideas, painted and visible philosophy are for once
as beautiful as Plato thought they must be, if one truly
apprehended them.   For note, above all, that with all his
wealth of antiquarian knowledge in detail, and with a .
perfect technique, it is after all the beauty, the grace of
poetry, of pagan philosophy, of religious faith that he
thus records.

Of religious faith also.   The Disputa, in which, under
the form of a council representative of all ages, he embodies the idea of theology, *divinarum rerum notitia*, as
constantly resident in the Catholic Church, ranks with the
" Parnassus" and the " School of Athens," if it does not
rather close another of his long lines of intellectual travail
—a series of compositions, partly symbolic, partly historical, in which the " Deliverance of St. Peter from
Prison," the " Expulsion of the Huns," and the " Coronation of Charlemagne," find their places; and by which,
painting in the great official chambers of the Vatican,
Raphael asserts, interprets the power and charm of the
Catholic ideal as realized in history.   A scholar, a student
of the visible world, of the natural man, yet even more
ardently of the books, the art, the life of the old pagan
world, the age of the Renaissance had been, through all
its varied activity, in spite of the weakened hold of
Catholicism on the critical intellect still under its influence,
the glow of it, as a religious ideal, and in the presence of
Raphael you cannot think it a mere after-glow.   Inde-
pendently, that is, of less or more evidence for it, the whole
creed of the Middle Age, as a scheme of the world as it
should be, as we should be glad to find it, was still welcome
to the heart, the imagination.   Now, in Raphael, all the
various conditions of that age discover themselves as characteristics of a vivid personal genius, which may be said
therefore to be conterminous with the genius of the Renaissance itself.   For him, then, in the breadth of his
immense cosmopolitan intelligence, for Raphael, who had
done in part the work of Luther also, the Catholic Church

—through all its phases, as reflected in its visible local center, the papacy—is alive still as of old, one and continuous, and still true to itself. Ah! what is local and visible, as you know, counts for so much with the artistic temper.

Old friends or old foes, with but new faces, events repeating themselves, as his large, clear, synoptic vision can detect, the invading King of France, Louis XII, appears as Attila: Leo X as Leo I: and he thinks of, he sees, at one and the same moment, the coronation of Charlemagne and the interview of Pope Leo with Francis I, as a dutiful son of the Church: of the deliverance of Leo X from prison, and the deliverance of St. Peter.

I have abstained from anything like description of Raphael's pictures in speaking of him and his work, have aimed rather at preparing you to look at his work for yourselves, by a sketch of his life, and therein especially, as most appropriate to this place, of Raphael as a scholar. And now if, in closing, I commend one of his pictures in particular to your imagination or memory, your purpose to see it, or see it again, it will not be the Transfiguration nor the Sixtine Madonna, nor even the " Madonna del Gran Duca," but the picture we have in London—the Ansidei, or Blenheim, Madonna. I find there, at first sight, with something of the pleasure one has in a proposition of Euclid, a sense of the power of the understanding, in the economy with which he has reduced his material to the simplest terms, has disentangled and detached its various elements. He is painting in Florence, but for Perugia, and sends it a specimen of its own old art—Mary and the babe enthroned, with St. Nicolas and the Baptist in attendance on either side. The kind of thing people there had already seen so many times, but done better, in a sense not to be measured by degrees, with a wholly original freedom and life and grace, though he perhaps is unaware, done better as a whole, because better in every minute particular, than ever before. The scrupulous scholar, aged twenty-three, is now indeed a master; but still goes carefully. Note, therefore, how much mere exclusion counts for in the positive effect of his work. There is a saying that the true artist is known best by what he omits. Yes, because the whole question of good taste is involved precisely in such jealous omission. Note this, for instance, in the familiar Apennine background, with its blue hills and brown towns, faultless, for once— for once only—and observe, in the Umbrian pictures around, how often such background is marred by grotesque, natural, or architectural detail, by incongruous or childish incident. In this cool, pearl-grey, quiet place, where color tells for double—the jeweled cope, the painted book in the hand of Mary, the chaplet of red coral—one is reminded that among all classical writers Raphael's preference was for the faultless Virgil. How orderly, how divinely clean and sweet the flesh, the vesture, the floor, the earth, the sky! Ah, say rather the hand, the method of the painter! There is an unmistakable pledge of strength, of movement and animation in the cast of the Baptist's countenance, but reserved, repressed. Strange, Raphael has given him a staff of transparent crystal. Keep, then, to that picture as the embodied formula of Raphael's genius. Amid all he has here already achieved, full, we may think, of the quiet assurance of what is to come, his attitude is still that of the scholar; he seems still to be saying, before all things, from first to last, "I am utterly purposed that I will not offend."

EDWARD JOHN PHELPS

THE SUPREME COURT AND POPULAR SOVEREIGNTY

[Address of Edward J. Phelps, lawyer, diplomatist, Minister to Great Britain, 1885-89 (born in Middlebury, Vt., July 11, 1822; died in New Haven, Conn., March 9, 1900), delivered at the centennial anniversary of the organization of the Supreme Court of the United States, February 4, 1890, held at the Metropolitan Opera-House, New York City, under the auspices of the New York State Bar Association. Grover Cleveland, as Chairman of the Executive Committee, presided.]

GENTLEMEN :—But few words remain to be added to those so well spoken by my distinguished brethren in concluding, on the part of the bar, the expression which this occasion calls for. We have thought it well to mark in a manner thus significant and conspicuous, the centennial anniversary of our highest and greatest tribunal; to review so far as the flying hour allows, its eventful and interesting history; to recall some of its memories, cherished and imperishable; and to consider in the light of a century's experience, what has been, and what is like to be hereafter, its place and its influence as an independent constitutional power in the Federal government of this country.

We cannot forget that in its origin it was an experiment, untried and uncertain. Judicial history has not furnished another example of a court created by an authority superior to legislation and beyond the reach of executive power, clothed with a jurisdiction above the law it was appointed to administer, and charged, not merely with the general course of public justice, but with the limitation of the powers of political government, and the adjustment of the conflicting claims of sovereign States. The hundred years that now terminate have tested the value of all American institutions. Fortunate as they have been for the most part, it will yet be the judgment of dispassionate history that no other has so completely justified the faith of its authors, or fulfilled with such signal success the purpose of its foundation.

What was that purpose? Not the limited original jurisdiction of the Court, dignified and important, but rarely invoked. Not chiefly, even, its ordinary appellate jurisdiction, extensive and beneficent as it is, most desirable, yet perhaps not indispensable. Not for these objects, great though they are, was it placed, or did it need to be placed, on the singular eminence it occupies. Its principal and largest function was designed to be, as it has been, the defence and preservation of the Constitution that created it as the permanent fundamental law on which our system of government depends. Had that instrument been left only directory to the legislature, to be construed and given effect as the exigencies of party or the purposes of the hour might demand; had it been referred to the conflicting determination of various courts, with no supreme arbiter to correct their mistakes, or to harmonize their disagreements, so that its meaning might depend upon the State or the tribunal in which the question happened to arise, it would speedily have become but the shadow of an authority that had no real existence, fruitful in a discord it was powerless to allay. American experience has made it an axiom in political science that no written constitution of government can hope to stand without a paramount and independent tribunal to determine its construction and to enforce its precepts in the last resort. This is the great and foremost duty cast by the Constitution, for the sake of the Constitution, upon the Supreme Court of the United States.

The jurisdiction of the Court over questions of this sort, and the dual sovereignty so skilfully divided between the States and the Federation, as they are the most striking are likewise the only entirely original features in the Constitution. All else found a precedent or at least a prototype, in previous institutions. In its other branches it is mainly the combination and adaptation of machinery that was known before. It was to be expected, therefore, that the earliest and most critical exercise of the new power conferred upon the Court would be displayed in dealing with the new form of sovereignty at the same time devised, and bringing into harmony those opposite forces that might so easily have resulted in conflict and disaster. The questions that have arisen in this field have been usually the most delicate, often the most difficult, always the most conspicuous of all that have engaged the attention of the Court. While it has been charged with the limitation of many other departments of governmental authority, here have been found hitherto its most permanent employment, and the most dangerful emergencies it has had to confront. Here have taken place its most celebrated judgments, the most signal triumphs of its wisdom, its foresight, as well as its moral courage—rarest of human virtues. It is to this sagacious judicial administration of the Constitution that we are principally indebted for the harmonious operation that has attended the Federal system, each party to it made supreme in its own sphere and at the same time strictly confined within it, neither transgressing nor transgressed. Looking back now upon this long series of determinations, it is easy to see how different American history might have been, had they proved less salutary, less wise, and less firm. The Court did not make the Constitution, but has saved it from destruction. Only in the one great conflict, generated by the single inherent weakness of the Constitution, and unhappily beyond judicial reach, has the Court failed to maintain inviolate all the borders and marches of contiguous jurisdiction and keep unbroken the peace of the Union.

But it still remains to be observed that the service of preserving, through the Constitution, the Union of the States, great and distinguished as it is, and vital as it is, has been wrought upon the machinery of government, not upon its essence. Beyond and above the question how a political system shall be maintained, lies the far larger question, Why should it be maintained at all? The forms of free government are valuable only as they effect its purpose. They may defend liberty, but they do not constitute it, nor necessarily produce it. Their ultimate permanence, therefore, among the men of our race, must depend, not on themselves, but on their results.

The true analysis of the function of the Supreme Court as the conservator of the Constitution involves, consequently, the further inquiry, What is the value of the Constitution to those who dwell under the shadow of its protection?

It rests upon the foundation stone of popular sovereignty. The true definition of that familiar and much-abused phrase is not always kept in view. The sovereignty of the people is not the arbitrary power or blind caprice of the multitude any more than of an aristocracy or a despot. It is not the right of any class, small or great, high or low, to wrong or oppress another. It is not a struggle between classes at all. It is simply recognition of the natural and equal rights of men as a basis of a government formed for their protection by its people, and regulated by law. A system under which every citizen, in the peace of God and of the State, shall be assured by indefeasible right and not by favor or sufferance, in the enjoyment of his life, his liberty, his property in all its forms, his home, his family relations, his freedom of conscience and of speech. The powers of government, in all their extent and elaboration, come down at last to this ultimate purpose. For this they exist, and on this foundation is raised all that renders social life desirable. "In my mind," said Lord Brougham, "he was guilty of no error, he was chargeable with no exaggeration, he was betrayed by his fancy into no metaphor, who once said that all we see about us, Kings, Lords, and Commons, the whole machinery of the State, all the apparatus of the system and its varied workings, end in simply bringing twelve good men into a box."

The world has seen empires and dynasties without number based upon arbitrary power. But for the most part it has seen them perish. They have illuminated the page of history, but with the light of the comet and the meteor, not of the stars. The civilization they have brought forth has been as transient as themselves. Neither government nor civilization contained any element of permanence, until they came to be founded upon

the principles of civil and religious liberty. Magna
Charta was therefore the starting-point, not merely of
free institutions, but of the only civilization that ever
did or ever could survive political systems and pass on
unimpaired from the ruins of the construction of another.
Its striking and memorable language no rhetoric has
been able to improve, no casuistry to obscure. When
it broke upon the world it proclaimed a new era, the
dawning of a better day for humanity, in which the rights
of man became superior to government, and their protection the condition of allegiance. The great thought matured with a slow but certain growth. Battles enough
were fought for it, but never in vain, until at last it came
to be established forever upon English soil, and among
the English race on every soil. And the highest eulogy
upon the British constitution was spoken when Chatham
said: "The poorest man may in his cottage bid defiance
to all the forces of the crown; it may be frail, its roof may
be shaky, the wind may blow through it; the storm may
enter, the rain may enter, but the King of England cannot
enter; all his forces dare not cross the threshold of the
ruined tenant." But the great orator could go no
further; he could not say that the British Parliament
might not enter the home of the subject, for all the judges
of England are powerless in the face of an Act of Parliament, whatever it may be. It was reserved for the American Constitution to extend the judicial protection of personal rights, not only against the rulers of the people, but
against the representatives of the people.

The history of the Saxon race exhibits few changes
more striking than the succession of power. First, in the
king; then when royal supremacy became intolerable, in
the hands of the barons, who struck the earliest blow for
freedom, and long stood between the throne and the
people, the supporters of the one, the protectors of the
other. When in the course of time that oligarchy had in
its turn abused its authority, it passed to the Parliament
chosen by the people. And when at last the founders of
our Constitution, driven to revolution by Parliamentary
oppression, had learned that even representative government cannot always be depended upon by those it represents, they placed the protection of personal rights beyond

the reach of the popular will, and found in a constitutional judiciary the true and final custodian of the liberty of the subject.

The maintenance of these rights against all Federal interference was conferred upon the Court by amendment, almost immediately after the adoption of the Constitution, and as soon as it was perceived that the power ought to be expressed, because it might fail to be implied. The protection of them against State invasion in one important particular,—the inviolability of contracts,—was provided in the original Constitution. And when, twenty-two years ago, the interference of the States with the rights of life, liberty, and property was forbidden by the Fourteenth Amendment, the jurisdiction of the Court over this great subject became complete, and will, beyond doubt, always remain so. But one exception still exists, in the power of Congress, within the limited scope of its authority, to pass a law, though it may impair the obligation of a pre-existing contract.

Other topics of constitutional interpretation will always remain. The time will never come when questions of conflicting authority between the States and the Nation will cease to rise. But that field must gradually grow smaller, and its inquiries less critical. The main landmarks have now been planted, the boundary lines traced, the cardinal rules strongly and clearly established. Future labor in that direction, though constant, will be easier and plainer than in the century that has passed away.

But new attacks upon individual rights in many forms and under many pretexts, are beginning to be heard of, and are to be looked for in an increasing measure. The accursed warfare of classes is the danger that appears chiefly to threaten the future. It requires little prescience to perceive that the burden of constitutional administration by the Court is to shift thereafter in a considerable degree from the preservation of the machinery of government, to the enforcing of its ultimate object; from conflicts between the States and the Federation, to those between the State and the citizen, involving the protection of property, of contracts, of personal rights. But the best assurance that the Court will be found equal to the emergencies that are to come, whatever they may prove to be, is seen in the success with which it has encountered those of the past. And that success is most clearly shown by the public confidence it has inspired. The people of this country have learned to have faith in the Court, and pride in it. Elevated and in a measure isolated as it is, they still feel it to be their own. Many a plain man has never seen it, nor ever expects to see it. He cannot discriminate its jurisdiction nor understand its procedure. The principles of its jurisprudence are not for his comprehension. But he reposes with a more confident security under the roof his industry has raised, and enjoys with a better assurance the liberty that has made him free, because he knows there is a limit which oppression cannot transgress; that he can never be disseized, nor outlawed, nor otherwise destroyed; that no agency of power can go upon him or send upon him, but by the judgment of his peers and the law of the land; and he believes that if the worst should come to the worst, and wrong and outrage should be found intolerable and yet without other redress, there is still laid up for him a remedy under the Constitution of his country, to be based in some way or other, in the Supreme Court of the United States.

Long and late may it be, sir, before that confidence is shaken. If it is sometimes child-like in its simplicity, it is always noble in its origin. Long and late may it be before even the suggestion shall penetrate the faith of common men that the highest American justice is not for them. May no consideration of convenience, no pressure of business, ever seek its relief in any limitation which shall carry the idea to the body of the people that there is reserved in this country for the powerful corporation, the millionaire, and the great financier, an ultimate justice that the humbler citizen cannot reach; that a ruinous case may be decided against him without redress; and yet the same judgment in the case of another man, whose dealings are larger in amount though smaller in relative consequence, may be reversed and set aside as unlawful and unjust. Lawyers know that purely constitutional questions are not measured by figures. But that discrimination between the special and the general jurisdiction can neither be made nor understood by the mass of men. And such questions form, after all, but a very small part of the administration of justice. Public confidence is a sensitive plant. No institution in a free government can afford to endanger it.

And thus, by the inexorable logic of sound constitutional principles, it has been brought to pass, that the rights of the people find their last and best security, not in the popular assembly, nor in any agency of its creation, but in that institution of government which is furthest of all beyond the popular reach, which is made, as far as any institution can be, independent of public feeling, and invulnerable to the attack of majorities. Having its origin in the sovereignty of the people it is the bulwark of the people against their own unadvised action, their own uninstructed will. It saves them not merely from their enemies but it saves them from themselves. And so it perpetuates the sovereignty from which it sprang; and which has best provided for its own supremacy by the surrender of a power it was dangerous to retain. For this purpose alone, aside from those necessary to its own maintenance, does the National government cross the line of the States. All merely legal rights of the citizen, outside of Federal affairs, are left dependent upon the authority of the State in which he is found. The only cardinal personal rights are taken in charge by the Nation, as between the Government and the individual, because only through that protection can be assured either the value or the permanence of a Constitution which is itself the government and itself the Union.

The experience of American free government has shown that it is the tendency of its legislative branches to decrease, and of its judicial power to rise, in public estimation. It has added a fresh demonstration to the truth that is as old as the history of freedom, that it must find its safety where it found its origin, in the exertions of those to whom truth is better than popularity, and right superior to gain. And it has proved again what has been proved so often, that the only liberty humanity can tolerate is the liberty that is under the law.

To you, our especial and most honored guests—Justices of the Court, whose nativity we celebrate—more than *Patres Conscripti* in our Republic—the Bar of this country, in all its length and breadth, has to-day but one greeting to offer, one message to convey. It is the assurance of their supreme respect, their unfaltering confidence, their cordial attachment. The relations of the Court with the advocates who have from time to time gathered about it, have been always among its happiest incidents. It has had the good fortune in an uncommon degree to inspire them not merely with respect but with a sincere personal affection. To this sentiment you have never been strangers, and you never will be. If the words of eulogy that have been so felicitously uttered by my brother have touched those who have gone before you rather than yourselves, it is because, and only because, they are with the dead and you are still among the living. Long may that restraint seal the lips of your eulogists.

Judges will be appointed and will pass away. One generation rapidly succeeds another. But whoever comes and whoever goes, the Court remains. The king may die, but still the king survives. Strong in its traditions, consecrated by its memories, fortified with the steadfast support of the profession that surrounds it, anchored in the abiding trust of its countrymen, the great Court will go on—and still go on, keeping alive through many a century that we shall not see, the light that burns with a constant radiance upon the high altar of American constitutional justice.

ALFRED S. PINKERTON

SPIRIT OF ODD-FELLOWSHIP

[Address by Alfred S. Pinkerton, lawyer (born in Lancaster, Pa., March 19, 1856; ———), delivered at Richmond, Va., in his capacity as Grand Sire of the Sovereign Grand Lodge of Odd Fellows, September 17, 1900.]

MR. CHAIRMAN, YOUR EXCELLENCY, MR. MAYOR, REPRESENTATIVES OF OUR ORDER, LADIES AND GENTLE-MEN:—This is not the first time that I have received the greetings of a Richmond audience and been the recipient of Virginian hospitality. I know the warmth of the one, the unbounded generosity of the other, and I voice the sentiment of every member of the Sovereign Grand Lodge when I say that each of us appreciates the splendid welcome you have given, and rejoices in the privilege that is his of visiting, under such happy auspices, this beautiful and historic State.

We knew that chivalry and knightly courtesy still existed in the Old Dominion; that Southern hearts would welcome us, and Southern hands be extended in fraternal greeting. Our anticipations have been realized, and we sit among you not as strangers, but as welcome guests, as neighbors, and as friends.

Representing an Order founded in man's nobility, we gladly assemble among a people whose ancestors first proclaimed the right of the individual man to direct his own affairs and destiny.

Before Plymouth Rock felt the touch of English feet the seeds of a nation had been sown at Jamestown. On Virginian soil representative government in America was born. The colonial charter of 1621 was the first grant of

964

self-government given by a hereditary ruler to dwellers
on this continent, given to those who dared assert that
English blood in Virginia meant a voice in Virginian rule.

As two centuries ago the people of England testified in
behalf of those bishops who but asserted their privileges
of self-respect; as then the flower of the British bar successfully pleaded for freedom of church; and freedom of
right; so in our fathers' time it was a country lawyer,
"who spoke as Homer wrote" who in the "parson's"
cause voiced that sentiment of Virginia which afterwards
flamed in syllabled fire from that old church still standing
in your city; he it was who ten years before a political
revolution that divided in government—but not in hearts
—the New World from the Old, offered the resolution by
which your General Assembly declared that it alone had
the right to tax Virginians. It was a Virginian who presided over the first American Congress, and from Virginian hands came another and immortal resolution, that
which declared that these colonies should be free and independent States.

I come from a community that has much in common
with this. Sprung from the same great freedom-loving
race, speaking the same language, sharing the glory of a
common descent and of a common literature, one in sentiment and in aspiration, the colonies of Virginia and Massachusetts were side by side in the contest for political
independence. Each called its land a "commonwealth,"
thus in the very title indicating the form of government
under which its people lived—the *common wealth*—the
home and rule of all the people—the union of all for the
benefit of each—the land of equal opportunities and equal
privileges. Yes, in the old days we were together. Virginia remembers—

" . . . . . how the Bay State, in answer to the call
Of her old House of Burgesses spoke out from Faneuil Hall
When, echoing back her Henry's cry, came pulsing on each breath
Of northern winds the thrilling cry of 'liberty or death.' "

Beneath the old elm still standing by Harvard College
the first soldier of Virginia—the first American—assumed
command of that army of "tradesmen, farmers, and mechanics," that in a spirit of sublime prophesy dared to call

itself " Continental," that won freedom from the trained soldiery of Europe and gave visible form to a government that has made good the name its soldiers bore. Then side by side our fathers fought; then side by side our statesmen sat; and the first name that appears upon that immortal Declaration of Independence, penned by a Virginian hand, and based upon Virginia's bill of rights, is that of a Massachusetts man, President of that Congress which gave to the world and to the godlike and aspiring soul this bible of the rights of man.

Hancock and Jefferson, Adams and Mason, Otis and Henry, united those two colonies that, more than any others, gave impulse to American thought and speech and action. There was Bunker Hill; here Yorktown. Nor do we forget that mighty lawyer, born of your blood and sleeping in your soil, the great interpreter of the written Constitution of our land, nor him, of Northern birth, that Constitution's eloquent defender—Marshall and Webster —great sons of the same proud race.

It was the civilization of Jamestown and of Plymouth that made possible this Government of ours, and though for a time the clouds lowered o'er our house, thank God we are once more as of yore; as, of old, they together "encountered Tarleton's charge of fire," so again have Virginia and Massachusetts struck hands—and this time in a deathless friendship; so again in the presence of a common danger, and in honor of a common flag, have our brothers touched elbows in the ranks, slept by the same camp-fires, and together offered upon the country's altar the rich libation of their blood. History is making fast. From the Western Hemisphere has departed every vestige of Castilian power. The starry flag has become a fixed constellation o'er Asiatic seas, but, better than all, we have learned to know our Motherland. The conquering English-speaking people have come closer together—and so have we at home. It was a good day for America when the soldier boy of New England and of the Northwest enlisted under a Virginian Lee, and when the star of Wheeler glistened upon a coat of army blue. Gone are the days of strife and bitterness and doubt; welcome the days of peace, of confidence, of lasting brotherhood.

We come to you in the closing hours of the Nineteenth

century, a century of wonderful development; a century of great achievements. Old empires have passed away; nations in swaddling-cloths have grown to manhood's state. Kings and czars have been born, have ruled, and been forgotten—boundaries of nations have been changed —thrones have fallen, and old dynasties been destroyed. Man everywhere is asserting the power and attributes of man. This Government of the people has shed its radiating light throughout the world. Europe, Asia, and Africa have felt its beneficent beams; individual man, under whatever government he may live, lifts his eyes higher than ever before, and while war and famine, and pestilence, and death still constitute a portion of our heritage, the path is upward, and never has God's light seemed so warm and bright to the great toiling masses of the earth as at this hour, when kingdoms and principalities and powers are but the instruments and not the destroyers of men.

Nor has the development been confined to the political world. In art, in science, in mechanics, has

> " Man put forth
> His pomp, his pride, his skill,
> And arts that made fire, flood, and earth,
> The vassals of his will."

The cotton-gin, the power-loom, the sewing-machine, the rotary printing-press, the reaper, the telegraph and telephone, the binding of electricity to man's common use, the thousand and one mechanical appliances that make our burdens light, and life more worth the living, are but a part of this century's tribute to the future. In letters and in literature what advances have been made! The printing-press has brought the richest thoughts of the best minds within easy reach of all, and the philosopher and the astronomer share their secrets with a thousand friends. Thought is purer than before, theology more simple and humane, religion more near the human heart and soul.

This is the age in which we live; this is the century that called into life that great humanitarian movement which we denominate Odd-Fellowship. It is the child of American spirit and life; it is a creation designed for daily food; it lives and moves among breathing men; it is for the closet and for the field; it is of practical use to a practical people; its secrets are a shield and not a sword; it believes in the royal heritage of man and in the divine right of self-advancement. Teaching loyalty to established government, and obedience to law, it holds that governments are made for man and that the citizen who controls himself, who recognizes the rights of, and has faith in, his fellow citizens is the best prop and support of such a government. It believes in truth, in honor, in temperance, in the overshadowing Fatherhood of God; in the lasting, eternal brotherhood of man; in charity in thought and charity in acts; to the cry of Cain it answers, "I am my brother's keeper," and in every hour of its existence it has blessed humanity and lessened human toil and suffering.

Bear with me for a moment. If I am correctly informed, the present total taxable valuation, real and personal, of this city is $69,215,240. Raze beautiful Richmond to the ground; convert into coin every foot of land within its corporate limits; let every stone and timber of every factory, every business block, every dwelling-house, contribute to the sum; into the crucible put your jewels and your stores of gold and silver; market the securities, bonds, and stocks of your people; and when you shall have done all this, when you shall have converted your city's soil and buildings into scrip, when you shall have stripped your citizens of all their taxable property, you will, even then, be over fifteen million dollars short of the amount of money that this Order has expended, since 1830, in brotherly relief. You will then be short a sum equal to seven-twelfths of the entire taxable valuation of the personal property here owned. At the present rate of charitable expenditure we distribute, for such purposes, the wealth of a Richmond every nineteen years; a distribution in which there is no expense account and in which every dollar finds the pocket of the beneficiary. Pardon the illustration, Mr. Mayor. We like your city too well to despoil it; we hope to come again; but the comparison made demonstrates the magnitude of this Order's silent charitable work.

Can you question the fraternal spirit of such a brotherhood? Dare you challenge its right to live? Can you define the future's bounds? It is not my purpose to enter into a discussion of the Order's principles, or to pronounce an eulogy upon its work. To-day it holds one million souls within its fond embrace. The streams of its unostentatious charity have flowed to every corner of our land; its white banner has led the march of fraternal life. To-day we salute our comrades across the seas; our flag is uplifted in the isles of the Pacific. Our faith has overleaped the barriers of States, nor has it been retarded by the artificial distinctions of society. Virginia's sons have shared our Order's struggles and its honors. They have taught its lessons on your soil, and " by their works ye shall know them."

We come to-day representing every State and Territory of this great Union in answer to Virginia's call, and in response to Richmond's welcome. With us as comrades, brothers, and friends are citizens of that northward land, with whose sons we claim kinship, whose national hymn is set to the same air as ours, and whose gentle ruler is Queen of American as well as of English hearts. Within our convention hall are clustered the flags of sixteen different lands wherein this Order dwells, and over all hangs the white flag of peace, emblazoned with the scarlet links of truth.

Such an Order it is my proud privilege to represent. In its name I accept your greeting, and in its name I thank you for it. Generous as have been the spoken words, more generous has been the manner of your salutation. From the moment we entered Virginia until this hour we have been the recipients of boundless hospitality. We have traveled your beautiful valleys with delight—we have shared in a true Virginia welcome—we are glad that we have come, and we shall bear to our several homes brightest recollections of the Old Dominion and of its sons and daughters.

To your Excellency, to you, Mr. Mayor, to the several representatives of our Order, and to you who represent our gentle sisterhood, I tender the thanks and the fraternal salutations of the Sovereign Grand Lodge, and I trust that our sojourn among you may be as pleasant to you as it is profitable and enjoyable to us.

Representatives: Virginia has formally welcomed us to

her heart; Richmond has opened wide her gates; our
brothers and sisters, the portals of their homes; let us
repay this courtesy by making this the most memorable
session of our history—memorable for the good we accomplish, for the inspiration given to our brotherhood, for the
assistance rendered to the weary soul.   As the gates of a
new century swing outward at our touch, let us lift our
flag to loftier heights, and let us dedicate our Order anew
to the great purposes that gave it birth.

We meet among a generous people and amid historic
surroundings.   Here, in more ancient days, people of our
blood and kin laid the foundations of a mighty power.
The history of this commonwealth is interwoven with that
of this nation and of the English-speaking race.   Its sons
have been conspicuous in the forum and on the battlefield.   Again and again has it sent forth its bravest to
build up other States, and to the nation it has given rulers
whose name and fame will live while centuries pass away.
We know its splendid history; we have faith in its bright
future, and—

> " Again we hail thee
>   Mother of States and unpolluted men,
>   Virginia, fitly named from England's manly Queen."

SARGENT SMITH PRENTISS

LAFAYETTE

[Eulogy by Sargent S. Prentiss, lawyer, orator, Member of Congress, from Mississippi (born in Portland, Maine, September 30, 1808; died in Laguerre, near Natchez, Miss., July 1, 1850), delivered in Jackson, Miss., August, 1835, after the death of Lafayette.]

Death, who knocks with equal hand at the door of the cottage and the palace gate, has been busy at his appointed work. Mourning prevails throughout the land, and the countenances of all are shrouded in the mantle of regret. Far across the wild Atlantic, amid the pleasant vineyards in the sunny land of France, there, too, is mourning; and the weeds of sorrow are alike worn by prince and peasant. Against whom has the monarch of the tomb turned his remorseless dart that such widespread sorrow prevails? Hark, and the agonized voice of Freedom, weeping for her favorite son, will tell you in strains sadder than those with which she " shrieked when Kosciusko fell " that Lafayette—the gallant and the good—has ceased to live.

The friend and companion of Washington is no more. He who taught the eagle of our country, while yet unfledged, to plume his young wing and mate his talons with the lion's strength, has taken his flight far beyond the stars, beneath whose influence he fought so well. Lafayette is dead! The gallant ship, whose pennon has so often bravely streamed above the roar of battle and the tempest's rage, has at length gone slowly down in the still and quiet waters. Well mightest thou, O Death, now recline beneath the laurels thou hast won; for never since, as the grim messenger of Almighty Vengeance, thou camest into this world, did a more generous heart cease to

heave beneath thy chilling touch, and never will thy in-
satiate dart be hurled against a nobler breast! Who does
not feel at the mournful intelligence, as if he had lost
something cheering from his own path through life; as if
some bright star, at which he had been accustomed frequently and fondly to gaze, had been suddenly extinguished in the firmament?

History's page abounds with those who have struggled
forth from the nameless crowd, and, standing forward in
the front ranks, challenged the notice of their fellow men;
but when, in obedience to their bold demands, we examine
their claims to our admiration, how seldom do we find
aught that excites our respect or commands our veneration. With what pleasure do we turn from the contemplation of the Cæsars and Napoleons of the human race to
meditate upon the character of Lafayette! We feel proud
that we belong to the same species; we feel proud that we
live in the same age; and we feel still more proud that our
own country drew forth and nurtured those generous
virtues which went to form a character that for love of
liberty, romantic chivalry, unbounded generosity and un-
wavering devotion, has never had a parallel.

The history of this wonderful man is engraved upon the
memory of every American, and I shall only advert to
such portions of it as will best tend to illustrate his character. In 1777 our fathers were engaged in rescuing from
the fangs of the British lion the rights which their sons
are now enjoying. It was the gloomiest period of the
Revolutionary struggle. Our army was feeble; an insolent and victorious enemy was pressing hard upon it;
despondency had spread through its ranks. It seemed as
if the last hope of Freedom was gone. Deep gloom had
settled over the whole country; and men looked with a
despairing aspect upon the future of a contest which their
best wishes could not flatter them was doubtful. It was
at this critical period that their hopes were renovated and
their spirits roused by the cheering intelligence that at
Charleston, in the State of South Carolina, there had just
arrived a gallant French nobleman of high rank and immense wealth, eager to embark his person and his fortunes
in the sacred cause of Liberty! New impulse was given
to the energies of our dispirited troops. As the first ray

of morning breaks upon the benighted and tempest-tossed mariner, so did this timely assistance cheer the hearts of the war-worn and almost despairing soldiers of Freedom. The enthusiastic Frenchman, though but a beardless youth, was immediately taken into the affections and the confidence of Washington. Soon, too, did he flash his maiden sword upon his hereditary foes and proved, upon the field of Brandywine, that his blood flowed as freely as his treasure in the cause he had espoused. That blood was the blood of the young Lafayette. But nineteen summers had passed over his brow, when he was thus found fighting side by side with the veteran warriors of Bunker Hill.

How came he here? Born to a high name and a rich inheritance; educated at a dissipated and voluptuous court; married to a young and beautiful woman;—how came he to break through the blandishments of love and the temptations of pleasure and thus be found fighting the battles of strangers, far away in the wilds of America? It was because, from his infancy, there had grown up in his bosom a passion more potent than all others: the love of liberty. Upon his heart a spark from the very altar of Freedom had fallen and he watched and cherished it with more than vestal vigilance. This passionate love of liberty; this fire which was thenceforth to glow unquenched and undimmed, impelled him to break asunder the ties both of pleasure and affection. He had heard that a gallant people had raised the standard of revolt against oppression and he hastened to join them. It was to him the Crusade of Liberty; and, like a Knight of the Holy Cross, he had enlisted in the ranks of those who had sworn to rescue her altars from the profane touch of the tyrant.

More congenial to him by far were the hardships, the dangers, and the freedom of the American wilds than the ease, the luxury, and the slavery of his native court. He exchanged the voice of love for the savage yell and the hostile shout; the gentle strains of the harp and lute for the trumpet and drum and the still more terrible music of clashing arms. Nor did he come alone or empty-handed. The people in whose cause he was about to peril his life and his fortune were too poor to afford him even the means of conveyance, and his own court threw every obstacle in the way of the accomplishment of his wishes. Did this dampen his ardor? Did this chill his generous aspiration? No; it added new vigor to each. " I will fit out a vessel myself," exclaimed the enthusiastic youth; and in spite of the sneers of the young and the cautions of the old the gallant boy redeemed his pledge. Soon a proud ship was seen flying fast and falcon-like across the wide Atlantic. She landed on our shores like a bird of promise; and by her present aid and hopes of future succor infused new vigor into our almost palsied arms.

Such was the commencement of a career destined to be more brilliant than any of which we read in tale or history, realizing the wildest wishes of youthful enthusiasm and showing how the romance of real life often exceeds the strangest fictions of the imagination. From the moment of joining our ranks the young hero became the pride and the boast of the army. He won the affections of the stern-browed and iron-souled warriors of New England and was received with open arms by the warm-hearted and chivalrous sons of the South. Though the down of manhood had scarcely begun to spring upon his cheek, yet were his counsels eagerly listened to by the hoary leaders and the scarred veterans of the war. On the field of battle he was impetuous and brave; in the council the wisdom of Nestor flowed from his lips.

But it is not my intention to go into a detailed account of the services rendered by Lafayette to the country of his adoption. Suffice it to say that, throughout the Revolutionary struggle, with unchanged fidelity and undeviating devotion, he continued to pour forth his blood and his treasure in the sacred cause he had espoused; and when at length, full of honors, without one single stain upon his bright escutcheon, he returned to his native land, the voices of millions of freemen were united in invoking the blessing of heaven upon his head. Thenceforth a halo of glory surrounded him, and he was hailed by all the world as the Apostle of Liberty! Full well did he deserve the title! For not more truly does the needle point to the pole than did all his feelings point to the great principles of civil freedom.

During the sanguinary scenes of the French Revolution, when the people had quaffed so deeply at the fountain of

liberty that they became drunk and frenzied with the
unusual draughts, Lafayette alone lost not his equanimity.
He alone dared to oppose the wild excesses of the Jaco-
bins; and though he was unable entirely to stem the mad-
dened torrent, which seemed let loose from hell itself, yet
many are the thanks due to his unwearied exertions to
restrain it within the banks of law and order. Throughout those troublesome times he was found at his post, by
the side of the Constitution and the laws; and when at
length the whole foundations of society were broken up
and the wild current of licentiousness and crime swept
him an exile into a foreign land, still did he hold fast his
integrity of soul. In the gloomy dungeons of Olmutz,
the flame of patriotism glowed as brightly and as warmly
in his breast as ever it did when fanned by the free breezes
of the mountains. The dungeons of Olmutz! What associations are connected with the name! They form a
part of the romance of history. For five long years was
the Friend of Liberty immured in the prison of the tyrant.
In vain did the civilized world demand his release. But
what nations could not effect, came near being accomplished by the devoted exertions of two chivalric young
men; and one of them was a South Carolinian whose
father had extended the hospitality of his house to Lafayette, when on his first visit to America he landed in
the city of Charleston. Strange, that, after the lapse of
so many years, the little child who had then climbed upon
his knee should now be periling his life for his rescue!
There is nothing in history to compare with this romantic
episode of real life, unless, perhaps, the story of the min-
strel friend of the lion-hearted Richard, wandering
through those very dominions, tuning his harp beneath
every fortress, till at length his strains were answered and
the prison of the royal Crusader discovered. But the
doors of the Austrian dungeon were at length thrown
open and Lafayette returned to France. Great changes,
however, had taken place in his absence. The flood of
the Revolution had subsided. The tempest of popular
commotion had blown over, leaving many and fearful evidences of its fury; and the star of the Child of Destiny had
now become lord of the ascendant. Small was the sympathy between the selfish and ambitious Napoleon and

Lafayette, the patriot and philanthropist. They could no more mingle than the pure lights of heaven and the unholy fires of hell. Lafayette refused with scorn the dignities proffered by the First Consul. Filled with virtuous indignation at his country's fate, he retired from the capital; and, devoting himself awhile to the pursuits of private life, awaited the return of better times.

Here we cannot but pause to contemplate these two wonderful men, belonging to the same age and to the same nation: Napoleon and Lafayette. Their names excite no kindred emotions; their fates no kindred sympathies. Napoleon—the Child of Destiny—the thunderbolt of war —the victor in a hundred battles—the dispenser of thrones and dominions; he who scaled the Alps and reclined beneath the pyramids, whose word was fate and whose wish was law. Lafayette—the volunteer of Freedom—the advocate of human rights—the defender of civil liberty—the patriot and the philanthropist—the beloved of the good and the free. Napoleon—the vanquished warrior, ignobly flying from the field of Waterloo, the wild beast, ravaging all Europe in his wrath, hunted down by the banded and affrighted nations and caged far away upon an ocean-girded rock. Lafayette, a watchword by which men excite each other to deeds of worth and noble daring; whose home has become the Mecca of freedom, toward which the pilgrims of Liberty turn their eyes from every quarter of the globe. Napoleon was the red and fiery comet, shooting wildly through the realms of space and scattering pestilence and terror among the nations. Lafayette was the pure and brilliant planet, beneath whose grateful beams the mariner directs his bark and the shepherd tends his flocks—Napoleon died and a few old warriors—the scattered relics of Marengo and of Austerlitz—bewailed their chief. Lafayette is dead and the tears of a civilized world attest how deep is the mourning for his loss. Such is, and always will be, the difference of feeling toward a benefactor and a conqueror of the human race.

In 1824, on Sunday, a single ship furled her snowy sails in the harbor of New York. Scarcely had her prow touched the shore, when a murmur was heard among the multitudes which gradually deepened into a mighty shout of joy.   Again and again were the heavens rent with the inspiring sound.   Nor did it cease; for the loud strain was carried from city to city and from State to State, till not a tongue was silent throughout this wide Republic from the lisping infant to the tremulous old man.   All were united in one wild shout of gratulation.   The voices of more than ten million freemen gushed up towards the sky and broke the stillness of its silent depths.   But one note and one tone went to form this acclamation.   Up in those pure regions clearly and sweetly did it sound: "Honor to Lafayette!"   "Welcome to the Nation's Guest!"   It was Lafayette, the war-worn veteran, whose arrival on our shores had caused this widespread, this universal joy.   He came among us to behold the independence and the freedom which his young arm had so well assisted in achieving; and never before did eye behold or heart of man conceive, such homage paid to virtue. Every day's march was an ovation.   The United States became for months one great festive hall.   People forgot the usual occupations of life and crowded to behold the benefactor of mankind.   The iron-hearted, gray-haired veterans of the Revolution thronged around him to touch his hand, to behold his face, and to call down Heaven's benisons upon their old companion-in-arms.   Lisping infancy and garrulous old age, beauty, talents, wealth, and power, all, for a while forsook their usual pursuits and united to pay a tribute of gratitude and welcome to the nation's guest.   The name of Lafayette was upon every lip, and wherever his name was, there, too, was an invocation for blessings upon his head.   What were the triumphs of the classic ages, compared with this unbought love and homage of a mighty people?   Take them in Rome's best days, when the invincible generals of the Eternal City returned from their foreign conquests, with captive kings bound to their chariot wheels and the spoils of nations in their train; followed by their stern and bearded warriors and surrounded by the endless multitudes of the seven-hilled city, shouting a fierce welcome home; what was such a triumph compared with Lafayette's?   Not a single city, but a whole nation riding as one man and greeting him with an affectionate embrace! One single day of such spontaneous homage were worth whole years of courtly adulation; one hour might well reward a man for a whole life of danger and of toil. Then, too, the joy with which he must have viewed the prosperity of the people for whom he had so heroically struggled! To behold the nation which he had left a little child, now grown up in the full proportions of lusty manhood! To see the tender sapling, which he had left with hardly shade enough to cover its own roots, now waxing into the sturdy and unwedgeable oak, beneath whose grateful umbrage the oppressed of all nations find shelter and protection! That oak still grows on in its majestic strength, and wider and wider still extends its mighty branches. But the hand that watered and nourished it while yet a tender plant is now cold; the heart that watched with strong affection its early growth has ceased to beat.

Virtue forms no shield to ward off the arrows of death. Could it have availed even when joined with the prayers of a whole civilized world, then, indeed, this mournful occasion would never have occurred and the life of Lafayette would have been as immortal as his fame. Yet, though he has passed from among us; though that countenance will no more be seen that used to lighten up the van of Freedom's battles as he led her eaglets to their feast; still has he left behind his better part: the legacy of his bright example, the memory of his deeds. The lisping infant will learn to speak his venerated name. The youth of every country will be taught to look upon his career and to follow in his footsteps. When hereafter a gallant people are fighting for freedom against the oppressor and their cause begins to wane before the mercenary bands of tyranny, then will the name of Lafayette become a watchword that will strike with terror on the tyrant's ear and nerve with redoubled vigor the freeman's arm. At that name many a heart before unmoved will wake in the glorious cause; and many a sword, rusting ingloriously in its scabbard, will leap forth to battle. But even amid the mourning with which our souls are shrouded, is there not some room for gratulation? Our departed friend and benefactor has gone down to the grave peacefully and quietly at a good old age. He had performed his appointed work. His virtues were ripe.

He had done nothing to sully his fair fame. No blot or soil of envy or calumny can now affect him. His character will stand upon the pages of history, pure and unsullied as the lilied emblem on his country's banner. He has departed from among us; but he has become again the companion of Washington. He has but left the friends of his old age to associate with the friends of his youth. Peace be to his ashes! Calm and quiet may they rest upon some vine-clad hill of his own beloved land! And it shall be called the Mount Vernon of France. And let no cunning sculpture, no monumental marble, deface with its mock dignity the patriot's grave; but rather let the unpruned vine, the wild flower and the free song of the uncaged bird, all that speaks of freedom and of peace be gathered round it. Lafayette needs no mausoleum. His fame is mingled with the nation's history. His epitaph is engraved upon the hearts of men.

JEAN FRANÇOIS RAFFAELLI

THE UNIVERSALITY OF ART

[Address by Jean François Raffaelli, painter, sculptor, and critic, Chevalier of the Legion of Honor (born in Paris, April 20, 1850; ———), delivered at the fourth celebration of Founder's Day, at the Carnegie Institute, Pittsburg, Pa., November 2, 1899. President W. N. Frew occupied the chair.]

MR. PRESIDENT AND FRIENDS:—I would have laughed much if I had been told, some twenty years ago, that I would consent to cross the ocean and come to America in order to act as a member of a jury in Pittsburg, and I would have hastened to consult the map about the situation of this city. For in France our geographical knowledge does not extend beyond Switzerland and Belgium, East and North, and Italy and Spain on the South. And, besides, twenty years ago, if I am to believe the most authoritative of your fellow citizens, Pittsburg did not exist for us; we, the artists, scarcely existed for Pittsburg. This fact was to be regretted both by the people of Pittsburg and by the artists. To speak the truth, if I have agreed to come among you, it was because your city really represents not only that genius of construction and invention which is peculiar to this nation, but because, thanks to Mr. Andrew Carnegie, it represents by the establishment of this Carnegie Institute an idea, a truly great idea.

If France has deserved some consideration in the history of nations, it is because she has, for a long time,—has ever struggled more for ideas than for material interests. Indeed, when Lafayette came to place himself on your side a hundred years ago, it was because you then represented in the human society, an idea, beautiful above all ideas, the idea of the liberty of the people. And if artists of some renown have come, and will come,—and submit to be more or less sick on a rough sea for fifteen long days— it is because Pittsburg, outside of her great industrial interests, which excell those of the largest industrial cities of the two worlds, represents to-day in the world of arts an idea. This idea is not only the idea of national but of international, universal art.

And allow me to claim here the priority of this idea for a small group of artists to whom I had the honor to belong in my youth. I refer to that group who were called Impressionists. Twenty years ago, in Paris, the Academy des Beaux Arts was all-powerful, just as in London is the Royal Academy. Now, at that time a dozen of artists united together, to use a Biblical expression. These artists, most of them poor, had a mutual admiration for each other, which is rather rare among artists. [Laughter.] They aimed to be the painters of their time, of their epoch, at a moment when Greek or Roman subjects alone were admired and rewarded. They grouped themselves, exhibited their works together, and the public, who did not understand them at that time, with laughter and mockery, called them " The Impressionists." None of us at first accepted this name, because we did not know, no more than we do to-day, what it meant. But it remained attached to us, and we had to keep it and to drag it along, just as dogs drag a saucepan which has been fastened to their tails. Thus we became what people called the Impressionists.

Now, do you know of whom this group was composed, each of whom was of a temperament totally different from that of his neighbor, just as the artists who were called the artists of the School of 1830—Corot, Eugene Delacroix, and Millet—differed? This little group was made up of Degas, whose mother was an Italian; of Claude Monet, a Frenchman; of Mary Cassatt, an American, whose family's cradle was in Pittsburg; of Sissley, whose mother was English; of Pissarro, from Holland; of Reneir, a Frenchman; and of your servant, whose grandfather was a Florentine. These were the members of the little group that has since agitated the world of arts. We represented—yes, we represented, without thinking of it, the art of all peoples, of all countries, the art of humanity. And this idea has triumphed everywhere. It has just triumphed here in Pittsburg; for years have followed years and here is disclosed what has meanwhile happened in the world of art.

In the first place, and under this influence of the Impressionists, a society was formed in Paris nearly ten years ago, called the National Society of Beaux Arts. This is eminently an International society, for the most famous of the artists who compose it are foreigners. To begin with the American artists: the admirable St. Gaudens, Dannat, Alexander, the excellent artist of Pittsburg; Humphrey-Johnston, MacMonnies, Walter Gay, Melchers, the great artist, Sargent, and many others. Yes, our beautiful National Society of Beaux Arts ought to be called by its true name—the International Society of Fine Arts, for the greatest artists of all countries show their work there.

Then, again, other societies were formed, and everywhere with this same idea of the internationality of art, pursuing thus what the Impressionists had begun. These societies are: the Society of Secession, in Munich; the Austrian Secession, in Vienna; the International Society of Fine Arts, in Venice; and finally the Carnegie Institute, of Pittsburg, where the art of all countries finds a generous refuge. And I remark here that this International Exhibition of Pittsburg is the only International Art Society existing in the United States. This is the idea which I have come to salute here: the idea of the internationality of art. [Applause.]

If we look back on the history of the past centuries, we shall see that every nation had, in its turn, a national art. But the nations were separated by long distances. To-day, on the contrary, by the numerous and rapid means of communication these distances are either altogether or greatly reduced. Yet, six days on board a steamer is still a long time, and, so far as I am concerned, I shall not come to see you again until the voyage is reduced to four days. Take my word for it! And since there are no more distances, or scarcely any, this art which the ancient nations transmitted to each other like a sacred relic, has no longer any reason for being national; it ought to be international and to belong, as the sacred mark of civilization, to all civilized nations. When I was asked in this country: "Is there an American art?" I answered: "There is no American art; no more than there is at present a French art. There is *the* art, that is all."

It was for the Americans, a national, cosmopolitan people, as no other, to defend this idea of the universal art. By this idea we artists become the champions of the alliance of all the civilized nations. A noble mission indeed. You must aid us to fulfil it worthily.

Therefore, let us salute here the man who has by his liberality made the splendid idea of a universal art possible in America—Mr. Andrew Carnegie. Let us salute also his co-workers, the officers and members of the Board of Trustees and the Director of Fine Arts. And I shall ask you to salute the excellent artist who for twenty years has devoted every moment to the art of which he is one of the noblest champions in this country—William M. Chase, who has done so much for art and eminent teaching in America. And let us congratulate one another in this idea. There is only one art in the world, as there is only one God. There is only one art, as there is only one ideal among civilized people. There is only one art, as there is only one brain in a head, as there is only one heart in a body, as there is only one soul in every one of us. [Applause.]

WILLIAM NORTH RICE

SCIENTIFIC THOUGHT IN THE NINETEENTH CENTURY

[Address by William North Rice, professor of geology in Wesleyan University (born in Marblehead, Mass., November 21, 1845; ———), delivered at the Centennial Celebration of the Connecticut Academy of Arts and Sciences, October 11, 1899.]

GENTLEMEN:—It is an interesting fact that the life of our Association is almost coextensive with that Nineteenth century of Christian civilization which is now drawing to a close. In intellectual, as in physical phenomena, we are tempted to overestimate the magnitude of near objects and to underestimate that of distant ones; but science and art tend to advance with accelerated velocity, and we are undoubtedly right in ranking the achievements of our age in science and its applications as far greater than those of any previous century.

When our predecessors assembled a hundred years ago to organize this Academy, they could avail themselves of no other means of transportation than those which were in use before the time of Homer. If they were required to traverse distances overland too great for convenient walking, they were carried or drawn by horses. If they had occasion to cross bodies of water, they used oars or sails. We have been brought to our destination to-day by the forces of steam and electricity. The harnessing of these mighty forces for man's use has transformed not only the modes of transportation, but also the processes of production of all kinds of commodities. It has wrought a revolution in the whole industrial system. The day of the small workshop is gone. The day of the great factory is come. Every phase of human life is affected by those arts which have arisen from the applications of science. Comforts and luxuries which a hundred years ago were beyond the reach of the most wealthy, are now available for the use of even the poor. Aniline dyes give to fabrics used for clothing or decoration colors beside which those of the rainbow are pale neutral tints. Sanitary science arrests the massacre of the innocents, and increases the average duration of human life. Anæsthetics and anti-septics take away from surgery its pain and its peril.

But, though our Association is an Academy of Arts and Sciences, it has, at least in its later life, devoted itself chiefly to the cultivation of pure science, leaving to other organi-zations the development of the applications of science. Fitly, then, our thoughts to-day dwell, not upon the vast progress of the useful arts, but upon the progress of pure science. Not the economic and the industrial, but the in-tellectual history of our century claims our attention.

I do not propose, in the few moments allotted to me this afternoon, to give an inventory of the important sci-entific discoveries of the Nineteenth century. The time would not suffice therefor, even were my knowledge of the various sciences sufficiently encyclopædic to justify me in the attempt. I wish rather to call your attention to a single broad, general aspect of the intellectual history of our age. I wish to remind you in how large a degree those general ideas which make the distinction btween the unscientific and the scientific view of nature have been the work of the Nineteenth century.

The first of these ideas is the extension of the universe in space. The unscientific mind looks upon the celestial bodies as mere appendages to the earth, relatively of small size, and at no very great distance. The scientific mind beholds the stellar universe stretching away, beyond meas-ured distances whose numerical expression transcends all power of imagination, into immeasurable immensities.

The second of these ideas is the extension of the uni-verse in time. To the unscientific mind, the universe has no history. Since it began to exist, it has existed substan-tially in its present condition. Among Christian peoples, until the belief was corrected by science, the Hebrew tra-dition of a creative week six thousand years ago was generally accepted as historic fact. If, on the other hand, unscientific minds not possessed of any supposed revelation in regard to the date of the world's origin, thought of the universe as eternal, that eternity was still conceived as an eternity of unhistoric monotony. The scientific mind sees in the present condition of the universe the monuments of a long history of progress.

The third of these ideas is the unity of the universe. To the unscientific mind the universe is a chaos. To the scientific mind it becomes a cosmos. To the unscientific mind, the processes of nature seem to be the result of forces mutually independent and often discordant. Polytheism in religion is the natural counterpart of the unscientific view of the universe. To the scientific mind, the boundless complexity of the universe is dominated by a supreme unity. One system of law, intelligible, formulable, pervades the universe, through all its measureless extension in space and time. The student of science may be theist or pantheist, atheist or agnostic; polytheist he can never be.

What then, let us ask ourselves, has been the contribution of our century to the development of these three ideas, which characterize the scientific view of nature:— the spatial extension of the universe, the historic extension of the universe, and the unity of the universe.

The development of the idea of the extension of the universe in space belongs mainly to earlier times than ours. The Greek geometers acquired approximately correct notions of the size of the earth and the distance of the moon. The Copernican astronomy in the Sixteenth century shifted the center of the solar system from the earth to the sun, and placed in truer perspective our view of the celestial spheres. But, though astronomy, the oldest of the sisterhood of the sciences, attained a somewhat mature development centuries ago, it has in our own century thrown new light upon the subject of the vastness of the universe. The discovery of Neptune has greatly increased the area of the solar system; the measurement of the parallax of a few of the brightest, and presumably the nearest, of the stars has rendered far more definite our knowledge of the magnitude of the stellar universe; and telescopes of higher magnifying power than had been used before have resolved many clusters of small and distant stars.

If the development of the idea of the spatial extension of the universe belongs mainly to an earlier period, the idea of its historic extension belongs mainly to our century. It is true, indeed, that Pythagoras and others of the ancient philosophers did not fail to recognize indications of change in the surface of the earth. And, in the beginning of the Renaissance, we find Leonardo da Vinci and others insisting that the fossils discovered in excavations in the stratified rocks were proof of the former existence of a sea teeming with marine life, where cultivated lands and populous cities had taken its place. Hutton's " Theory of the Earth," which in an important sense marks the beginning of modern geological theorizing, appeared in the Edinburgh " Philosophical Transactions " in 1788, but was not published as a separate work till seven years later. Not till 1815 was published William Smith's Geological Map of England, the first example of systematic stratigraphic work extended over any large area.

To the beginning of our century belong also the classical and epoch-making researches of Cuvier upon the fossil fauna of the Paris basin. By far the larger part, therefore, of the development of geologic science, with its far-reaching revelations of continental emergence and submergence, mountain growth and decay, and evolution and extinction of successive faunas and floras, belongs to the Nineteenth century. Far on into our century extended the conflict with theological conservatism, in which the elder Silliman, James L. Kingsley, and others of the early members of our Academy bore an honorable part, and which ended in the recognition, by the general public, as well as by the select circle of scientific students, of an antiquity of the earth far transcending the limits allowed by venerable tradition.

To our century also belongs chiefly the development in astronomy of the idea of the history of the solar system. It is, indeed, true that, in the conception of the nebular hypothesis, Laplace, whose " Théorie de la Monde " was published in 1796, was preceded by Kant and Swedenborg. But the credit of a discovery belongs not so much to the first conception of an idea as to its development into a thoroughly scientific theory.   Our century, moreover, has added to those evidences of the nebular theory which Laplace derived from the analogies of movement in the solar system, the evidence furnished by the spectroscope, which finds in the nebulæ matter in some such condition as that from which the solar system is supposed to have been evolved.

But by far the most important contribution of this century to the intellectual life of man is the share which it has had in developing the idea of the unity of nature.   The greatest step prior to this century in the development of that idea (and probably the most important single discovery in the whole history of science) was Newton's discovery of universal gravitation two hundred years ago; but the investigations of our century have revealed, with a fulness not dreamed of before, a threefold unity in nature—a unity of substance, a unity of force, and a unity of process.

Spectrum analysis has taught us somewhat of the chemical constitution, not only of the sun, but also of the distant stars and nebulæ; and has thus revealed a substantial identity of chemical constitution throughout the universe.   Profoundly interesting, from this point of view, is the recent discovery, in uraninite and some other minerals, of the element helium, previously known only by its line in the spectrum of the sun.   Profoundly interesting will be, if confirmed by further researches, the still more recent alleged discovery of terrestrial coronium.

The doctrine of the conservation of energy formulates a unity of force in all physical processes.   In this case, as in others, prophetic glimpses of the truth came to gifted minds in earlier times.   Lord Bacon declared heat to be a species of motion.   And Huyghens, in the Seventeenth century, distinctly formulated the theory of light as an undulation, though the mighty influence of Newton maintained the emission theory in general acceptance for a century and a half.

When Lavoisier exploded the phlogiston theory, and laid the foundation of modern chemical philosophy, it was seen that, in every chemical change, there is a complete equation of matter.   But there was in the phlogiston theory a distorted representation of a truth which the chemical theory of Lavoisier and his successors ignored. They could give no account of the light and heat and electricity so generally associated with chemical transformations. These "imponderable agents," as they were called, believed to be material, yet so tenuous as to be destitute of weight, haunted like ghosts the workshop of the artisan and the laboratory of the scientist, wonderfully important in their effects, but utterly unintelligible in their nature. It was almost exactly at the beginning of our century that the researches of Rumford discovered the first words of the spell by which these ghosts were destined to be laid. When Rumford declared, in his interpretation of his experiments, "Anything which any insulated body or system of bodies can continue to furnish without limitation, cannot possibly be a material substance," the fate of the supposed imponderable fluid caloric was sealed; but it was not till near the middle of our century that Joule completed the work of Rumford by the determination of the mechanical equivalent of heat. About the same time, Foucault's measurement of the velocity of light in air and in water afforded conclusive proof of the undulatory theory of light. In these great discoveries was laid the strong foundation for the magnificent generalization of the conservation of energy—a generalization which the sagacious intuition of Mayer and Carpenter and Le Conte at once extended beyond the realm of inorganic nature to the more subtile processes of vegetable and animal life. In this connection, I may be permitted to refer to the work of some of my colleagues, with the Atwater-Rosa calorimeter, which has given more complete experimental proof than had previously been given of the conservation of energy in the human body.

But by far the greatest of the intellectual achievements of our age has been the development of the idea of the unity of process pervading the whole history of nature. The word which sums up in itself the expression of the most characteristic and fruitful intellectual life of our age is the word evolution. The latter half of our century has been so dominated by that idea in all its thinking, that it may well be named the Age of Evolution. We may give as the date of the beginning of the new epoch the year 1858; and the Wittenberg theses of the intellectual reformation of our time were the twin papers of Darwin and Wallace, wherein was promulgated the theory of natural selection.

And yet, of course, the idea of evolution was not new, when these papers were presented to the Linnæan Society. Consciously or unconsciously, the aim of science at all times must have been to bring events that seemed isolated into a continuous development. To exclude the idea of evolution from any class of phenomena, is to exclude that class of phenomena from the realm of science.

In the former half of our century, evolutionary conceptions of the history of inorganic nature had become pretty well established. The nebular hypothesis was obviously a theory of planetary evolution. The Lyellian geology, which took the place of the catastrophism of the last century, was the conception of evolution applied to the physical history of the earth. Nor had there been wanting anticipations of evolution within the realm of biology. The author of that sublime Hebrew psalm of creation preserved to us as the first chapter of Genesis, was in his way a good deal of an evolutionist. " Let the earth bring forth,"—" let the waters bring forth,"—are words that point to a process of growth rather than to a process of manufacture in the origination of living beings. In crude and vague forms, the idea of evolution was held by some of the Greek philosophers. Just at the beginning of our century Lamarck developed the idea of evolution into something like a scientific theory.

Yet it is no less true that the epoch of evolution in human thought began with Darwin. Manifold suggestions there were of genetic relationships between different organisms, whether organic forms were studied by the systematist or the embryologist, the geographer or the paleontologist; but each and all found the path to any credible theory of organic evolution blocked by the stubborn fact that variations in species appeared everywhere to be limited in degree, and to oscillate about a central average type, instead of becoming cumulative from generation to generation. In the Darwinian principle of natural selection, for the first time, was suggested a force, whose existence in nature could not be doubted, and whose tendency, conservative in stable environment, progressive in changing environment, would account at once for the permanence of species through long ages, and for epochs of relatively rapid change. However Darwin's work may be discredited by the exaggerations of Weismannism, however it may be minified by Neo-Lamarckians, it is the theory of natural selection which has so nearly removed the barrier in the path of evolution, impassable before, as to lead, first the scientific world, and later the world of thought in general, to a substantially unanimous belief in the derivative origin of species. Certain it is that no discovery since Newton's discovery of universal gravitation has produced so profound an effect upon the intellectual life of mankind. The tombs of Newton and Darwin lie close together in England's Valhalla, and together their names must stand as the two great epoch-making names in the history of science.

Darwin's discovery relates primarily to the origin of species by descent with modification from preëxisting species. It throws no direct light upon the question of the origin of life. But analogy is a guide that we may reasonably follow in our thinking, provided only we bear in mind that she is a treacherous guide and sometimes leads astray. Conclusions that rest only on analogy must be held tentatively and not dogmatically. Yet it would be an unreasonable excess of caution that would refuse to recognize the direction in which analogy points. When we trace a continuous evolution from the nebula to the dawn of life, and again a continuous evolution from the dawn of life to the varied flora and fauna of to-day, crowned with glory by the appearance of man himself, we can hardly fail to accept the suggestion that the transition from the lifeless to the living was itself a process of evolution. Though the supposed instances of spontaneous generation all resolve themselves into errors of experimentation, though the power of chemical synthesis, in spite of the vast progress it has made, stops far short of the complexity of protoplasm, though we must confess ourselves unable to imagine any hypothesis for the origin of that complex apparatus which the microscope is revealing to us in the infinitesimal laboratory of the cell, are we not compelled to believe that the law of continuity has not been broken, and that a probable theory of the method of natural transition from the lifeless to the living may yet be within reach of human discovery?

Still further.   Are we content to believe that evolution began with the nebula?   Are we satisfied to assume our chemical atoms as an ultimate and inexplicable fact? Herschel and Maxwell, indeed, have reasoned, from the supposed absolute likeness of atoms of any particular element, that they bear "the stamp of a manufactured article," and must therefore be supposed to have been specially created at some definite epoch of beginning. But, when we are speaking of things of which we know so little as we know of atoms, there is logically a boundless difference between saying that we know no difference between the atoms of hydrogen, and saying that we know there is no difference.   Is it not legitimate for us to recognize here again the direction in which analogy points, and to ask whether those fundamental units of physical nature, the atoms themselves, may not be products of evolution? Thus analogy suggests to us the question, whether there is any beginning of the series of evolutionary changes which we see stretching backward into the remote past; whether the nebulæ from which systems have been evolved were not themselves evolved; whether existing forms of matter were not evolved from other forms that we know not; whether creative Power and creative Intelligence have not been eternally immanent in an eternal universe. I cannot help thinking that theology may fitly welcome such a suggestion, as relieving it from the incongruous notion of a benevolent Deity spending an eternity in solitude and idleness.   The contemplation of his own attributes might seem a fitting employment for a Hindoo Brahm.   It hardly fits the character of the Heavenly Father, of whom we are told that He " worketh hitherto."

In the last suggestion I have ventured outside the realm of science.   But most men are not so constituted that they can carry their scientific and their philosophical and religious beliefs in compartments separated by thought-proof bulkheads.   Scientific and philosophic and religious thought, in the individual and in the race, must act and react upon each other.   It was, therefore, inevitable that our century of scientific progress should disturb the religious beliefs of men.   When conceptions of the cosmos with which religious beliefs had been associated were rudely shattered, it was inevitable that those religious beliefs themselves should seem to be imperiled. And so, in the early years of the century, it was said, " If the world is more than six thousand years old, the Bible is a fraud, and the Christian religion a dream." And later, it was said, " If physical and vital forces are correlated with each other, there is no soul, no distinction of right and wrong, and no immortality." And again it was said, " If species have originated by evolution, and not by special creation, there is no God." So it had been said centuries before, " If the earth revolves around the sun, Christian faith must be abandoned as a superstition." But in the Nineteenth century, as in the Sixteenth, the scientific conclusions won their way to universal acceptance, and Christian faith survived. It showed a plasticity which enabled it to adapt itself to the changing environment. The magically inerrant Bible may be abandoned, and leave intact the faith of the church in a divine revelation. The correlation of forces acting in the human cerebrum with those of inorganic nature may be freely admitted; and yet we may hold that there are other forms of causation in the universe than physical energy, and that the inexpugnable belief of moral responsibility is more valid than the strongest induction. The " carpenter God " of the older natural theology may vanish from a universe, which we have come to regard as a growth and not a building; but there remains the immanent Intelligence—

> " Whose dwelling is the light of setting suns,
> And the round ocean, and the living air,
> And the blue sky, and in the mind of man ";—

the God in whom " we live and move and have our being."

The church has learned wisdom. The persecution of Galileo is not likely to be repeated, nor even the milder forms of persecution which assailed the geologists at the beginning, and the evolutionists in the middle, of our century. And science, too, has learned something. In all its wealth of discovery, it recognizes more clearly than ever before the fathomless abysses of the unknown and unknowable. It stands with unsandaled feet in the presence of mysteries that transcend human thought. Religion never so tolerant. Science never so reverent. Nearer than ever before seems the time when all souls that are loyal to truth and goodness shall find fellowship in freedom of faith and in service of love.

THEODORE ROOSEVELT

THE STRENUOUS LIFE

[Address by Theodore Roosevelt, twenty-fifth President of the United States, Author, Statesman, former Governor of New York (1898-1900) born in New York city, October 27, 1858; —— delivered at the Appomatox Day Celebration of the Hamilton Club, at Chicago, Ill., April 10th, 1899. President Hope Reed Cody of the club occupied the chair. Mr. Roosevelt, then Governor of New York, was the central figure and chief speaker at the celebration.]

GENTLEMEN :—In speaking to you, men of the greatest city of the West, men of the State which gave to the country Lincoln and Grant, men who preëminently and distinctly embody all that is most American in the American character, I wish to preach not the doctrine of ignoble ease but the doctrine of the strenuous life; the life of toil and effort; of labor and strife; to preach that highest form of success which comes not to the man who desires mere easy peace but to the man who does not shrink from danger, from hardship, or from bitter toil, and who out of these wins the splendid ultimate triumph.

A life of ignoble ease, a life of that peace which springs merely from lack either of desire or of power to strive after great things, is as little worthy of a nation as of an individual. I ask only that what every self-respecting American demands from himself, and from his sons, shall be demanded of the American nation as a whole. Who among you would teach your boys that ease, that peace is to be the first consideration in your eyes—to be the ultimate goal after which they strive? You men of Chicago have made this city great, you men of Illinois have done your share, and more than your share, in making America great, because you neither preach nor practice such a doctrine. You work yourselves, and you bring up your sons to work. If you are rich, and are worth your salt, you will teach your sons that though they may have leisure, it is not to be spent in idleness; for wisely used leisure merely means that those who possess it, being free from the necessity of working for their livelihood, are all the more bound to carry on some kind of non-remunerative work in science, in letters, in art, in exploration, in historical research—work of the type we most need in this country, the successful carrying out of which reflects most honor upon the nation.

We do not admire the man of timid peace. We admire the man who embodies victorious effort; the man who never wrongs his neighbor; who is prompt to help a friend; but who has those virile qualities necessary to win in the stern strife of actual life. It is hard to fail; but it is worse never to have tried to succeed. In this life we get nothing save by effort. Freedom from effort in the present, merely means that there has been stored up effort in the past. A man can be freed from the necessity of work only by the fact that he or his fathers before him have worked to good purpose. If the freedom thus purchased is used aright, and the man still does actual work, though of a different kind, whether as a writer or a General, whether in the field of politics or in the field of exploration and adventure, he shows he deserves his good fortune. But if he treats this period of freedom from the need of actual labor as a period not of preparation but of mere enjoyment, he shows that he is simply a cumberer on the earth's surface; and he surely unfits himself to hold his own with his fellows if the need to do so should again arise. A mere life of ease is not in the end a satisfactory life, and above all it is a life which ultimately unfits those who follow it for serious work in the world.

As it is with the individual so it is with the nation. It is a base untruth to say that happy is the nation that has no history. Thrice happy is the nation that has a glorious history. Far better it is to dare mighty things, to win glorious triumphs, even though checkered by failure, than to take rank with those poor spirits who neither enjoy much nor suffer much because they live in the gray twilight that knows neither victory nor defeat. If in 1861 the men who loved the Union had believed that peace was the end of all things and war and strife a worst of all things, and had acted up to their belief, we would have saved hundreds of thousands of lives, we would have saved hundreds of millions of dollars. Moreover, besides saving all the blood and treasure we then lavished, we would have prevented the heart-break of many women, the dissolution of many homes; and we would have spared the country those months of gloom and shame when it seemed as if our armies marched only to defeat. We could have avoided all this suffering simply by shrinking from strife. And if we had thus avoided it we would have shown that we were weaklings and that we were unfit to stand among the great nations of the earth. Thank God for the iron in the blood of our fathers, the men who upheld the wisdom of Lincoln and bore sword or rifle in the armies of Grant! Let us, the children of the men who proved themselves equal to the mighty days—let us, the children of the men who carried the great Civil War to a triumphant conclusion, praise the God of our fathers that the ignoble counsels of peace were rejected, that the suffering and loss, the blackness of sorrow and despair, were unflinchingly faced and the years of strife endured; for in the end the slave was freed, the Union restored, and the mighty American Republic placed once more as a helmeted queen among nations.

We of this generation do not have to face a task such as that our fathers faced, but we have our tasks, and woe to us if we fail to perform them! We cannot, if we would, play the part of China, and be content to rot by inches in ignoble ease within our borders, taking no interest in what goes on beyond them; sunk in a scrambling commercialism; heedless of the higher life, the life of aspiration, of toil and risk; busying ourselves only with the wants of our bodies for the day; until suddenly we should find, beyond a shadow of question, what China has already found, that in this world the nation that has trained itself to a career of unwarlike and isolated ease is bound in the end to go down before other nations which have not lost the manly and adventurous qualities. If we are to be a really great people, we must strive in good faith to play a great part in the world. We cannot avoid meeting great issues. All that we can determine for ourselves is whether we shall meet them well or ill. Last year we could not help being brought face to face with the problem of war with Spain. All we could decide was whether we should shrink like cowards from the contest or enter into it as beseemed a brave and high-spirited people; and, once in, whether failure or success should crown our banners. So it is now. We cannot avoid the responsibilities that confront us in Hawaii, Cuba, Porto Rico, and the Philippines. All we can decide is whether we shall meet them in a way that will redound to the national credit, or whether we shall make of our dealings with these new problems a dark and shameful page in our history. To refuse to deal with them at all merely amounts to dealing with them badly. We have a given problem to solve. If we undertake the solution there is, of course, always danger that we may not solve it aright, but to refuse to undertake the solution simply renders it certain that we cannot possibly solve it aright.

The timid man, the lazy man, the man who distrusts his country, the overcivilized man, who has lost the great fighting, masterful virtues, the ignorant man and the man of dull mind, whose soul is incapable of feeling the mighty lift that thrills " stern men with empires in their brains "— all these, of course, shrink from seeing the nation undertake its new duties; shrink from seeing us build a navy and army adequate to our needs; shrink from seeing us do our share of the world's work by bringing order out of chaos in the great, fair tropic islands from which the valor of our soldiers and sailors has driven the Spanish flag. These are the men who fear the strenuous life, who fear the only national life which is really worth leading. They believe in that cloistered life which saps the hardy virtues in a nation, as it saps them in the individual; or else they are wedded to that base spirit of gain and greed which recognizes in commercialism the be-all and end-all of national life, instead of realizing that, though an indispensable element, it is after all but one of the many elements that go to make up true national greatness. No country can long endure if its foundations are not laid deep in the material prosperity which comes from thrift, front business energy and enterprise, from hard unsparing effort in the fields of industrial activity; but neither was any nation ever yet truly great if it relied upon material prosperity alone. All honor must be paid to the architects of our material prosperity; to the great captains of industry who have built our factories and our railroads; to the strong men who toil for wealth with brain or hand; for great is the debt of the nation to these and their kind. But our debt is yet greater to the men whose highest type is to be found in a statesman like Lincoln, a soldier like Grant. They showed by their lives that they recognized the law of work, the law of strife; they toiled to win a competence for themselves and those dependent upon them; but they recognized that there were yet other and even loftier duties—duties to the nation and duties to the race.

We cannot sit huddled within our own borders and avow ourselves merely an assemblage of well-to-do hucksters who care nothing for what happens beyond. Such a policy would defeat even its own end; for as the nations grow to have ever wider and wider interests and are brought into closer and closer contact, if we are to hold our own in the struggle for naval and commercial supremacy, we must build up our power without our own borders. We must build the Isthmian canal, and we must grasp the points of vantage which will enable us to have our say in deciding the destiny of the oceans of the East and the West.

So much for the commercial side. From the standpoint of international honor, the argument is even stronger. The guns that thundered off Manila and Santiago left us echoes of glory, but they also left us a legacy of duty. If we drove out a mediæval tyranny only to make room for savage anarchy, we had better not have begun the task at all. It is worse than idle to say that we have no duty to perform and can leave to their fates the islands we have conquered. Such a course would be the course of infamy. It would be followed at once by utter chaos in the wretched islands themselves. Some stronger, manlier power would have to step in and do the work; and we would have shown ourselves weaklings, unable to carry to successful completion the labors that great and high-spirited nations are eager to undertake. The work must be done. We cannot escape our responsibility, and if we are worth our salt, we shall be glad of the chance to do the work—glad of the chance to show ourselves equal to one of the great tasks set modern civilization. But let us not deceive ourselves as to the importance of the task. Let us not be misled by vainglory into underestimating the strain it will put on our powers. Above all, let us, as we value our own self-respect, face the responsibilities with proper seriousness, courage, and high resolve. We must demand the highest order of integrity and ability in our public men who are to grapple with these new problems. We must hold to a rigid accountability those public servants who show unfaithfulness to the interests of the nation or inability to rise to the high level of the new demands upon our strength and our resources.

Of course, we must remember not to judge any public servant by any one act, and especially should we beware of attacking the men who are merely the occasions and not the causes of disaster. Let me illustrate what I mean by the army and the navy. If twenty years ago we had gone to war, we should have found the navy as absolutely unprepared as the army. At that time our ships could not have encountered with success the fleets of Spain any more than nowadays we can put untrained soldiers, no matter how brave, who are armed with archaic black-powder weapons against well-drilled regulars armed with the highest type of modern repeating rifle. But in the early '80s the attention of the nation became directed to our naval needs. Congress most wisely made a series of appropriations to build up a new navy, and under a succession of able and patriotic Secretaries, of both political parties, the navy was gradually built up, until its material became equal to its splendid personnel, with the result that last summer it leaped to its proper place as one of the most brilliant and formidable fighting navies in the entire world. We rightly pay all honor to the men controlling the navy at the time it won these great deeds, honor to Secretary Long and Admiral Dewey, to the Captains who handled the ships in action, to the daring Lieutenants who braved death in the smaller craft, and to the heads of bureaus at Washington who saw that the ships

were so commanded, so armed, so equipped, so well en-
gined, as to insure the best results. But let us also keep
ever in mind that all of this would not have availed if it
had not been for the wisdom of the men who during the
preceding fifteen years had built up the navy. Keep in
mind the Secretaries of the Navy during those years; keep
in mind the Senators and Congressmen who by their votes
gave the money necessary to build and to armor the ships,
to construct the great guns, to train the crews; remember
also those who actually did build the ships, the armor, and
the guns; and remember the Admirals and Captains who
handled battle-ship, cruiser, and torpedo boat on the high
seas, alone and in squadrons, developing the seamanship,
the gunnery, and the power of acting together, which their
successors utilized so gloriously at Manila and off Santiago.

And, gentlemen, remember the converse, too. Remember that justice has two sides. Be just to those who
built up the navy, and for the sake of the future of the
country keep in mind those who opposed its building up.
Read the "Congressional Record." Find out the Senators and Congressmen who opposed the grants for building the new ships, who opposed the purchase of armor,
without which the ships were worthless; who opposed
any adequate maintenance for the Navy Department, and
strove to cut down the number of men necessary to man
our fleets. The men who did these things were one and
all working to bring disaster on the country. They have
no share in the glory of Manila, in the honor of Santiago.
They have no cause to feel proud of the valor of our sea
Captains, of the renown of our flag. Their motives may
or may not have been good, but their acts were heavily
fraught with evil. They did ill for the national honor;
and we won in spite of their sinister opposition.

Now, apply all this to our public men of to-day. Our
army has never been built up as it should be built up. I
shall not discuss with an audience like this the puerile suggestion that a nation of seventy millions of freemen is in
danger of losing its liberties from the existence of an
army of 100,000 men, three-fourths of whom will be employed in certain foreign islands, in certain coast for-
tresses, and on Indian reservations. No man of good

sense and stout heart can take such a proposition seriously. If we are such weaklings as the proposition implies, then we are unworthy of freedom in any event. To no body of men in the United States is the country so much indebted as to the splendid officers and enlisted men of the regular army and navy; there is no body from which the country has less to fear; and none of which it should be prouder, none which it should be more anxious to upbuild.

Our army needs complete reorganization—not merely enlarging—and the reorganization can only come as the result of legislation. A proper general staff should be established, and the positions of ordnance, commissary, and quartermaster officers should be filled by detail from the line. Above all, the army must be given a chance to exercise in large bodies. Never again should we see, as we saw in the Spanish War, Major Generals in command of divisions who had never before commanded three companies together in the field. Yet, incredible to relate, the recent Congress has showed a queer inability to learn some of the lessons of the war. There were large bodies of men in both branches who opposed the declaration of war, who opposed the ratification of peace, who opposed the upbuilding of the army, and who even opposed the purchase of armor at a reasonable price for the battle-ships and cruisers, thereby putting an absolute stop to the building of any new fighting ships for the navy. If during the years to come any disaster should befall our arms, afloat or ashore, and thereby any shame come to the United States, remember that the blame will lie upon the men whose names appear upon the roll-calls of Congress on the wrong side of these great questions. On them will lie the burden of any loss of our soldiers and sailors, of any dishonor to the flag; and upon you and the people of the country will lie the blame, if you do not repudiate, in no unmistakable way, what these men have done. The blame will not rest upon the untrained commander of untried troops; upon the civil officers of a department, the organization of which has been left utterly inadequate; or upon the Admiral with insufficient number of ships; but upon the public men who have so lamentably failed in forethought as to refuse to remedy these evils long in advance, and upon the nation that stands behind those public men.

So at the present hour no small share of the responsibility for the blood shed in the Philippines, the blood of our brothers and the blood of their wild and ignorant foes, lies at the thresholds of those who so long delayed the adoption of the treaty of peace, and of those who by their worse than foolish words deliberately invited a savage people to plunge into a war fraught with sure disaster for them—a war, too, in which our own brave men who follow the flag must pay with their blood for the silly, mock-humanitarianism of the prattlers who sit at home in peace.

The army and navy are the sword and the shield which this nation must carry if she is to do her duty among the nations of the earth—if she is not to stand merely as the China of the Western Hemisphere. Our proper conduct toward the tropic islands we have wrested from Spain is merely the form which our duty has taken at the moment. Of course, we are bound to handle the affairs of our own household well. We must see that there is civic honesty, civic cleanliness, civic good sense in our home administration of city, State, and Nation. We must strive for honesty in office, for honesty towards the creditors of the nation and of the individual; for the widest freedom of individual initiative where possible, and for the wisest control of individual initiative where it is hostile to the welfare of the many. But because we set our own household in order, we are not thereby excused from playing our part in the great affairs of the world. A man's first duty is to his own home, but he is not thereby excused from doing his duty to the State; for if he fails in this second duty it is under the penalty of ceasing to be a freeman. In the same way, while a nation's first duty is within its own borders, it is not thereby absolved from facing its duties in the world as a whole; and if it refuses to do so it merely forfeits its right to struggle for a place among the peoples that shape the destiny of mankind.

In the West Indies and the Philippines alike we are confronted by most difficult problems. It is cowardly to shrink from solving them in the proper way; for solved they must be, if not by us, then by some stronger and more manful race; if we are too weak, too selfish, or too foolish to solve them, some bolder and abler people must undertake the solution. Personally I am far too firm a believer in the greatness of my country and the power of my countrymen to admit for one moment that we shall ever be driven to the ignoble alternative.

The problems are different for the different islands. Porto Rico is not large enough to stand alone. We must govern it wisely and well, primarily in the interest of its own people. Cuba is, in my judgment, entitled ultimately to settle for itself whether it shall be an independent State or an integral portion of the mightiest of republics. But until order and stable liberty are secured, we must remain in the island to insure them; and infinite tact, judgment, moderation, and courage must be shown by our military and civil representatives in keeping the island pacified, in relentlessly stamping out brigandage, in protecting all alike, and yet in showing proper recognition to the men who have fought for Cuban liberty. The Philippines offer a yet graver problem. Their population includes half caste and native Christians, warlike Moslems, and wild pagans. Many of their people are utterly unfit for self-government and show no signs of becoming fit. Others may in time become fit, but at present can only take part in self-government under a wise supervision at once firm and beneficent. We have driven Spanish tyranny from the islands. If we now let it be replaced by savage anarchy, our work has been for harm and not for good. I have scant patience with those who fear to undertake the task of governing the Philippines, and who openly avow that they do fear to undertake it, or that they shrink from it because of the expense and trouble; but I have even scanter patience with those who make a pretense of humanitarianism to hide and cover their timidity, and who cant about "liberty" and the "consent of the governed," in order to excuse themselves for their unwillingness to play the part of men. Their doctrines if carried out would make it incumbent upon us to leave the Apaches of Arizona to work out their own salvation and to decline to interfere in a single Indian reservation. Their doctrines condemn your forefathers and mine for ever having settled in these United States.

England's rule in India and Egypt has been of great benefit to England, for it has trained up generations of men accustomed to look at the larger and loftier side of public life. It has been of even greater benefit to India and Egypt. And finally, and most of all, it has advanced the cause of civilization. So, if we do our duty aright in the Philippines, we will add to that national renown which is the highest and finest part of national life; will greatly benefit the people of the Philippine Islands; and, above all, we will play our part well in the great work of uplifting mankind. But to do this work, keep ever in mind that we must show in a high degree the qualities of courage, of honesty, and of good judgment. Resistance must be stamped out. The first and all-important work to be done is to establish the supremacy of our flag. We must put down armed resistance before we can accomplish anything else, and there should be no parleying, no faltering in dealing with our foe. As for those in our own country who encourage the foe, we can afford contemptuously to disregard them; but it must be remembered that their utterances are saved from being treasonable merely from the fact that they are despicable.

When once we have put down armed resistance, when once our rule is acknowledged, then an even more difficult task will begin, for then we must see to it that the islands are administered with absolute honesty and with good judgment. If we let the public service of the islands be turned into the prey of the spoils politician we shall have begun to tread the path which Spain trod to her own destruction. We must send out there only good and able men, chosen for their fitness and not because of their partisan service, and these men must not only administer impartial justice to the natives and serve their own government with honesty and fidelity, but must show the utmost tact and firmness, remembering that with such people as those with whom we are to deal weakness is the greatest of crimes, and that next to weakness comes lack of consideration for their principles and prejudices.

I preach to you, then, my countrymen, that our country calls not for the life of ease, but for the life of strenuous endeavor. The Twentieth century looms before us big with the fate of many nations. If we stand idly by, if we seek merely swollen, slothful ease, and ignoble peace, if we shrink from the hard contests where men must win at hazard of their lives and at the risk of all they hold dear, then the bolder and stronger peoples will pass us by and will win for themselves the domination of the world. Let us therefore boldly face the life of strife, resolute to do our duty well and manfully; resolute to uphold righteousness by deed and by word; resolute to be both honest and brave, to serve high ideals, yet to use practical methods. Above all, let us shrink from no strife, moral or physical, within or without the nation, provided we are certain that the strife is justified; for it is only through strife, through hard and dangerous endeavor, that we shall ultimately win the goal of true national greatness.

LORD ROSEBERY

ROBERT BURNS

[Address of Archibald Philip Primrose, Earl of Rosebery, statesman, orator, British Prime Minister 1894-95 (born in London, May 7, 1847; ———), delivered in St. Andrew's Hall, Glasgow, July 21, 1896, being the occasion of the Burns Centenary celebration at Dumfries, Scotland.]

I cannot perhaps deny that to-day has been a labor, but it has been a labor of love. [The speaker had delivered an address in the morning before the tomb of Burns, at Dumfries.] It is, it must be, a source of joy and pride to see our champion Scotsman receive the honor and admiration and affection of humanity, to see as I have seen this morning the long processions bringing homage and tribute to the conquering dead. But these have only been signs and symptoms of world-wide reverence and devotion. That generous and immortal soul pervades the universe to-day. In the humming city and in the crowd of men, in the backwood and in the swamp, where the sentinel paces the black frontier or the sailor smokes the evening pipe, or where, above all, the farmer and his men pursue their summer toil, whether under the Stars and Stripes or under the Union Jack, the thought and sympathy of men are directed to Robert Burns.

I have sometimes asked myself, if a roll-call of fame were read over at the beginning of every century, how many men of eminence would answer a second time to their names. But of our poet there is no doubt or question. The *adsum* of Burns rings out clear and unchallenged. There are few before him on the list, and we cannot now conceive a list without him. He towers high, and yet he lived in an age when the average was sublime. It sometimes seems to me as if the whole Eighteenth century was a constant preparation for a constant working up to the great drama of the Revolution which closed it. The scenery is all complete when the time arrives—the dark volcanic country, the hungry, desperate people, the firefly nobles, the concentrated splendor of the Court; in the midst, in her place as heroine, the dazzling queen; and during lone previous years brooding nature has been producing not merely the immediate actors, but figures worthy of the scene. What a glittering procession it is! We can only mark some of the principal figures. Burke leads the way by seniority; then come Fox, and Goethe, Nelson and Mozart, Schiller, Pitt and Burns, Wellington and Napoleon, and among these Titans Burns is a conspicuous figure—a figure which appeals most of all to the imagination and affection of mankind. Napoleon looms larger to the imagination, but on the affection he has no hold. It is in the combination of the two powers that Burns is supreme. What is his secret? We are always discussing him and endeavoring to find it out. Perhaps, like the latent virtue of some medical baths, it may never be satisfactorily explained, but at any rate let us discuss him again.

That is, I presume, our object to-night. What pleasanter or more familiar occupation can there be for Scotsmen? But the Scotsmen who enjoy it have generally, perhaps, more time than I. Pardon, then, the imperfections of my speech, for I speak of a subject which no one can altogether compass, and which a busy man has, perhaps, no right to attempt.

The clue to Burns' extraordinary hold on mankind is possibly a complicated one. It has, perhaps, many developments. If so, we have no time to consider it to-night; but I personally believe the causes are, like most great causes, simple, though it might take long to point out all the ways in which they operate. The secret, as it seems to me, lies in two words—inspiration and sympathy. But if I wished to prove my contention I should go on quoting from his poems all night, and his admirers would still declare that I had omitted the best passages. I must proceed, then, in a more summary way. There seem to be two great natural forces in British literature—I use the safe adjective of "British" [laughter and applause]—and your applause shows me that I was right to do so. [Renewed applause.] I use it partly because hardly any of Burns' poetry is strictly English, partly because he hated and was perhaps the first to protest against the use of the word English as including Scottish. There are, I say, two great forces, which seem sheer inspiration and nothing else—I mean Shakespeare and Burns. This is not the place or the time to speak of the miracle called Shakespeare, but one must say a word of the miracle called Burns.

Try and reconstruct Burns as he was—a peasant born in a cottage that no sanitary inspector in these days would tolerate for a moment [laughter]; struggling with desperate effort against pauperism, almost in vain; snatching at scraps of learning in the intervals of toil, as it were with his teeth; a heavy, silent, lad, proud of his plough. All of a sudden, without preface or warning, he breaks out into exquisite song like a nightingale from the brushwood, and continues singing as sweetly, in nightingale pauses, till he dies. The nightingale sings because he cannot help it. He can only sing exquisitely, because he knows no other. So it was with Burns. What is this but inspiration? One can no more measure or reason about it than measure or reason about Niagara, and, remember, the poetry is only a fragment of Burns. Amazing as it may seem, all contemporary testimony is unanimous that the man was far more wonderful than his works. "It will be the misfortune of Burns' reputation," writes an accomplished lady, who might well have judged him harshly, "in the records of literature, not only to future generations and to foreign countries, but even with his native Scotland and a number of his contemporaries, that he has been regarded as a poet and nothing but a poet. Poetry," she continues—" I appeal to all who had the advantage of being personally acquainted with him—was actually not his forte. None certainly ever outshone Burns in the charms—the sorcery I would almost call it—of fascinating conversation, the spontaneous eloquence of social argument, or the unstudied poignancy of brilliant repartee," and she goes on to describe the almost superhuman fascination of his voice and of his eyes—"those balls of black fire which electrified all on whom they rested."

It seems strange to be told that it would be an injustice to judge Burns by his poetry alone, but as to the magnetism of his presence and conversation there is only one verdict. "No man's conversation every carried me so completely off my feet," said the Duchess of Gordon, the friend of Pitt and of the London wits, the queen of Scottish society. Dugald Stewart says that "all the faculties of Burns' mind were, so far as I could judge, equally vigorous, and his predilection for poetry was rather the result of his own enthusiastic and impassioned temper than of a genius exclusively adapted to that species of composition. From his conversation I should have pronounced him to be fitted to excel in whatever walk or ambition he had chosen to exert his abilities." And of his prose compositions the same severe judge speaks thus: "Their great and various excellences render some of them scarcely less objects of wonder than his poetical performances." The late Dr. Robertson used to say that, considering his education, the former seemed to him the more remarkable of the two. "I think Burns," said Dr. Robertson, to a friend, "was one of the most extraordinary men I ever met with. His poetry surprised me very much, his prose surprised me still more, and his conversation surprised me more than both his poetry and his prose." We are told, too, that he felt a strong call towards oratory, and all who heard him speak—and some of them were excellent judges—admitted his wonderful quickness of apprehension and readiness of eloquence. All this seems to me marvelous. It surely satisfies the claim of inspiration without the necessity of quoting a line of his poetry. [Cheers.]

I pass then to his sympathy. If his talents were universal his sympathy was not less so. His tenderness was no mere selfish tenderness for his own family, for he loved all mankind, except the cruel and base—nay, we may go further and say that he placed all creation, especially the suffering and depressed part of it, under his protection. The oppressor in every shape, even in the comparatively innocent embodiment of the factor and the sportsman, he regarded with direct and personal hostility. But, above

all, he saw the charm of the home.   He recognized it as
the basis of all society.   He honored it in its humblest
form, for he knew, as few know, how sincerely the family
in the cottage is welded by mutual love and esteem.   "I
recollect," once said Dugald Stewart, speaking of Burns,
"he told me when he was admiring a distant prospect in
one of our morning walks, that the sight of so many
smoking cottages gave pleasure to his mind, which none
could understand who did not witness, like himself, the
happiness and worth which they contained."

He dwells repeatedly on the primary sacredness of the
home and family, the responsibility of fatherhood and marriage.   "Have I not," he once wrote to Lord Mar, "a
more precious stock in my country's welfare than the
richest dukedom in it?   I have a large family of children,
and the prospect of many more."   The lines in which he
tells his faith are not less memorable than the stately
stanzas in which Gray sings of the "short and simple annals of the poor."   I must quote them again, often quoted
as they are :—

> "To make a happy fireside chime
>   To weans and wife,
> That's the true pathos and sublime
>   Of human life."

His verses then go straight to the heart of every home;
they appeal to every father and mother; but that is only
the beginning, perhaps the foundation, of his sympathy.
There is something for everybody in Burns.   [Cheers.]
He has a heart even for vermin; he has pity even for the
arch-enemy of mankind.   And his universality makes his
poems a treasure-house in which all may find what they
want.   Every wayfarer in the journey of life may pluck
strength and courage from it as he pauses.   The sore, the
weary, the wounded will all find something to heal and
soothe.   For this great master is the universal Samaritan.
Where the priest and the Levite may have passed by in
vain this eternal heart will still afford resource.

But he is not only for the sick in spirit.   The friend, the
patriot, will all find their choicest refreshment in Burns.
His touch is everywhere the touch of genius; nothing

comes amiss to him. What was said of the debating power of his eminent contemporary, Dundas, may be said of his poetry: "He went out in all weathers"; and it may be added that all weathers suited him, that he always brought back something that cannot die! [Cheers.]

He is, then, I think, a universal friend in a unique sense, but was, poetically speaking, the special friend of Scotland in a sense which recalls a profound remark of another eminent Scotsman—I mean Fletcher of Saltoun. In an account of a conversation between Lord Cromartie, Sir Edward Seymour, and Sir Christopher Musgrave, Fletcher writes: "I said I knew a very wise man, so much of Sir Christopher's sentiment that he believed if a man were permitted to make all the ballads, he need not care who should make the laws of a nation." This may be readily paraphrased, that it is more important to make the songs of a nation than frame its laws, and this again may be interpreted, that in former days, at any rate in the days of Fletcher, even to the days of Burns, it is the familiar songs of a people that mold their thoughts, their manners and their morals. [Cheers.] If this be true, can we exaggerate the debt that Scotland owes Burns? He has bequeathed to his country the most exquisite casket of songs in the world—primarily to his country, but others cannot be denied their share. I will give only one example but that is a signal one. From distant Rumania the queen of that country wrote to Dumfries to-day that she has no copy of Burns with her, but that she knows his songs by heart. [Cheers.]

We must remember that there is more than this to be said. Many of Burns' songs were already in existence in the lips and minds of the people, rough and coarse, and obscene. Our benefactor takes them, and with a touch of inspired alchemy transmutes them and leaves them pure gold. He loved the old catches and the old tunes, and into these gracious molds he poured his exquisite gifts of thought and expression. But for him these ancient airs, often wedded to words which no decent man could recite, would have perished from that corruption if not from neglect. He rescued them for us by his songs, and in doing so he hallowed life and sweetened the breath of Scotland. [Cheers.]

I have also used the words patriot and lover. These draw me to different lines of thought. The word patriot leads me to the political side of Burns. There is no doubt that he was suspected of being a politician, and he is even said to have sometimes wished to enter Parliament. [Laughter.] That was perhaps an excusable aberration, and my old friend Professor Masson has, I think, surmised that had he lived he might have been a great Liberal pressman. [Laughter.] My frail thought shall not dally with such surmise, but it conducts us naturally to the subject of Burns' politics. From his sympathy for his own class, from his indignation against nobles like the Duke of Queensberry, and from the toasts that cost him so dear it might be considered easy to infer his political opinions.

But Burns should not be claimed for any party. A poet, be it remembered, is never a politician, and a politician is never a poet [laughter and cheers]—that is to say, a politician is never so fortunate as to be a poet, and a poet is so fortunate as never to be a politician. [Renewed laughter.] I do not say that the line of demarcation is never passed. A politician may have risen for a moment, or a poet may have descended, but where there is any confusion between the two callings it is generally because the poet thinks he discerns or the politician thinks he needs something higher than politics. Burns' politics were entirely governed by the imagination. He was at once a Jacobite and a Jacobin. He had the sad sympathy which most of us have felt for the hapless house of Stuart, without the least wish to be governed by it. He had much the same spirit of abstract sympathy with the French Revolution when it was setting all Europe to rights, but he was prepared to lay down his life to prevent its putting this island to rights. [Laughter.] And then came his official superiors of the Excise, who, notwithstanding Mr. Pitt's admiration of his poetry, snuffed out his politics without remorse.

The name of Pitt leads me to add that Burns had some sort of relation with three Prime Ministers. Colonel Jenkinson, of the Cinque Ports Fencible Cavalry, and afterwards minister for fifteen years under the title of Liverpool, was on duty at Burns' funeral, though we are told—the good man—that he disapproved of the poet and

declined to make his acquaintance. Pitt, again, passed on
Burns one of his rare and competent literary judgments,
so eulogistic, indeed, that one wondered that a powerful
Minister could have allowed one he admired so much to
exist on an exciseman's pay, when well, and an exciseman's half-pay when he died. [Cheers.] And from
Addington, another Prime Minister, Burns elicited a son-
net which in the Academy of Lagado would have surely
been held a signal triumph of the art of extracting sunshine from cucumbers. [Laughter.]

So much for politics in the party sense. "A man's a
man for a' that." Is not Burns' politics the assertion of
the rights of humanity? In a sense far wider than party
politics it erects all mankind, it is the charter of its self-
respect, and it binds, it heals, it invigorates, it sets the
bruised and broken on their legs, it refreshes the stricken
soul, it is the salve and tonic and character, it cannot be
narrowed into party politics. Burns' politics are indeed
nothing but the occasional overflow of his human sympathy into past history and current events.

And now having discussed two trains of thought suggested by the words friend and patriot, I come to a more
dangerous word, lover. There is an eternal controversy
which it appears no didactic oil will ever assuage as to
Burns' private life and morality. Some maintain that
these have nothing to do with his poems, some maintain
that his life must be read in his works, and again some
think that his life damns his poems, while others aver that
his poems cannot be fully appreciated without his life.
Another school thinks that his vices have been exaggerated, while their opponents scarcely think such exaggeration possible. It is impossible to avoid taking a side. I
walk on the ashes, knowing fire beneath and unable to
avoid them, for the topic is inevitable. I must confess
myself, then, one of those who think that the life of Burns
doubles the interest of his poems, and I doubt whether the
failings of his life have been much exaggerated, for contemporary testimony on that point is strong, though a
high and excellent authority, Mr. Wallace, has recently
taken the other side with much power and point. But the
life of Burns, which I love to read with his poems, does
not consist in his vices. They lie outside it. It is a life of

work and truth and tenderness, and though like all lives
it has its light and shade, remember that we know all the
worst as well as the best.

His was a soul bathed in crystal. He hurried to avow
everything. There was no reticence in him. The only
obscure passage in his life is the love-passage with High-
land Mary, and as to that he was silent not from shame,
but because it was a sealed and sacred episode. "What a
flattering idea," he once wrote, "is a world to come.
There shall I with speechless agony or rapture recognize
my lost, my ever dear Mary, whose bosom was fraught
with truth, honor, constancy and love." But he had, as
the French say, the defects of his qualities. His imagination was a supreme and celestial gift, but his imagination often led him wrong and never more than with
woman. The chivalry that made Don Quixote see the
heroic in all the common events of life made Burns (as
his brother tells us) see a goddess in every girl he approached; hence many love affairs, and some guilty ones;
but even these must be judged with reference to time and
circumstances. This much is certain—had he been devoid of genius they would not have attracted attention.
It is Burns' pedestal that affords a target. And why, one
may ask, is not the same treatment measured out to Burns
as to others? The illegitimate children of great captains
and statesmen and princes are treated as historical and ornamental incidents. They strut the scene of Shakespeare
and ruffle it with the best. It is for the illegitimate children of Burns, though he and his wife cherished them as
if born in wedlock, that the vials of wrath are reserved.
They were two brilliant figures both descended from the
Stuarts who were alive during Burns' life. We occupy
ourselves endlessly and severely with the offences of
Burns, we heave an elegant sigh over the hundred lapses
of Charles James Fox and Charles Edward Stuart.
[Cheers.]

Again, it is quite clear that, though exceptionally sober
in his earlier years, he drank too much in later life, but
this, it must be remembered, was but an occasional con-
descendence to the vice and habit of the age. The
gentry who pressed him to their houses and who were all
convivial have much to answer for. His admirers who

thronged to see him, and who could only conveniently sit with him in a tavern, are also responsible for this habit so perilously attractive to men of genius, from the decorous Addison and the brilliant Bolingbroke onward. The Eighteenth century records hard drinking as the common incident of intellectual eminence. To a man who had shone supreme in the most glowing society, and who was now an exciseman in a country town, with a home which cannot have been very exhilarating, with the nervous system highly strung, the temptation of the warm tavern and the admiring circle there may well have been almost irresistible.

Some attempt to say that his intemperance was exaggerated. I neither affirm nor deny it. If he succumbed it was to good-fellowship and cheer. Remember, I do not seek to palliate or excuse, and, indeed, none will be turned to dissipation by Burns' example—he paid too dearly for it. But I will say this, that it all seems infinitely little, infinitely remote. Why do we strain at this distance to discern this dim spot on the poet's mantle? Shakespeare and Ben Jonson took their cool tankard at the "Mermaid." We cannot afford, in the strictest view of dietary responsibility, to quarrel with them for it. When we consider Pitt and Goethe we do not concentrate our vision on Pitt's bottles of port or Goethe's bottles of Moselle. Then why, we ask, is there such a chasm between the "Mermaid" and the "Globe"; and why are the vintages of Wimbledon and Weimar so much more innocent than the simple punch-bowl of Inverary marble and its contents? [Cheers.]

I should like to go a step further and affirm that we have something to be grateful for even in the weaknesses of men like Burns. Mankind is helped in its progress almost as much by the study of imperfection as by the contemplation of perfection. Had we nothing before us in our futile and halting lives but saints and the ideal, we might well fail altogether. We grope blindly along the catacombs of the world, we climb the dark ladder of life, we feel our way to futurity, but we can scarcely see an inch around or before us. We stumble and falter and fall, our hands and knees are bruised and sore, and we look up for light and guidance. Could we see nothing but distant,

unapproachable impeccability we might well sink pros-
trate in the hopelessness of emulation, and the weariness
of despair. Is it not then, when all seems blank and light-
less and lifeless, when strength and courage flag, and when
perfection seems remote as a star, is it not then that imperfection helps us? When we see that the greatest and
choicest images of God have had their weaknesses like
ours, their temptations, their hour of darkness, their
bloody sweat, are we not encouraged by their lapses and
catastrophes to find energy for one more effort, one more
struggle? Where they failed, we feel it a less dishonor
to fail; their errors and sorrows make, as it were, an easier
ascent from infinite imperfection to infinite perfection.

Man, after all, is not ripened by virtue alone. Were
it so, this world were a paradise of angels. No. Like
the growth of the earth, he is the fruit of all seasons, the
accident of a thousand accidents, a living mystery moving
through the seen to the unseen; he is sown in dishonor;
he is matured under all the varieties of heat and cold, in
mists and wrath, in snow and vapors, in the melancholy of
autumn, in the torpor of winter as well as in the rapture
and fragrance of summer, or the balmy affluence of
spring, its breath, its sunshine; at the end he is reaped, the
product not of one climate but of all, not of good alone
but of sorrow, perhaps mellowed and ripened, perhaps
stricken and withered and sour. How, then, shall we
judge any one?—how, at any rate, shall we judge a giant,
great in gifts and great in temptation, great in strength,
and great in weakness? Let us glory in his strength and
be comforted in his weakness, and when we thank Heaven
for the inestimable gift of Burns, we do not need to remember wherein he was imperfect, we cannot bring ourselves to regret that he was made of the same clay as ourselves. [Cheers.]

CARL SCHURZ

THE TRUE AMERICANISM

[Address by Carl Schurz, publicist and statesman (born at Liblar, near Cologne, Germany, March 2, 1829; ———), delivered in New York City at a meeting of the Chamber of Commerce of the State of New York, January 2, 1896, Mr. Schurz rising to second the resolutions embodied in a report to the Chamber by its Committee on Foreign Commerce and the Revenue Laws upon the then pending Venezuelan question.]

MR. PRESIDENT:—As an honorary member of the Chamber of Commerce, I am thankful for the privilege of seconding the resolutions offered by the Committee. I yield to no one in American feeling or pride; and, as an American, I maintain that international peace, kept in justice and honor, is an American principle and an American interest. As to the President's recent message on the Venezuela case, opinions differ. But I am sure that all good citizens, whether they approve or disapprove of it, and while they would faithfully stand by their country in time of need, sincerely and heartily wish that the pending controversy between the United States and Great Britain be brought to a peaceable issue.

I am well aware of the strange teachings put forth among us by some persons, that a war, from time to time, would by no means be a misfortune, but rather a healthy exercise to stir up our patriotism, and to keep us from becoming effeminate. Indeed, there are some of them busily looking round for somebody to fight, as the crazed Malay runs amuck looking for somebody to kill. The idea that the stalwart and hard-working American people, engaged in subduing to civilization an immense continent,

CARL SCHURZ

Photogravure after a photograph from life

need foreign wars to preserve their manhood from dropping into effeminacy, or that their love of country will flag unless stimulated by hatred of somebody else, or that they must have bloodshed and devastation as an outdoor exercise in the place of other sports—such an idea is as preposterous as it is disgraceful and abominable.

It is also said that there are some American citizens of Irish origin, who wish the United States to get into a war with England, because they believe such a war would serve to relieve Ireland of the British connection. We all value the willingness of the Irish-born American citizens to fight for their adopted country if need be; and nobody will deny that their hearty love for their native land is, as such, entirely natural and entitled to respect. But as American citizens, having sworn exclusive allegiance to the United States, not one of them should ever forget that this Republic has a right to expect of all its adopted citizens, as to their attitude toward public affairs, especially questions of peace or war, the loyal and complete subordination of the interests of their native countries to the interests of the United States.

There are also corrupt politicians eager to plunder the public under a cheap guise of patriotism, and unscrupulous speculators looking for gambling and pilfering opportunities in their country's trouble, and wishing for war as the piratical wrecker on his rocky shore wishes for fogs or hurricanes. They deserve the detestation of every decent man.

But aside from these classes it may safely be assumed that all seriously minded American citizens earnestly hope for a continuance of the long-existing friendly relations between this country and Great Britain. General Sherman, whose memory is dear to us all, is reported to have said, in his vigorous way: "You want to know what war is? War is hell." And nobody who has seen war as he had, and as some of us have, will question the truthfulness of this characteristic saying. True, war sometimes develops noble emotions and heroic qualities in individuals or in a people; but war is hell for all that. If our boasted civilization and Christianity are to mean anything, they should mean this: No war is justifiable unless its cause or object stand in just proportion to its cost in blood, in destruction, in human misery, in waste, in political corruption, in social demoralization, in relapse of civilization; and even then it is justifiable only when every expedient of statesmanship to avert it has been thoroughly exhausted.

I shall not discuss now whether those who honestly think that our present difference with Great Britain would, as to cause or object, justify war, or those who think the contrary, are right. I expect them both to co-operate in an earnest endeavor to encourage those expedients of statesmanship by which war may be averted in either case. Confronting a grave emergency, we must, as practical men, look at the situation, not as it might have been or ought to be, but as it is. For several years our Government has been seeking to bring a boundary dispute between Venezuela and British Guiana to a friendly settlement, but without success. Last summer, the President, through the Secretary of State, in a despatch reviewing the case at length, and containing an elaborate disquisition on the Monroe Doctrine, asked the British Government whether it " would consent or decline to submit the Venezuelan question in its entirety to impartial arbitration," calling for "a definite decision." Lord Salisbury, after some delay, replied, in a despatch also discussing the Monroe Doctrine from his point of view, that the Venezuela question might be in part submitted to arbitration, but he refused to submit it in its entirety as asked for. Thereupon President Cleveland sent a message to Congress recommending appropriations for a Commission to be appointed by the Executive, which Commission "shall make the necessary investigation" of the boundary dispute, and report to our government; and when such report is made and accepted, it will, in the President's opinion, "be the duty of the United States to resist, by every means, the appropriation by Great Britain of any lands, or the exercise of any governmental jurisdiction over any territory, which, after investigation, we have determined of right belongs to Venezuela." And Congress, by unanimously voting the appropriation asked for, without qualification, virtually made the position taken by the President its own.

This correspondence and this message, by their tone

as well as their substance, have essentially changed the situation. It is no longer a mere question of boundary, or of the status of the Monroe Doctrine, but after a demand and a call for a definite decision, and a definite refusal of the thing demanded, and in answer to this something that may be understood as a threat of war, it has assumed the most ticklish form of an international difference—the form of a question of honor. Questions of fact, of law, of interest, of substantial justice and right it may sometimes be difficult to determine; but there are rules of evidence, of legal construction, of equity, and precedents to aid us. A question of honor is often inaccessible to these aids, for it is a matter of sentiment. Affairs of honor have caused as many follies as affairs of love. It is a strange fact, that while the mediæval conception of honor which regarded the duel as the only adequate settlement of a question of that nature, has yielded to more enlightened and more moral views in several highly civilized countries, nations are in such cases still apt to rush to arms as the only means of satisfaction.

It is generally said, in Great Britain as well as here, that there will be no war. The belief is born of the wish. It is so general because almost everybody feels that such a war would be a disaster not only calamitous but also absurd and shameful to both nations. From the bottom of my heart I trust the prediction will prove true. But the prediction itself, with the popular sentiment prompting it, will not be alone sufficient to make it true. Bloody wars have happened in spite of an earnest popular desire for peace on both sides, especially when points of honor inflamed the controversy. It may be in vain to cry "Peace! Peace!" on both sides of the ocean, if we continue to flaunt the red rag in one another's faces.

The Commission just appointed by the President indeed consists of eminent, patriotic and wise men. They will, no doubt, conduct their inquiry with conscientious care and fairness. So we think here. But we have to admit that after all it is a one-sided contrivance, and as such lacks an important element of authority. Suppose the report of the Commission goes against the British contention. Suppose then we say to Great Britain: "*Our* investigation shows this, and *we* decide accordingly.

Take this, or fight!" How then? It is quite possible
that a vast majority of the British people care very little
about the strip of territory in dispute, and would have
been satisfied to let the whole of it go to arbitration. It
is not impossible even that Lord Salisbury himself, in view
of the threatening complications in Europe and other
parts of the world, and of the manifold interests involved,
might at last rather let it be so submitted than have a
long quarrel about it. But it may well be doubted
whether any statesman at the head of the British or any
other great government would think that he could afford
to yield what he otherwise would be disposed to yield,
under a threat of war. Similar circumstances would produce similar effects with us. The fact is, therefore, that
however peaceable the popular temper may be on both
sides of the water, the critical moment will come at the
time when the Commission reports, and if that Commission remains one-sided as it is now the crisis may become
more exciting and dangerous than ever.

But in the meantime there will be something calling for
the most earnest attention of the business world on both
sides of the Atlantic. While that critical period is im-
pending there will be—who knows how long—a dark
cloud of uncertainty hanging over both nations, an uncertainty liable to be fitfully aggravated on occasions, or even
without occasion, by speculative manufacturers of rumors.
Every business calculation will be like taking a gambler's
chance. The spirit of enterprise will be depressed by
vague anxiety as to the future, by the apprehension-
paralysis, and I need not tell you as experienced business
men what all this means as to that confidence which is
necessary to set in motion the rich man's money and the
poor man's labor, and thus to develop general prosperity.
It is of the highest importance, therefore, that this uncertainty be removed, or at least lessened as much and as
soon as possible; and the peace sentiment prevailing here
as well as in England, of which the friendly message from
the Chamber of Commerce in Edinburgh is so cheering an
evidence, may perhaps be practically set to work for the
accomplishment of that end.

A thought occurred to me when studying President
Cleveland's Venezuela message, which, indeed, may well

have occurred, at least in general outline, to many others
at the same time, because it seems so natural. I am glad
to notice that something in the same line was suggested
by an English journal. The President has appointed an
American Commission to inquire into British claims as to
the Venezuela boundary. As I have already pointed out,
the findings of that Commission will, owing to its one-
sided origin, lack an essential element of the moral authority required to command general credit. This authority would be supplied if an equal number of eminent
Englishmen, designated by the British Government, were
joined to the Commission to co-operate in the examination of the whole case, and if the two parties, to prevent
deadlocks between them, agreed upon some distinguished
person outside to preside over and direct their delibera-
tions and to have the casting vote—the joint commission
to be not a court of arbitration, and as such to pronounce
a final and binding decision of the whole case—the thing
which Lord Salisbury objected to—but an advisory council, to report the results of its inquiry into the whole case,
together with its opinions, findings and recommendations
to the two governments for their free acceptance or rejection.

It may be said that such an arrangement would not
entirely remove the uncertainty as to the final outcome. I
believe, however, that it would at least very greatly lessen
that uncertainty. I think it probable that the finding
and recommendations of a Commission so constituted
would have high moral authority, and carry very great
weight with both governments. They would be likely to
furnish, if not a complete and conclusive decision, at least
a basis for a friendly agreement. The very appointment
of such a Joint Commission by the two governments
would be apt at once to remove the point of honor, the
most dangerous element, from the controversy, and thus
go very far to relieve the apprehension of disastrous possibilities which usually has so unsettling and depressing an
effect.

I do not know, of course, whether such a plan would
be accepted by either government. I think, however,
that each of them could assent to it without the slightest
derogation to its dignity, and that if either of them re-

ceived it, upon proper presentation, even with an informal manifestation of favor, the way would easily be opened to a mutual understanding concerning it. At any rate, it seems to me worth the while of a public spirited and patriotic body like this, and of other friends of peace here or abroad, to consider its expediency, and at the close of my remarks I shall move a tentative resolution to that effect, in addition to the one now pending.

I repeat, I am for peace—not, indeed, peace at any price, but peace with honor. Let us understand, however, what the honor of this great American Republic consists in. We are a very powerful people—even without an army or navy immediately ready for action, we are, in some respects, the most powerful people on earth. We enjoy peculiar advantages of inestimable value. We are not only richer than any European nation in men, in wealth and in resources yet undeveloped, but we are the only nation that has a free hand, having no dangerous neighbors and no outlying and exposed possessions to take care of. We are, in our continental position, substantially unassailable. A hostile navy may destroy what commercial fleet we have, blockade our ports, and even bombard our seaboard towns. This would be painful enough, but it would only be scratching our edges. It would not touch a vital point. No foreign power or possible combination could attack us on land without being overwhelmed on our own soil by immensely superior numbers. We are the best fitted, not, perhaps, for a war of quick decision, but for a long war. Better than any other nation we can, if need be, live on our own fat. We enjoy the advantage of not having spent our resources during long periods of peace on armaments of tremendous cost without immediate use for them, but we would have those resources unimpaired in time of war to be used during the conflict. Substantially unassailable in our continental fastness, and bringing our vast resources into play with the patriotic spirit and the inventive genius and energy of our people, we would, on sea as well as on land, for offensive as well as defensive warfare, be stronger the second year of a war than the first, and stronger the third than the second, and so on. Owing to this superiority of our staying power, a war with the United States would be to any foreign nation practically a war without end. No foreign power or possible combination in the Old World can, therefore, considering in addition to all this the precarious relations of every one of them with other powers and its various exposed interests, have the slightest inclination to get into a war with the United States, and none of them will, unless we force it to do so. They will, on the contrary, carefully avoid such a quarrel as long as they can, and we may be confident that without firing a gun, and even without having many guns ready for firing, we shall always see our rights respected and our demands, if they are just and proper—may be, after some diplomatic sparring—at last fully complied with.

What is the rule of honor to be observed by a power so strong and so advantageously situated as this Republic is? Of course, I do not expect it meekly to pocket real insults if they should be offered to it. But, surely, it should not, as our boyish jingoes wish it to do, swagger about among the nations of the world, with a chip on its shoulder, and shaking its fist in everybody's face. Of course, it should not tamely submit to real encroachments upon its rights. But, surely, it should not, whenever its own notions of right or interest collide with the notions of others, fall into hysterics and act as if it really feared for its own security and its very independence. As a true gentleman, conscious of his strength and his dignity, it should be slow to take offense. In its dealings with other nations it should have scrupulous regard, not only for their rights, but also for their self-respect. With all its latent resources for war, it should be the great peace power of the world. It should never forget what a proud privilege and what an inestimable blessing it is not to need and not to have big armies or navies to support. It should seek to influence mankind, not by heavy artillery, but by good example and wise counsel. It should see its highest glory, not in battles won, but in wars prevented. It should be so invariably just and fair, so trustworthy, so good tempered, so conciliatory, that other nations would instinctively turn to it as their mutual friend and the natural adjuster of their differences, thus making it the greatest preserver of the world's peace.

This is not a mere idealistic fancy. It is the natural

position of this great Republic among the nations of the
earth. It is its noblest vocation, and it will be a glorious
day for the United States when the good sense and the
self-respect of the American people see in this their "manifest destiny." It all rests upon peace. Is not this peace
with honor? There has, of late, been much loose speech
about "Americanism." Is not this good Americanism?
It is surely to-day the Americanism of those who love
their country most. And I fervently hope that it will be
and ever remain the Americanism of our children and
our children's children.

GENERAL SHERMAN

[Address by Carl Schurz at a special meeting of the Chamber of
Commerce of the State of New York, February 17, 1891, upon second-
ing resolutions before the Chamber on the death of General William
Tecumseh Sherman.]

GENTLEMEN:—The adoption by the Chamber of Commerce of these resolutions which I have the honor to second, is no mere perfunctory proceeding. We have been
called here by a genuine impulse of the heart. To us General Sherman was not a great man like other great men,
honored and revered at a distance. We had the proud
and happy privilege of calling him one of us. Only a
few months ago, at the annual meeting of this Chamber,
we saw the familiar face of our honorary member on this
platform by the side of our President. Only a few weeks
ago he sat at our banquet table, as he had often before, in
the happiest mood of conviviality, and contributed to the
enjoyment of the night with his always unassuming and
always charming speech. And as he moved among us
without the slightest pomp of self-conscious historic dignity, only with the warm and simple geniality of his nature,
it would cost us sometimes an effort of the memory to
recollect that he was the renowned captain who had mar-
shaled mighty armies victoriously on many a battlefield,
and whose name stood, and will forever stand, in the very
foremost rank of the saviors of this Republic, and of the

great soldiers of the world's history. Indeed, no American could have forgotten this for a moment; but the affection of those who were so happy as to come near to him, would sometimes struggle to outrun their veneration and gratitude.

Death has at last conquered the hero of so many campaigns; our cities and towns and villages are decked with flags at half-mast; the muffled drum and the funeral cannon-boom will resound over the land as his dead body passes to the final resting-place; and the American people stand mournfully gazing into the void left by the sudden disappearance of the last of the greatest men brought forth by our war of regeneration—and this last also finally become, save Abraham Lincoln alone, the most widely beloved. He is gone; but as we of the present generation remember it, history will tell all coming centuries the romantic story of the famous "March to the Sea"—how, in the dark days of 1864, Sherman, having worked his bloody way to Atlanta, then cast off all his lines of supply and communication, and, like a bold diver into the dark unknown, seemed to vanish with all his hosts from the eyes of the world, until his triumphant reappearance on the shores of the ocean proclaimed to the anxiously expecting millions, that now the final victory was no longer doubtful, and that the Republic would surely be saved.

Nor will history fail to record that this great general was, as a victorious soldier, a model of republican citizenship. When he had done his illustrious deeds, he rose step by step to the highest rank in the army, and then, grown old, he retired. The Republic made provision for him in modest republican style. He was satisfied. He asked for no higher reward. Although the splendor of his achievements, and the personal affection for him, which every one of his soldiers carried home, made him the most popular American of his day, and although the most glittering prizes were not seldom held up before his eyes, he remained untroubled by ulterior ambition. No thought that the Republic owed him more ever darkened his mind. No man could have spoken to him of the "ingratitude of Republics," without meeting from him a stern rebuke. And so, content with the consciousness of a great duty nobly done, he was happy in the love of his fellow citizens.

Indeed, he may truly be said to have been in his old age, not only the most beloved, but also the happiest of Americans. Many years he lived in the midst of, posterity. His task was finished, and this he wisely understood. His deeds had been passed upon by the judgment of history, and irrevocably registered among the glories of his country and his age. His generous heart envied no one, and wished every one well; and ill-will had long ceased to pursue him. Beyond cavil his fame was secure, and he enjoyed it as that which he had honestly earned, with a genuine and ever fresh delight, openly avowed by the charming frankness of his nature. He dearly loved to be esteemed and cherished by his fellow men, and what he valued most, his waning years brought him in ever increasing abundance. Thus he was in truth a most happy man, and his days went down like an evening sun in a cloudless autumn sky. And when now the American people, with that peculiar tenderness of affection which they have long borne him, lay him in his grave, the happy ending of his great life may soothe the pang of bereavement they feel in their hearts at the loss of the old hero who was so dear to them, and of whom they were and always will be so proud. His memory will ever be bright to us all; his truest monument will be the greatness of the Republic he served so well; and his fame will never cease to be prized by a grateful country, as one of its most precious possessions.

THOMAS JENKINS SEMMES

PERSONAL CHARACTERISTICS OF THE CHIEF JUSTICES

[Address by Thomas J. Semmes, lawyer, one time professor of Civil Law in the University of Louisiana, President of the American Bar Association 1886 (born in Georgetown, D. C., December 16, 1824; died in New Orleans, La., June 23, 1899), delivered at the Centennial celebration of the Supreme Court of the United States, at the Metropolitan Opera-House, New York City, February 4, 1890. Grover Cleveland, as Chairman of the Executive Committee, occupied the chair.]

MR. PRESIDENT:—During the century of its existence seven persons, exclusive of the present incumbent, filled the office of Chief Justice of the Supreme Court of the United States: Jay, Rutledge, Ellsworth, Marshall, Taney, Chase, and Waite. Most of these were appointed in the prime of life. Taney at fifty-nine, was the oldest; Jay resigned when he was but fifty years of age. Marshall and Taney presided in the Court for sixty-three years— Marshall from 1801 to July, 1835, and Taney from 1836 to 1864.

Marshall was appointed by John Adams about a month before the inauguration of President Jefferson; it was said that his appointment was due to his defence in Congress of the Administration in the case of Jonathan Robbins, who claimed to be an American citizen and who had been delivered up, by order of the President, to the British Government as a deserter, and was hanged at the yard-arm of a British man-of-war. Taney was appointed by Andrew Jackson shortly before the accession of Mr. Van Buren, and it is said he was appointed because of his aid to General Jackson on the bank question, and espe-

1029

cially as a reward for the act of removing the public deposits. Marshall was a legacy left by the defeated Federalists to the victorious Republicans of that day; Taney, with the address that he had prepared for the President, was a legacy left by General Jackson to the people of the United States. Taney had been nominated by General Jackson as an Associate Justice of the Supreme Court while Marshall was Chief Justice; the Senate under the domination of party spirit indefinitely postponed the nomination, although we know from a letter addressed to Benjamin Watkins Leigh, then a Senator from Virginia, that Marshall desired the appointment of Taney to be confirmed.

These two men were born, Marshall on one side of the Potomac, in the year 1755, in Fauquier County, Virginia, and Taney on the other side of the Potomac, in the year 1777, in Calvert County, Maryland. Marshall was a member of the Protestant Episcopal Church; Taney was a devout Roman Catholic.

Marshall was assailed by the Republicans of his day because of decisions in the case of Marbury vs. Madison, and on the trial of Aaron Burr. Taney met the same fate from the Republicans of his day because of his decisions in the case of Dred Scott, and in the Merryman *habeas corpus* case.

The criticism of Mr. Jefferson on the opinion of Marshall in the case of Marbury vs. Madison is not altogether unfounded. The Chief Justice having reached the conclusion that the Supreme Court had no power to issue a writ of mandamus to the Secretary of State, it being an exercise of original jurisdiction not warranted by the Constitution, could have, and perhaps should have, abstained from entering upon the discussion of other questions not necessary to be decided; it is this discussion which Mr. Jefferson sarcastically called an obiter dissertation. However that may be, Marshall vindicated the opinion entertained of him by the Federalists of that day, when he held that an act of Congress repugnant to the Constitution is not law, and that it is the province and duty of the Judicial Department to say what the law is; that the Constitution is to be considered in Courts as the paramount law, and that any other principle would subvert the foundation of all written constitutions, and would give to the legislature a practical and real omnipotence, while the Constitution professed to restrict their powers within narrow limits. Before this decision was made there had been hesitancy and halting among judges as to the power of the Court to declare an act of Congress void because of its repugnancy to the Constitution. This decision invested the Supreme Court with, or rather secured to it, a power which no Court ever before possessed; and the possession of such power has elicited from a distinguished foreigner the remark that the Court is not only a most interesting but virtually unique creation of the founders of the Constitution. Ever since the decision rendered in the case of Marbury vs. Madison, except during a paroxysm of passion, the eyes of the nation have been fixed on the Court as the guardian of the National Constitution and the harmonious regulator of inter-state relations. The Romans regarded their Prætor " as the living voice of the civil law "; the Supreme Court is in fact the living voice of the Constitution; that is to say, it voices the will of the people as expressed in the Constitution. The Court is the conscience of the people who, to restrain themselves from hasty and unjust action have placed their representatives under the restrictions of paramount law. It is the spirit and tone of the people in their best moments. It is the guarantee of the minority against the vehement impulses of the majority.

The Court also exercises veto power on State action more potent than that proposed in the convention, although much less distasteful. Its veto power is constantly exerted, not, it is true, to annul State laws, but to declare in more euphemistic language that a State statute is no law, because it is repugnant to the Constitution.

Jefferson hated Marshall, who reciprocated his dislike. During the trial of Burr, Marshall did not hesitate to issue a subpœna *duces tecum* to the President, requiring him to appear in Court and produce a certain letter of General Wilkinson.

The determination of Marshall to decide Burr's case according to law, unawed by public clamor or by the denunciations of those in power, is manifested in that part of his opinion where he says: " That this Court does not

usurp power is most true.   That this Court does not shirk
from its duty is no less true.   No man, might he let the
bitter cup pass from him without reproach, would drain
it to the bottom.   But if he has no choice in the case, if
there is no alternative presented to him but a dereliction
of duty or the opprobrium of those who are denominated
'the world,' he merits the contempt as well as the indignation of his country who can hesitate which to embrace."

Marshall's sturdy conduct as a member of the commission to France in 1797 gave origin to the celebrated din-
ner-toast: "Millions for defence, but not a cent for
tribute."   Pickering, whose pen was usually dipped in
gall, said: "Of the three envoys to France, the conduct
of Marshall has been entirely satisfactory, and ought to
be marked by the most decided approbation of the public."   And Patrick Henry, his political opponent, alluding
to the bearing of Marshall as one of the envoys to France,
says: "His temper and disposition were always pleasant,
his talents and integrity unquestioned.   I love him because he felt and acted as a Republican, as an American."

Chief Justice Marshall when appointed, had reached the
age of forty-five.   William Wirt thus describes him:—

"The Chief Justice of the United States is in his person tall, meagre,
emaciated; his muscles so relaxed as not only to disqualify him apparently for any vigorous exertion of body, but destroy everything like
harmony in his whole appearance and demeanor, dress, attitude, gesture; sitting, standing or walking he is as far removed from the
idolized graces of Lord Chesterfield as any other gentleman on earth.
His head and face are small in proportion to his height; his complexion swarthy; the muscles of his face being relaxed make him
appear to be fifty years of age—nor can he be much younger.   His
countenance has a faithful expression of good-humor and hilarity,
while his black eyes, that unerring index, possess an irradiating spirit,
which proclaims the imperial powers of the mind that sits enthroned
within."

In this man what a legacy the dying Federalists bequeathed to the country!   When Wolcott heard of the
appointment, he said that, although Marshall was a man
of virtue and distinguished talents, "he will think much
of the State of Virginia, and is too much disposed to govern the world according to rules of logic; he will read and

expound the Constitution as if it were a penal statute, and will sometimes be embarrassed with doubts of which his friends will not see the importance."

What has been the result? To use the language of Mr. Bryce: "It is hardly an exaggeration to say that the American Constitution as it now stands, with the mass of fringing decisions that explain it, is a far more complete and finished instrument than it was when it came fire-new from the hands of the convention. It is not merely their work, but the work of the Judges, and most of all of one man—the great Chief Justice Marshall."

In 1775, when rumors were in circulation of the occurrences near Boston, Marshall, not then twenty years of age, marched to the muster-field of the militia twenty miles distant, wearing a plain blue hunting-shirt and trousers of the same material fringed with white, and a round black hat mounted with the buck's-tail for a cockade. Elected a lieutenant he, with his men, joined Patrick Henry in his march on Williamsburg. With promoted rank, he was personally engaged in the battles of Iron Hill, Brandywine, Germantown, and Monmouth, and with Washington's exhausted troops he went into winter quarters at Valley Forge, where, says Slaughter: "He was the best-tempered man I ever knew. During his sufferings nothing discouraged, nothing disturbed him. If he had only bread to eat, it was just as well; if only meat, it made no difference. If any of the officers murmured at their deprivations, he would shame them by good-natured raillery, or encourage them by his own exuberance of spirits. He was an excellent companion and idolized by the soldiers and his brother officers, whose gloomy hours were enlivened by his inexhaustible fund of anecdote."

He was with Wayne at the assault on Stony Point, and subsequently covered Major Lee's retreat after his surprise of the enemy at Powle's Hook, July 19, 1779. His military career terminated in 1781, having in the interval served under Baron Steuben, and aided in defeating Arnold's invasion of Virginia. In the year 1780, while waiting in Williamsburg for the organization of a new corps of troops, he studied law under Chancellor Wythe.

It was during the summer after the war that he walked to Philadelphia in order to be inoculated for the smallpox, and on his arrival he was refused admission to one of the hotels because of his shabby appearance, long beard, and worn-out garments. Some years afterwards his rustic appearance lost him a fee. A gentleman who wished to retain a lawyer met Marshall one morning strolling through the streets of Richmond, attired in a plain linen roundabout and shorts, with hat under his arm, from which he was eating cherries; and although Marshall had been recommended to him, the careless, languid air of the young lawyer created such an unfavorable impression that the gentleman did not engage him. He was always easy, frank, friendly, and cordial in his manners, and social in his habits. He was never very studious. Although temperate in his habits he was very fond of his bottle of Madeira at dinner. Without possessing beauty of style, melody of voice, grace of person, or charm of manner, he became a distinguished advocate and achieved rapid and extraordinary success at the bar.

Yet Mr. Wirt says: " This extraordinary man, without the aid of fancy, without the advantages of person, voice, attitude, gesture, or any of the ornaments of an orator, deserves to be considered as one of the most eloquent men in the world, if eloquence may be said to consist in the power of seizing the attention with irresistible force, and never permitting it to elude the grasp until the hearer has received the conviction which the speaker intends. His voice is dry and hard; his attitude, in his most effective orations, is often extremely awkward; while all his gestures proceed from his right arm and consist merely in a perpendicular swing of it, from about the elevation of his head to the bar, behind which he is accustomed to stand. As to fancy, if she holds a seat in his mind at all, his gigantic genius tramples with disdain on all her flower-decked plats and blooming parterres. How then, you will ask, how is it possible that such a man can hold the attention of an audience enchained through a speech of even ordinary length? I will tell you. He possesses one original and almost supernatural faculty: the faculty of developing a subject by a single glance of his mind, and detecting at once the very point on which every controversy depends. No matter what the question, though ten times more knotted than ' the gnarled oak,' the lightning of heaven is not more rapid or more resistless than his astonishing penetration. Nor does the exercise of it seem to cause him an effort. On the contrary, it is as easy as vision. I am persuaded that his eyes do not fly over a landscape and take its various objects with more promptitude and facility, than his mind embraces and analyses the most complex subject."

Marshall married Miss Ambler, one of the colonial belles of Williamsburg, whom he courted while he was a young soldier. This union endured more than forty years. She died December 25, 1831. The tender and assiduous attention he paid to her is one of the most interesting and striking features of his domestic life. Bishop Meade says: "She was nervous in the extreme. The least noise was sometimes agony to her whole frame, and his perpetual endeavor was to keep the house and outhouses from slightest cause of distressing her, walking himself at times about the house and yard without shoes." Judge Story said: "She must have been a very extraordinary woman, and I think he is the most extraordinary man I ever saw for the depth and tenderness of his feelings." I cannot forbear to quote in full a tribute to her memory, written by himself, December 25, 1832, and found among his papers:—

"This day of joy and festivity to the whole Christian world is, to my sad heart, the anniversary of the keenest affliction which humanity can sustain. While all around is gladness, my mind dwells on the silent tomb and cherishes the remembrance of the beloved object which it contains. On December 25, 1831, it was the will of Heaven to take to itself the companion who has sweetened the choicest part of my life, has rendered toil a pleasure, has partaken of all my feelings and was enthroned in the inmost recess of my heart. Never can I cease to feel the loss and to deplore it. Grief for her is too sacred ever to be profaned on this day, which shall be, during my existence, marked by a recollection of her virtue.

"On January 3, 1783, I was united by the holiest bonds to the woman I adored. From the moment of our union to that of our separation, I never ceased to thank Heaven for this, its best gift. Not a moment passed in which I did not consider her as a blessing from which the chief happiness of my life was derived. This never-dying sentiment, originating in love, was cherished by a long and close observation of as amiable and estimable qualities as ever adorned the female bosom. To a person which in youth was very attractive, to manners uncommonly pleasing, she added a fine understanding, and the sweetest temper which can accompany a just and modest sense of what was due to herself. She was educated with a profound reverence for religion, which she preserved to her last moments. This sentiment among her earliest and deepest impressions, gave a coloring to her whole life; hers was the religion taught by the Savior of men. She was a firm believer in the faith inculcated by the church (Episcopal) in which she was bred.

"I have lost her and with her I have lost the solace of my life. Yet she remains still the companion of my retired hours, still occupies my inmost bosom. When alone and unemployed, my mind still recurs to her. More than one thousand times since December 25, 1831, have I repeated to myself the beautiful lines written by General Burgoyne, under a similar affliction, substituting 'Mary' for 'Anna':—

> "'Encompassed in an angel's frame
> An angel's virtues lay;
> Too soon did heaven assert its claim
> And take its own away.
>
> "'My Mary's worth, my Mary's charms
> Can nevermore return.
> What now shall fill these widowed arms?
> Ah! me, my Mary's urn—
> Ah! me, ah! me, my Mary's urn.'"

One of his descendants, a great-grandchild, writes me that the family knew well she would learn from others that he was a great man; "they told me he was only a good one. My father spent many Christmas holidays with his grandparents. His grandmother was an invalid and intolerant of the slightest noise, but his grandfather was ever ready to be his playfellow and companion. Every morning and evening he would take him by the hand and bid him be very quiet; then on tiptoe, with finger on his lips, he would take him to her room to say good-morning and good-night. He was a devoted lover every day of her life. He was a humble but devoted Christian. And he said he never failed nightly to say the little prayer, 'Now I lay me down to sleep,' which he learned at his mother's knee as soon as he could lisp."

With Marshall, the Chief Justices who had participated in the Revolution ended. Taney, though born during the

Revolution, was twenty-two when Washington died. At fifty-nine he was Chief Justice; he died in the eighty-eighth year of his age in Washington.

Taney was a man of iron will and undaunted courage, braved public opinion boldly when he thought it his duty, and, though naturally vehement and passionate, he used no harsh or vindictive language toward his traducers, and his temper was kept under perfect control. Even when engaged in politics, the harshest expressions ever used by him were at a public meeting called by his political friends to greet him after his nomination as Secretary of the Treasury had been rejected by the Senate. It was the first time in the history of the Government that the Senate had refused to confirm a Cabinet Minister nominated by the President. Mr. Webster, in a speech at a public dinner, had alluded to Taney as "the pliant instrument of the President, ready to do his bidding"; for Taney, as Secretary of the Treasury, had ordered the removal of the public deposits from the United States Bank. At the meeting to which I refer Taney said: "Neither my principles nor my habits lead me to bandy words of reproach with Mr. Webster or any one else. But it is well known that he has found the bank a profitable client, and I submit to the public whether the facts I have stated do not furnish ground for believing that he has become its 'pliant instrument' and is prepared on all occasions to do its bidding whenever and wherever it may choose to require him. In the situation in which he has placed himself before the public, it would far better become him to vindicate himself from imputations to which he stands justly liable than to assail others."

He had advised General Jackson in 1832 to veto the bill renewing the charter of the United States Bank, and he aided in preparing the veto message; in fact, he was the only member of the Cabinet who favored the veto. The correspondence between General Jackson and Taney in August, 1833, has convinced every one that the removal of the public deposits from the United States Bank was not the act of the pliant instrument of the President, but of a Cabinet Minister in execution of a policy which he had urged upon the President.

The opinion in the Dred Scott case elicited storms of

disapprobation from heated partisans; the political leaders in paroxysms of rage traduced the Court and the Chief Justice, and, for the first time in the history of the nation, a political party through its platform of principles and the President elected by them, inculcated the doctrine " that if the policy of the government upon vital questions affecting the whole people is to be irrevocably fixed by decisions of the Supreme Court, the instant they are made in ordinary litigation between parties in personal actions the people will have ceased to be their own rulers, having to that extent practically resigned their government into the hands of that eminent tribunal."

The arbitrament of the Supreme Court being rejected, nothing was left but the sword. The judgment delivered in the Dred Scott case has been tried, as in the olden times, by an appeal to the wager of battle, and in that way it has been reversed.

When war came, Taney was not deterred by clamor, nor by flaming swords, nor by the insolence of power, nor by threats, from the performance of his official duty.

A distinguished gentleman of the Baltimore bar, who witnessed the trial of the Merryman *habeas corpus* case in Baltimore, thus described the scene to me:—

" I do not think that there ever was a more striking illustration of judicial dignity and self-restraint than what occurred at the hearing of the celebrated *habeas corpus* case of John Merryman in 1861. It would not be easy to conceive a more remarkable manifestation of the control which one old and infirm man could exercise over a large and highly-excited crowd by the mere force of his own personality and his hold on the public respect and affection. Long before the hour of the hearing the streets leading to the Court-house were filled with a dense mass of people. It was not long after April 19, 1861, and the popular mind had lost but little of the excitement of that occasion. The crowd, nevertheless, was comparatively quiet, but the suppression of feeling only added to its intensity. It would have needed but a word to start a popular movement which would not have been checked, in any way, by the knowledge that a very considerable body of regular troops was at Fort McHenry. As the Chief Justice came down for the meeting of the Court he was leaning upon the arm of his young grandson. As he approached the crowd, half a square from the court-room, every man lifted his hat, and a pathway was opened through the dense mass of people for him and his companion to pass. As the Chief Justice walked through, the whole crowd uncovered themselves, and they continued uncovered until he entered the Court-house. The immediate approach to the entrance was so closely packed that the Chief Justice was compelled to pass down the side of the Court-house to a private entrance, which gave him access to the bench from the rear of the building. The court-room itself was so much crowded that I think it would have been difficult to pack a half dozen more men in it.

"When the Chief Justice came in the most absolute silence prevailed. He asked the clerk in his usual quiet and low tones, whether any return had been made to the writ. The officer whom General Cadwalader had made the bearer of his return proceeded to read it. His manner was not calculated to diminish the feeling of indignation and resentment, which was caused by the avowed determination of the General to disobey the mandate of the Court and disregard the rights of Mr. Merryman as a citizen. An intense but subdued excitement became visible throughout the court-room, though the dead silence continued. The same excitement was soon communicated to the people outside. Nothing but the manner and bearing of the Chief Justice, and the veneration in which he was held, prevented an outbreak on the spot, of which General Cadwalader's messenger would probably have been the victim. So great, however, was the silent influence of the Chief Justice, and the respect for his person and authority, that no demonstration of any kind was made, and the city was thus saved from a catastrophe which, in the then state of the public mind, could not have been otherwise than very disastrous, both in itself and its consequences. It was very difficult to conceive, without witnessing it, that in a case involving the liberty of the citizen, and the legal and constitutional guarantees that secure it, any judicial officer impressed with the responsibility of the occasion, and indignant, as he must have been, at the defiance of his mandate and the asserted supremacy of the Federal Executive over the Constitution and laws, could have so dealt with the matter that the most careful observer would trace no departure, in the slightest degree, from the tranquil dignity which characterized the Court in the daily exercise of its ordinary jurisdiction."

Taney was not ambitious of political office; political life did not suit his taste, because he was a thoroughly trained lawyer and devoted to his profession. He was a classical scholar and studied English with uncommon care. His style was simple and severe; in perspicuity of finish and language he was unsurpassed. He was a constant student; his studies embracing literature ancient and modern. His memory was surprising and his mind so logical that its power of subtle analysis, says Mr. Justice Curtis, exceeded that of any man he ever knew. He was a man of high breeding, and of extraordinary delicacy and courtesy; though vehement by nature, he was gentle in manners, generous to his opponents, and Mr. Justice Curtis says, " as absolutely free from vanity or self-conceit as any man he ever knew."

The touch of romance in his nature was exhibited by his fondness for flowers, and his beautiful devotion to the memory of his mother, by whose side he wished to be buried. Though shy and reserved in his manners, he was most attractive at home, being to a large extent the companion of his daughters, for he had no sons. He married Miss Key, the sister of the author of the " Star-Spangled Banner." His love for her is portrayed in the following letter, dated January 7, 1852, at Washington:—

" I cannot, my dearest wife, suffer the seventh of January to pass without renewing to you the pledges of love which I made to you on January 7th forty-six years ago, and although I am sensible that in that long period I have done many things which I ought not to have done, and have left undone many things that I ought to have done, yet in constant affection to you I have never wavered, never being insensible how much I owe to you, and now pledge to you again a love as true and sincere as that I offered on January 7, 1806."

She died of yellow fever in 1855 at Old Point Comfort. Her death was a sore affliction to him; in a letter addressed to Mr. Justice Curtis, November 3, 1855, he says: " The chastisement with which it has pleased God to visit me has told sensibly on a body already worn by age as well as upon the mind; I shall meet you with a broken heart and with a broken spirit."

Religion was prominent in his life; he was a regular communicant in the Catholic Church: in a letter to his kinsman, he says: " Most thankful am I that the reading, reflection, studies, and experience of a long life have strengthened and confirmed my faith in the Catholic Church, which has never ceased to teach her children how they should live and how they should die."

He prized official integrity to a degree which is hardly appreciated by those not so delicate as he was; hence he refused, while Secretary of the Treasury, to accept a box of cigars as a present from the Collector of the Port of New York; he declined the dedication to him of Mr.

Seward's speech on the French Spoliation Claims, lest its acceptance might be construed into interference in a measure pending before Congress. He never spoke ill of any man; he espoused the cause of the oppressed; and was charitable to the poor; he liberated the slaves that came to him as an inheritance, aided them in their employments and took care of them when in want.

He was tall in stature, pale, thin, looked infirm and ready to drop into the grave. Near-sightedness gave him a sort of immobility of expression. He was affected with a morbid sensibility caused by delicate health from early youth; toward the end of his life he looked like a disembodied spirit, for his mind was not affected by his age or the infirmities of his body. He died October 12, 1864, in the eighty-eighth year of his age, and was buried by the side of his mother. He died in Washington poor and neglected; his life went out like a candle expiring in its socket in a deserted chamber.

The lines of Horace attached by him to his autograph sent on June 24, 1864, to Mrs. Alice Key Pendleton, are characteristic of the man:—

> Justum et tenacem propositi virum
> Non civium ardor prava jubentium
> Non vultus instantis tyranni
> Mente quatit solida.

The judicial life of Jay, Rutledge, and Ellsworth was so short that the interest attached to them as Chief Justices is diminished by the admiration they elicit as leaders of the Revolution, and as statesmen.

All three were appointed by Washington. The judiciary bill was approved September 24, 1789. Jay was nominated and confirmed two days afterward. So great was the opinion entertained of his character and abilities that Washington gave him a choice of the offices under the Government. He preferred the office of Chief Justice as more in accord with his taste, his education, and his habits. Before this he had been Minister to Spain, and President of Congress, and Secretary of State, and had negotiated the Treaty of Peace in 1782-83; he had also filled the office of Chief Justice of the State of New York; and, as a

member of the New York Convention, had taken a leading part in framing the Constitution of that State in 1777.

It was he who prepared the address of the Continental
Congress to the people of Great Britain, a vigorous, patriotic paper which fixed the eyes of the people upon him.

His skill in negotiating the Treaty of Peace is universally recognized.   He induced Franklin to concur with
him and John Adams, in disregarding the instructions of
Congress, to act in concert with our ally, the King of
France, because he believed Vergennes, the French Minister, was playing a double part, injurious to the interests
of the United States.   At the time the propriety of his
conduct was questioned, but subsequent disclosures of
contemporary correspondence have vindicated his sagacity.   While holding the office of Chief Justice he was
appointed Minister to Great Britain, and negotiated the
celebrated treaty which, though approved by Washington,
was so much condemned by the public.   On his return
from England, having resigned the office of Chief Justice,
he was elected Governor of New York, which office he
filled for two terms.   During his second term the political
tide was turning against the Federalist party to which he
belonged.

The Republicans in the New York Legislature introduced a bill to divide the State into election districts, and
provide for the choice of Presidential electors by the people in the respective districts; this was defeated by the
Federalist majority on Constitutional grounds.   After the
adjournment of the Legislature, it was thought that the
district system would best promote the political interests
of the Federal party.   Hamilton, in a letter dated May 7,
1800, proposed to Jay that he should reconvene the Legislature for the purpose of having passed the very bill
which they had just defeated.   Hamilton urged Jay not
to be over-scrupulous, and that to the extraordinary nature of the crisis scruples of delicacy and propriety ought
to give way.   This letter was found among Jay's papers
thus endorsed: "Proposing a measure for party purposes which I do not think it becomes me to adopt."

Washington placed the untried Constitution under the
guardianship of a Chief Justice who was not only a lawyer,
but a statesman and a diplomatist, and especially a man

familiar with the practical difficulties encountered in the administration of government during the Revolution, and under the régime of the Confederation.

Although the decision rendered by Jay in Chisholm vs. Georgia was reversed by the Constitutional amendment adopted in 1798, yet the tone of the decision, and the logical deduction from its principles, were significant of the change in the structure of the Government erected by the Constitution. The country was startled by the claim that the people of the United States, as the sovereign people of a nation, had established a Constitution by which it was their wish that the States should be bound, and to which the State Constitutions should be made to conform; that the sovereignty of the nation is in the people of the nation, and the residuary sovereignty of each State in the people of each State. This was really the only important case decided by the Court while Jay was Chief Justice.

He sat on the bench robed in the traditionary gown of the English judges, but he discarded the wig to wear the hair off the forehead, tied behind into a cue. He was a little less than six feet in height, well-formed but thin, his complexion without color, his eyes blue and penetrating, his nose aquiline, and his chin pointed. His dress was black; his manner gentle and unassuming, but somewhat chilled by the dignity of the statesman. His style of speaking was quiet and limpid without gesture. He was philanthropic, and desired the extinction of slavery in accordance with a sentiment then prevalent even in the South, whose leading men at that time, especially those of Virginia, as Mr. Webster tells us, " felt and acknowledged that it was a moral and political evil; that it weakened the arm of the free man and kept back the progress and success of free labor."

Jay married in 1774 Miss Livingston who, it is said, was very beautiful. She was the life of fashionable society in Philadelphia while he was Secretary of Foreign Affairs under the Confederacy. Several children were the fruit of this marriage. His wife having suffered from delicate health for several years, died shortly after his retirement from public life.

Jay was by nature of a quick temper, but he kept it under control; he was straightforward and sincere; he had strong family and local attachments; he had an elevated sense of justice; was tenacious in his friendships and in his enmities; his mind was vigorous, exact, and logical; penetration was its characteristic; but he was not a full or learned man, nor did imagination enlarge the compass of his thought or impart grace and flexibility to his mind. The Bible was his constant study and his religion was a part of his being and displayed itself in the uniform tenor of his life. But the religion which descended to him from his ancestors came tinctured with the spirit of intolerance, which Buckle tells us characterized the Huguenots wherever they had power in France, the result, as he says, of that *odium theologicum* which is one of the characteristics of civil government when controlled by ecclesiastical influences. Mr. Jay proposed in the New York Convention to exclude Roman Catholics from the privileges of citizenship, but fortunately the proposition was defeated by the spirit of the Revolution, which was stronger than the expiring fanaticism of the age.

When Jay resigned in 1795, Washington at once appointed John Rutledge, of South Carolina, to succeed him. He held the office but six months, having been rejected by the Senate on account of his violent opposition to Jay's treaty with Great Britain, and also, it is believed, on account of mental infirmity, caused by exposure in the swamps of South Carolina during the Revolutionary War. He was a very interesting and remarkable man. His intellectual abilities were great, and his character earnest and resolute. His father was an Irish physician who settled in Charleston in 1734. He soon married a young lady of fortune who was a mother at fifteen and a widow at twenty-six. John was born in 1739 and was the oldest of seven children. Having been fairly educated in the classics, he commenced the study of law at seventeen. After two years he went to London and entered as a student in the Temple. Mansfield was presiding then in the King's Bench; Henley, afterward Lord Northington, was Lord Keeper; Pratt, afterward Lord Chancellor and Earl of Camden, was Attorney-General; and Burke was just rising to fame, and Thurlow was just emerging from obscurity. He remained three years in the Temple, and having been called to the bar, returned to Charleston in

1761. He commenced practice at the Charleston bar when he was twenty-two. His success was immediate. Instead of rising by degrees, he burst forth at once an able lawyer and an accomplished orator. His ideas were clear and strong; his utterance rapid, but distinct; his active and energetic manner of speaking forcibly impressed his sentiments on the mind and heart; he successfully used both argument and wit.

When the news of the passage of the Stamp Act reached Charleston he was chosen, by an assembly of the people, one of the delegates to the first Congress held in New York. Afterward, in 1774, he was sent with his brother, Edward Rutledge, to the Continental Congress. At the meeting to appoint delegates, question arose as to the power which should be conferred on them. Rutledge insisted that they should have plenary discretion, with power to pledge the people of South Carolina to abide by whatever the delegates would agree to; some one asked what must be done in case the delegates made a bad use of their power? His laconic answer was, " Hang them."

The Province of South Carolina on March 26, 1776, adopted a State Constitution and established a State government; Rutledge was chosen President, or Governor. When the British fleet of forty vessels approached Charleston, early in June, 1776, the decision and energy of the Governor caused the superiority of his genius to be acknowledged by all. In the course of a few days five or six thousand men were assembled for the defence of Charleston. General Charles Lee, who had been appointed by Congress to take command in the Southern Department, said that Fort Moultrie was a slaughter pen, and advised Governor Rutledge to order its abandonment. Rutledge declined to give the order, and wrote thus to Moultrie: " General Lee wishes you to evacuate the fort, you will not do so without an order from me. I would sooner cut off my right hand than write one."

In 1780 Charleston fell, and no one could say when the Legislature might again be able to meet. That body, before its adjournment, clothed " the Governor and such of his council as he could conveniently consult with power to do everything necessary for the public good, except take away the life of a citizen without a legal trial."

Hence he was called " Dictator John." The British over-
ran South Carolina, drove Rutledge from the State and
defeated Gates. But Rutledge did not despair; he applied
all his energies to the task of reorganizing the army; he
commissioned Sumter as a Brigadier-General, he conferred elevated rank on Pickens and Marion, procured
from Congress a commission for Morgan, so that when
Greene arrived he found Morgan at the head of his rifle-
men in Gates's army. Greene, in a letter written after the
battle of Cowpens, describes the wretched condition of
affairs, and then says: "We are obliged to subsist ourselves by our industry, aided by the influence of Governor
Rutledge, who is one of the first characters I ever met."
In January, 1782, he called the Legislature together and
surrendered his powers, because he thought them too
great to be vested in any man in a free country, except
to meet a pressing emergency temporarily.

No complaint was ever preferred against him for his
administration while Dictator. He was an active and
prominent member of the Convention which framed the
Constitution of the United States; he overcame the opposition which the Constitution met with in South Carolina,
when it was submitted for ratification to the State Convention. He filled the office of Chancellor of the Equity
Courts of his State and in 1791 was appointed Chief Justice of its law court. He was appointed by Washington
and confirmed by the Senate as an Associate Justice of the
Supreme Court of the United States immediately on its
organization in September, 1789, his commission being
first in date. Having been appointed Chief Justice of
South Carolina in February, 1791, he resigned the office
of Associate Justice of the Supreme Court. In 1792 he
lost his wife, an event that touched the deepest feelings of
his heart, for he was both gentle and tender by nature.
He died July 18, 1800, leaving eight children, six sons and
two daughters.

He was tall, well-framed and robust; his forehead broad,
his eyes dark and piercing; his mouth indicated firmness
and decision; his hair, combed back according to the fashion of the day, was powdered and tied behind. His aspect
was resolute, and wore an expression of thought and determination. His feelings were warm and ardent, and he

had an impulsive energy which, however, was controlled by a vigorous common sense. Earnestness was the secret of his power; the supreme element of his character was "force."

Ellsworth was appointed March 4, 1796, and he too, like Jay, while holding the office of Chief Justice, was sent on a foreign mission. He was selected by President Adams as one of the envoys to France on February 2, 1799, and left for Paris in the fall of that year. He attained eminence at the bar very early in life, but he cut no figure in the Revolution until he took his seat in Congress in the fall of 1778; from that period till 1782 he was an active member of the Committee of Appeals and aided Robert Morris in his financial schemes. After the Revolutionary war he was a conspicuous member of the Convention of 1787. He was jealous of the dominance of the larger States, and to his unyielding pertinacity the country is indebted for the final compromise of the Constitution, which gave to each State equality of representation in the Senate. He always urged the necessity of preserving the existence and agency of the State governments; the only chance, said he, of maintaining a general Government lies in creating it on those of the individual States. To the sarcasm of Wilson, "that we are forming a government for men and not for imaginary beings called States," and to the invective of King against "the phantom of State sovereignty," he replied "that his happiness depended on the States as much as a new born infant on its mother for nourishment." In the Convention of his State called to ratify the Constitution he made an admirable speech, urging union as the only mode of saving Connecticut from the rapacity of New York on one side and of Massachusetts on the other. He said: "If we do not unite shall we not be like Issachar of old, a strong ass crouching down between two burdens?"

Elected to the Senate under the new Constitution, he framed the Judiciary Act of 1789, which alone is a monument to his skill and intellectual vigor. While he presided in the Court but little business came before it, and no case of great importance was decided.

Ellsworth was tall, erect, with firm and penetrating blue eyes, and of dignified demeanor. His manners were plain, simple, and unaffected. Patient, attentive, and laborious he was endowed with great power of reflection, investigation, and argument. President Adams speaks of him " as a great man of business." He himself said that he had no imagination nor had he any fertility of mind or opulence of knowledge. It might be said of him what Hazlitt said of Pope: " He would be more delighted with a patent lamp than with the

' Pale reflex of Cynthia's brow,'

that fills the sky with its soft silent lustre, that trembles through the cottage window, and cheers the watchful mariner on the lonely wave."

In Ellsworth's speeches there is no fancy, no grace, no splendor of diction, no genius; for genius is a mind in which imagination, intelligence, and feeling exist in an elevated proportion and in exact equation. It has a penetrating view of ideas, and incarnates them powerfully in brass, in marble, or in language. Ellsworth was a man who studied one subject at a time and kept at it till he mastered it; he seldom worked with other men's tools; he had great penetration, remarkable power of analysis, and, like most men of intellect without much culture, he seized on the strong point, and left it for no other—like Hercules with his club, armed with a single weapon, but that one powerful and massive. He was earnest in tone, energetic in manner, lucid and simple in language, illustrating by a diagram, not a picture. In early life he was intended for the ministry, and studied theology a year after he graduated from Princeton College. He was called to the bar in 1771, and married shortly afterward Miss Wolcott. Having nothing to live on, his father gave him a lease of a small, wild, uncultivated farm near Hartford. After three years' struggle with poverty, success at the bar was attained. Although a grave and religious man of the New England type, he had conversational talents, and was agreeable in the social circle. He was a domestic man and especially fond of little children. Both of these traits are portrayed in the following letter written to his wife while he was Senator in the first Congress when sitting in New York:—

" The family in which I live have no white children. But I often amuse myself with a colored one about the size of our little daughter, who peeps into my door now and then with a long story, which I cannot more than half understand. Our two sons I sometimes fancy that I pick out among the little boys playing at marbles in the street. Our eldest daughter is, I trust, alternately employed between her book and her wheel. You must teach her what is useful; the world will teach her enough of what is not. The nameless little one I am hardly enough acquainted with to have much idea of; yet I think she occupies a corner of my heart, especially when I consider her at your breast."

The story told of him by one of his biographers I can scarcely credit. After a protracted absence in Europe, he returned home. The whole family, who were expecting his arrival, descried him at a distance in his carriage, and hastened forth to welcome him. The biographer says he alighted from his carriage; but he spoke not to his wife, nor did he embrace his children. He glanced not even at his twin boys; but leaning over the gate and covering his face, he silently breathed a prayer in gratitude to God. The picture may be true; but it is not natural. Any man, except, perhaps, Simeon Stylites, would have kissed his wife and children first.

Chase, when made Chief Justice in 1864, though younger than Taney, older than Marshall, in face, figure and majestic presence, was more distinguished than either. He was less a lawyer than Taney, but he brought to the bench a stock of learning equal to that which Marshall had begun with. His health failed in 1870; his eyes lost their lustre, and his face became wan and emaciated, so that in fact his judicial life practically terminated several years before his death in 1873. When appointed he had been for many years engaged in political affairs, and it was difficult for him to throw off the hopes and aspirations and love of power which political life engenders. He was, in fact, an able politician, and felt that he could best serve his country as a statesman. He gives this estimate of himself in a letter to the Rev. Joshua Leavitt, dated October 7, 1863. " I really feel," he says, "as if with God's blessing I could administer the government of this country so as to secure and imperdibilize (there's a new word for you) our institutions, and create a party fundamentally and thoroughly democratic, which would guarantee a succession of successful administrations."

This aspiration was not entirely suppressed while he was robed in the ermine of justice. Mr. Justice Clifford says: "Appointed, as it were, by common consent, he seated himself easily and naturally in the chair of justice, and gracefully answered every demand upon the station, whether it had respect to the dignity of the office or to elevation of the individual character of the incumbent, or to his firmness, purity, or vigor of mind. From the first moment he drew the judicial robes around him he viewed all questions submitted to him, as a judge, in the calm atmosphere of the bench, and with the deliberate consideration of one who feels that he is determining issues for the remote and unknown future of a great people. Throughout his judicial career he always maintained that dignity of courage and that calm, noble, and unostentatious presence that uniformly characterized his manners and deportment; in the social circle and in his intercourse with his brethren, his suggestions were always couched in friendly terms, and were never marred by severity or harshness."

The faculty of reason was very broad and strong in him, yet without being vast or surprising; his education had all been of a kind to discipline and invigorate his natural powers; his oratory was vigorous, with those qualities of clearness, force, and earnestness which produce conviction. His force of will was prodigious; his courage to brave and his fortitude to endure were absolute. His adhesion to the Christian faith was constant and sincere, and he accepted it as the master and ruler of his life. He had devout confidence in the moral government of the world by a personal God, as a present and real power controlling and directing all human affairs. He was all his life a great student of the Scriptures, and no modern speculations ever shook his belief.

Chief Justice Waite was a native of the State of Connecticut, and a graduate of Yale College. His father held a high judicial position in Connecticut. Having studied law he emigrated to Ohio, prompted, no doubt, by the sturdy independence of his own nature. He achieved marked success in his profession, which caused him to be made one of the counsel of the United States in the matter of the Geneva arbitration. His argument in reply to that of Sir Roundell Palmer attracted some attention, but he was almost unknown to the profession and to the country when appointed Chief Justice by President Grant in January, 1874. He was not a great man, nor was he born to be the leader of men; nor had he any great ambition; nor any of that genius which in its struggle for supremacy seeks to surmount the world and say, like Lucifer: "Place my throne by the throne of God." But to a certain extent his elevation reinforced his character. There is no man called suddenly into public life who, in passing from his own house to preside in the capital of the Union over the most dignified, if not the most powerful, tribunal on earth, has not been changed—transfigured. If he has not been it is an evidence of such hopeless mediocrity that even the hand of God would hardly be able to produce anything from it.

Waite was trained in the ways of the law and of the courts; his opinions do not convey the impression of a commanding intellect, but they are clear, terse, vigorous and judicial. He was absorbed in the obligations and responsibilities of his office, having no ambition beyond it. He was in manner plain, unattractive, and unostentatious; his genial and social nature, combined with amiable courtesy, endeared him to the members of the bar. He was an upright and impartial judge, a good man, and a pious Christian.

JOHN CAMPBELL SHAIRP

THE LITERARY THEORY OF CULTURE

[Address by John Campbell Shairp, poet, critic, and essayist, Principal of the United College, St. Andrew's (born in Houstoun, West Lothian, July 30, 1819; died at Ormsary in Argyll, September 18, 1885), delivered as one of a series of addresses on Culture and Religion, before the University of St. Andrew's.]

A true poet and brilliant critic of the present time, admired by all for his fine and cultivated genius, and to me endeared by never-fading memories of early companionship, has identified his name with a very different view of culture from that which I brought before you the last time I addressed you. If Professor Huxley's is the exclusively scientific view of culture, Mr. Arnold's may be called the literary or æsthetic one. In discussing the former theory, I attempted to examine it in the light of facts, and to avoid applying to it any words which its author might disown. For mere appeal to popular prejudice should have no place in discussions about truth, and he who has recourse to that weapon in so far weakens the cause he advocates. If, however, I was constrained to call attention to some not unimportant facts of human nature which that theory fails to account for, this should be regarded not as appeal to unreasoning prejudice, but as a statement of omitted facts.

But whatever might be said of Professor Huxley's view, as leaving out of sight the spiritual capacities and needs of man, the same objection cannot equally be urged against Mr. Arnold's theory of culture. He fully recognizes religion as an element, and a very important one, in his theory; only we may see cause to differ from him in the place which he assigns to it. Though I believe Mr. Arnold's theory to be defective when taken as a total philosophy of life, yet so large-minded and generous are the views it exhibits, so high and refined are the motives it urges for self-improvement, that I believe no one can seriously and candidly consider what he says without deriving good from it. As a recent writer has truly said, "The author of this theory deserves much praise for having brought the subject before men's minds, and forced a little unwilling examination on the 'self-complacent but very uncultured British public.'"

Many who now hear me may have probably read in Mr. Arnold's several works all his pleadings for culture. To these the recapitulation of his views which I shall give may be somewhat tedious, but I hope those who know his writings will bear with me while I briefly go over his views for the sake of those of my hearers who may be less acquainted with them.

In Mr. Arnold's view, the aim of culture is not merely to render an intelligent being more intelligent, to improve our capacities to the uttermost, but, in words which he borrows from Bishop Wilson, "to make reason and the kingdom of God prevail." It is impelled not merely by the scientific desire to see things as they are, but rather by the moral endeavor to know more and more the universal order, which seems intended in the world, that we may conform to it ourselves, and make others conform to it; in short, that we may help to make the will of God prevail in us and around us. In this, he says, is seen the moral, social, beneficent nature of culture, that while it seeks the best knowledge, the highest science that is to be had, it seeks them in order to make them tell on human life and character.

The aim of culture, therefore, is the perfection of our human nature on all its sides, in all its capacities. First, it tries to determine in what this perfection consists, and in order to solve this question, it consults the manifold human experience that has expressed itself in such diverse ways, throughout science, poetry, philosophy, history, as well as through religion. And the conclusion which culture reaches is, Mr. Arnold holds, in harmony with the voice of religion. For it places human perfection in an internal

condition of soul, in the growth and predominance of our
humanity proper, as distinguished from our animality.

Again, it does not rest content with any condition of
soul, however excellent, but presses ever onward to an
ampler growth, to a gradual harmonious expansion of
those gifts of thought and feeling which make the peculiar
dignity, wealth, and happiness of human nature.   Not a
having and resting, but a growing and becoming, is the
true character of perfection as culture conceives it.
Again, in virtue of that bond of brotherhood which binds
all men to each other, whether they will it or not, this
perfection cannot be an isolated individual perfection.
Unless the obligation it lays on each man to consider
others as well as himself is recognized, the perfection attained must be a stunted, ignoble one, far short of true
perfection.

In all these three considerations the aim of culture, Mr.
Arnold thinks, coincides with the aim of religion.

First, in that it places perfection not in any external
good, but in an internal condition of soul—" The kingdom
of God is within you."

Secondly, in that it sets before men a condition not of
having and resting, but of growing and becoming as the
true aim—" Forgetting those things which are behind,
and reaching forth unto those things which are before."

Thirdly, in that it holds that a man's perfection cannot
be self-contained, but must embrace the good of others
equally with his own, and as the very condition of his own
—" Look not every man on his own things, but every man
also on the things of others."

These three notes belong alike to the perfection which
culture aims at and to that which religion enjoins.

But there is a fourth note of perfection as conceived by
culture, in which, as Mr. Arnold thinks, it transcends the
aim of religion.   " As an harmonious expansion of all the
powers which make the beauty and worth of human nature," Mr. Arnold holds that it " goes beyond religion, as
religion is generally conceived among us."   For religion,
Mr. Arnold thinks, aims at the cultivation of some, and
these, no doubt, the highest powers of the soul, at the expense, even at the sacrifice, of other powers, which it
regards as lower.   So it falls short of that many-sided,

even-balanced, all-embracing totality of development
which is the aim of the highest culture.

Mark well this point, for, though I cannot stop to discuss it now, I must return to it after I have set before you
Mr. Arnold's view in its further bearings.

After insisting, then, that culture is the study of perfection, harmonious, all-embracing, consisting in becoming
something rather than in having something, in an inward
condition of soul rather than in any outward circumstances, Mr. Arnold goes on to show how hard a battle
culture has to fight in this country, with how many of our
strongest tendencies, our most deep-rooted characteristics, it comes into direct, even violent collision. The
prominence culture gives to the soul, the inward and
spiritual condition, as transcending all outward goods put
together, comes into conflict with our worship of a mechanical and material civilization. The social aspirations
it calls forth for the general elevation of the human family
conflict with our intense individualism, our "every man
for himself." The totality of its aim, the harmonious expansion of all human capacities, contradicts our inveterate
one-sidedness, our absorption each in his own one pursuit.
It conflicts, above all, with the tendency so strong in us
to worship the means and to forget the ends of life.

Everywhere, as he looks around him, Mr. Arnold sees
this great British people chasing the means of living with
unparalleled energy, and forgetting the inward things of
our being, which alone give these means their value. We
are, in fact, idol-worshippers without knowing it. We
worship freedom, the right to do every man as he chooses,
careless whether the thing we choose to do be good or
not. We worship railroads, steam, coal, as if these made
a nation's greatness, forgetting that

> " .   .   . by the soul
> Only the nations shall be great and free."

We worship wealth, as men have done in all ages, in
spite of the voices of all the wise, only, perhaps, never
before in the world's history with such unanimity, such
strength and consistency of devotion, as at this hour, in
this land. I must quote the words in which he makes

culture address the mammon-worshippers—those who have either gotten wealth, or, being hot in the pursuit of it, regard wealth and welfare as synonymous:—

"Consider," he makes culture say, "these people, their way of life, their habits, their manners, the very tones of their voice; look at them attentively, observe the literature they read (if they read any), the things that give them pleasure, the words which come forth from their mouths, the thoughts which make the furniture of their minds; would any amount of wealth be worth having with the condition that one was to become like these people by having it? Thus," he says, "culture begets a dissatisfaction which is of the highest possible value in stemming the common tide of men's thoughts in a wealthy and industrious community, and which saves the future, as one may hope, from being wholly materialized and vulgarized, if it cannot save the present." Against all this absorbing faith in machinery, whatever form it takes, whether faith in wealth or in liberty, used or abused, or in coals and railroads, or in bodily health and vigor, or in population, Mr. Arnold lifts up an earnest protest.

It is an old lesson, but one which each age forgets and needs to be taught anew, men forgetting the inward and spiritual goods, and setting their hope on the outward and material ones. Against this all the wise of the earth have, each one in his day, cried aloud—the philosophers, moralists, and satirists of Greece and Rome, Plato, Epictetus, Seneca, and Juvenal, not less than Hebrew prophets and Christian apostles, up to that divine voice which said, "What shall it profit a man if he gain the whole world and lose his own soul?"

This same old lesson Mr. Arnold repeats, but in modern language, and turns against the shapes of idol-worship, which he sees everywhere around him. In contrast, then, to all the grosser interests that absorb us, he pleads for a mental and spiritual perfection, which has two sides, or prominent notes—beauty and intelligence—or, borrowing words which Swift first used, and which, since Mr. Arnold reproduced them, have become proverbial, "Sweetness and Light"—" An inward and spiritual activity having for its characters increased sweetness, increased light, increased life, increased sympathy."

The age of the world in which these two, "sweetness and light," were preëminently combined was, Mr. Arnold thinks, the best age of Athens—that which is represented in the poetry of Sophocles, in whom "the idea of beauty and a full-developed humanity" took to itself a religious and devout energy, in the strength of which it worked. But this was but for a moment of time, when the Athenian mind touched its acme. It was a hint of what might be when the world was ripe for it, rather than a condition which could then continue. In our own countrymen, Mr. Arnold believes, partly from the toughness and earnestness of the Saxon nature, partly from the predominance in our education of the Hebrew teaching, the moral and religious element has been drawn out too exclusively. There is among us an entire want of the idea of beauty, harmony, and completely rounded human excellence. These ideas are either unknown to us, or entirely misapprehended.

Mr. Arnold then goes on to contrast his idea of a perfectly and harmoniously developed human nature with the idea set up by Puritanism, and prevalent amid our modern multifarious churches. He grants that the church organizations have done much. They have greatly helped to subdue the grosser animalities, they have made life orderly, moral, serious. But when we go beyond this, and look at the standards of perfection which these religious organizations have held up, he finds them poor and miserable, starving more than a half, and that the finest part of human nature. He turns to modern religious life, as imaged in the "Noncomformist," or some other religious newspaper of the hour, and asks, What do we find there? "A life of jealousy of other churches, disputes, tea-meetings, openings of chapels, sermons." And then he exclaims, "Think of this as an ideal of human life, completing itself on all sides, and aspiring with all its organs after sweetness, light, and perfection!" "How," he asks, "is the ideal of a life so unlovely, so unattractive, so narrow, so far removed from a true and satisfying ideal of human perfection, . . . to conquer and transform all the vice and hideousness" that we see around us? "Indeed, the strongest plea for the study of perfection as pursued by culture, the clearest proof of the actual inade-

quacy of the idea of perfection held by the religious
organizations—expressing, as I have said, the most wide-
spread effort which the human race has yet made after
perfection—is to be found in the state of our life and
society with these in possession of it, and having been in
possession of it I know not how many years. We are all
of us included in some religious organization or other;
we all call ourselves, in the sublime and aspiring language
of religion, children of God. Children of God—it is an
immense pretension!—and how are we to justify it? By
the works which we do, and the words which we speak.
And the work which we collective children of God do,
our grand center of life, our city, is London! London,
with its unutterable external hideousness, and with its
internal canker, *publicè egestas, privatim opulentia*, unequaled in the world!"

These are severe words, yet they have a side of truth
in them. They portray our actual state so truly that,
though they may not be the whole truth, it is well we
should remember them, for they cannot be altogether
gainsaid.

I have now done with the exposition of Mr. Arnold's
theory. Before going on to note what seems to me to be
its radical defect, let me first draw attention to two of its
most prominent merits. His pleading for a perfection
which consists in a condition of soul, evenly and harmoniously developed, is but a new form of saying, "A
man's life consisteth not in the abundance of the things
which he possesseth." You will say, perhaps, Is not this
a very old truth? Why make such ado about it, as though
it were a new discovery? Has it not been expressed far
more strongly in the Bible than by Mr. Arnold? True,
it is an old truth, and we all know it is in the Bible. But
it is just these old truths which we know so well by the
ear, but so little with the heart, that need to be reiterated
to each age in the new language which it speaks. The
deepest truths are always becoming commonplaces, till
they are revivified by thought. And they are true thinkers and benefactors of their kind who, having thought
them over once more, and passed them through the
alembic of their own hearts, bring them forth fresh
minded, and make them tell anew on their generation.

And of all the old proverbs that this age needs applied to it, none is more needed than that which Mr. Arnold has proclaimed so forcibly.

Again, as to the defects which Mr. Arnold charges against our many and divided religious organizations, it cannot be denied that the moral and social results we see around us are far from satisfactory. In this state of things we cannot afford to neglect whatever aid that culture or any other power offers—to ignore those sides and forces of human nature which, if called into play, might render our ideal at once more complete and more efficient. There is much to excuse the complaints which highly educated men are apt to make, that religious minds have often been satisfied with a very partial and narrow development of humanity, such as does not satisfy, and ought not to satisfy, thoughtful and cultivated men. The wise and truly religious thing to do is not to get angry at such criticisms, and give them bad names, but to be candid, and listen to those who tell us of our shortcomings—try to see what justice there may be in them, and to turn whatever truth they may contain to good account.

Mr. Arnold sets before us a lofty aim ; he has bid us seek our good in something unseen, in a spiritual energy. In doing this he has done well. But I must hold that he has erred in his estimate of what that spiritual energy is, and he has missed, I think, the true source from which it is to be mainly derived. For in his account of it he has placed that as primary which is secondary and subordinate, and made that secondary which by right ought to be supreme.

You will remember that when describing his idea of the perfection to be aimed at he makes religion one factor in it—an important and powerful factor, no doubt, still but one element out of several, and that not necessarily the ruling element, but a means toward an end, higher, more supreme, more all-embracing than itself. The end was a many-sided, harmonious development of human nature, and to this end religion was only an important means. In thus assigning to religion a secondary, however important, place, this theory, as I conceive, if consistently acted on, would annihilate religion. There are things which are either ends in themselves or they are nothing; and such, I conceive, religion is. It either is supreme, a good in itself and for its own sake, or it is not at all. The first and great commandment must either be so set before us as to be obeyed, entered into, in and for itself, without any ulterior view, or it cannot be obeyed at all. It cannot be made subservient to any ulterior purpose. And herein is instanced "a remarkable law of ethics, which is well known to all who have given their minds to the subject." I shall give it in the words of one who has expressed it so well in his own unequaled language that it has been proposed to name it after him, Dr. Newman's law: "All virtue and goodness tend to make men powerful in this world; but they who aim at the power have not the virtue. Again: Virtue is its own reward, and brings with it the truest and highest pleasures; but they who cultivate it for the pleasure-sake are selfish, not religious, and will never gain the pleasure, because they never can have the virtue."

Apply this to the present subject. They who seek religion for culture-sake are æsthetic, not religious, and will never gain that grace which religion adds to culture, because they never can have the religion. To seek religion for the personal elevation, or even for the social improvement it brings, is really to fall from faith which rests in God and the knowledge of Him as the ultimate good, and has no by-ends to serve. And what do we see in actual life? There shall be two men, one of whom has started on the road of self-improvement from a mainly intellectual interest, from the love of art, literature, science, or from the delight these give, but has not been actuated by a sense of responsibility to a Higher than himself. The other has begun with some sense of God, and of his relation to Him, and starting from this center has gone on to add to it all the moral and mental improvement within his reach, feeling that, beside the pleasure these things give in themselves, he will thus best fulfil the purpose of Him who gave them, thus best promote the good of his fellow men, and attain the end of his own existence. Which of these two will be the highest man, in which will be gathered up the most excellent graces of character, the truest nobility of soul? You cannot doubt it. The sense that a man is serving a Higher than himself, with a service which will become ever more and more perfect freedom, evokes more profound, more humbling, more exalted emotions than anything else in the world can do.

The spirit of man is an instrument which cannot give out its deepest, finest tones, except under the immediate hand of the Divine Harmonist. That is, before it can educe the higher capacities of which human nature is susceptible, culture must cease to be merely culture, and pass over into religion. And here we see another aspect of that great ethical law already noticed as compassing all human action, whereby "the abandoning of some lower object in obedience to a higher aim is made the very condition of securing the said lower object." According to this law it comes that he will approach nearer to perfection, or (since to speak of perfection in such as we are sounds like presumption) rather let us say, he will reach farther, will attain to a truer, deeper, more lovely humanity, who makes not culture, but oneness with the will of God, his ultimate aim. The ends of culture, truly conceived, are best attained by forgetting culture and aiming higher. And what is this but translating into modern and less forcible language the old words, whose meaning is often greatly misunderstood, "Seek ye first the kingdom of God, and all other things will be added unto you?" But by seeking the other things first, as we naturally do, we miss not only the kingdom of God, but those other things also which are only truly attained by aiming beyond them.

Another objection to the theory we have been considering remains to be noted. Its starting-point is the idea of perfecting self; and though, as it gradually evolves, it tries to forget self, and to include quite other elements, yet it never succeeds in getting clear of the taint of self-reference with which it set out. While making this objection, I do not forget that Mr. Arnold, in drawing out his view, purposes as the end of culture to make reason and the kingdom of God prevail; that he sees clearly, and insists strongly, that an isolated self-culture is impossible; that we cannot make progress toward perfection ourselves unless we strive earnestly to carry our fellow men along with us. Still may it not with justice be said that these unselfish elements—the desire for others' good, the desire to advance God's kingdom on earth—are in this theory awakened, not simply for their own sakes, not chiefly because they are good in themselves, but because they are clearly discerned to be necessary to our self-perfection—elements apart from which this cannot exist?

And so it comes that culture, though made our end never so earnestly, cannot shelter a man from thoughts about himself, cannot free him from that which all must feel to be fatal to high character—continual self-consciousness. The only forces strong enough to do this are great truths which carry him out of and beyond himself, the things of the spiritual world sought, not mainly because of their reflex action on us, but for their own sakes, because of their own inherent worthiness. There is, perhaps, no truer sign that a man is really advancing than that he is learning to forget himself, that he is losing the natural thoughts about self in the thought of One higher than himself, to whose guidance he can commit himself and all men. This is no doubt a lesson not quickly learned; but there is no help to learning it in theories of self-culture which exalt man's natural self-seeking into a specious and refined philosophy of life.

Again, it would seem that in a world made like ours culture, as Mr. Arnold conceives it, instead of becoming an all-embracing bond of brotherhood, is likely to be rather a principle of exclusion and isolation. Culture such as he pictures is at present confessedly the possession of a very small circle. Consider, then, the average powers of men, the circumstances in which the majority must live, the physical wants that must always be uppermost in their thoughts, and say if we can conceive that, even in the most advanced state of education and civilization possible, high culture can become the common portion of the multitude. And with the few on a high level of cultivation, the many, to take the best, on a much lower, what is the natural result? Fastidious exclusiveness on the part of the former, which is hardly human, certainly not Christian. Take any concourse of men, from the House of Commons down to the humblest conventicle, how will the majority of them appear to eyes refined by elaborate culture, but not humanized by any deeper sentiment? To such an onlooker will not the countenances of most seem unlovely, their manners repulsive, their modes of thought commonplace—it may be, sordid? By any such concourse the man of mere culture will, I think, feel himself repelled, not attracted. So it must be, because culture, being mainly a literary and æsthetic product, finds little in the unlettered multitude that is akin to itself. It is, after all, a dainty and divisive quality, and cannot reach to the depths of humanity. To do this takes some deeper, broader, more brotherly impulse, one which shall touch the universal ground on which men are one, not that in which they differ —their common nature, common destiny, the needs that poor and rich alike share. For this we must look elsewhere than to culture, however enlarged.

The view I have been enforcing will appear more evident if from abstract arguments we turn to the actual lives of men. Take any of the highest examples of our race, those who have made all future generations their debtors. Can we imagine any of these being content to set before themselves, merely as the end of their endeavors, such an aim as the harmonious development of human nature? A Goethe, perhaps, might: and if we take him as the highest, we will take his theory likewise. Hardly, I think, Shakespeare, if we can conceive of him as ever having set before himself consciously any formal aim. But could we imagine St. Paul doing so, or Augustine, or Luther, or such men as Pascal or Archbishop Leighton? Would such a theory truly represent the ends they lived for, the powers that actuated them, the ideal whence they drew their strength? These men changed the moral orbit of the world, but by what lever did they change it? Not by seeking their own perfection, nor even by making the progress of the race their only aim. They found a higher, more permanent world on which to plant the lever that was to move this one. They sought first the advancement of the kingdom of God and truth for its own sake, and they knew that this embraced the true good of man and every other good thing.

Indeed, of culture put in the supreme place, it has been well said that it holds forth a hope for humanity by enlightening self, and not a hope for humanity by dying to self. This last is the hope which Christianity sets before us. It teaches, what indeed human experience in the long run teaches too, that man's chief good lies in ceasing from the individual self, that he may live in a higher personality, in whose purpose all the ends of our true personality are secure. The sayings in the Gospels to this effect will readily occur to every one. Some glimpse of the same truth had visited the mind of the speculative Greek poet four hundred years before the Christian era when he said:

> Τίς οἶδεν εἰ τό ζῆμ μέν ἐστι κατθανεῖν,
> Τὸ κατθανεῖν δὲ ζῆν;

> "Who knoweth whether life may not be death,
> And death itself be life?"

There is but one other thought I would submit to you. Those who build their chief hope for humanity on culture rather than on religion would raise men by bringing them into contact and sympathy with whatever of best and greatest the past has produced. But is not a large portion of what is best in the literature and the lives of past generations based on faith in God, and on the reality of communion with him as the first and chief good? Would this best any longer live and grow in men if you cut them off from direct access to its fountain-head, and confined them to the results which it has produced in past ages— if, in fact, you made the object of the soul's contemplation not God, but past humanity? Are we of these latter days to be content with the results of the communion of others, and not have direct access to it ourselves—to read and admire the high thoughts of à Kempis, Pascal, Leighton, and such men, and not to go on and drink for ourselves from the same living well-heads from which they drank? Not now, any more than in past ages, can the most be made of human character, even in this life, till we ascend above humanity—

> "Unless above himself he can
> Erect himself, how poor a thing is man!"

I cannot close without expressing a feeling which I dare say has been present to the minds of many here, as throughout this discourse they listened to the oft-repeated word *perfection*. Perfection! the very word seems like mockery when applied to such as we. For how poor a thing must any perfection be that is reached this side the grave! Far truer is that word of St. Augustine—"That is the true perfection of a man to find out his own imperfection." Yes, the highest perfection any one will attain in this life is to be ever increasingly sensible how imperfect he is. As perfection is put forward in the theory I have been examining, one cannot but feel that there is a very inadequate notion of the evil in the human heart that is to be cured, and of the nature of the powers that are needed to cope with it. And in this respect we cannot but be struck with how greatly Christianity differs from culture, and differs only to surpass it; its estimate of the disease is so much deeper, and the remedy to which it turns so far transcends all human nostrums. Christianity, too, holds out perfection as the goal. But in doing so its view is not confined to time, but contemplates an endless progression in far-on ages. The perfection the Culturists speak of, if it does not wholly exclude the other life, seems to fix the eye mainly on what can be done here, and not to take much account of what is beyond. That was a higher and truer idea of perfection which Leighton had: "It is a union with a Higher Good by love, that alone is endless perfection. The only sufficient object for man must be something that adds to and perfects his nature, to which he must be united in love; somewhat higher than himself, yea, the highest of all, the Father of spirits. That alone completes a spirit and blesses it—to love Him, the spring of spirits."

To sum up all that has been said, the defect in Mr. Arnold's theory is this: It places in the second and subordinate place that which should be supreme, and elevates to the position of command a power which, rightly understood, should be subordinate and ministrant to a higher than itself. The relation to God is first, this relation is last, and culture should fill up the interspace—culture, that is, the endeavor to know and use aright the nature which he has given us, and the world in which he has placed us. Used in such a way, culture is transmuted into something far higher, more beneficent, than it ever could become if it set up for itself and claimed the chief place.

I might now conclude, but there is a poem of Archbishop Trench's, one of his earliest, and most interesting, which so well embodies much that I have said, that I hope you will bear with me while I read a somewhat lengthy passage from it. The lines are simple, not greatly elaborated, but they are true, and they may, perhaps, fix the attention of some who by this time have grown weary of abstract and prosaic argument—according to that saying—

> "A verse may find him who a sermon flies."

A youth, a favored child of culture, when he has long sought and not found what he expected to find in culture, wanders forth desolate and desponding into the eastern desert. The irrevocable past lies heavy on him—his baffled purpose, his wasted years, his utter misery. So heart-forlorn is he that he is on the verge of self-destruction. At length, as he sits inconsolable beside a ruined temple in the desert, an old man stands by his side, and asks, "What is your sorrow?" The youth, lured by some strange sympathy in the old man's mien and voice, unburdens to him his grief, tells how he has tried to make and keep himself wise and pure and elevated above the common crowd, that in his soul's mirror he might find—

> "A reflex of the eternal mind,
> A glass to give him back the truth,"

how he has followed after ideal beauty, to live in its light, dwell beneath its shadow, but at length has found that this too is vanity and emptiness.

> "Till now, my youth yet scarcely done,
> The heart which I had thought to steep
> In hues of beauty, and to keep
> Its consecrated home and fane,
> That heart is soiled with many a stain,
> Which from without or from within
> Has gathered there till all is sin,
> Till now I only draw my breath,
> I live but in the hope of death."

After an interval the old man replies:—

" Ah me, my son,
A weary course your life has run;
And yet it need not be in vain
That you have suffered all this pain; . . 。
Nay, deem not of us as at strife,
Because you set before your life
A purpose, and a loftier aim
Than the blind lives of men may claim
For the most part; or that you sought,
By fixed resolve and solemn thought,
To lift your being's calm estate
Out of the range of time and fate.
Glad am I that a thing unseen,
A spiritual Presence, this has been
Your worship, this your young heart stirred.
But yet herein you proudly erred,
Here may the source of woe be found,
You thought to fling yourself around
The atmosphere of light and love
In which it was your joy to move;
You thought by efforts of your own
To take at last each jarring tone
Out of your life, till all should meet
In one majestic music sweet;
And deemed that in your own heart's ground
The root of good was to be found,
And that by careful watering
And earnest tendance we might bring
The bud, the blossom, and the fruit,
To grow and flourish from that root.
You deemed you needed nothing more
Than skill and courage to explore
Deep down enough in your own heart,
To where the well-head lay apart,
Which must the springs of being feed,
And that these fountains did but need
The soil that choked them moved away,
To bubble in the open day.
But thanks to Heaven it is not so:
That root a richer soil doth know
Than our poor hearts could e'er supply—
That stream is from a source more high;
From God it came, to God returns,
Not nourished from our scanty urns,
But fed from His unfailing river,
Which runs and will run on forever."

GOLDWIN SMITH

THE LAMPS OF FICTION

[Address of Goldwin Smith, author and professor of history (born in Reading, England, August 23, 1823; ———), delivered on the centenary of the birth of Sir Walter Scott.]

Ruskin has lighted seven lamps of Architecture to guide the steps of the architect in the worthy practice of his art. It seems time that lamps should be lighted to guide the steps of the writer of Fiction. Think what the influence of novelists now is, and how some of them use it! Think of the multitudes who read nothing but novels; and then look into the novels which they read! I have seen a young man's whole library consisting of thirty or forty of those paper-bound volumes, which are the bad tobacco of the mind. In England, I looked over three railway bookstalls in one day. There was hardly a novel by an author of any repute on one of them. There were heaps of nameless garbage, commended by tasteless, flaunting woodcuts, the promise of which was no doubt well kept within. Fed upon such food daily, what will the mind of a nation be? I say that there is no flame at which we can light the Lamp of Fiction purer or brighter than the genius of him in honor to whose memory we are assembled here to-day. Scott does not moralize. Heaven be praised that he does not. He does not set a moral object before him, nor lay down moral rules. But his heart, brave, pure, and true, is a law to itself; and by studying what he does, we may find the law for all who follow his calling. If seven lamps have been lighted for architecture, Scott will light as many for Fiction.

1068

I. The Lamp of Reality.—The novelist must ground his work in faithful study of human nature. There was a popular writer of romances, who, it was said, used to go round to the fashionable watering-places to pick up characters. That was better than nothing. There is another popular writer who, it seems, makes voluminous indices of men and things, and draws on them for his material. This also is better than nothing. For some writers, and writers dear to the circulating libraries too, might, for all that appears in their works, lie in bed all day, and write by night under the excitement of green tea. Creative art, I suppose they call this, and it is creative with a vengeance. Not so, Scott. The human nature which he paints, he has seen in all its phases, gentle and simple, in burgher and shepherd, Highlander, Lowlander, Borderer, and Islesman; he had come into close contact with it; he had opened it to himself by the talisman of his joyous and winning presence; he had studied it thoroughly with a clear eye and an all-embracing heart. When his scenes are laid in the past, he has honestly studied history. The history of his novels is perhaps not critically accurate, not up to the mark of our present knowledge, but in the main it is sound and true—sounder and more true than that of many professed historians, and even than that of his own historical works, in which he sometimes yields to prejudice, while in his novels he is lifted above it by his loyalty to his art.

II. The Lamp of Ideality.—The materials of the novelist must be real; they must be gathered from the field of humanity by his actual observation. But they must pass through the crucible of the imagination; they must be idealized. The artist is not a photographer, but a painter. He must depict, not persons, but humanity; otherwise he forfeits the artist's name, and the power of doing the artist's work in our hearts. When we see a novelist bring out a novel with one or two good characters or the same few characters over and over again, we may be sure that he is without the power of idealization. He has merely photographed what he has seen, and his stock is exhausted. It is wonderful what a quantity of the mere lees of such writers, more and more watered down, the

libraries go on complacently circulating, and the reviews
go on complacently reviewing. Of course, this power
of idealization is the great gift of genius. It is that which
distinguishes Homer, Shakespeare, and Walter Scott from
ordinary men. But there is also a moral effort in rising
above the easy work of mere description to the height of
art. Need it be said that Scott is thoroughly ideal, as well
as thoroughly real? There are vague traditions that this
man and the other was the original of some character of
Scott. But who can point out the man of whom a character in Scott is a mere portrait? It would be as hard
as to point out a case of servile delineation in Shakespeare. Scott's characters are never monsters or carica-
tures. They are full of nature; but it is universal nature.
Therefore they have their place in the universal heart,
and will keep that place forever. And mark that even in
his historical novels he is still ideal. Historical romance
is a perilous thing. The fiction is apt to spoil the fact,
and the fact the fiction; the history to be perverted and
the romance to be shackled; daylight to kill dreamlight,
and dreamlight to kill daylight. But Scott takes few
liberties with historical facts and characters; he treats
them with the costume and the manners of the period, as
the background of the picture. The personages with
whom he deals freely are the Peverils and the Nigels; and
these are his lawful property, the offspring of his own
imagination, and belong to the ideal.

III. The Lamp of Impartiality.—The novelist must look
on humanity without partiality or prejudice. His sympathy, like that of the historian, must be unbounded, and
untainted by sect or party. He must see everywhere the
good that is mixed with evil, the evil that is mixed with
good. And this he will not do, unless his heart be right.
It is in Scott's historical novels that his impartiality is most
severely tried and is most apparent, though it is apparent
in all his works. Shakespeare was a pure dramatist;
nothing but art found a home in that lofty, smooth, idealistic brow. He stands apart, not only from the political
and religious passions, but from the interests of his time,
seeming hardly to have any historical surroundings, but to
shine like a planet suspended by itself in the sky. So it is

with that female Shakespeare in miniature, Miss Austen.
But Scott took the most intense interest in the political
struggles of his time.   He was a fiery partisan, a Tory in
arms against the French Revolution.   In his account of
the coronation of George IV, a passionate worship of
monarchy breaks forth, which, if we did not know his
noble nature, we might call slavish.   He sacrificed ease,
and at last life, to his seignorial aspirations.   On one occasion he was even carried beyond the bounds of propriety
by his opposition to the Whig chief.   The Cavalier was his
political ancestor; the Covenanter, the ancestor of his
political enemy.   The idols which the Covenanting icono-
clast broke were his.   He would have fought against the
first revolution under Montrose, and against the second
under Dundee.   Yet he is perfectly, serenely just to the
opposite party.   Not only is he just, he is sympathetic.
He brings out their worth, their valor, such grandeur of
character as they have, with all the power of his art, making no distinction in this respect between friend and foe.
If they have a ridiculous side he uses it for the purposes of
his art, but genially, playfully, without malice.   If there
was a laugh left in the Covenanters, they would have
laughed at their own portraits as painted by Scott.   He
shows no hatred of anything but wickedness itself.   Such
a novelist is a most effective preacher of liberality and
charity; he brings our hearts nearer to the Impartial
Father of us all.

IV. The Lamp of Impersonality.—Personality is lower
than partiality.   Dante himself is open to the suspicion
of partiality; it is said, not without apparent ground, that
he puts into hell all the enemies of the political cause,
which, in his eyes, was that of Italy and God.   A legend
tells that Leonardo da Vinci was warned that his divine
picture of the Last Supper would fade, because he had
introduced his personal enemy as Judas, and thus dese-
crated art by making it serve personal hatred.   The
legend must be false,—Leonardo has too grand a soul.   A
wretched woman in England, at the beginning of the last
century, Mrs. Manley, systematically employed fiction as
a cover for personal libel; but such an abuse of art as this
could be practised or countenanced only by the vile.

Novelists, however, often debase fiction by obtruding their
personal vanities, favoritisms, fanaticisms, and antipathies.
We had, the other day, a novel, the author of which introduced himself almost by name as a heroic character, with
a description of his own personal appearance, residence,
and habits, as fond fancy painted them to himself.   There
is a novelist, who is a man of fashion, and who makes the
age of the heroes in his successive novels advance with his
own, so that at last we shall have irresistible fascination
at threescore years and ten.   But the commonest and the
most mischievous way in which personality breaks out is
pamphleteering under the guise of fiction.   One novel is
a pamphlet against lunatic asylums, another against model
prisons, a third against the poor-law, a fourth against the
government offices, a fifth against trade-unions.   In these
pretended works of imagination, facts are coined in support of a crotchet, of an antipathy with all the license of
fiction; calumny revels without restraint, and no cause is
served but.that of falsehood and injustice.   A writer takes
offense at the excessive popularity of athletic sports; instead of bringing out an accurate and conscientious
treatise to advocate moderation, he lets fly a novel painting the typical boating-man as a seducer of confiding
women, the betrayer of his friend, and the murderer of
his wife.   Religious zealots are very apt to take this
method of enlisting imagination, as they think, on the side
of truth.   We had once a high Anglican novel in which
the Papist was eaten alive by rats, and the Rationalist and
Republican was slowly seethed in molten lead, the fate of
each being, of course, a just judgment of heaven on those
who presumed to differ from the author.   Thus the voice
of morality is confounded with that of tyrannical petulance
and self-love.   Not only is Scott not personal, but we
cannot conceive his being so.   We cannot think possible
that he should degrade his art by the indulgence of ego-
tism, or crotchets, or party piques.   Least of all can we
think it possible that his high and gallant nature should
use art as a cover for striking a foul blow.

V. The Lamp of Purity.—I heard Thackeray thank
Heaven for the purity of Dickens.   I thanked Heaven for
the purity of a greater than Dickens—Thackeray himself.

We may all thank Heaven for the purity of one still
greater than either—Sir Walter Scott.   I say still greater
morally, as well as in power as an artist, because in Thackeray there is cynicism, though the more genially and
healthy element predominates; and cynicism, which is not
good in the great writer, becomes very bad in the little
reader.   We know what most of the novels were before
Scott.   We know the impurity, half-redeemed, of Field-
ing, the unredeemed impurity of Smollett, the lecherous
leer of Sterne, the coarseness even of Defoe.   Parts of
Richardson himself could not be read by a woman without
a blush.   As to French novels, Carlyle says of one of the
most famous of the last century, that after reading it you
ought to wash seven times in Jordan; but after reading
the French novels of the present day, in which lewdness
is sprinkled with sentimental rosewater, and deodorized,
but by no means disinfected, your washings had better be
seventy times seven.   There is no justification for this; it
is mere pandering, under whatever pretense, to evil pro-
pensities; it makes the divine art of fiction " procuress to
the Lords of Hell."   If our established morality is in any
way narrow and unjust, appeal to Philosophy, not to
Comus; and remember that the mass of readers are not
philosophers.   Coleridge pledges himself to find the deepest sermons under the filth of Rabelais; but Coleridge
alone finds the sermons, while everybody finds the filth.
Impure novels have brought and are bringing much
misery on the world.   Scott's purity is not that of cloistered innocence and inexperience, it is the manly purity of
one who had seen the world, mingled with men of the
world, known evil as well as good; but who, being a true
gentleman, abhorred filth, and teaches us to abhor it too.

VI. The Lamp of Humanity.—One day we see the walls
placarded with the advertising woodcut of a sensational
novel, representing a girl tied to a table and a man cutting
off her feet into a tub.   Another day we are allured by
a picture of a woman sitting at a sewing-machine and a
man seizing her from behind by the hair, and lifting a club
to knock her brains out.   A French novelist stimulates
your jaded palate by introducing a duel fought with
butchers' knives by the light of lanterns.   One genius sub-

sists by murder, as another does by bigamy and adultery. Scott would have recoiled from the blood as well as from the ordure, he would have allowed neither to have defiled his noble page. He knew that there was no pretense for bringing before a reader what is merely horrible; that by doing so you only stimulate passions as low as licentiousness itself—the passions which were stimulated by the gladiatorial shows in degraded Rome, which are stimulated by the bullfights in degraded Spain, which are stimulated among ourselves by exhibitions the attraction of which really consists in their imperiling human life. He knew that a novelist had no right even to introduce the terrible except for the purpose of exhibiting human heroism, developing character, awakening emotions which, when awakened, dignify and save from harm. It is want of genius and of knowledge of their craft that drives novelists to outrage humanity with horrors. Miss Austen can interest and even excite you as much with the little domestic adventures of Emma as some of her rivals can with a whole Newgate calendar of guilt and gore.

VII. The Lamp of Chivalry.—Of this briefly. Let the writer of fiction give us humanity in all its phases, the comic as well as the tragic, the ridiculous as well as the sublime; but let him not lower the standard of character or the aim of life. Shakespeare does not. We delight in his Falstaffs and his clowns as well as in his Hamlets and Othellos; but he never familiarizes us with what is base and mean. The noble and chivalrous always holds its place as the aim of true humanity in his ideal world. Perhaps Dickens is not entirely free from blame in this respect; perhaps Pickwickianism has in some degree familiarized the generation of Englishmen who have been fed upon it with what is not chivalrous, to say the least, in conduct, as it unquestionably has with slang in conversation. But Scott, like Shakespeare, wherever the thread of his fiction may lead him, always keeps before himself and us the highest ideal which he knew, the ideal of a gentleman. If any one says there are narrow bounds wherein to confine fiction, I answer there has been room enough within them for the highest tragedy, the deepest pathos, the broadest humor, the widest range of character, the most moving incident that the world has ever enjoyed. There has been room within them for all the kings of pure and healthy fiction—for Homer, Shakespeare, Cervantes, Molière, Scott! "Farewell, Sir Walter," says Carlyle at the end of his essay, "farewell, Sir Walter, pride of all Scotchmen." Scotland has said farewell to her mortal son. But all humanity welcomes him as Scotland's noblest gift to her, and crowns him, as on this day, one of the heirs of immortality.

JOHN LANCASTER SPALDING

OPPORTUNITY

[Address by Bishop J. L. Spalding, Roman Catholic Bishop of Peoria, Ill., since 1877 (born in Lebanon, Pa., June 3, 1840; ———), delivered at the opening of the Spalding Institute, Peoria, December 6, 1899.]

How shall I live? How shall I make the most of my life and put it to the best use? How shall I become a man and do a man's work? This, and not politics or trade or war or pleasure, is the question. The primary consideration is not how one shall get a living, but how he shall live, for if he live rightly, whatever is needful he shall easily find. Life is opportunity, and therefore its whole circumstance may be made to serve the purpose of those who are bent on self-improvement, on making themselves capable of doing thorough work. Opportunity is a word which, like so many others that are excellent, we get from the Romans. It means near port, close to haven. It is a favorable occasion, time, or place for learning or saying or doing a thing. It is an invitation to seek safety and refreshment, an appeal to make escape from what is low and vulgar and to take refuge in high thoughts and worthy deeds, from which flows increase of strength and joy. It is omnipresent. What we call evils, as poverty, neglect, and suffering, are, if we are wise, opportunities for good. Death itself teaches life's value not less than its vanity. It is the background against which its worth and beauty stand forth in clear relief. Its dark form follows us like our shadow, to bid us win the prize while yet there is time; to teach that if we live in what is permanent, the destroyer cannot blight what we know and love; to urge us, with a

power that belongs to nothing else, to lay the stress of all
our hoping and doing on the things that cannot pass away.
"Poverty," says Ouida, "is the north wind that lashes
men into Vikings." "Lowliness is young ambition's ladder." What is more pleasant than to read of strong-
hearted youths, who, in the midst of want and hardships
of many kinds, have clung to books, feeding, like bees to
flowers? By the light of pine-logs, in dim-lit garrets, in
the fields following the plough, in early dawns when others
are asleep, they ply their blessed task, seeking nourishment for the mind, athirst for truth, yearning for full
sight of the high worlds of which they have caught faint
glimpses; happier now, lacking everything save faith and
a great purpose, than in after years when success shall
shower on them applause and gold.

Life is good, and opportunities of becoming and doing
good are always with us. Our house, our table, our tools,
our books, our city, our country, our language, our business, our profession,—the people who love us and those
who hate, they who help and they who oppose—what is
all this but opportunity? Wherever we be there is opportunity of turning to gold the dust of daily happenings. If
snow and storm keep me at home is not here an invitation to turn to the immortal silent ones who never speak
unless they are addressed? If loss or pain or wrong
befal me, shall they not show me the soul of good there
is in things evil? Good fortune may serve to persuade us
that the essential good is a noble mind and a conscience
without flaw. Success will make plain the things in which
we fail; failure shall spur us on to braver hope and striving. If I am left alone, yet God and all the heroic dead
are with me still. If a great city is my dwelling place, the
superficial life of noise and haste shall teach me how
blessed a thing it is to live within in the company of true
thoughts and high resolves. Whatever can help me to
think and love, whatever can give me strength and
patience, whatever can make me humble and serviceable,
though it be a trifle light as air, is opportunity, whose
whim it is to hide in unconsidered things, in chance acquaintance and casual speech, in the falling of an apple,
in floating weeds, or the accidental explosion in a chemist's
mortar.

Wisdom is habited in plainest garb, and she walks modestly, unheeded of the gaping and wondering crowd. She rules over the kingdom of little things, in which the lowly-minded hold the places of privilege. Her secrets are revealed to the careful, the patient, and the humble. They may be learned from the ant or the flower that blooms in some hidden spot or from the lips of husbandmen and housewives.

He is wise who finds a teacher in every man, an occasion to improve in every happening, for whom nothing is useless or in vain. If one whom he has trusted prove false, he lays it to the account of his own heedlessness and resolves to become more observant. If men scorn him, he is thankful that he need not scorn himself. If they pass him by, it is enough for him that truth and love still remain. If he is thrown with one who bears himself with ease and grace, or talks correctly in pleasantly modulated tones, or utters what can spring only from a sincere and generous mind—there is opportunity. If he chance to find himself in the company of the rude, their vulgarity gives him a higher estimate of the worth of breeding and behavior. The happiness and good fortune of his fellows add to his own. If they are beautiful or wise or strong, their beauty, wisdom, and strength shall in some way help him. The merry voices of children bring gladness to his heart; the songs of birds wake melody there. Whoever anywhere, in any age, spoke noble words or performed heroic deeds, spoke and wrought for him. For him Moses led the people forth from bondage; for him the three hundred perished at Thermopylæ; for him Homer sang; for him Demosthenes denounced the tyrant; for him Columbus sailed the untraveled sea; for him Galileo gazed on the starry vault; for him the blessed Savior died. He knows that whatever diminishes his good-will to men, his sympathy with them, even in their blindness and waywardness, makes him poorer, and he therefore finds means to convert their faults even into opportunities for loving them more. The rivalries of business and politics, the shock of conflicting aims and interests, the prejudices and perversities of men, shall not cheat him of his own good by making him less just or kind. He stands with the

Eternal for righteousness, and will not suffer that fools or criminals divert him to lower ends.

If we have but the right mind, all things, even those that hurt, help us. "That which befits us," says Emerson, "embosomed in beauty and wonder as we are, is cheerfulness and courage, and the endeavor to realize our aspirations. The life of man is the true romance which when it is valiantly conducted, yields the imagination a higher joy than any fiction." May we not make the stars and the mountains and the all-enduring earth minister to tranquillity of soul, to elevation of mind, and to patient striving? Have not the flowers and the human eye and the look of heaven when the sun first appears or departs, power to show us that God is beautiful and good? Shall not the great, calm Mother whose fair face, despite the storms and battles of all the ages, is still full of repose and strength, teach us the wisdom of brave work without noise or hurry? It seems scarcely possible to live in the presence of nature and not be cured of vanity and conceit. When we see how gently and patiently she effaces or beautifies all traces of convulsions, agonies, defeats, and enmities, we feel that we are able to overcome hate and envy and all ignoble passions.

Since life is great, nay, of inestimable value, no opportunity by which it may be improved can be small. Higher things remain to be done than have yet been accomplished. God and His universe still wait on each individual soul, offering opportunity. In the midst of the humble and inevitable realities of daily life each one must seek out for himself the way to better worlds. Our power, our worth will be proportionate to the industry and perseverance with which we make right use of the ever-recurring minor occasions whether for becoming or for doing good. Opportunity is not wanting—there is place and means for all —but we lack will, we lack faith, hope, and desire, we lack watchfulness, meditation, and earnest striving, we lack aim and purpose. Do we imagine that it is not possible to lead a high life in a lowly room? That one may not be hero, sage, or saint in a factory or a coal-pit, at the handle of the plough or the throttle of the engine? We are all in the center of the same world and whatever happens to us is great, if there be greatness in us. The dis-

believers in opportunity are voluble with excuses. They
cannot; they have no leisure; they have not the means.
But they can if they will; leisure to improve one's self is
never wanting, and they who seek find the means. There
is always opportunity to do right though he who does it
stand alone, like Abdiel,—

> " Among innumerable false, unmoved,
> Unshaken, unseduced, unterrified."

Let a man but have an aim, a purpose, and opportunities
to attain his end shall start forth like buds at the kiss of
spring. If we do not know what we want, how shall anything be made to serve us? The heedless walk through
deserts in which the observant find the most precious
things. Little is to be hoped for from the weavers of
pretexts, from those who tell us what they should do, if
circumstances were other. What hinders helps, where
souls are alive. Say not thou lackest talent. What talent
had any of the great ones better than their passionate trust
in the efficacy of labor?

The important thing is to have an aim and to pursue it
with perseverance. What is the aim the wise should propose to themselves? Not getting and possessing, but
becoming and being. Man is not only more than anything that can belong to him; he is greater than planets
and solar systems. We easily persuade ourselves that
were circumstances more favorable we should be better
and happier. It may be so, but the mood is weak and
foolish. There is never a question of what might have
been where true men think and act. The past is irrecover-
able. It is our business to do what we can here and now,
and regrets serve but to enfeeble and distract us. The
boundless good lies near each one, and though a thousand
times it has eluded us, let us believe that now we shall
hold it fast. From failure to failure we rise toward truth
and love. The ascent is possible even for the lowliest of
God's creatures. When, indeed, we look backward
through long years of life, lost opportunities rise before
us like mocking fiends crying, Too late, too late, Nevermore, nevermore; but the wise heed no voice that bids
them lose heart. They look ever forward, they press

toward the mark, knowing that the present moment is the only opportunity. Now is the day of salvation, now is the day of doom. The individual is but as a bubble that rises from out the infinite ocean of being and bursts in the inane; but his life is nevertheless enrooted in the Absolute, and all the circumstances by which his existence is surrounded and attended are but meant to awaken in him a knowledge and appreciation of his abiding and inestimable worth. They all, therefore, are or may be made opportunities. The paramount consideration is not what will procure for him more money, finer houses, better machines, more rapid or more destructive engines, but what will make him wiser, stronger, holier, more loving, more godlike. The useful is not the best; or shall I say that the most useful is that which serves divine ends, which though it provide not bed or board, illumines, exalts, and enriches the life of man? Emerson rightly affirms that they are beggars who live but to the useful.

All things exist for God and to educate man into his likeness. If one were but high and pure enough he would scatter blessings as the flower fragrance, and all who came near him would depart made sweet and rich as the air the flower has kissed. To rise daily out of one's self toward truth and beauty and goodness is the secret of becoming day by day more like unto God.

We imagine that we lack material things, but what we really need is more and diviner life. Money is but a remedy for poverty, and poverty is but one of many evils; and if we give our hearts chiefly to riches, we leave ourselves exposed to all the ills that make man miserable, save one.

We find ourselves where we seek ourselves—in matter or in mind, in the low world of mere sensation and base desire, or in that where souls are transfigured by truth and love. Perfection, indeed, is beyond our reach, but they who seriously strive to become perfect acquire excellences and virtues, taste a peace and a joy of which the many have hardly a conception. When we act in the light of the ideal of human perfection, all the ways of life become plain, and opportunity is ever present and appealing. We find it in youth and in age, in glad days and in sad days, in health and in sickness, in poverty and in

wealth, in the panorama of nature with its change of seasons, its sunsets and dawns, its mountains and oceans, its
plains and rivers, and in the only less marvelous world of
literature and art.   What are the senses but permanent
opportunities, inviting us to look that we may see and
know, to listen that we may hear and understand?   What
is success but a command to attempt still higher things?
What is failure but an exhortation to the all-hoping heart
of man to make another venture?   At whatsoever moment we awaken to the meaning and worth of life there
is work for us to do.   No one, it may be, will pay us for it,
but God and nature are always with us, assisting us in
every effort to become wise, strong, and virtuous.   If we
cannot do great things, there is ever-present opportunity
of doing small things well; and great occasions come to
those alone who make good use of the hundred minor
offices and occurrences with which the lives of all are
filled.   If we fail in the dangers and temptations which
none escape, it is because there is some fault in our daily
life, in our habitual state.

Everything has a meaning, has truth and nourishment
for those who are wholly alive, and opportunities come
crowding in upon them—opportunities to learn, to admire,
to love, to cheer, to console, to enlighten and guide.   Is
there not always opportunity to deny one's self, to refrain
from facile and cheap pleasures that we may make ourselves capable of pure joy?   Pleasure is the bait on
Nature's hook and they who bite are caught.   Pleasure
is death's forager.   If we are but true and high in the
common affairs, nothing shall have power to harm us.   Is
opportunity lacking to be polite, obliging, discreet and
amiable, to listen with attention or to speak what is better
than silence, to observe carefully, to bear bravely and to
do right?   Is it difficult to find occasion for being sincere
and honest?   Honesty is the best policy, because an honest man, whether or not he get place or money, is a
genuine man, self-approved, and pleasing to God.   In
poverty he is rich, in prison he is free.   Whatever his outward fate and fortune, failure cannot touch him, for to be
a genuine man is the highest we may know on earth.   Is
opportunity lacking to speak truth and to live within one's
means—to obey the two great commandments, Do not lie,

Do not go into debt? Lying makes us vile in our own eyes, and debt makes us slaves.

What innumerable blessings we miss through lack of sensibility, of openness to light, of fair-mindedness, of insight, of teachableness,—virtues which it is possible for all to cultivate! The best is not ours, not because it is far away and unattainable, but because we ourselves are indifferent, narrow, short-sighted, and unsympathetic. To make our world larger and fairer it is not necessary to discover or acquire new objects, but to grow into conscious and loving harmony with the good which is ever-present and inviting. How much of life's joy we lose from want of a fearless and cheerful spirit. The brave and glad-hearted, like the beautiful, are welcome in all companies.

It is our own fault if beauty is not ours. A fair and luminous mind creates a body after its own image. With health and a soul, nor man nor woman can be other than beautiful, whatever the features. The most potent charm is that of expression. As the moonlight clothes the rugged and jagged mountain with loveliness so a noble mind transfigures its vesture.

There is little truth in Voltaire's assertion that opportunity for doing mischief is found a hundred times a day; of doing good, once a year. Doubtless it is easy to fall, easy to descend the downward and open way that leads to ruin, and hard to retrace one's steps; and they who seek occasions for gross indulgence or aught else that is unworthy, find them. Life is full of beauty, it is full of hideousness. To each one is left the choice whether he shall take the good or the evil. They who prefer darkness to light, lies to truth, hatred to love, strife to peace, pleasures to joy, do not lack occasions. Indeed, virtue is difficult, vice easy. Disease, not health, is contagious. Folly comes unsought, wisdom only when entreated.

Evil association more surely corrupts than good improves. Occasion makes the thief, not the honest man. To be idle is pleasant, and the idle are easily tempted and quickly yield. In fact, opportunity is servile and compliant. What use is to be made of it depends on him to whom it is offered. He may adore or he may mock, he may love or he may scorn, he may get understanding or steep himself in denser ignorance, he may play the hero or prove a coward, become saint or devil. On him it depends whether or not he shall know the right moment, receive the heavenly messenger, and be made glad and strong by the fair countenance of truth.

" This could but have happened once,
And we missed it, lost it forever."

A noble character produces no impression on a vulgar mind.. The pure and innocent awaken coarse thoughts in sensual natures. No place is so sacred, no being so holy as not to be perverted to base uses by base men.

The man himself is the best part of the opportunity. The starlit heaven is not sublime when there is no soul capable of awe; the spring is not fair where there is no glad heart to see and feel. Opportunity is living correspondence with one's environment. Where there is no correspondence there is no opportunity. For ages the exhaustless resources of America lay unknown and unutilized, because the right kind of man was not here. The Kimberly diamonds were but worthless pebbles, the playthings of the children of savages, until it chanced that they fell under the eye of one who knew how to look.

All nature is crammed with precious, nay, divine things, for those who can see. Innumerable men and women had seen the kettle boil, but it occurred to only one that the force which lifted the lid might be confined and made to do human service. The man finds or makes his opportunities, and in turn they help to make him. The multitude will not lay hold on opportunity unless it be thrust upon them; and even then they are listless and unresolved; and therefore are they condemned to remain inferior. The few who rise above the crowd are ever alert to discover how they may improve themselves, and become helpers and leaders.

We are born to grow—this is the word which religion, philosophy, literature and art ceaselessly utter; and we can grow only by keeping ourselves in vital communion with the world within and without us. Use or lose is Nature's law; also, use and improve. If a little money is taken from us we make ourselves miserable, and all the while we

are permitting the wealth which enriches the mind to slip
from us as though it were the dirt from which the gold
has been sifted.

There are few whom routine work keeps busy more
than ten hours in the twenty-four. Allow eight hours for
sleep and two for meals, and there remain four for self-
improvement. How is it possible, you ask, to live without
recreation and amusement? Find them in the effort to
upbuild your being, and joy and fulness of life shall be
yours beyond the reach of kings. Learn to think, and
you shall never lack pleasant occupation. Bring your
mind into unison with the currents of thought which are
found in the books of power, and you need be neither
lonely nor depressed. The transfusion of thought is more
quickening than the transfusion of blood. As in the
midst of battle the soldier is often unconscious of his
wounds, so they who have a purpose and seriously pursue
it, easily become indifferent to the troubles which make
weaker men wretched.

Games and other amusements doubtless have their
uses, especially for the young, and for all who are feeble
in body or in mind, but when we consider that they are
generally occasions for wasting time, and so, a chief obstacle to human advancement, it is difficult not to condemn
the apathy, the indifference to the meaning and worth of
life which makes possible their universal prevalence.
They are least harmful in the home, and even there what
irreparable loss they involve! Economy of time is more
indispensable than economy of money; for it is a means
not only of getting money, but of getting what is vastly
higher and more precious—wisdom and virtue. All else
may be made good, but time misspent is lost forever. It
is the element in which life exists, and to squander it is to
dissipate vital force. What increases health and strength
of body is good unless it diminish vigor of mind or weaken
the will to devote one's self to right human ends. The
passion and persistence with which athletic sports are followed in our colleges and universities undermine moral
and intellectual ambition just at the time when the formation of character and the acquisition of knowledge are of
the highest importance. Those whose ideal is athletic
are in danger of not looking higher than the prize-ring.

True human power is not physical; its seat is in the mind, in the will, in the conscience. Let our schoolboys be happy and joyous, let them divert themselves, in a free spirit, like gentlemen, but let them not lay the stress of their attention and admiration on rowing or leaping or kicking a ball or hitting it with a bat, nor imagine that great skill of this kind is helpful or desirable. It is generally an accomplishment of those whose spiritual being is callous or superficial. These sports are not the best means even for promoting health and physical culture, which are the result of moderate, not violent exercise, of temperance, cleanliness, sleep, cheerful thoughts and worthy aims followed in a brave and generous spirit. Mere strength of body is not a test either of endurance or of vitality. We die from sensual excess, or from despondency, or from both. Indulgence and disappointment kill more than work, which if it be full of joy and hope, brings length of days. Worry, whatever its source, weakens, takes away courage, and shortens life. Our sons murder us, said a rich man, speaking of a friend who had just died.

The sweet idleness praised by poets and lovers is not idleness, but leisure to give one's self to high thoughts and loftier moods. The really idle are oppressed by a sense of fatigue, and therefore tiresome to themselves and others. Let those who complain of having to work undertake to do nothing. If this do not convert them, nothing will. Those who live in inaction on the fruits of the labors of others lose the power to enjoy, come to feel existence to be a burden, and fall a prey to life-weariness. He sits uneasy at the feast who thinks of the starving; he is not comfortable at his own fireside who remembers those who have none. To know that life is good one must be conscious that he is helping to make it good at least for a few.

Work, not play, is the divine opportunity. The outcome of civilization, if we continue to make progress, must be that to each and every one work shall be given to do, which while it provides the necessaries and comforts of life, will cheer, strengthen, console, purify, and enlighten; and when this day comes the Nineteenth century shall appear to have been but little better than the Ninth;

for a society in which millions are condemned to do dehumanizing work or starve is barbarous.

The century which is now drawing to end has been so filled with wonders, with progress in science and wealth, with discoveries and inventions, that it seems to illumine the pages of history with a blaze of glory. But it is not all light. The failure is as serious as the success is great. The individual has not risen as his knowledge has widened and his environment improved. What he is, is still held to be less important than what he possesses and uses. In the mad race for wealth multitudes are sacrificed as pitilessly as in warfare; they are dragged by competition to the verge of starvation; they are driven to work under conditions which dehumanize. Greed has led to a worldwide struggle as cruel as that of nature, in which only the strongest or the most cunning and conscienceless survive. Our society makes criminals, and our penal institutions harden them in wrong-doing. The people are taxed to support vast armies and to supply them with more and more expensive and effective instruments of murder; and wars are waged not to liberate and uplift weaker races, but to rob and oppress them; and these crimes are committed in the name of religion and civilization. The great powers of Europe look on in stolid indifference while helpless populations are massacred; and America, which has always meant good-will to men and opportunity for all, seems to be drifting away from what Americans have loved and lived for into the evil company of these Old-World nations, drunken with lust for conquest and lust for gold. While knowledge grows, while man's control over the forces of nature increases, the individual seems to be losing his hold on the principles which underlie right life. The power of sustained thought, of persevering labor for high and unselfish ends, the spirit of sacrifice and devotion, faith and hope, the love of liberty and independence are, it is to be feared, diminishing.

There is still evil enough in the world to save us from self-complacency, from the foolish and vulgar habit of self-laudation, but the triumphs of the Nineteenth century have been sufficiently real and great to inspire confidence and courage in the young who are preparing to take their place in the Twentieth as strong and faithful workers in every righteous cause. Here in America, above all, the new age approaches offering opportunity. Here only a beginning has been made; we have but felled the forest, and drained the marsh, and bridged the river and built the road; but cleared the wildwood and made wholesome the atmosphere for a more fortunate race, whom occasion shall invite to greater thoughts and more godlike deeds. We stand in the front rank of those who face life, dowered with all the instruments of power which the labors of the strongest and wisest in all time and place have provided.

We might have been born savages or slaves, in a land of cannibals or tyrants; but we enter life welcomed by all that gives worth and joy, courage and security to man. There is inspiration in the air of America. Here all is fresh and young, here progress is less difficult, here there is hope and confidence, here there is eagerness to know and to do. Here they who are intelligent, sober, industrious and self-denying may get what money is needed for leisure and independence, for the founding of a home and the right education of children,—the wealth which strengthens and liberates, not the excess which undermines and destroys. The material is good but in so far as it is a means to spiritual good. The power to think and appreciate the thoughts of others, to love and to be happy in the joy, the courage, the beauty, and the goodness of others, lifts us above our temporal environment, and endows us with riches of which money can never be the equivalent. A great thought or a noble love, like a beautiful object, bears us away from the hard and narrow world of our selfish interests, dips us in the clear waters of pure delight, and makes us glad as children who lie in the shade and catch the snowy blossoms as they fall.

No true man ever believes that it is not possible to do great things without great riches. When, therefore, we say with Emerson, that America is but a name for opportunity, we do not emphasize its material resources or the facility with which they may be made available. He who knows that the good of life lies within and that it is infinite, capable of being cherished and possessed more and more by whoever seeks it with all his heart, understands that a little of what is external is sufficient and is not hard to acquire. He, therefore, neither gives himself to the pursuit of wealth or fame or pleasure or position, nor thinks those fortunate who are rich in these things.   He feels that the worst misfortune is not the loss of money or friends or reputation, but the loss of inner strength and wholeness, of faith in God and man, of self-respect, of the desire for knowledge and virtue.   The darkened mind, the callous heart, the paralytic will—these are the root evils. Is man a real being, with an element of freedom, responsibility and permanence in his constitution, or is he but a phantom, a bubble that rises and floats for a moment, and then bursts in the boundless inane, where all things disappear and are no more?   This is the radical question, for if the individual wholly ceases to be at death, the race itself is but a parasite of a planet which is slowly perishing; and life's formula is—from nothing to nothing.   But nothingness is inconceivable, for to think is to be conscious of being: something exists; therefore something has always existed.   Being is a mental conception; and when we affirm that it is eternal we affirm the eternity of mind, that mind is involved in the nature of things.   It is the consciousness of this that makes it impossible for the soul to accept a mechanical theory of the universe or to rest content with what is material.   It is akin to the infinite Spirit, and for man opportunity is opportunity to develop his true self, to grow in wisdom and love.   What he yearns for in his deepest heart is not to eat and drink, but to live in ever-increasing conscious communion with the vital truth which is the soul's nourishment, the element in which faith and hope and freedom thrive.

The modern mind, having gained a finer insight into the play of the forces of nature, which are ceaselessly being transformed into new modes of existence, seems threatened with loss of the power of perceiving the Eternal. But this enfeeblement and perturbation are temporary, and on our wider knowledge we shall build a nobler and more glorious temple wherein to believe and serve, to love and pray.   That man, who lives but a day and is but an atom, should imagine that he partakes of the attributes of the eternal and absolute Being, would seem to be absurd. None the less all that is most real and highest in him impels to this belief.   To lose it is to lose faith in the meaning and worth of life; is to abandon the principle that issues in the heroic struggles and sufferings, by which freedom, civilization, art, science, and religion have been won and secured as the chief blessings of the race. It is not possible to find true joy except in striving for the infinite, for something we have not yet, which we can never have, here at least. Hence, whatever purpose a man cherish, whatever task he set himself, he finds his work stretching forth endlessly. The more he attains the more clearly he perceives the boundless unattained. His success is ever becoming failure, his riches poverty, his knowledge ignorance, his virtue vice. The higher he rises in power of thought and love, the more what he thinks and loves seems to melt away and disappear in the abysmal depths of the All-perfect Being, who is forever and forever, of whom he is born, and whom to seek through endless time were a blessed lot. It is the hope of finding Him that lures the soul to unseen worlds, lifts it out of the present, driving it to the past and the future, that it may live with vanished saints and heroes, or with the diviner men who yet shall be.

The best moments are those in which we stay within ourselves, alone with God and all His world of truth and beauty. This is the sage's delight; this the student's. This is the ever-welling source of joy for all who cherish the soul and bear it company. This is the solitude which for open minds and pure hearts is peopled with high thoughts and blissful yearnings. In the crowd, in the society even of one or two these heavenly visitations never or seldom come. By the harvest we reap from the inner eye's contemplations we are nourished and strengthened to bear and do our share in the sufferings and achievements of the wise and good. Lovers themselves feel most the blessedness of love when they are parted, left to visions and dreams of the ideals by which they are haunted.

"Where a man can live, he can also live well; but he may have to live in a palace," says Marcus Aurelius, implying that right life is most difficult in high places. Why, then, should we wish to dwell in a great city or to have great wealth or notoriety? These things are distractions and hindrances. They draw us from out the depths of the soul and thrust us into the midst of noise and confusion, of

strife and envy, or they lead us into the pitfalls of sensuality, taking us away from ourselves to make us the sport
of the mob of time-servers and idlers.   To live for an hour
alone with God gives us a more intimate sense of the value
and sacredness of life than to dwell for years in the company of worldlings.   O highest and best, source of all, of
all father, guide, and nourisher, from out the midst of
infinite mystery and suffering we look to Thee!   On Thee
our faith and hope and love, on Thee our need and despair
still call.   We cannot grasp Thy being or comprehend
Thy ways.   We can but know Thy truth, Thy goodness,
and Thy beauty.   It is enough: Thou art with us; in
Thee we live.   What Thou doest is eternally right; on
Thee we throw the burden of our lives.   Thou art, Thou
hast ever been, Thou shalt be forever; Thou holdest us
in Thy sight whether we live or whether we die.

The measure of the value of opportunity is its influence
on religious and moral life.   We are athirst for God, and
finding Him not we harden to mere materialists, or sink
into lethargy, or drown consciousness in the sloughs of
sensuality.   In the end, each one has but himself, and if
God be not in that self, he is poor and wretched, though he
possess a universe; for with a few spadefuls of earth on
his head it will all be over, forever.   The vanity, the nothingness of the individual, when his existence is thrown
against the background of eternity and infinity, is appalling, but when it is lifted into the light and life of the
Almighty Father, who is truth and love and righteousness,
it acquires divine meaning and worth.

To throw away life is the greatest crime we can commit.   It is our duty to live; therefore it is our duty to live
in ever-increasing completeness of faith and love, of wisdom and power; for if we cease to grow, we begin to die.
The body indeed is doomed to decay, but the soul was
made to rise toward God throughout eternity.   The only
right opportunities, then, are those which help to make
us god-like—strong, patient, active, fair, wise, benevolent,
useful, and holy.

Genuine progress is spiritual.   The man has higher
value than the machine.   Nietsche holds that it would be
right and admirable to sacrifice all men actually existing, if
it were possible thereby to originate a stronger species.

This, he says, would be real progress. But if there is no divine Being, no immortal life, this mightier superhuman, who would also have keener insight, would but see more clearly the misery and futility of existence. Let us rather listen to Matthew Arnold, when he declares that whatever progress may be made in science, art, and literary culture, however much higher, more general and more effective than at present the value for them may become, Christianity will be still there, as what these rest against and imply; as the indispensable background, the three-fourths of life. It is only when we walk in the spirit and follow in the footsteps of the Son of God, that we come to understand that life is opportunity, rich as earth, wide as heaven, deep as the soul.

We weary of everything,—of labor, of rest, of pleasure, of success, of the company of friends, and of our own, but not of the divine presence uttering itself in hope and love, in peace and joy. They who live with sensual thoughts and desires soon come to find them a burden and a blight; but the lowly-minded and the clean in heart, who are busy with whatsoever things are true and fair and good, feel themselves in a serene world where it is always delightful to be. When we understand that all is from God and for Him, and turn our wills wholly to Him, trouble, doubt, and anxiety die away, and the soul rests in the calm and repose that belong to whatever is eternal. He sees all and is not disturbed. Why should we be filled with apprehension because there are ripples in the little pond where our life-boat floats?

Since He has made us for everlasting bliss, He has made us to be happy now in the work that lies at our hand or in the sorrow and suffering we must bear. Whatever brings a high thought or a gentle or a generous mood is consecrated as though wafted to us from the wings of angels. Had we the power to gratify every wish and whim, human life would become impossible. God's love is as manifest when He hems us in as when He enlarges the bounds in which He permits us to move. We ask blindly for many things, when all that we need is that He guide us. "Thy will be done," is the sum of all true worship and right prayer. The rest is aside from the divine purpose, and could it be realized would make the world

a chaos or a desert.   We should not love the flowers if it
were always spring; and our purest pleasures would pall
did not pain and loss come to teach us their worth.

Life is action; but to be passive, awaiting the utterances
of God, through whatever medium they may come, is often
the highest wisdom.   To souls that are calmly expectant,
whisperings become audible, as in the silence of serene
nights, which tell of diviner worlds, where it is eternally
well with the gentle, the loving, and the pure of heart.

There is no worse perversion of Christian truth than to
maintain that the Savior taught that to make one's self
miserable here is the means of attaining future blessedness.   They who follow Him walk in the way of peace and
joy.   They are unafraid.   They dwell in a heavenly kingdom.   The Omnipotent is their father, with them in death
as in life.   They need little, nor fear to lack that little.
Suffering makes them wise and strong.   They are able to
be of help, for they think not of themselves.   They do no
evil, and therefore can suffer none.   They despise not this
present life, for they are conscious that even now they are
with God and are immortal.   Since universal love is the
law of Christ's religion, they thrust forth whatever may
foster the spirit of distrust and alienation.   It is weakness
and ignorance to imagine that to dislike those who have
a creed or a country other than ours, is proof of piety and
patriotism.   The bitterness we cherish against others
makes our own lives bitter; the wrong we do them we ourselves must suffer.   We play the Pharisee when we think
or believe as though we were superior to the rest of men.

The followers of the Divine Master best know that true
men need not great opportunities.   He himself met with
no occasions which may not be offered to any one.   His
power and goodness are most manifest amidst the simplest
and lowliest surroundings.   To beggars, fishermen, and
shepherds He speaks words which resound throughout the
ages and still awaken in myriad hearts echoes from higher
worlds.   Whether He walks amid the cornfields, or sits
by the well, or from a boat or a hillside speaks to the multitude; whether He confronts the elders who bring Him
the guilty woman, or stands before Pilate, or hangs on the
cross, He is equally noble, fair, and God-like.   The lesson He teaches by word and deed is that we should not

wait for opportunity, but that the secret of true life and best achievement lies in doing well the thing the heavenly Father gives us to do.   He who throws himself resolutely and with perseverance into a course of worthy action will at last hear the discords of human existence die away into harmonies; for if the voice within whispers that all is well, it is fair weather, however the clouds may lower or the lightning play.   What we habitually love and live by, will, in due season, bud, blossom, and bear fruit.

Whatever opportunity is favorable to genuine life, to its joy, purity, beauty, and power, is good; whatever occasion is hurtful to such life is evil.   In each one's path through the world there are a thousand pitfalls, into any one of which he may step unawares.   Let us take heed therefore and choose our way.

Let a man have a purpose, let him resolve and labor to make of himself a good mechanic, or merchant, or farmer, or lawyer, or doctor, or teacher, or priest; but first of all let him have the will and the courage to make of himself a true man, for else there shall be no worth in him.   On the miser, the drunkard, the liar, the lecher, the thief, no blessings can fall.   Our value is measured by that of the things we believe, know, love, and strenuously strive to accomplish.   Make no plans, entertain no schemes. Think and do day by day the best thou art able to think and do.   This is the open secret, which all might learn and which only a few know.   But to them it reveals the way to the highest and the holiest.

Busy thyself not with what should be corrected or abolished; but give thyself wholly to learning, loving, and diffusing what is good and fair.   The spirit of the creator is more joyful and more potent than that of the critic or reformer.   Budding life pushes away the things that are dead; and if thou art a wellspring of vital force, thou shouldst not be a grave-digger.   The test of a man's strength and worth is not so much what he accomplishes as what he overcomes.   When circumstances favor, the lesser man may do the greater work, as cowards who are armed conquer heroes who are weaponless.   He who has made his own the spiritual wealth of all the ages, knows more and can do more than the mighty men of the past, who excelled him in natural endowment and in virtue.

The wise therefore are not exalted in their own conceit by the advantages and opportunities they enjoy, but they are made humble rather when they remember the greater and worthier men who, lacking all save honest minds and true hearts, hewed their way through a thousand obstacles to freedom and light.

Few can utter words of wisdom, but opportunity to speak kind words is offered to every one; and they are more helpful. When we are thrown with persons who have feeble mental culture, but who are mild, simple, and true, we feel how little intellectual accomplishments contribute to form what is best in man. They who have the mother virtues are not injured by their ignorance of the objections which would discredit all virtue. The best is within the reach of all; therefore it is not to be found in great possessions or exalted position or abstruse thoughts. The reward of all right life is increase of the power of living rightly. The world can give to the hero or the saint nothing that is comparable to the growing strength and joy there is in being a hero or a saint. "To be spiritually minded is life and peace." Opportunity for many things may be lacking, but it is always possible to do what belongs to one's condition; and if it be only to wait and suffer, the right spirit will make this enough.

Whatever is inevitable or irremediable is, in so far, part of the divine purpose, and to accept it with a grave trustfulness is the only wisdom; but let us be slow to believe that a thing is inevitable or irremediable. Walk perseveringly in the light of a great purpose, and difficulties shall disappear, even as the horizon recedes before the advancing step. Have faith in thyself and in God, and thou shalt be borne upward and onward as by invisible tireless wings fanning the ethereal element, where the soul breathes its proper atmosphere and knows nor doubt nor fear. If small things are given thee to do, do them as though they were great, since for thee their significance is infinite.

We are the slaves of our needs—the fewer they are, the freer are we; the higher they are, the nobler the masters we serve. Not independence, but interdependence, is the law of our life. It is only in ministering to one another, in bearing one another's burdens, in sharing one another's joys, that we become human and truly live. Let us draw closer together, that we may feel the pulsings of divine sympathy and love in one another's hearts. If we stand apart we shall be stranded in the great river, we shall miss the good of living, we shall lose God. Life is communion and helpfulness; death is disintegration and impotence. A spiritual empire, a heavenly kingdom can be constituted and sustained only by the moral and mental union and communion of its citizens, and this can be brought about and kept vital only by right education. When a noble faith and great thoughts strike root in the heart and mind of a people, it is held together by bonds which no catastrophe, no conquest, no dismemberment or dispersion can loosen; and without a noble faith and great thoughts neither military power nor vast territory nor wealth can give to a people a permanent place in history or a lasting influence on the progress of the race. All else passes and becomes as though it had not been, but what the world once recognizes and accepts as a vital truth, as an ideal of human perfection which cannot be outgrown, remains a possession forever to purify and enrich life.

Opportunity in the highest sense of the word is opportunity for education, for making ourselves men. This end every occasion should serve, since for this we are born. "We should, as far as it is possible," says Aristotle, "make ourselves immortal, and strive to live by that part of ourselves which is most excellent." Now, the testimony of the wise of all ages agrees that a virtuous life is the best and the happiest. Choose and follow it then though thou find it hard; for custom will make it easy and pleasant. Piety nourishes faith, hope, and love, and therefore sustains life. If thou seekest for what is new and also permanently interesting, live with the old truths, until they strike root in thy being and break into new light and power. The happenings of the day and year are but novelties, but bubbles that burst in the vacant air; that which is forever new is ancient as God. It is that whereby the soul lives. It was with the first man when first he blossomed forth from eternity; it is with thee now and shall be with all men until the end. It is the source whence thy being springs: its roots dip into infinity; its flowers make the universe glad and sweet; it is the power

which awakens the soul to the consciousness of its kinship with Him who is all in all, who is life and truth and
love, who the more He is sought and loved doth seem to
be the more divinely beautiful and good.   Learn to live
with the thoughts which are symbols of His Eternal Being,
and thou shalt come to feel that nothing else is so fresh
or fair.   As a sound may suggest light and color, a per-
fume recall forgotten worlds; as a view, disclosed by a
turn in the road may carry us across years and oceans to
scenes and friends long unvisited; as a bee weaving his
winding path from flower to flower may bring back the
laughter of children, the songs of birds, and the visionary
clouds fallen asleep in the voluptuous sky of June; so the
universe will come to utter for us the voice of the Creator,
who is our Father.   Nothing touches the soul but leaves
its impress, and thus, little by little, we are fashioned into
the image of all we have seen and heard, known and
meditated; and if we learn to live with all that is fairest
and purest and best, the love of it all will in the end become
our very life.

EDMUND CLARENCE STEDMAN

THE WORK OF ROBERT LOUIS STEVENSON

[Address by Edmund Clarence Stedman, poet and critic (born in Hartford, Conn., October 8, 1833; ———), delivered in Carnegie Hall, New York City, January 4, 1895, at a memorial meeting held to do honor to the memory of Robert Louis Stevenson. The meeting was given under the auspices of the Uncut Leaves Society. Mr. Stedman presided, and the list of fifty vice-presidents included many notable names.]

LADIES AND GENTLEMEN:—Such an assemblage—in the chief city of the Western World—is impressive from the fact that we have not come together for any civic, or political, or academic purpose. I have been thinking, too, of its significance in view of considerations quite apart from the sorrowful cause of our gathering. But of these this is not the time to speak. On its face, this demonstration is a rare avowal of the worth of literary invention. It shows a profound regard for the career of a writer who delighted us, a sense of loss instantaneously awakened by the news of his taking-off. For the moment we realize how thoroughly art and song and letters have become for us an essential part of life—a common ground whereupon we join our human love and laughter and tears, and at times forego all else to strew laurel and myrtle for one who has moved us to these signs and emotions.

Yes, we are brought together by tidings, almost from the antipodes, of the death of a beloved writer in his early prime. The work of a romancer and poet, of a man of insight and feeling, which may be said to have begun but fifteen years ago, has ended, through fortune's sternest cynicism, just as it seemed entering upon even more splendid achievement. A star surely rising, as we thought, has suddenly gone out. A radiant invention shines no more; the voice is hushed of a creative mind, expressing its fine imaginings in this, our peerless English tongue. His expression was so original and fresh from Nature's treasure-house, so prodigal and various its too brief flow, so consummate through an inborn gift made perfect by unsparing toil that mastery of the art by which Robert Louis Stevenson conveyed those imaginings to us: so picturesque, yet wisely ordered, his own romantic life—and now, at last, so pathetic a loss, which renews

> The Virgilian cry,
> The sense of tears in mortal things,

that this assemblage has gathered, at the first summons, in tribute to a beautiful genius, and to avow that with the putting out of that bright intelligence the reading world experiences a more than wonted grief.

Stevenson was not of our own people, though he sojourned with us and knew our continent from east to west as few of this large audience can know it. But a British author now, by statutory edict, is of our own. Certainly his fame is often made by the American people—yes, and sometimes unmade. Theirs is the great amphitheatrum. They are the ultimate court of review. All the more we are here " for the honor of literature "; and so much the more it is manifest that the writer who lightens our hearts, who takes us into some new wonderland of his discovery, belongs, as I say, to the world. His name and fame are, indeed, a special glory of the country that bore him, and a vantage to his native tongue. But by just so much as his gift is absolute, and therefore universal, he belongs in the end to the world at large. Above all, it is the recounter—and the Greeks were clear-headed in deeming him a maker, whether his story be cast in prose or verse—who becomes the darling of mankind. This has been so whether among the Grecian isles, or around the desert camp-fires, or in the gardens of Italy; and is so when he brings us his romance, as in our modern day, from our Pacific Eldorado, or from Indian barracks and jungle, or from the land of the Stuarts, or, like Stevenson and our own Melville before him, from palm-fringed beaches of the Southern Seas.

Judged by the sum of his interrupted work, Stevenson had his limitations. But the work was adjusted to the scale of a possibly long career. As it was, the good fairies brought all gifts, save that of health, to his cradle, and the gift-spoiler wrapped them in a shroud. Thinking of what his art seemed leading to—for things that would be the crowning efforts of other men seemed 'prentice-work in his case—it was not safe to bound his limitations. And now it is as if Sir Walter, for example, had died at forty-four, with the "Waverley Novels" just begun! In originality, in the conception of action and situation, which, however fantastic, are seemingly within reason, once we breathe the air of his Fancyland; in the union of bracing and heroic character and adventure; in all that belongs to tale-writing pure and simple, his gift was exhaustless. No other such charmer, in this wise, has appeared in his generation. We thought the stories, the fairy tales, had all been told, but "Once upon a time" meant for him our own time, and the grave and gay magic of Prince Florizel in dingy London or sunny France. All this is but one of his provinces, however distinctive. Besides, how he buttressed his romance with apparent truth! Since Defoe, none had a better right to say: "There was one thing I determined to do when I began this long story, and that was to tell out everything as it befel."

One or two points are made clear as we look at the shining calendar of Stevenson's productive years. It strengthens one in the faith that work of the first order cannot remain obscure. If put forth underhanded it will be found out and will make its way. In respect of dramatic force, exuberant fancy, and ceaselessly varying imagination on the one hand, and on the other of a style wrought in the purest, most virile and most direct temper of English narrative prose, there has been no latter-day writing more effective than that of Stevenson's longer fictions— "Kidnapped," with its sequel, "David Balfour"; "The Master of Ballantrae," and that most poetic of absolute romances, "Prince Otto." But each of his shorter tales as well, and of his essays—charged with individuality—has a quality, an air of distinction, which, even though the thing appeared without signature, differentiated it from other people's best, set us to discovering its authorship, and made us quick to recognize that master-hand elsewhere.

Thus I remember delighting in two fascinating stories of Paris in the time of François Villon, anonymously reprinted by a New York paper from a London magazine. They had all the quality, all the distinction, of which I speak. Shortly afterward I met Mr. Stevenson, then in his twenty-ninth year, at a London club, where we chanced to be the only loungers in an upper room. To my surprise he opened a conversation—you know there could be nothing more unexpected than that in London—and thereby I guessed that he was as much, if not as far, away from home as I was. He asked many questions concerning "the States"; in fact, this was but a few months before he took his steerage passage for our shores. I was drawn to the young Scotsman at once. He seemed more like a New Englander of Holmes's Brahmin caste, who might have come from Harvard or Yale. But as he grew animated I thought, as others have thought, and as one would suspect from his name, that he must have Scandinavian blood in his veins—that he was of the heroic, restless, strong and tender Viking strain, and certainly from that day his works and wanderings have not belied the surmise. He told me that he was the author of that charming book of gipsying in the Cévennes which just then had gained for him some attentions from the literary set. But if I had known that he had written those two stories of Sixteenth-century Paris—as I learned afterward when they reappeared in the "New Arabian Nights" —I would not have bidden him good-by as to an "unfledged comrade," but would have wished indeed to "grapple him to my soul with hooks of steel."

Another point is made clear as crystal by his life itself. He had the instinct, and he had the courage, to make it the servant, and not the master, of the faculty within him. I say he had the courage, but so potent was his birth-spell that doubtless he could not otherwise. Nothing commonplace sufficed him. A regulation stay-at-home life would have been fatal to his art. The ancient mandate, "Follow thy Genius," was well obeyed. Unshackled free-

dom of person and habit was a prerequisite; as an imaginary artist he felt—Nature keeps her poets and story-
tellers children to the last—he felt, if he ever reasoned it
out, that he must " gang his own gait," whether it seemed
promising, or the reverse, to kith, kin, or alien.   So his
wanderings were not only in the most natural but in the
wisest consonance with his creative dreams.   Wherever
he went, he found something essential for his use,
breathed upon it, and returned it fourfold in beauty and
worth.   The longing of the Norseman for the tropic, of
the pine for the palm, took him to the South Seas.   There,
too, strange secrets were at once revealed to him, and
every island became an " Isle of Voices."   Yes, an additional proof of Stevenson's artistic mission lay in his careless, careful, liberty of life; in that he was an artist no less
than in his work.   He trusted to the impulse which possessed him—that which so many of us have conscientiously
disobeyed and too late have found ourselves in reputable
bondage to circumstances.

But those whom you are waiting to hear will speak more
fully of all this—some of them with the interest of their
personal remembrance—with the strength of their affection for the man beloved by young and old.   In the
strange and sudden intimacy with an author's record which
death makes sure, we realize how notable is the list of
Stevenson's works produced since 1878; more than a score
of books—not fiction alone, but also essays, criticism,
biography, drama, even history, and, as I need not remind
you, that spontaneous poetry which comes only from a
true poet.   None can have failed to observe that, having
recreated the story of adventure, he seemed in his later
fiction to interfuse a subtler purpose—the search for character, the analysis of mind and soul.   Just here his summons came.   Between the sunrise of one day and the sun-
set of the next he exchanged the forest study for the
mountain grave.   There, as he had sung his own wish,
he lies " under the wide and starry sky."   If there was
something of his own romance, so exquisitely capricious,
in the life of Robert Louis Stevenson, so, also, the poetic
conditions are satisfied in his death, and in the choice of
his burial-place upon the top of Pala.   As for the splendor
of that maturity upon which we counted, now never to be

fulfilled on sea or land, I say—as once before, when the great New England romancer passed in the stillness of the night:—

> What though his work unfinished lies? Half bent
> The rainbow's arch fades out in upper air;
> The shining cataract half-way down the height
> Breaks into mist; the haunting strain, that fell
> On listeners unaware,
> Ends incomplete: but through the starry night
> The ear still waits for what it did not tell.

CHARLES WILLIAM STUBBS

SHAKESPEARE AS A PROPHET

[Address by the Very Reverend Charles William Stubbs, D. D., Dean of Ely, since 1894 (born in Liverpool, England, September 3, 1845; ———), delivered in New York, in November, 1899, during his American lecture tour through the season of 1899-1900.]

I have to speak to you to-day of *Shakespeare as a National Prophet*. You will rightly ask me in what sense I use this term. Let me answer you in the words of two modern poets.

In his magnificent prose essay on "The Defence of Poetry," the poet Shelley thus compares the functions of the poet and the prophet:—

"Poets, according to the circumstance of the age and nation in which they appeared, were called in the earlier epochs of the world, legislators or prophets. A poet essentially comprises and unites both these characters. For he not only beholds intensely the present as it is, and discovers those laws according to which present things ought to be ordered, but he beholds the future in the present, and his thoughts are the germs of the flower and fruit of latest time. Not that I assert poets to be prophets in the gross sense of that word, or that they can foretell the form as surely as they foreknow the spirit of events. Such is the pretence of superstition which would make poetry an attribute of prophecy, rather than prophecy an attribute of poetry."

And this is how the great American poet, Russell Lowell, has expressed a similar thought in imperishable verse:—

1104

"To know the heart of all things was his duty,
 All things did speak to him to make him wise,
And with a sorrowful and conquering beauty
 The soul of all looked grandly from his eyes.
He gazed on all within him and without him,
 He watched the flowing of Time's steady tide,
And shapes of glory floated all about him
 And whispered to him, and he prophesied.
Than all men he more fearless was, and freer,
 And all his brethren cried with one accord—
'Behold the holy man! behold the seer!
 Him who hath spoken with the unseen Lord.' "

But you will ask me very probably, and some of you perhaps with some surprise—Can you really speak of Shakespeare, even in this sense, as a prophet? Can you speak of him in any sense even as a religious man? My friends, I should not care to speak of him in this place at all if I did not think that he was both.

If the underlying and almighty essence of this world be good, then it is likely—is it not?—that the writer who most deeply approached to that essence will be himself good. There is a religion of week-days as well as of Sundays, a religion of "cakes and ale" as well as of pews and altar-cloths. This England lay before Shakespeare as it lies before us all, with its green fields, and its long hedgerows, and its many trees, and its great towns, and its endless hamlets, and its motley society, and its long history, and its bold exploits and its gathering power; and he saw that they were good. To him, perhaps, more than to any one else, has it been given to see that they were a great unity, a great religious object; that if you could only descend to the inner life, to the deep things, to the secret principles of its noble vigor, to the essence of character, to what we know of Hamlet and seem to fancy of Ophelia, we might, so far as we are capable of so doing, understand the Nature which God has made. Let us, then, think of Shakespeare, not as a teacher of dry dogmas, or a sayer of hard sayings, but as

" A priest to us all
Of the wonder and bloom of the world "—

a teacher of the hearts of men and women; one from

whom may be learnt something of that inmost principle
that ever modulates

> " With murmurs of the air,
> And motions of the forest and the sea,
> And voice of living beings, and woven hymns
> Of night and day and the deep heart of man."

Shakespeare was not a prophet or preacher, of course,
in the same sense as Mrs. Barbauld, or Dr. Doddridge, or
Dr. Watts, or even John Keble. But perhaps he was
something better and higher. He rises above mere
morals, and preaches to us, prophesies to us of life.

The Gospel of Jesus Christ, remember, is not morality
only, not a book of morals, but the story of a life; a life
in which all men can see the perfection of human character, the divinity of forgiveness, of perpetual mercy, of
constant patience, of endless peace, of everlasting gentleness; and is there any prophet of our modern dispensa-
tion who knew these things better, or could prophesy of
them more vividly through life, than did Shakespeare?

In an evil day too, remember, Shakespeare prophesied;
he taught the most gracious and gentle precepts—too
good I fancy almost to have been listened to, if men had
quite known what they were receiving. There are some
things in Shakespeare I almost fancy he might have been
burnt for had he been a theologian—just as, certainly,
there are things about politics, about civil liberty, which,
had he been a politician or a statesman, would have
brought him to the block.

It is argued by some critics from certain indications in the plays
(the Jack Cade scenes, for example, in 2, " Henry VI ") that Shakespeare had no sympathy with political freedom, or with democratic
ideas; had indeed, a very wholesome feudal disdain of the many-
headed monster. And it is true, no doubt, that Shakespeare was not
a modern democrat. But it is equally true, that there was not a modern democracy in "the spacious days of great Elizabeth." In the
Tudor period the People had not emerged. Representative democracy is, in fact, an entirely modern institution, which throws out of
court therefore all interested appeals to the sad fate of democratic
(so-called) institutions in old days. And there are certainly those
among Shakespeare students (Werner, for example, in his "Jahr-
buch") who discover in the author of " Hamlet " and " Lear " a

thinker in the foremost ranks of modern and patriotic spirits; a fore-runner of the struggle for freedom in which England was to engage first among the nations of Europe. But Shakespeare was too human, and too permanent—shall we say too " eternal "?—to be a party poli-tician. " A plague on both your houses! " is his nearest to a political cry. A poet of the Nineteenth century, of course, who had no care for political theories and philosophies of history, would show himself to be lacking in that very sympathy with humanity which made Shake-speare what he was. But Shakespeare himself dealt with men, and not with ideas. He has no abstract political principles to apply, even in his story of the contest of Lancaster and York. And the nearest to a political principle you can get anywhere in Shakespeare is the con-sciousness of his faith in the divine right of the kingliest nature to be king. Indeed, in this respect, I think we may guess that Shake-speare in the Nineteenth century would echo the noble words of Keats:—

> " Where is the poet? show him, show him,
>   Muses nine, that I may know him.
>   It is the man who with a man
>   Is an equal, be he king
>   Or poorest of the beggar clan,
>   Or any other wondrous thing
>   A man may be ' twixt ape and Plato.' "

But God made him a player and neither of these other things. And so he could teach a message to his age which it much needed, lessons of peace, gentleness, mercy, pa-tience, long-suffering.

He was no priest, it is true, he waved no censer, yet who can tell, when we consider the thousands of souls who have learnt the lessons of Shakespeare, how much he has done to humanize, nay, to Christianize mankind. His doctrine may not be preached to me in set dogma and maxim. It may rather perhaps distil as dew. Yet many a man who has read " The Merchant of Venice," or pon-dered over that sad drama of a sinful soul in " Macbeth," or watched that terrible attempt of the wicked King to pray, in " Hamlet," or in " Measure for Measure " has grasped the key to that marvelously sad but most moral story in the lines—

> " He who the sword of Heaven would bear
>   Must be holy as severe,"

has heard sermons more precious probably than any homilies of the pulpit, lessons I venture to think, as sweet, or sweeter than any that have fallen on the world since the days of the Apostles. For think of it for a moment in this way.

We are all familiar with the thought that it is Christ's life which gives to the Master's words their force, and we confess that love of Jesus Himself is the only motive strong enough to make men keep His Commandments. St. John sums up the significance of all that in the phrase —"The word was made flesh."

It is not irreverence, I think, to point out that Shakespeare's teaching has the same advantage over that of the ordinary preacher that the teaching of the Evangelists has over the teaching of Solomon. He gives us a man to know instead of a proverb. It is through words made flesh that he teaches us.

The time at our disposal is all too short, alas! to make this special interpretation of Shakespeare's method as a teacher, as a national prophet, plain to you. But let me take two concrete examples of his method, which will, at any rate furnish I think each one of us with two practical lessons for our own every-day working lives. And the first lesson is an appropriate one for St. George's Day. For it is a lesson of chivalry.

I am sure that many of you must be familiar with that noble passage in Mr. Ruskin's "Sesame and Lilies" in which that great writer calls attention to the fact that, in the strict sense of the word, Shakespeare has no heroes— only heroines. "There is not one entirely heroic figure," Mr. Ruskin says, "in all his plays, except the slight sketch of Henry V. . . . Whereas there is hardly a play that has not a perfect woman in it, steadfast in grave hope, and errorless purpose; Cordelia, Desdemona, Isabella, Hermione, Imogen, Queen Catherine, Perdita, Sylvia, Viola, Rosalind, Helena, and last, and perhaps loveliest, Virgilia, are all faultless; conceived in the highest heroic type of humanity.

Now the lesson of this fact is not, I think, what Mr. Ruskin apparently conceives it to be. It is not, that is to say, that women are perfect in character—"infallibly faithful and wise counsellors—incorruptibly just and pure examples—strong always to sanctify, even when they cannot save "—in a way which is not possible to men. But the lesson is surely this: That Shakespeare evidently thought them so. That is the point to be grasped. Shakespeare kept true through his whole life to the youthful, the chivalric. ideal of a good woman, expressed in words which, in "Measure for Measure," he puts into the mouth of the jesting Lucio, describing Isabella—in her virginal strength and self-possessed dignity, perhaps the noblest of all the heroines of the plays:—

> "I hold you as a thing enskyed and sainted;
> By your renouncement, an immortal spirit;
> And to be talked with in sincerity,
> As with a saint."

And, my friends, what is worth remembering about this reverence of Shakespeare for women, which surrounds them for him to the end of his days—it is in "Winter's Tale," one of his latest plays, that he draws for us the gracious simplicity, the wifely perfection, of Hermione, and in "The Tempest," the latest of his plays, the peerless purity, the maiden sweetness, of the most admired Miranda—with an almost divine light and glamour, is that it is just what the ordinary man of the world too often despises as the mistake of his inexperienced youth. And yet who was more "the man of the world" than Shakespeare? His knowledge of human nature was immense and infallible, and in no sense did he avoid the world and its temptations. He lived, too, in the midst of London town life, of theatrical life, such as we know it to have been in Elizabeth's day, coarse, corrupt, feculent, and yet he preserved in his heart the feeling, natural, I venture to assert, to uncorrupted youth, of the divinity and sacredness of womanhood, so that in his latest as in his earliest plays his strong spirit, so keen to detect human weakness and sin, pays woman the involuntary homage of laying aside, in face of her excellence, its weapon of criticism. It is Iago, who is nothing if not critical, who dares to doubt of Desdemona's truth. He, it is true, as Mrs. Jameson says in her "Characteristics of Women," would have "bedeviled an angel." But alas! there are men in our own day, who, with none of Iago's wickedness, in either intention or act, are still tainted by the evil spirit of the world, and in their inmost thought dare to judge as he did of the virtue of woman. But such a man was not Shakespeare. He, at fifty years of age, still feels, in presence of his heroines, like a lover before his first love.

Seriously, then, do I beg you to ponder this fact, that the reverence for woman, which too many men affect to lose in their teens, was retained by the myriad-minded Shakespeare, to the end of his days.

One further word and lesson. You remember the character of Prospero in "The Tempest." Did it ever strike you to identify that great enchanter with Shakespeare himself in the closing years of life? The thought is surely a fruitful one. For "The Tempest," the latest of all his plays, is an ideal allegory of human life, with undermeanings everywhere, in every line of it, for those who have eyes to see, and ears to hear; but with all its lessons unforced, unsophisticated, illusive, unperceived indeed by those whose eyes are closed, whose ears are dull of hearing: the scene of it nowhere, anywhere, for it is in the Fortunate Island of the soul of man, that vexed land of Imagination hung between the upper and the nether world; the characters of it, types, abstractions—Womanhood, Youth, the People,—all of them, more or less, victims of illusion, all of them losing their way in this enchanted Realm of Life, except only Prospero, the great mage, absolute lord of the Island, who could summon to his service, at a moment's notice, every shape of merriment or of passion, every figure in the great tragi-comedy of life, and who, being none other surely than Shakespeare himself, "not one, but all mankind's epitome," could run easily through the whole scale of human passion and thought, from "Nature's woodnotes wild," or the homely commonplaces of existence, the chimney-corner wisdom of "Master Goodman Dull," to the transcendental subtilties of—

> "No, Time, thou shalt not boast that I do change,
> Thy pyramids built up with newer light
> To me are nothing novel, nothing strange,
> They are but dressings of a former sight."

It is not only because Prospero was a great enchanter, about to break his magic staff, to " drown his book deeper than ever plummet sounded," to dismiss his " airy spirits," and to return to the practical service of the State, that we identify the Philosopher Duke with Shakespeare the Poet Prophet. It is rather because the temper of Prospero is the temper of Shakespeare in those last days, when he came back to the dear old English home here in Stratford, to its sweetest, simplest, homeliest things, finding the daily life of this little place, the men and women here, the Nature all around, the green fields, the sweet hedgerow flowers, the quiet woods, the softly flowing Avon, good enough for him; despising nothing as common or unclean; curious of all things and of all men, but never scornful; humorous, sympathetic, tolerant; his wide-viewing mind at last looking back from the altitudes of thought to which he had attained, on all the pageantry of the lower world which he had abandoned, through a strange, pathetic, ideal light.

> " Our revels now are ended: these our actors,
>   As I foretold you, were all spirits, and
>   Are melted into air, into thin air:
>   And, like the baseless fabric of this vision,
>   The cloud-capp'd towers, the gorgeous palaces,
>   The solemn temples, the great globe itself,
>   Yea, all which it inherit, shall dissolve;
>   And, like this insubstantial pageant faded,
>   Leave not a rack behind.   We are such stuff
>   As dreams are made of, and our little life
>   Is rounded with a sleep.   Sir, I am vex'd;
>   Bear with my weakness; my old brain is troubled.
>   Be not disturb'd with my infirmity:
>   If you be pleased, retire into my cell,
>   And there repose; a turn or two I'll walk,
>   To still my beating mind."

And so he ends—Prospero or Shakespeare. In the epilogue to the play you have the keynote of this self-mastered character, this self-possessed grandeur of a completely disciplined will which is common to both,—to Shakespeare as to Prospero—Forgiveness and Freedom.

"And my ending is despair,
Unless I be relieved by prayer;
Which pierces so, that it assaults
Mercy itself, and frees all faults."

And so, too, I will end—how better?—with those lessons
of Freedom and Forgiveness: the true Freedom which
only comes from service, the true Pardon which only
comes to those who forgive, because they have been forgiven.

Have you learnt those lessons? The root of all true
religion, believe me, lies there. What do you know of
the true "service which is perfect freedom"? What is
your definition of life? How do you conceive of it to
yourself? Is it, do you think, as Shakespeare has elsewhere said,—"a tale told by an idiot, signifying nothing"? or is it a mission of service to your fellows for
Christ's sake? God grant you may answer—Life is service! Life is duty! Life is a mission! All for Love and
the world well lost. For Jesus said—"Whosoever would
save his life shall lose it; but whosoever shall lose his life
for My sake shall save it."

And the lesson of Pardon—have you made that, too,
yours? "The tongues of dying men"—our poet says—
"enforce attention like deep harmony." And from the
Cross of Jesus and His last dying prayer—"Father, forgive them; for they know not what they do"—we have
all learnt—God grant it!—to recognize the ethical beauty
of the spirit of forgiveness; but do we equally acknowledge its moral power? its redeeming power? "Father!
. . . forgive us our trespasses, as we forgive them
that trespass against us." So daily we pray. Brothers!
Sisters! do we truly realize this power of forgiveness, this
social power of remitting or retaining sins, this priestly
power of humanity? Ah! believe me, just so far as we
exercise it lovingly and wisely in our lives and with our
lips we help men away from sin: just so far as we do not
exercise it, or exercise it wrongly, we drive men into sin.
And, my friends, from which of your Christian teachers
will you learn of that unstrained "quality of mercy"—of
that earthly power of free forgiveness "which then shows
likest God's when mercy seasons justice"—more un-

erringly than you will from Shakespeare? He was no priest, I repeat, he waved no censer. But just as in regard to that other lesson of Freedom, Shakespeare does seem to give to each one of us courage, and energy, and strength to dedicate ourselves and our work to that service, to that mission—whatever it may be—which life has revealed to us as best, and highest, and most real,—so, also, with regard to this other lesson of the Redemptive Power of a priestly Humanity, this social force of true forgiveness, I do not hesitate to say that in Shakespeare's genius there burns truly, and fragrantly, and steadily—

> " Such incense as of right belongs
>   To the true shrine,
> Where stands the Healer of all wrongs,
>   In light Divine."

DAVID SWING

THE NOVEL IN LITERATURE

[Address by David Swing, clergyman, and platform speaker, founder of the Central (Independent) Church, Chicago, of which he remained minister until his death. He was born in Cincinnati, Ohio, August 23, 1830; died in Chicago, Ill., October 3, 1894.]

In speaking of the novel, it is not my purpose to eulogize nor to decry it, but simply in an impartial manner, to inquire as to the position in literature that the novel should occupy. I shall speak only of the ideal novel, and shall say little of it in the concrete.

Every branch of fine art springs out of something within human nature. All of the arts are the external expression of something in the spirit, and literature, being one of the arts, must also be the external expression of something within. In seeking for the cause of some branches of the fine arts, it is often essential that we fall back upon our rights as human beings, and placing our hands upon our hearts, say, "I love this or I love that because—I do." None of you can rise in your place and tell why you love music.

Very often we have to be like the young man who was walking in the garden among the Romans—I am sure it was in the Roman days—with an old philosopher, and, having come to a bed of poppies, the young man said, "Father, why is it the poppy makes people sleepy?" Now, the custom of these old Latin and Greek professors was never to admit ignorance of anything, but always to know the whole reason—and there are men yet living of that class, theologians generally. The old philosopher

From "Old Pictures of Life." Copyright, by Stone & Kimball, and published by Herbert S. Stone & Co.

looking upon the ground said: "My son, the poppy makes people sleepy because it possesses a soporific principle"; and the young man was happy. Walking through this garden of literature, this flower called the novel—not this poppy, for the sermon is the true poppy of literature—this rose rises up before you and asks if you can tell the source of its gorgeous coloring. In doing this it is necessary to go back.

First, having found out what literature is, we may infer whether the novel is a part of true literature. Literature is that thought which is universal. True literature must be universal truth appealing to man as man, not to man as a Methodist, Calvinist, an Englishman, or an American. Hence the writings of Shakespeare, of Homer, of Milton pass into all languages, because the great thoughts of those writers belong to the human heart. But the element of universality is not sufficient, because the truths of the multiplication table are universal. The whole human family believe that twice two makes four. Besides the universality, you will find that all the thoughts of literature spring from the soul, that is, from the emotions, from the sentiments, rather than from the intellect alone. So that in literature you must have a universality of thought, and thought ornamented, thought decorated—the thoughts of the heart. This is sufficiently inclusive, if it includes poetry, the drama, the great histories, the great essays, and religion, and is sufficiently exclusive if it throws out encyclopedias, "The Congressional Globe," and, what is better yet, arithmetic, and also dogmatic theology—which is no part of literature.

Secondly, all the fine arts spring from a basis of sentiment. They are the outward expressions of sentiment, and for the most part all fine arts spring from a single sentiment, that of the beautiful. Music, statuary, painting, architecture are the outward expressions of our sense of beauty. Literature is nothing else than thought ornamented. Where, then, is this element of beauty that makes the novel a part of literature, and secures for it an admittance into the great world of art? Go back with me, if you choose, two thousand years, and you will see upon the walls of every old temple, of every palace, of every dwelling-house a certain form or figure, and the likeness is—woman. The forehead is not high, as our girls used to think twenty years ago—I believe the notion has perished, that thought made the forehead high; nor is the hair black, as our girls still think, but brown. The cheek, the chin, the nose, the shoulders all express beauty in the undulating lines that are supposed to convey it.

The Greeks called this image Andromeda, or Helen. Along came the Latins and called it Minerva, or Zenobia. Along came the Italians and called it Beatrice. The Bible built a beautiful garden around it and called it Eve. But call this creature what you may, this is the Atlas upon whose shoulders the world of the novel turns and passes through the vicissitudes of day and night, summer and winter. This is the element of beauty that entered into that part of literature, and for the most part acts as the adorning element, the decoration of the thought.

I affirm, therefore, that of the novel woman is the satisfactory explanation, the ample apology. The novel is that part of literature which is decorated, for the most part, by the beauty of woman. It is the woman in literature. I mean by this, not that woman is the whole subject-matter. She cannot be; but she is the inspiration, the central figure in the group, the reason of the grouping, the apology for it, the explanation of it, the decoration, the golden light flung over the thought. Let me illustrate. While Madame Récamier lived the great men of France—generals, statesmen, scientific men, literary men of every kind, and even clergymen—met in her parlors every day at four o'clock. Not because they loved her or she them—for it is said she loved nobody deeply—and they met not because of her conversation, for she said little, but they convened every day because there was an inspiration in her presence, something that sweetly molded the hour. They met because her beauty, her friendship, was a glorious flag under which to convene, and when she departed from life those great men convened no more. Not because the questions of war or theology had been answered, but because their hearts had been freed from that charming entanglement. This is all. What a power to inspire has the single sentiment called "love"! I believe that is the best name for it—or friendship. What an influence it does exert upon all our years between fifteen and—and—eighty. We have all known the poor sewing-girl to bend over her machine and sing far into the night, not because sewing-machines and poverty are sweet, but because there is something in that deep attachment she has to some human being which will take up a life of varied cares and sorrows and will baptize them all into its great flowing river and make this very life all beauty by its coloring.

This, then, is what I mean by saying that woman is the inspiration of that part of literature called the novel. The great Hindoo nation produced a beautiful system of morals and quite a good system of scientific thought and truth, but no novel. Why? Because the reason of the novel had not been permitted to exist. The Hindoo world denied the existence of woman as a mental and spiritual being, and thus, having held back the cause, the effect failed to put in an appearance. The novel rose up out of the land which emancipated woman; and ever since that day the novel has been the photograph of woman, beautiful as she is beautiful, wretched where she declines. In the days of Sir Walter Scott it was nothing but the history of a green country courtship long drawn out and full of monotony, that is, to the rest of mankind. Had not Sir Walter Scott woven into his novels a vast amount of scenery and costume and history, his works to-day would be entirely crowded from our shelves. In Sir Walter Scott's day the entire effort of genius in this line was to postpone a wedding. Just think of it! Escapes from bandits, Indians, poisoning, and mothers-in-law enabled the novel writer then to accumulate stuff enough for two volumes, and then came a wedding or a funeral.

Every novel, too, must have its hero, as well as its heroine. But candor compels me—I emphasize the word—the sense of justice compels me to say that there is not in the masculine faith or nature the element of beauty that will ever enable it to become the basis of fine art. It is discouraging, but true.

When any painter wishes to place upon canvas his idea of beauty, he never asks men to sit. Who ever saw Faith, Hope, and Charity pictured as three men?

I now proceed to the most difficult part of my discussion, viz., that the more the novel gets away from woman the greater the book. This I suppose you will think is heresy, but I expect to show you it is orthodox. That is, the more she is made the priestess of the religion without herself becoming the religion the greater the book. In his preface Montaigne says, "I have gathered flowers from everybody's field, and nothing is mine except the string that binds them." So, the modern novel, that is, the ideal novel—and the modern novel is approaching the ideal novel—is a book in which the truth is gathered from every field, from science, from religion, from politics, and woman is the white ribbon that binds them for us. That is all.

To illustrate: Let us take the German novel by Richter. Who was Richter? Was he some young man trying to palm off on the public an account of his courtship? By no means. For fifty or sixty years had the sun gone down in beauty along the Rhine in his sight. For fifty years he had been a sincere follower of Jesus Christ. The hair hung snow-white upon his shoulders when he sat down to commit to writing his deepest thoughts regarding education, and religion, and the development of character; and he chose Linda, a beautiful being, and set her down in the midst of his thought after weaving around her all the flowers of his mind's best moments, and we are all allured along by her shining figure through the deepest thoughts of that German philosopher. In George Mac-Donald our religion is reinstated. The religion of the past is all reconstructed—not overthrown, but beautifully reconstructed. In his works the gates of hell are made a little narrower, so that not quite so big a crowd are forced therein. In his works the gates of heaven are made a good deal larger, so that millions of beings whom our ancestors shut out forever from this blessed abode all come crowding in there, a happy throng, through its pearly gates. What need I say of Bulwer, and George Eliot, and all this modern school? I will only say this, that they are gates of beauty through which often appear the holiest truths of life.

Now, if education were simply the accumulation of truths I should not be willing to enter this plea, but education is never the accumulation of facts. Otherwise all the books we would need would be the encyclopedia, the dictionary, the daily press. Education is the awakening of the heart: it is life, vitality, the arousing of the spirit. And hence all the arts come beside the truths of life. Education, being the power to think, the power to act, what we need is not information only, but awakening something that moves the sluggish blood in our hearts and makes us truly alive. This is what we all need, because man is not only by nature totally depraved, but totally lazy. Edmund Burke was indeed a man that knew much, but you can find many a German professor in his garden that knew ten times as much. So Daniel Webster; but Daniel Webster felt deeply some of the truths of life. They flowed all through his blood, tingled in his finger-ends—liberty for example, the Union. Education, there-fore, is not the amassing of truths, but it is the deep reali-zation of truth, and hence around the great forehead of Daniel Webster all the shouts of liberty in all the ages of the past echoed a great music in the upper air. This was education, the power to think and to feel deeply.

I speak with feeling upon this point, because one of the great calamities with which we all have to battle is nar-rowness, that is, we all become attached to our little path in life, and we think that is the God-appointed life. The physician feels that if only the whole human family would read some of the rules regarding health, they would need little else. They would not need much daily newspaper, or preaching, or magazine. He has come to feel that the wisdom of the world is all along his path. It is so with the lawyer, and who is an exception to this? I am not sure but that the editor of the daily paper—the best in the land—feels that if we would all take his paper—and it is the best in the land—we would need nothing else. And then along comes a clergyman, and he is perfectly certain —if the clergyman ever has an assurance of faith, it is on this point—that if the whole world were brought before his pulpit every Sunday morning, it would need very little of the novel, or the newspaper, or the magazine, for does he not know it all?—and so cheap! It is the fine art that helps the newspaper, and the newspaper that helps the fine art, and the pulpit the same, and he has the educated

soul who permits all these rays of light to fall right down
through his intellect upon his heart.

The question, Who should read novels? is perfectly
absurd.   There are in all the arts the high and the low.
The wit of Rabelais is low, or Cervantes lofty.   The paintings of the old Dutch school were humble, being most of
them scenes in grog-shops, but in the Düsseldorf school
lofty, being for the most part great scenes from the world
of nature.   The poetry of Swinburne is low for the most
part, that of Bryant lofty.   These two colors, white and
black, run through all the arts everywhere, and it is for
us to choose.   Who should read the novel?   Everybody
should read the novel where woman decorates the great
truths of life; but where the novel is the simple history
of love, nobody.   And especially should those read novels
who the most don't want to; they the most need them.
And there ought to be a law requiring a certain class of
people to read one novel a year—persons who through
some narrowness of law, or of medicine, or of merchan-
dise, or, what is most probable, of theology, have been
reduced to the condition of pools of water in August—
stationary, sickly, scum-covered, and just about to go dry.

Nor are we to love only the novel in the day when history has become so deep, so broad, so grand, not being
the history of wars any more, but of thought, of science,
of art.   In such a day, to love only the novel, and to read
only the novel, is to offer an insult alike to God and to
man; but even Tyndall ought to turn away from his
perpetual analyses of drops of water, everlasting weighing
of dust, and over the pages of "John Halifax" pass from a
world of matter to a world of spirit.   So must you all live,
with all the beautiful things and the powerful things of
God's world falling right into your open hearts, feeding
the great flame of life.   As miners look up a long shaft
and see a little piece of sky which they call heaven, so
there are men who look through a long punched-elder,
very long and very slim, and they see through the other
end of it a spot, and call it a world.   It must be the effort
of our lives to get right away from this imprisonment.   To
be too near any one thing—that is fanaticism.   It is the
eclipse of God's great Heavens in favor of our tallow
candle.

LEW WALLACE
Photogravure after a photograph

LEW WALLACE

RETURN OF THE FLAGS

[Address by General Lew Wallace, lawyer, soldier, author (born in Brookville, Ind., April 10, 1827; ———), delivered at Indianapolis, Ind., July 4, 1866, on the occasion of the return to the State of the colors of all its commands that took part in the Civil War. A vast multitude was gathered at the ceremony, which was conducted with great splendor. To this presentation address of General Wallace the Governor of Indiana, Oliver P. Morton, made an appropriate response.]

GOVERNOR:—The Soldiers' Association of the State have had it in mind to signalize in some especial manner the happy conclusion of the recent Civil War. This they have thought to accomplish by a ceremonious return of the colors with which their respective commands were entrusted: and, not without a dash of poetry, they have chosen this as a proper day for the celebration. For them, therefore, and for the great body of comrades, present and absent, whom they represent, I have the honor to give you back their flags, with the request that measures be taken by the next General Assembly to preserve them forever.

Sir, I shall never forget my first interview with you upon the subject of the war. It was a day or two after the fall of Sumter. The National Government had not recovered from that blow, and we were in nowise better off. You told me that the President had called for six regiments of volunteers from Indiana, and asked me to accept the Adjutant-Generalcy, and help you raise them, and I agreed to. It may be to our shame now, but truth requires the admission that we spoke of the matter then as one of

doubt. The President hoped, yet feared, and so did we.
Ah, sir, that there should have been a suspicion of our
people or a dread that they would fail their Government!
Yet had a prophet told us then what proportions the war
would assume, what other quotas it would demand, what
others exhaust, I much fear we would not have been
stout enough to put despair aside.

Now, I congratulate you upon the firmness with which
you did your duty. I congratulate you also upon having
a State whose people never failed their Governor. I return you the colors of thirteen regiments of cavalry,
twenty-six batteries, and one hundred and fifty-six regiments of infantry. Have I not reason to congratulate you
upon the glory acquired by our native State during your
administration—a glory which you in a great part share—
a glory which will live always?

Most of the flags I return are grandly historical. I
would like to tell their stories separately, because it would
so much enhance the renown of the brave men to whom
they belonged: that, however, is impossible; time forbids
it; or rather it is forbidden by the number of flags. As
the next best way to gratify curiosity concerning them, it
is arranged that the sacred relics shall each be displayed
before the audience, accompanied with a recital of the
principal battles in which they figured. Still, I must be
permitted to indulge in a kind of recapitulatory reference to them. There may be some citizen present who
does not realize how necessary his State was in the great
work of suppressing the Rebellion—perhaps some soldier
who has yet to learn what a hero he really was.

When the war began, the military fame of Indiana, as
you remember, was under a cloud. It was in bad repute,
particularly with the Southern people. Why? It is un-
necessary to say. Such was the case. I allude to it now
to call attention to the fact that those sections in which
our repute was worst bear to-day the deepest marks of
our armed presence. A little over five years ago on this
very spot a gallant regiment was sworn to "Remember
Buena Vista"; to-day it can be said, with a truth which
the long array of storied flags shortly to be displayed
will eloquently attest, the slander of Buena Vista has been
more than remembered—it is avenged. By a chance,

much grumbled at in the beginning by the soldiers, much complained of by the historian, whose narrative it sadly complicates, our regiments were more scattered than those of any other State. Indeed, it is not too much to say that there has not been in the five years a military department without one or more of them; nor an army corps that has not borne some of them on its rolls; nor a great battle in which some of them have not honorably participated.

As true lovers of our brave native State, let us rejoice at that distribution. It enabled our soldiers to serve the Union everywhere; it enabled them to convince all foemen, as well as friends, of their courage, endurance, and patriotism; it is the means by which the name of Indiana is or will be written upon every battle monument— through its chances every victory, wherever or by whomsoever won, in any degree illustrative of Northern valor, is contributive to her glory.

Three of our regiments took part in the first battle of the war; while another, in view of the Rio Grande, fought its very last battle. The first regiment under Butler to land at the wharf at New Orleans was the 21st Indiana. The first flag over the bloody parapet at Fort Wagner, in front of Charleston, was that of the 13th Indiana. The first to show their stars from the embattled crest of Mission Ridge were those of the 79th and 86th Indiana. Two of our regiments helped storm Fort McAllister, down by Savannah. Another was amongst the first in the assaulting line at Fort Fisher. Another, converted into engineers, built all of Sherman's bridges from Chattanooga to Atlanta, from Atlanta to the sea, and from the sea northward. Another, in line of battle on the beach of Hampton Roads, saw the frigate " Cumberland " sink to the harbor's bed rather than strike her flag to the " Merrimac "; and, looking from the same place next day, cheered, as never men cheered, at sight of the same " Merrimac " beaten by a single gun in the turret of Worden's little " Monitor."

Others aided in the overthrow of the savages, red and rebel, at Pea Ridge, Arkansas. Three from Washington, across the Peninsula, within sight of Richmond evacuated, to Harrison's Landing, followed McClellan to his fathomless fall.   Five were engaged in the salvation of Washington at Antietam.   Four were with Burnside at Fredericksburg, where some of Kimball's Hoosiers were picked up lying nearer than all others to the pitiless embrasures. Five were at Chancellorsville, where Stonewall Jackson took victory out of Hooker's hand and carried it with him to his grave.   Six were almost annihilated at Gettysburg. One, an infantry regiment, marched nearly ten thousand miles; literally twice around the Rebellion, fighting as it went.   Four were part of the besom with which Sheridan swept the Shenandoah Valley.

Finally, when Grant, superseding Halleck, transferred his headquarters to the East, and began the last grand march against Richmond, four of our regiments, joined soon after by another, followed him faithfully, leaving their dead all along the way—in the Wilderness, at Laurel Hill, at Spottsylvania, at Po River, at North Anna River, at Bethesda Church, at Cold Harbor, in front of Petersburg, down to Clover Hill—down to the final halt in the war in which Lee yielded up the sword of the Rebellion.

Sir, it is my opinion that our regiments were all equally brave and patriotic; that some achieved a wider distinction than others, was because their opportunities were better and more frequent.   Such being my belief, I hope to be forgiven if I stop here and make special mention of the 7th, 13th, 14th, 19th, and 20th regiments.   Theirs was a peculiar lot.   Throughout the war they served in the East as our representatives.   Commanded entirely by Eastern officers, who were naturally less interested in them than in the people of their own States, it was their fate to be little mentioned in reports and seldom if ever heard of in Eastern papers.   In fact, they were our lost children; as effectually lost in the mazes of the great Eastern campaigns as De Soto and his people were lost in the wilderness of the New World, and like them again, wandering here and there, never at rest, seldom halting except to fight.   The survivors—alas! that they should come back to us so broken and so few—were in the service nearly five years, and of that time they lived quite three years on the march, in the trenches, in rifle-pits, "on the rough edge of battle," or in its very heart.

But, sir, most of the flags returned to you belong to the

regiments whose theater of operations cannot well be ter-
ritorially described; whose lines of march were backward
and forward, through fifteen States of the Union.

If one seeks the field in which the power of our State,
as well as the valor of our people, had the finest exempli-
fication, he must look to the West and South.   I will not
say that Indiana's contributions to the cause were indispensable to its final success.   That would be unjust to the
States more populous and wealthy and equally devoted.
But I will say, that her quotas precipitated the result;
without them the war might yet be in full progress and
doubtful.

Let us consider this proposition a moment.   At Shiloh,
Indiana had thirteen regiments; at Vicksburg, she had
twenty-four; at Stone River, twenty-five; at Chickamauga,
twenty-seven; at Mission Ridge, twenty; in the advance
from Chattanooga to Atlanta, fifty; at Atlanta, Sherman
divided them so that exactly twenty-five went with him
down to the sea, while twenty-five marched back with
Thomas, and were in at the annihilation of Hood at Nash-
ville.   What a record is thus presented!   Ask Grant or
Rosecrans or Sherman if from the beginning to the end
of their operations there was a day for which they could
have spared those regiments.   No; without them, Bragg
might yet be on Lookout Mountain; or Sherman still tilt-
ing like a Titan among the gorges of Kenesaw and Re-
saca; or, worse yet, Halleck, that only one of all our generals who never saw a battle, might be General-in-Chief,
waiting for the success at Vicksburg to reduce him to his
proper level—chief of an unnamed staff.

I regret that time limits me to such a meagre analysis
of the services of our soldiers.   Still it is enough to challenge inquiry concerning them; enough at least to show
how sacred these flags are.   I know you will receive them
reverently.   I know you will do all in your power to have
them put where no enemy other than time can get at them.
Yet, with shame be it said, there are men who deny their
sanctity.   We have neighbors, all of us, who see or affect
to see in them nothing but hated symbols of venality, ambition, and murder.   God pity such a wretched delusion!
The conflict is gone, let us hope never to return; but what
a sum of human hopes and promises was involved in it!

What a sum of human good will result from it! Its conclusion was a renewal of our liberty—a proclamation of
eventual liberty to all mankind—a yielding up forever of
that unhallowed thing called Christian slavery.

Put them away tenderly. They are suggestive mementoes of a glorious cause magnificently maintained.
They will serve many good purposes yet. In the years to
come the soldiers will rally around them, not as formerly
called from fitful slumbers by the picket's near alarm, or
in the heat and fury of the deadly combat; but in the calm
of peace, and in the full enjoyment of all they struggled
for. If only from habit, where the flags are the veterans
will come; and they will look at them through tear-
dimmed eyes, and tell where they flew on such a day;
what well-remembered comrades bore them through such
a fight; who were wounded; who died under them. If
only to make the veterans glad, and enable them, it may
be, in old age to renew their youth, and with each other
to march their marches and fight their battles over again,
I pray you put the holy relics safely away.

Sir, we do not realize the war just ended; we only
remember it while in progress; we only think of it by
piecemeal. Our most vivid impressions of it are derived
from mere incidents. Not merely what is thought of it
now, but what has been said and written about it is colored
by the misconceptions, prejudices, and partialities of the
hour. But this will be changed. The day will come when
the volumes of facts now under lock and key and with-
held from fear, affection, or policy will be exposed; and
there will be historians to collate and refine them, and
poets to exalt them, and artists to picture them, and philosophers to analyze their effects upon society, religion,
and civilization.

Then, and not until then, will the struggle be wholly
realized. Meantime it will grow in the estimation of each
succeeding generation, and be continually more and more
sanctified. And in those days mementoes will be in request. There are unjeweled swords, not worth the looking at now, that will be fortunes then. Bullets, gleaned
by the plowmen from famous fields, will wear shining
labels in richest cabinets; and letters, at present not as
valuable as old colonial deeds, will then be of inestimable

virtu because they are originals from the hand of a Lincoln or a Grant, written in the crisis of the great Rebellion. In that day what a treasure will this collection of flags be to our successors! And what pilgrimages there will be to see the tattered, shot-torn, blood-stained fragments which streamed so often with more than a rainbow's beauty through the vanished clouds of the dreadful storm! And at sight of them, how men will be reminded of the thousand battles fought; of Shiloh, that tournament to the death in which the vaunting chivalry of the Southwest met for the first time the despised chivalry of the Northwest, and were overthrown in the very midst of a supposed victory; of Vicksburg, that operation the most daring in conception, most perfect in execution, and the most complete in results of modern warfare; of the advance to Atlanta, in which the genius of the general was so well supported by the splendid endurance of the soldier; and of the march to the sea, memorable chiefly as a cold, rigid, retributive triumph in which the horrors of a ruthless progress were so strangely blent with the prayers and blessings of a race raised so sublimely and after such ages of suffering from the plantation to the school, from slavery to freedom, from death to life!

You know, sir, how prone men are in prosperity to forget the pangs of adversity. Ordinarily, what cares the young spendthrift, happy in the waste of his father's fortune, for that father's life of toil and self-denial? It is to be hoped these flags will prevent such indifference on the part of our posterity. Think of them grouped all in one chamber! What descendant of a loyal man could enter it, and look upon them, and not feel the ancestral sacrifices they both attest and perpetuate? And when the foreigner, dreaming, it may be, of invasion or conquest, or ambition, political or military, more dangerous now than all the kings, shall come into their presence, as come they will; though they be not oppressed with reverence, or dumb-stricken with awe, as you and I and others like us may be, doubt not that they will go away wiser than they came; they will be reminded of what the Frenchman had not heard when he landed his legions on the palmy shore of Mexico; of what a ruler of England overlooked when he was willing to make haste to recognize the Rebellion;

of what the trained leaders of the Rebellion themselves took not into account when they led their misguided followers into the fields of war; they will be reminded that this people, so given to peace, so devoted to trade, mechanics, agriculture, so occupied with schools and churches and a Government which does their will through the noiseless agency of the ballot-box, have yet when roused a power of resistance sufficient for any need however great; that this nationality, yet in youth's first freshness, is like a hive of human bees—stand by it quietly and you will be charmed by its proofs of industry, its faculty of appliance, its well-ordered labor; but touch it, shake it rudely, menace its population, or put them in fear, and they will pour from their cells an armed myriad whom there is no confronting —or rather that it is like the ocean, beautiful in calm, but irresistible in storm.

Fellow soldiers! Comrades: When we come visiting the old flags, and take out those more especially endeared to us because under them we each rendered our individual service, such as it was, we will not fail to be reminded of those other comrades—alas! too many to be named— who dropped one by one out of the ranks or the column to answer at roll-call nevermore; whose honorable discharges were given them by fever in the hospital or by a bullet in battle; whose bones lie in shallow graves in the cypress swamp, in the river's deepening bed, in the valley's Sabbath stillness, or on the mountain's breast, blackened now by tempests—human as well as elemental. For their sakes let us resolve to come here with every recurrence of this day, and bring the old colors to the sunlight, and carry them in procession, and salute them martially with roll of drums and thunder of guns. So will those other comrades of whom I speak know that they are remembered at least by us; and so will we be remembered by them.

In the armies of Persia there was a chosen band called the Immortals. They numbered ten thousand; their ranks were always full, and their place was near the person of the king. The old poets sing of this resplendent host as clad in richest armor, and bearing spears pointed with pomegranates of silver and gold. We, too, have our Immortals! Only ours wear uniforms of light, and they

number more than ten times ten thousand, and instead of
a king to serve, they have for leader and lover that man
of God and the people, Lincoln, the martyr.   On their
rolls shine the heroic names without regard to such paltry
distinctions as rank or state.   Among them are no officers, no privates!   In the bivouacs of Heaven they are
all alike Immortals.   Of such are Ellsworth, Baker, Wads-
worth, Sedgwick and MacPherson.   Of such, also, are
our own Hackleman, Gerber, Tanner, Blinn, and Carroll,
and that multitude of our soldiers who, victims of war,
are now " at the front," while we are waiting " in reserve."

CHARLES DUDLEY WARNER

GEORGE WILLIAM CURTIS, LITTERATEUR

[Address by Charles Dudley Warner, critic, novelist, man of letters (born in Plainfield, Mass., September 12, 1829; died in Hartford, Conn., October 20, 1900), delivered at a meeting of the Unitarian Club of New York, held in memory of George William Curtis, November 14, 1892.]

MR. CHAIRMAN:—We all loved him. This is about what I would like to say and about the sum and substance of it all. I should not like to stand here for criticism, if that were necessary, with a knife in my hand even if it were a gilt-edged one. To-night I feel only a great emotion of gratitude that I knew him, and that I had in some measure the privilege of his confidence in certain things. You have had a very complete setting forth of what Mr. Curtis was, and the estimation in which he was held, not only by his own religious body, to which he was such an honor, but by the country at large; and I have been asked to say something about him on his literary side.

Mr. Curtis was born with a literary gift. That is a very distinct gift. I do not think it is ever simulated by anybody; and if anybody does get, by advertisement, a little reputation of that kind, it does not last long after the advertisements have grown cold and been paid for. Mr. Curtis was born, as I judge from his early sketches, something of a dreamer. He liked to lounge about the Providence wharf and smell the molasses, rum, and other things that came from foreign coasts. He always saw the foreign coasts, and never lost sight of them. He saw them when he came into the large and practical affairs of life. There was that dreaminess in the boy, I judge, and I suppose that is what made him go to Brook Farm. There must have been something peculiar in a youth of that age which should lead him into such a purely roseate and humanitarian experiment as that idylic attempt to live by the work of one's own hands—milking and things of that kind—at Brook Farm. If the cows had been always liberal, and the soil had been a little better, I think the experiment might have succeeded. Mr. Curtis went from there, fortunately for him, with apparently a very inadequate school training, to Europe, for four years. Europe was his university; and to a poor man, with such high ideals as that boy had, it was probably the best university that he could have had; because he saw the best there; he evidently consorted with the best people, and he got out of history the best that was to be learned, both for warning and inspiration. The first that the world knew of him was after his return from Europe, when the first fruits of his culture were laid before the public in a little volume called " Nile Notes of Howadji." We did not then know—most of us—what a howadji was: but the Notes were so entirely delightful, and such a perfect continuation of the life which we all hope to lead somewhere in our " Arabian Nights," that we judged that a howadji must be a most agreeable and charming person. You will remember that he went by the name of Howadji Curtis for a long time; and we all recognized it. There grew up (I do not know how—of course it was in the man) in the public mind everywhere a certain notion of a very cultivated, dainty, chivalrous, and yet manly person, out of those " Nile Notes." Those Notes are not critical; they are not archæological, but much what the " Arabian Nights" entertainers might themselves have spun about the things in Egypt which please the fancy, and do not appear even to satiate.

But after Mr. Curtis came back and began to live the life of this country, his attention was almost immediately attracted to a state of things here which received evidently more attention at that time than it would command now. I should say that it would take about forty persons at that time to produce the impression upon Mr. Curtis's mind which it needs four hundred now to produce. That was

about the proportion of social impression which he had:
and out of that impression came, in the first place, a very
startling indictment, called "Our Best Society," which
was followed by the delineation of one of the most charming women of antiquity, Mrs. Potiphar.   There grew out
of that "The Potiphar Papers."   I was looking them
over the other day (I had remembered them in my time as
being on the whole rather a genial satire), and I was surprised, when I came to read them again, to find how much
of a very decided sincerity and earnestness there was in
them.   There is no mincing matters at all in them.   If
you read them by the light of to-day you will find that in
them things are called by their right names, and the bad
is held up to retribution without any mincing at all.

About the same time, however, and almost contemporary with these papers, began to appear a series of as
delightful sketches of a life that we all would like to lead,
or at least ought to like to lead, as we have ever had in
this country; these sketches conveyed a notion of the
idylic life of "Prue and I."   Now, the noticeable thing
about them was not that the style was charming, but that
here was the first evidence that he had the divine gift.
The style, the charm, was there.   It was the same that
we saw afterwards when he entered the field as a lecturer.
It was grace; it was witchery; it was the last thing that we
want in the orator or the lecturer.   It was not that alone
in "Prue and I"; but here was a statement made under
playful aspect, that after all there was something better
than money, something better than fine equipage; that
on the whole it was just as well to see Aurelia go out in
her fine clothes and her beautiful attire, as it was to go
yourself—provided you hadn't the money.   There was a
most exquisite and beautiful gospel of common life in
those early sketches; and you will notice the characteristic
of them—which was the characteristic of everything of
that day—and I was surprised when I came to think about
it—it was their democracy, their absolute democracy.
Our good friends who did not like civil service reform
(unless they had the arrangement of it entirely within
themselves) used to sneer a good deal at Mr. Curtis as
being non-American, and a dude, and I do not know
what else—and it is not necessary to repeat the fine

phrases. But there was the beginning of the man and he never changed in that respect from being the most intensely American and democratic writer of that day! You must remember that that was a day of sentimentality. If you will look back to the time from 1840 onward to 1850, you will be as much pleased as delighted, perhaps, with the amount of gush that we contrived to get out, in that period. It was a mawkish, sentimental era, almost altogether. You all remember about the old garret, and the rain on the roof, and the old yellow letters that the woman got out of the old garret, and the baby—why the baby was harder work than anything else—and the baby's shoes, the little shoes that you all know: why, we gushed and cried all over the place, about the baby's shoes, for a long time. They were not real tears; nobody pretended that they were; but we wanted something to cry about, and so we cried about those things. That was the era of extreme sentiment and gush,—or what would now be called "swash." In that era Mr. Curtis struck that perfectly pure and strong American note.

There was one thing to be said about those papers. I had remembered them as delicate satire. Mr. Curtis was a master of irony in his later years; with the most exquisite irony he used to cut off the heads of these fellows here in New York, and they never found it out. Some of them think they are alive now. They believe that a man is alive long after he has forfeited public esteem. Mr. Curtis had a most exquisite irony, but in those early papers it was not so fine; it was so downright, so sledge-hammery, that it could not be mistaken. Most noticeable was the change that came as he went along in life, as he grew in years, and grew in mastery of his weapon until he flowered out in those papers in Harper's "Monthly," which he continued for thirty years, and which, whenever the occasion required, were very masterpieces in delicate satire, and good-humored irony, which is always the best sort, because men hate much more to be laughed at than to be sworn at.

I cannot of course go into any criticism of Mr. Curtis's work. I hold literature in great esteem in the great places in the world, because I think it is the most important thing we have, believing as I do, and as you know, that the most valuable thing in literature is nothing but a record of the thought of the world and of its emotions.   Now, it is quite possible that on the highest plane of literary perform- ance Mr. Curtis may take a place somewhere lower than we estimate him, in the warmth of our affection; but there is one thing which is perfectly certain, and that is, that the best, the most enduring literature, is that which most con- cerns and has the strongest relation to life.   The notice- able thing about Mr. Curtis is, that all the time his litera- ture, without ever ceasing to be high-class literature, in whatever way he turned his pen, or his tongue, became more and more intimately and radically blended with the deepest interests of human life.   And so, whether the first efforts of Mr. Curtis endure, as some lyrics, as some pieces of old literature, will endure, the real essence and sub- stance of the literature which he so thoroughly put into everything that he did, is one of our most enduring and valuable national possessions.   Mr. Curtis never ceased to be a literary man.   You all know the story—you know what " The Potiphar Papers " cost him; you know what his early stand in anti-slavery matters cost him.   They cost him what they cost Phillips, and what they cost every- body who was manly enough to stand up in that day and brave social opinion.   But Mr. Curtis went on without any break at all in the use of that literary gift; and when he went up there to Middletown, in the early days of the anti-Nebraska excitement, and made an oration to the young students there it was a trumpet-call to the young men of the country, to go out and join in the great move- ment which this nation was bound to make for its emanci- pation from evil and from slavery.   When he made that effort it was just as distinctly a literary performance as was " Prue and I," or " The Potiphar Papers," or as any Egyptian paper that he ever wrote.   It was, in the first place, eloquent—and if you read it to-day you will find that it was eloquent in the highest sense of finished literary effort.   I remember the effect it had; it was not merely the nature of the appeal; others were making that appeal in a thousand newspapers; but it was the clean, high, com- manding literary note in that oration, which called the young men up to a higher plane of action and of life than they had ever been on before.

I could talk a great while (but it is useless) about Mr. Curtis in various ways. I think that no one ever went to him that did not feel that his greeting of him was somehow a benediction. On the most trivial matters, if you went to speak to him, or if you went to consult him about any serious thing, there was always the same—never any condescension—but always the same recognition of your dignity, and always the same affability, grace and charm of manner. I do not know but it increased our self-esteem—perhaps that was it; we felt that we were so much finer than we thought we were before, or so graceful a person would not treat us with so much consideration. But whatever it was, I always came away from a little or a long talk with Mr. Curtis with the feeling that I had somehow been refreshed, cleansed, purified and very often baptized with a new purpose in well-doing. [Applause.]

BOOKER T. WASHINGTON

PROGRESS OF THE AMERICAN NEGRO

[Address by Professor Booker Taliaferro Washington, principal of the Tuskegee Normal and Industrial Institute, Tuskegee, Ala., since 1881 (born near Hale's Ford, Virginia, 1859; ———), delivered at the opening of the Cotton States and International Exposition at Atlanta, Ga., September 18, 1895.]

MR. PRESIDENT AND GENTLEMEN OF THE BOARD OF DIRECTORS, AND CITIZENS:—One-third of the population of the South is of the Negro race. No enterprise seeking the material, civil, or moral welfare of this section can disregard this element of our population and reach the highest success. I but convey to you, Mr. President and Directors, the sentiment of the masses of my race when I say that in no way have the value and manhood of the American Negro been more fittingly and generously recognized than by the managers of this magnificent Exposition at every stage of its progress. It is a recognition that will do more to cement the friendship of the two races than any occurrence since the dawn of our freedom. Not only this, but the opportunity here afforded will awaken among us a new era of industrial progress. Ignorant and inexperienced, it is not strange that in the first years of our new life we began at the top instead of at the bottom; that a seat in Congress or the State Legislature was more sought than real estate or industrial skill; that the political convention or stump speaking had more attractions than starting a dairy-farm or truck-garden.

A ship lost at sea for many days suddenly sighted a friendly vessel. From the mast of the unfortunate vessel was seen a signal: "Water, water; we die of thirst!"

The answer from the friendly vessel at once came back:
" Cast down your bucket where you are." A second time
the signal, " Water, water; send us water!" ran up from
the distressed vessel, and was answered: " Cast down
your bucket where you are." And a third and fourth
signal for water was answered: " Cast down your bucket
where you are." The captain of the distressed vessel, at
last heeding the injunction, cast down his bucket, and it
came up full of fresh, sparkling water from the mouth of
the Amazon River. To those of my race who depend on
bettering their condition in a foreign land, or who underestimate the importance of cultivating friendly relations
with the Southern white man, who is their next door
neighbor, I would say: " Cast down your bucket where
you are "—cast it down in making friends in every manly
way of the people of all races by whom we are surrounded.

Cast it down in agriculture, mechanics, in commerce, in
domestic service, and in the professions. And in this connection it is well to bear in mind that whatever other sins
the South may be called to bear, when it comes to business,
pure and simple, it is in the South that the Negro is given
a man's chance in the commercial world, and in nothing is
this Exposition more eloquent than in emphasizing this
chance. Our greatest danger is, that in the great leap
from slavery to freedom we may overlook the fact that
the masses of us are to live by the productions of our
hands, and fail to keep in mind that we shall prosper in
proportion as we learn to dignify and glorify common
labor and put brains and skill into the common occupations of life; shall prosper in proportion as we learn to
draw the line between the superficial and the substantial,
the ornamental gewgaws of life and the useful. No race
can prosper till it learns that there is as much dignity in
tilling a field as in writing a poem. It is at the bottom
of life we must begin, and not at the top. Nor should
we permit our grievances to overshadow our opportunities.

To those of the white race who look to the incoming of
those of foreign birth and strange tongue and habits for
the prosperity of the South, were I permitted I would
repeat, what I say to my own race, " Cast down your
bucket where you are." Cast it down among the 8,000,-

ooo Negroes whose habits you know, whose fidelity and love you have tested in days when to have proved treacherous meant the ruin of your firesides. Cast down your bucket among these people who have, without strikes and labor wars, tilled your fields, cleared your forests, builded your railroads and cities, and brought forth treasures from the bowels of the earth, and helped make possible this magnificent representation of the progress of the South. Casting down your bucket among my people, helping and encouraging them as you are doing on these grounds, and to education of head, hand, and heart, you will find that they will buy your surplus land, make blossom the waste places in your fields, and run your factories. While doing this, you can be sure in the future, as in the past, that you and your families will be surrounded by the most patient, faithful, law-abiding, and unresentful people that the world has seen. As we have proved our loyalty to you in the past, in nursing your children, watching by the sick-bed of your mothers and fathers, and often following them with tear-dimmed eyes to their graves, so in the future, in our humble way, we shall stand by you with a devotion that no foreigner can approach, ready to lay down our lives, if need be, in defense of yours, interlacing our industrial, commercial, civil, and religious life with yours in a way that shall make the interests of both races one. In all things that are purely social we can be as separate as the fingers, yet one as the hand in all things essential to mutual progress.

There is no defense or security for any of us except in the highest intelligence and development of all. If anywhere there are efforts tending to curtail the fullest growth of the Negro, let these efforts be turned into stimulating, encouraging, and making him the most useful and intelligent citizen. Effort or means so invested will pay a thousand per cent. interest. These efforts will be twice-blessed—" blessing him that gives and him that takes."

There is no escape through law of man or God from the inevitable :—

> The laws of changeless justice bind
>   Oppressor with oppressed;
> And close as sin and suffering joined
>   We march to fate abreast.

Nearly sixteen millions of hands will aid you in pulling the load upwards, or they will pull against you the load downwards. We shall constitute one-third and more of the ignorance and crime of the South, or one-third its intelligence and progress; we shall contribute one-third to the business and industrial prosperity of the South, or we shall prove a veritable body of death, stagnating, depressing, retarding every effort to advance the body politic.

Gentlemen of the Exposition, as we present to you our humble effort at an exhibition of our progress, you must not expect overmuch. Starting thirty years ago with ownership here and there in a few quilts and pumpkins and chickens, remember the path that has led from these to the inventions and production of agricultural implements, buggies, steam-engines, newspapers, books, statuary, carving, paintings, the management of drug stores and banks has not been trodden without contact with thorns and thistles. While we take pride in what we exhibit as a result of our independent efforts, we do not for a moment forget that our part in this exhibition would fall far short of your expectations but for the constant help that has come to our educational life, not only from the Southern States, but especially from Northern philanthropists, who have made their gifts a constant stream of blessing and encouragement.

The wisest among my race understand that the agitation of questions of social equality is the extremest folly, and that progress in the enjoyment of all the privileges that will come to us must be the result of severe and constant struggle rather than of artificial forcing. No race that has anything to contribute to the markets of the world is long in any degree ostracized. It is important and right that all privileges of the law be ours, but it is vastly more important that we be prepared for the exercises of these privileges. The opportunity to earn a dollar in a factory just now is worth infinitely more than the opportunity to spend a dollar in an opera-house.

In conclusion, may I repeat that nothing in thirty years has given us more hope and encouragement, and drawn us so near to you of the white race, as the opportunity offered by this Exposition; and here bending, as it were, over the altar that represents the results of the struggles

of your race and mine, both starting practically empty-
handed three decades ago, I pledge that in your effort to
work out the great and intricate problem which God has
laid at the doors of the South you shall have at all times
the patient, sympathetic help of my race; only let this be
constantly in mind that, while from representations in
these buildings of the product of field, of forest, of mine,
of factory, letters, and art, much good will come: yet far
above and beyond material benefits will be that higher
good, that let us pray God will come, in a blotting out of
sectional differences and racial animosities and suspicions,
in a determination to administer absolute justice, in a willing obedience among all classes to the mandates of law.
This, coupled with our material prosperity, will bring into
our beloved South a new heaven and a new earth.

THE AMERICAN STANDARD

[Address by Professor Booker Taliaferro Washington at the Harvard
Alumni gathering, Cambridge, June 24, 1896, after receiving the honorary degree of Master of Arts from the University.]

MR. PRESIDENT AND GENTLEMEN:—It would in some
measure relieve my embarrassment if I could, even in a
slight degree, feel myself worthy of the great honor which
you do me to-day. Why you have called me from the
Black Belt of the South, from among my humble people,
to share in the honors of this occasion, is not for me to
explain; and yet it may not be inappropriate for me to
suggest that it seems to me that one of the most vital
questions that touch our American life, is how to bring
the strong, wealthy, and learned into helpful touch with the
poorest, most ignorant, and humble, and at the same time
make the one appreciate the vitalizing, strengthening influence of the other. How shall we make the mansions
on yon Beacon street feel and see the need of the spirits
in the lowliest cabin in Alabama cotton-fields or Louisiana
sugar-bottoms? This problem Harvard University is

solving, not by bringing itself down, but by bringing the masses up.

If through me, a humble representative, seven millions of my people in the South might be permitted to send a message to Harvard—Harvard that offered up on death's altar, young Shaw, and Russell, and Lowell and scores of others, that we might have a free and united country, that message would be, " Tell them that the sacrifice was not in vain. Tell them that by the way of the shop, the field, the skilled hand, habits of thrift and economy, by way of industrial school and college, we are coming. We are crawling up, working up, yea, bursting up. Often through oppression, unjust discrimination, and prejudice, but through them all we are coming up, and with proper habits, intelligence, and property, there is no power on earth that can permanently stay our progress."

If my life in the past has meant anything in the lifting up of my people and the bringing about of better relations between your race and mine, I assure you from this day it will mean doubly more. In the economy of God, there is but one standard by which an individual can succeed— there is but one for a race. This country demands that every race measure itself by the American standard. By it a race must rise or fall, succeed or fail, and in the last analysis mere sentiment counts for little. During the next half century and more, my race must continue pass- ing through the severe American crucible. We are to be tested in our patience, our forbearance, our perseverance, our power to endure wrong, to withstand temptations, to economize, to acquire and use skill; our ability to compete, to succeed in commerce, to disregard the superficial for the real, the appearance for the substance, to be great and yet small, learned and yet simple, high and yet the servant of all. This, this is the passport to all that is best in the life of our Republic, and the Negro must possess it, or be debarred.

While we are thus being tested, I beg of you to re- member that wherever our life touches yours, we help or hinder. Wherever your life touches ours, you make us stronger or weaker. No member of your race in any part of our country can harm the meanest member of mine, without the proudest and bluest blood in Massachusetts being degraded.   When Mississippi commits crime, New England commits crime, and in so much lowers the standard of your civilization.   There is no escape—man drags man down, or man lifts man up.

In working out our destiny, while the main burden and center of activity must be with us, we shall need in a large measure in the years that are to come, as we have in the past, the help, the encouragement, the guidance that the strong can give the weak.   Thus helped, we of both races in the South, soon shall throw off the shackles of racial and sectional prejudices and rise as Harvard University has risen and as we all should rise, above the clouds of ignorance, narrowness, and selfishness, into that atmosphere, that pure sunshine, where it will be our highest ambition to serve man, our brother, regardless of race or previous condition.

HENRY WATTERSON

FRANCIS SCOTT KEY

[Oration by Henry Watterson, journalist and orator, editor of the Louisville "Courier-Journal" since 1868 (born in Washington, D. C., February 16, 1840; ———), delivered at the dedication of the monument over the grave of Francis Scott Key, the author of the "Star-Spangled Banner," at Frederick, Md., August 9, 1898.]

The Key Monument Association, to which is due the act of tardy justice whose completion we are here to celebrate, has reason to be proud of the success which has crowned its labor of love. Within something less than four years from the date of its organization, it has reared this beautiful and imposing memorial to the author of the "Star-Spangled Banner." Beneath it lie the mortal remains of Francis Scott Key and of his wife, Mary Tayloe Key. Hitherto unmarked, except in the humblest way, their final resting place on earth has been at last separated from among the surrounding multitude of less distinguished graves, to be at once an altar and a shrine, known among men, wherever liberty makes her home, and consecrate to all hearts wherein the love of liberty dwells.

One cannot help thinking it something more than a coincidence that this monument is erected, and that these services are held, at a moment when not alone is the country engaged in foreign war, but also at a moment when the words of Key's immortal anthem ring in the memory and start to the lips of all the people of all the States and sections of the Union. But a little while ago this seemed a thing impossible of realization during the life of the generation of men which is passing away. Years of embittered civil strife, with their wounds kept open by years of succeeding political controversy, were never before thus ended; nor did ever a people so promptly obey the laws alike of reason, race, and nature, from which, as from some magic fountain, the American Republic sprang.

Nothing in romance, or in poetry, surpasses the wondrous story of this Republic. Why Washington, the Virginia planter, and why Franklin, the Pennsylvania printer? Another might have been chosen to lead the Continental armies; a brilliant and distinguished soldier; but, as we now know, not only a corrupt adventurer, but a traitor, who preceded Arnold, and who, had he been commander of the forces at Valley Forge, would have betrayed his adopted country for the coronet which Washington despised. In many ways was Franklin an experiment, and, as his familiars might have thought, a dangerous experiment, to be appointed the representative of the colonies in London and in Paris, for, as they knew, and as we now know, he was a stalwart, self-indulgent man, apparently little given either to prudence or to courtliness. What was it that singled out these two men from all others and designated them to be the Chiefs of the Military and Diplomatic establishments set up by the provincial gentlemen, whose Declaration of Independence was not merely to establish a new nation, but to create a new world? It was as clearly the inspiration of the Almighty as, a century later, was the faith of Lincoln in Grant, whom he had never seen and had reason to distrust. It was as clearly the inspiration of the Almighty as that, in every turn of fortune, God has stood by the Republic; not less in the strange vicissitudes of the Wars of the Revolution and of 1812, than in those of the War of Sections; in the raising up of Paul Jones and Perry, of Preble and Hull, when, discouraged upon the land, the sea was to send God's people messages of victory, and in the striking down of Albert Sidney Johnston and Stonewall Jackson, when they were sweeping all before them. Inscrutable are the ways of Providence to man. Philosophers may argue as they will, and rationalism may draw its conclusions; but the mysterious power unexplained by either has, from the beginning of time, ruled the destinies of men.

Back of these forces of life and thought there is yet another force equally inspired of God and equally essential to the exaltation of man, a force without which the world does not move except downward, the force of the imagination which idealizes the deeds of men and translates their meaning into words.   It may be concluded that Washington at Monmouth and Franklin at Versailles were not thinking a great deal of what the world was like to say. But there are beings so constituted that they cannot act, they can only think, and these are the Homers who relate in heroic measure, the Shakespeares who sing in strains of heavenly music.   Among the progeny of these was Francis Scott Key.

The son of a revolutionary soldier, he was born the 9th of August, 1780, not far away from the spot where we are now assembled, and died in Baltimore the 11th of January, 1843.   His life of nearly sixty-three years was an unbroken idyl of tranquil happiness; amid congenial scenes; among kindred people; blessed by wedded love and many children, and accompanied by the successful pursuit of the learned profession he had chosen for himself.   Goldsmith's sketch of the village preacher may not be inaptly quoted to describe his unambitious and unobtrusive career:—

> "Remote from towns he ran his godly race,
> Nor e'er had changed, nor wished to change, his place."

Yet it was reserved for this constant and modest gentleman to leave behind him a priceless legacy to his countrymen and to identify his name for all time with his country's flag.

The "Star-Spangled Banner" owed very little to chance. It was the emanation of a patriotic fervor as sincere and natural as it was simple and noble.   It sprang from one of those glorious inspirations which, coming to an author unbidden, seizes at once upon the hearts and minds of men.   The occasion seemed to have been created for the very purpose.   The man and the hour were met, and the song came; and truly was song never yet born amid such scenes.   We explore the pages of folk-lore, we read the story of popular music, in vain, to find the like. Even the authorship of the English national anthem is in dispute.   The "Marseillaise" did indeed owe its being to

the passions of war and burst forth in profuse strains of
melody above the clang of arms; but it was attended by
those theatrical accessories which preside over and minister to Latin emotions, and seem indispensable to its
developments, and it is believed to have derived as much
of its enthusiasm from the wine-cup as from the drum-beat.
Key's song was the very child of battle. It was rocked
by cannon in the cradle of the deep. Its swaddling-cloths
were the Stars and Stripes its birth proclaimed. Its coming was heralded by shot and shell, and, from its baptism
of fire, a nation of freemen clasped it to its bosom. It
was to be thenceforth and forever freedom's Gloria in
Excelsis.

The circumstances which ushered it into the world,
hardly less than the words of the poem, are full of patriotic
exhilaration. It was during the darkest days of our second war of independence. An English army had invaded
and occupied the seat of the National Government and had
burned the Capitol of the Nation. An English squadron
was in undisputed possession of the Chesapeake Bay.
There being nothing of interest, or value left within the
vicinity of Washington to detain them, the British were
massing their land and naval forces for other conquests,
and, as their ships sailed down the Potomac, Dr. William
Beanes, a prominent citizen of Maryland, who had been
arrested at his home in Upper Marlboro charged with
some offense, real or fancied, was carried off a prisoner.

It was to secure the liberation of this gentleman, his
neighbor and friend, that Francis Scott Key obtained
leave of the President to go to the British Admiral under
a flag of truce. He was conveyed by the cartel boat used
for the exchange of prisoners and accompanied by the
flag-officer of the Government. They proceeded down
the bay from Baltimore and found the British fleet at the
mouth of the Potomac.

Mr. Key was courteously received by Admiral Coch-
rane; but he was not encouraged as to the success of his
mission until letters from the English officers wounded at
Blandensburg and left in the care of the Americans were
delivered to the friends on the fleet to whom they had
been written. These bore such testimony to the kindness
with which they had been treated that it was finally agreed

that Dr. Beanes should be released; but, as an advance
upon Baltimore was about to be made, it was required
that the party of Americans should remain under guard
on board their own vessel until these operations were concluded.   Thus it was that, the night of the 14th of September, 1814, Key witnessed the bombardment of Fort
McHenry, which his song was to render illustrious.

He did not quit the deck the long night through.   With
his single companion, the flag-officer, he watched every
shell from the moment it was fired until it fell, "listening
with breathless interest to hear if an explosion followed."
Whilst the cannonading continued they needed no further
assurance that their countrymen had not capitulated.
"But," I quote the words of Chief Justice Taney, repeating the account given him by Key immediately after, "it
suddenly ceased some time before day; and, as they had
no communication with any of the enemy's ships, they did
not know whether the fort had surrendered, or the attack
upon it had been abandoned.   They paced the deck the
residue of the night in painful suspense, watching with
intense anxiety for the return of day, and looking every
few minutes at their watches to see how long they must
wait for it; and, as soon as it dawned and before it was
light enough to see objects at a distance, their glasses
were turned to the fort, uncertain whether they should see
there the Stars and Stripes or the flag of the enemy."
Blessed vigil! that its prayers were not in vain; glorious
vigil! that it gave us the "Star-Spangled Banner"!

During the night the conception of the poem began to
form itself in Key's mind.   With the early glow of the
morning, when the long agony of suspense had been
turned into the rapture of exultation, his feeling found
expression in completed lines of verse, which he wrote
upon the back of a letter he happened to have in his possession.   He finished the piece on the boat that carried
him ashore and wrote out a clear copy that same evening
at his hotel in Baltimore.   Next day he read this to his
friend and kinsman, Judge Nicholson, who was so pleased
with it that he carried it to the office of the "Baltimore
American," where it was put in type by a young appren-
tice, Samuel Sands by name, and thence issued as a broad-
side.   Within an hour after it was circulating all over the

city, hailed with delight by the excited people. Published
in the succeeding issue of the "American," and elsewhere
reprinted, it went straight to the popular heart. It was
quickly seized for musical adaptation. First sung in a
tavern adjoining the Holliday Street Theater in Baltimore,
by Charles Durang, an actor, whose brother, Ferdinand
Durang, had set it to an old air, its production on the
stage of that theater was the occasion of spontaneous and
unbounded enthusiasm. Wherever it was heard its effect
was electrical, and thenceforward it was universally accepted as the National anthem.

The poem tells its own story, and never a truer, for
every word comes direct from a great heroic soul, powder-
stained and dipped, as it were, in sacred blood.

> "O say, can you see by the dawn's early light
> What so proudly we hailed at the twilight's last gleaming?
> Whose broad stripes and bright stars through the perilous fight,
> O'er the ramparts we watched were so gallantly streaming!"

The two that walked the deck of the cartel boat
had waited long. They had counted the hours as they
watched the course of the battle. But a deeper anxiety
yet is to possess them. The firing has ceased. Ominous
silence! Whilst cannon roared they knew that the fort
held out. Whilst the sky was lit by messengers of death
they could see the National colors flying above it.

> ". . . the rocket's red glare, the bombs bursting in air,
> Gave proof through the night that our flag was still there."

But there comes an end at last to waiting and watching;
and as the first rays of the sun shoot above the horizon
and gild the Eastern shore, behold the sight that gladdens
their eyes as it—

> ". . . catches the gleam of the morning's first beam,
> In full glory reflected, now shines on the stream"—

for there, over the battlements of McHenry, the Stars
and Stripes float defiant on the breeze, whilst all around
evidences multiply that the attack has failed, that the
Americans have successfully resisted it, and that the Brit-

ish are withdrawing their forces. For then, and for now, and for all time, come the words of the anthem—

> "O thus be it ever when freemen shall stand
> Between their loved homes and the war's desolation!
> Blest with vict'ry and peace, may the Heaven-rescued land
> Praise the Power that hath made and preserved us a nation."

for—

> ". . . conquer we must, when our cause it is just,
> And this be our motto, 'In God is our trust';
> And the Star-Spangled Banner in triumph shall wave
> O'er the land of the free and the home of the brave!"

The Star-Spangled Banner! Was ever flag so beautiful, did ever flag so fill the souls of men? The love of woman; the sense of duty; the thirst for glory; the heart-throbbing that impels the humblest American to stand by his colors fearless in the defense of his native soil and holding it sweet to die for it—the yearning which draws him to it when exiled from it—its free institutions and its blessed memories, all are embodied and symbolized by the broad stripes and bright stars of the nation's emblem, all live again in the lines and tones of Key's anthem. Two or three began the song, millions join the chorus. They are singing it in Porto Rican trenches and on the ramparts of Santiago, and its echoes, borne upon the wings of morning, come rolling back from far-away Manila; the soldier's message to the soldier; the hero's shibboleth in battle; the patriot's solace in death! Even to the lazy sons of peace who lag at home—the pleasure-seekers whose merry-making turns the night into day—those stirring strains come as a sudden trumpet-call, and above the sounds of revelry, subjugate for the moment to a stronger power, rises wave upon wave of melodious resonance, the idler's aimless but heartfelt tribute to his country and his country's flag.

Since the "Star-Spangled Banner" was written nearly a century has come and gone. The drums, and tramplings of more than half its years have passed over the grave of Francis Scott Key. Here at last he rests forever. Here at last his tomb is fitly made. When his eyes closed upon the scenes of this life their last gaze beheld the ensign of the Republic "full-high advanced, its arms and trophies streaming in their original lustre, not a stripe erased or polluted nor a single star obscured." If happily they were spared the spectacle of a severed Union, and "a land rent by civil feud and drenched in fraternal blood," it may be that somewhere beyond the stars his gentle spirit now looks down upon a Nation awakened from its sleep of death and restored to its greater and its better self, and known and honored, as never before throughout the world. Whilst Key lived there was but a single paramount issue, about which all other issues circled, the Constitution and the Union. The problems of the Constitution and the Union solved, the past secure, turn we to the future; no longer a huddle of petty sovereignties, held together by a rope of sand; no longer a body of mercenary shopkeepers worshiping rather the brand upon the dollar than the eagle on the shield; no longer a brood of provincial laggards, hanging with bated breath upon the movements of mankind, afraid to trust themselves away from home, or to put their principles to the test of progress and of arms; but a Nation, and a leader of nations; a world power which durst face Imperialism upon its own ground with Republicanism, and with it dispute the future of Civilization. It is the will of God; let not man gainsay. Let not man gainsay until the word of God has been carried to the furthermost ends of the earth; not until freedom is the heritage of all His creatures; not until the blessings which he has given us are shared by His people in all lands; not until Latin licentiousness fostered by modern wealth and culture and art, has been expiated by fire, and Latin corruption and cruelty have disappeared from the government of men; not until that sober-suited Anglo-Saxonism, which, born at Runnymede, was to end neither at Yorktown nor at Appomattox, has made, at one and the same time, another map of Christendom and a new race of Christians and yeomen, equally soldiers of the Sword and of the Cross, even in Africa and in Asia, as we have made them here in America. Thus, and thus alone, and wherever the winds of heaven blow, shall fly the spirit if not the actuality of the blessed symbol we have come here this day to glorify; ashamed of nothing that God has sent, ready for everything that God may send! It was not a singer of the fireside, but a heartless wanderer, who put in all hearts the Anglo-Saxon's simple " Home, Sweet Home." It was a poet, not a warrior, who gave to our Union the Anglo-American's homage to his flag. Even as the Prince of Peace who came to bring eternal life was the Son of God, were these His ministering angels; and, as each of us, upon his knees, sends up a prayer to Heaven for " Home, Sweet Home," may he also murmur, and teach his children to lisp, the sublime refrain of Key's immortal anthem—

> " 'Tis the Star-Spangled Banner, O, long may it wave
> O'er the land of the free and the home of the brave! "

DANIEL WEBSTER

AMERICAN GOVERNMENT UNIQUE

[Oration by Daniel Webster, statesman and orator (born in Salisbury, N. H., January 18, 1782; died in Marshfield, Mass., October 24, 1852), delivered in Fryeburg, Maine, July 4, 1802, when Webster was but twenty years of age, and at the time principal of the Fryeburg Academy. This oration is referred to in Webster's Autobiography as unpublished, and so it remained till eighty years after its delivery, when the original manuscript was found, with a mass of Webster's private papers, in a junk-shop in Boston, and rescued from destruction. Passing then into appreciative hands, it was issued in pamphlet form in 1882, the centennial year of Webster's birth. The impression created by this early effort of the orator upon the minds of the townspeople who heard it, was deep and lasting, and it has been said that its sentiments were remembered and repeated by some of them after a lapse of more than fifty years. An interesting fact is seen in the strikingly similar peroration to the last speech made by Webster in the Senate of the United States on July 17, 1850.]

FELLOW CITIZENS:—It is at the season when nature hath assumed her loveliest apparel that the American people assemble in their several temples to celebrate the birthday of their nation. Arrayed in all the beauties of the year, the Fourth of July once more visits us. Green fields and a ripening harvest proclaim it, a bright sun cheers it, and the hearts of freemen bid it welcome. Illustrious spectacle! Six millions of people this day surround their altars, and unite in an address to Heaven for the preservation of their rights. Every rank and every age imbibes the general spirit. From the lisping inhabitant of the cradle to the aged warrior whose gray hairs are fast sinking in the western horizon of life, every voice is, this day, tuned to the accents of Liberty! Washington! My Country!

Festivals established by the world have been numerous. The coronation of a king, the birth of a prince, the marriage of a princess, have often called wondering crowds together. Cities and nations agree to celebrate the event which raises one mortal man above their heads, and beings called men stand astonished and aghast while the pageantry of a monarch or the jeweled grandeur of a queen poses before them. Such a festival, however, as the Fourth of July is to America, is not found in history; —a festival designed for solemn reflection on the great events that have happened to us; a festival in which freedom receives a nation's homage, and Heaven is greeted with incense from ten thousand hearts.

In the present situation of our country, it is, my respected fellow citizens, matter of high joy and congratulation that there is one day in the year on which men of different principles and different opinions can associate together. The Fourth of July is not an occasion to compass sea and land to make proselytes. The good sense and the good nature which yet remain among us will, we trust, prevail on this day, and be sufficient to chain, at least for a season, that untamed monster, Party Spirit— and would to God that it might be chained forever, that, as we have but one interest, we might have but one heart and one mind!

You have hitherto, fellow citizens, on occasions of this kind, been entertained with the discussion of national questions; with inquiries into the true principles of government; with recapitulations of the War; with speculations on the causes of our Revolution, and on its consequences to ourselves and to the world. Leaving these subjects, it shall be the ambition of the speaker of this day to present such a view of your Constitution and your Union as shall convince you that you have nothing to hope from a change.

This age has been correctly denominated an age of experiments. Innovation is the idol of the times. The human mind seems to have burst its ancient limits, and to be traveling over the face of the material and intellectual creation in search of improvement. The world hath become like a fickle lover, in whom every new face inspires a new passion. In this rage for novelty many things are made better, and many things are made worse. Old errors are discarded, and new errors are embraced. Governments feel the same effects from this spirit as everything else. Some, like our own, grow into beauty and excellence, while others sink still deeper into deformity and wretchedness. The experience of all ages will bear us out in saying that alterations of political systems are always attended with a greater or less degree of danger. They ought, therefore, never to be undertaken unless the evil complained of be really felt and the prospect of a remedy clearly seen. The politician that undertakes to improve a Constitution with as little thought as a farmer sets about mending his plow is no master of his trade. If that Constitution be a systematic one, if it be a free one, its parts are so necessarily connected that an alteration in one will work an alteration in all; and this cobbler, however pure and honest his intentions, will, in the end, find that what came to his hands a fair and lovely fabric goes from them a miserable piece of patchwork.

Nor are great and striking alterations alone to be shunned. A succession of small changes, a perpetual tampering with minute parts, steal away the breath though they leave the body; for it is true that a government may lose all its real character—its genius and its temper—without losing its appearance. You may have a despotism under the name of a republic. You may look on a government and see it possess all the external essential modes of freedom, and yet see nothing of the essence, the vitality, of freedom in it: just as you may behold Washington or Franklin in wax-work,—the form is perfect, but the spirit, the life, is not there.

The first thing to be said in favor of our system of government is that it is truly and genuinely *free*, and the man has a base and slavish heart that will call any government good that is *not free*. If there be, at this day, any advocate for arbitrary power, we wish him the happiness of living under a government of his choice. If he is in love with chains, we would not deny him the gratification of his passion. Despotism is the point where everything bad centers, and from which everything good departs.

As far as a government is distant from this point, so far it is good; in proportion as it approaches towards this, in the same proportion it is detestable. In all other forms there is something tolerable to be found; in despotism there is nothing. Other systems have some amiable features, some right principles, mingled with their errors; despotism is all error; it is a dark and cheerless void, over which the eye wanders in vain in search of anything lovely or attractive.

The true definition of despotism is government without law. It may exist, therefore, in the hands of many as well as of one. Rebellions are despotisms; factions are despotisms; loose democracies are despotisms. These are a thousand times more dreadful than the concentration of all power in the hands of a single tyrant. The despotism of one man is like the thunderbolt, which falls here and there, scorching and consuming the individual on whom it lights; but popular commotion, the despotism of a mob, is an earthquake, which in one moment swallows up everything. It is the excellence of our government that it is placed in a proper medium between these two extremes, that it is equally distant from mobs and from thrones.

In the next place our government is good because it is *practical*. It is not the sick offspring of closet philosophy. It did not rise, vaporous and evanescent, from the brains of Rousseau and Godwin, like a mist from the ocean. It is the production of men of business, of experience, and of wisdom. It is suited to what man is and what it is in the power of good laws to make him. Its object—the just object of all governments—is to secure and protect the weak against the strong, to unite the force of the whole community against the violence of oppressors. Its power is the power of the nation; its will is the will of the people. It is not an awkward, unshapely machine which the people cannot use when they have made it, nor is it so dark and complicated that it is the labor of one's life to investigate and understand it. All are capable of comprehending its principles and its operations. It admits, too, of a change of men and of measures. At the will of a majority, we have seen the government of the nation pass from the hands of one description of men into those of another. Of the comparative merits of those different men, of their honesty, their talents, their patriotism, we have here nothing to say. That subject we leave to be decided before the impartial tribunal of posterity. The fact of a change of rulers, however, proves that the government is manageable, that it can in all cases be made to comply with the public will. It is, too, an equal government. It rejects principalities and powers. It demolishes all the artificial distinctions which pride and ambition create. It is encumbered with no lazy load of hereditary aristocracy. It clothes no one with the attributes of God; it sinks no one to a level with brutes: yet it admits those distinctions in society which are natural and necessary. The correct expression of our Bill of Rights is that men are born equal. It then rests with themselves to maintain their equality by their worth. The illustrious framers of our system, in all the sternness of republicanism, rejected all nobility but the nobility of talents, all majority but the majority of virtue.

Lastly, the government is one of our choice; not dictated to us by an imperious Chief Consul, like the governments of Holland and Switzerland; not taught us by the philosophers, nor graciously brought to us on the bayonets of our magnanimous sister republic on the other side the ocean. It was framed by our fathers for themselves and for their children. Far the greater portion of mankind submit to usurped authority, and pay humble obedience to self-created law-givers; not that obedience of the heart which a good citizen will yield to good laws, but the obedience which a harnessed horse pays his driver, an obedience begotten by correction and stripes.

The American Constitution is the purchase of American valor. It is the rich prize that rewards the toil of eight years of war and of blood: and what is all the pomp and military glory, what are victories, what are armies subdued, fleets captured, colors taken, unless they end in the establishment of wise laws and national happiness? Our Revolution is not more renowned for the brilliancy of its scenes than for the benefit of its consequences. The Constitution is the great memorial of the deeds of our ancestors. On the pillars and on the arches of that dome their names are written and their achievements recorded. While that lasts, while a single page or a single article can be found, it will carry down the record to future ages. It will teach mankind that glory, empty, tinkling glory, was not the object for which Americans fought. Great Britain had carried the fame of her arms far and wide. She had humbled France and Spain; she had reached her arm across the Eastern Continent, and given laws on the banks of the Ganges. A few scattered colonists did not rise up to contend with such a nation for mere renown. They had a nobler object, and in pursuit of that object they manifested a courage, constancy, and union that deserve to be celebrated by poets and historians while language lasts.

The valor of America was not a transient, glimmering ray shot forth from the impulse of momentary resentment. Against unjust and arbitrary laws she rose with determined, unalterable spirit. Like the rising sun, clouds and mists hung around her, but her course, like his, brightened as she proceeded. Valor, however, displayed in combat is a less remarkable trait in the character of our countrymen than the wisdom manifested when the combat was over. All countries and all ages produce warriors, but rare are the instances in which men sit down coolly at the close of their labors to enjoy the fruits of them. Having destroyed one despotism, nations generally create another; having rejected the dominion of one tyrant, they make another for themselves. England beheaded her Charles, but crowned her Cromwell. France guillotined her Louises, but obeys her Bonapartes. Thanks to God, neither foreign nor domestic usurpation flourishes on our soil!

Having thus, fellow citizens, surveyed the principal features of our excellent Constitution and paid an inadequate tribute to the wisdom which produced it, let us consider seriously the means of its preservation. To perpetuate the government we must cherish the love of it. One chief pillar in the republican fabric is the spirit of patriotism. But patriotism hath, in these days, become a good deal questionable. It hath been so often counterfeited that even the genuine coin doth not pass without suspicion. If one proclaims himself a patriot, this uncharitable, misjudging world is pretty likely to set him down for a knave, and it is pretty likely to be right in this opinion. The

rage for being patriots hath really so much of the ridiculous in it that it is difficult to treat it seriously.   The preaching of politics hath become a trade, and there are many
who leave all other trades to follow it.   Benevolent, dis-
interested men!   With Scriptural devotion they forsake
houses and lands, father and mother, wife and children,
and wander up and down the community to teach mankind that their rulers oppress them!   About the time
when it was fashionable in France to cut off men's heads,
as we lop away superfluous sprouts from our apple-trees,
the public attention was excited by a certain monkey, that
had been taught to act the part of a patriot to great perfection.   If you pointed at him, says the historian, and
called him an aristocrat or a monarchist, he would fly at
you with great rage and violence; but, if you would do
him the justice to call him a good patriot, he manifested
every mark of joy and satisfaction.   But, though the
whole French nation gazed at this animal as a miracle, he
was, after all, no very strange sight.   There are, in all
countries, a great many monkeys who wish to be thought
patriots, and a great many others who believe them such.
But, because we are often deceived by appearances, let us
not believe that the reality does not exist.   If our faith is
ever shaken, if the crowd of hypocritical demagogues lead
us to doubt, we will remember Washington and be convinced; we will cast our eyes around us, on those who
have toiled and fought and bled for their country, and
we will be persuaded that there is such a thing as real
patriotism, and that it is one of the purest and noblest
sentiments that can warm the heart of man.

To preserve the government we must also preserve a
correct and energetic tone of morals.   After all that can
be said, the truth is that liberty consists more in the habits
of the people than in anything else.   When the public
mind becomes vitiated and depraved, every attempt to
preserve it is vain.   Laws are then a nullity, and Constitutions waste paper.   There are always men wicked enough
to go any length in the pursuit of power if they can find
others wicked enough to support them.   They regard not
paper and parchment.   Can you stop the progress of a
usurper by opposing to him the laws of his country? then
you may check the careering winds or stay the lightning

with a song. No. Ambitious men must be restrained by
the public morality: when they rise up to do evil, they
must find themselves standing alone. Morality rests on
religion. If you destroy the foundation, the superstruc-
ture must fall. In a world of error, of temptation, of
seduction; in a world where crimes often triumph, and
virtue is scourged with scorpions,—in such a world, certainly, the hope of a hereafter is necessary to cheer and
to animate. Leave us, then, the consolations of religion.
Leave to man, to frail and feeble man, the comfort of
knowing that, when he gratifies his immortal soul with
deeds of justice, of kindness and of mercy, he is rescuing
his happiness from final dissolution and laying it up in
Heaven.

Our duty as citizens is not a solitary one. It is connected with all the duties that belong to us as men. The
civil, the social, the Christian virtues are requisite to render
us worthy the continuation of that government which is
the freest on earth. Yes, though the world should hear
me, though I could fancy myself standing in the congregation of all nations, I would say: "Americans, you are
the most privileged people that the sun shines on. The
salutary influences of your climate are inferior to the
salutary influences of your laws. Your soil, rich to a
proverb, is less rich than your Constitution. Your rivers,
large as the oceans of the old world, are less copious than
the streams of social happiness which flow around you.
Your air is not purer than your civil liberty, and your
hills, though high as heaven and deep as the foundations
of the earth, are less exalted and less firmly founded than
that benign and everlasting religion which blesses you
and shall bless your offspring. Amidst these profuse
blessings of nature and of Providence, beware! Standing in this place, sacred to truth, I dare not undertake to
assure you that your liberties and your happiness may not
be lost. Men are subject to men's misfortunes. If an
angel should be winged from Heaven, on an errand of
mercy to our country, the first accents that would glow
on his lips would be, 'Beware! be cautious! you have
everything to lose; you have nothing to gain.'" We live
under the only government that ever existed which was
framed by the unrestrained and deliberate consultations

of the people. Miracles do not cluster. That which has happened but once in six thousand years cannot be expected to happen often. Such a government, once gone, might leave a void, to be filled, for ages, with revolution and tumult, riot and despotism.

The history of the world is before us. It rises like an immense column, on which we may see inscribed the soundest maxims of political experience. These maxims should be treasured in our memories and written on our hearts. Man, in all countries, resembles man. Whereever you find him, you find human nature in him and human frailties about him. He is, therefore, a proper pupil for the school of experience. He should draw wisdom from the example of others,—encouragement from their success, caution from their misfortunes. Nations should diligently keep their eye on the nations that have gone before them. They should mark and avoid their errors, not travel on heedlessly in the path of danger and of death while the bones of their perished predecessors whiten around them. Our own times afford us lessons that admonish us both of our duty and our danger. We have seen mighty nations, miserable in their chains, more miserable when they attempted to shake them off. Tortured and distracted beneath the lash of servitude, we have seen them rise up in indignation to assert the rights of human nature; but, deceived by hypocrites, cajoled by demagogues, ruined by false patriots, overpowered by a resistless mixed multitude of knaves and fools, we have wept at the wretched end of all their labors. Tossed for ten years in the crazy dreams of revolutionary liberty, we have seen them at last awake, and, like the slave who slumbers on his oar and dreams of the happiness of his own blessed home, they awake to find themselves still in bondage. Let it not be thought that we advert to other nations to triumph in their sufferings or mock at their calamities. Would to God the whole earth enjoyed pure and rational liberty, that every realm that the human eye surveys or the human foot treads were free! Wherever men soberly and prudently engage in the pursuit of this object, our prayers in their behalf shall ascend unto the Heavens and unto the ear of Him who filleth them. Be they powerful or be they weak, in such a cause they deserve success. Yes, "The poorest being that crawls on earth, contending to save itself from injustice and oppression, is an object respectable in the eyes of God and man." Our purpose is only to draw lessons of prudence from the imprudence of others, to argue the necessity of virtue from the consequences of their vices.

Unhappy Europe! the judgment of God rests hard upon thee. Thy sufferings would deserve an angel's pity if an angel's tears could wash away thy crimes! The Eastern Continent seems trembling on the brink of some great catastrophe. Convulsions shake and terrors alarm it. Ancient systems are falling; works reared by ages are crumbling into atoms. Let us humbly implore Heaven that the wide-spreading desolation may never reach the shores of our native land, but let us devoutly make up our minds to do our duty in events that may happen to us. Let us cherish genuine patriotism. In that, there is a sort of inspiration that gives strength and energy almost more than human. When the mind is attached to a great object, it grows to the magnitude of its undertaking. A true patriot, with his eye and his heart on the honor and happiness of his country, hath an elevation of soul that lifts him above the rank of ordinary men. To common occurrences he is indifferent. Personal considerations dwindle into nothing in comparison with his high sense of public duty. In all the vicissitudes of fortune, he leans with pleasure on the protection of Providence and on the dignity and composure of his own mind. While his country enjoys peace, he rejoices and is thankful; and, if it be in the counsel of Heaven to send the storm and the tempest, his bosom proudly swells against the rage that assaults it. Above fear, above danger, he feels that the last end which can happen to any man never comes too soon if he falls in defence of the laws and liberties of his country.

JOHN WEISS

THE TASK OF RELIGION

[Address by John Weiss, clergyman, lecturer, essayist (born in Boston, June 28, 1818; died there, March 9, 1879), delivered before the graduating class of the Divinity School of Harvard University, June 27, 1869.]

GENTLEMEN OF THE GRADUATING CLASS:—You linger a while, between the midsummer of the grass and the trees, elate as the season, infecting it with your own hope and confidence, just as if hearts outside were not swelling with the suppressed tears of desire to be at home with God. In what places do they await the coming of some modern and untrammeled word, to have enthusiasm snatch their hand away from doubts, and lay it warm in the hand that offers divine friendship? Whither do you journey—into what knowledge of distrust, what discovery of deep alienation from the ideal life, what revolt of souls against their own bondage,—but also into what delight, as you see all kinds of people acquiring truth for themselves, and turning it to life! Your scholarly reverie is almost over: this alarm that interrupts it is beaten by hearts at the front, on the contested line between the body and the spirit.

Your active ministry begins at a period of great mental disturbance, which marks a passage from one position of intelligence to another. Whatever may be your outfit of knowledge, or the depth of spiritual experience which you may have reached, it is safe to say that your education passes to its most important work, since you are about to meet men and women face to face. In doing this, you face for the first time the real problems of the spiritual life. Human nature is learning to ask very intelligent and

embarrassing questions, while its religious exigencies are
the same that they ever were, and have to be harmonized
with knowledge. Here you may have been taught to
gauge and appreciate past epochs of spiritual development,
and to note their connection with various mental states,
and you have indulged religious feelings. But now you
are about to discern, by contact with men in vital society,
what is essential religion, in order that your service may
be timely for this race and country. The past may be
the soil that holds your roots, but not a ball and chain
around the ankle. If you undertake to drag the dogmatic
life of nineteen centuries across the face of the country,
your traces will be marked by denudation of the fertility
that would prefer your bold husbandry. You go forth to
quicken the native germs that lie waiting to succeed the
old crops, when decay or the ax shall clear the land.
"Instead of the thorn shall come up the fir-tree, and
instead of the brier shall come up the myrtle-tree."

Cheap publications of every kind spread the moods of
the period far and wide. Their range passes through all
the speculative forms, and all the emotions which the
world at any time has known. The very richness is a
cause of the distraction. Thought is unconsciously embarrassed as so many departments throw wide open their
doors at once, and display their collections. And there is
no statement too scientific to resist the intentions of popular treatment. It is macerated, dissected, volatilized, put
up in packages for the trapper and emigrant. Every condition of half-knowledge appropriates it. People who are
troubled with imperfect nutrition will snatch, at every
railway station, a gulp of spectrum analysis, primeval man,
the correlation of forces, spontaneous generation, social
statics, Carl Vogt's impetuous atheism, Mr. Darwin's pan-
genesis, Professor Huxley's non-committal protoplasm,
and the last message from the summer-land. Such a meal
cannot be matched at the most indigestible depot in
America. Westward the tide of empire runs and reads.

The scientific mind is making the whole world at once
its laboratory and auditorium; and among the hearers
there is no distinction of person, color, sex, or previous
preparation. Is it at all wonderful that religion finds herself ill at ease in this promiscuous assembly, especially

when a spirit rules to assign her to the pauper's gallery, as not quite presentable close to the stage of brilliant analysis! She sits and sees motion converted into heat, the lines of Orion's atmosphere described, chronology knocked away from under Adam's feet and fall, the cerebral and nervous system hunted down to within an inch of her life, and the final stroke only suspended out of regard to her feelings, but in amazement that she is present there at all. She listens to the proof of her functional position as the efflorescence of the polyp through a vast gradation of improving epochs. The Perseus of science, behind his fossil shield, waits till she, too, petrifies.

We need not trouble ourselves with the confusion of tongues which has descended upon theology. That is no longer of consequence while human nature is laid waste by this incursion of all the facts and all the conjectures. They penetrate into the solemn presence of our primitive beliefs, where that senate sits in composed silence. One of them, bolder than the rest, stretches forth his hand towards the Ancient of Days, and then a slaughter of the whole is easy.

When we look closely at the mental confusion that prevails, we find that it can be classified, dropping out the consideration of varying intelligence, and noting only its relation to spiritual ideas. There is a class of persons to whom the phrase, "invisible world," has no meaning. They have learned to consider that the universe is occupied with the functions of matter, and that whatever these displace is superfluous and fantastical. There are more things in heaven and earth than we dream of; but, as fast as they are discovered, we find they are only things. This is the class that gets accentuated according to temperament, or divided into sub-classes; such as the one whose special distinction is to derive the moral law from the combinations of birth and physical organization, and to reduce accountability to a table of probable recurrences of vice and virtue. The distinction of another is to be incapable of conceiving of a personal continuance after the bodily functions are exhausted, or even of a transformation of its elemental force into some other element. And others surmise that the emotions of the friend, the lover, the poet and musician, the gladness that rises from the heart's meadow and sings its path deep into the sky, the profound regret of self-dissatisfaction, the hungry and eager scent of the imagination upon some trail, the music as it opens, the straining of the body's leash outward towards some depth, and down through some perspective, to overtake fulfilment,—that all this is molecular distribution and arrangement, as the nimble atoms of the organism cling or fly apart, and assemble in varying ratios to condense a protean force. Whatever a man thinks that he feels is nothing but the rotation of these microscopic spheres. His most sanguine aspirations have been only the lifting of his brain, as the increased action of the heart sends blood to make it fit closely to the skull. And when it shrinks, that is his only mortification and regret. And when he is flush with perfectly assimilated food, it is his only manliness and ethical ability, his capacity for patriotism, to sacrifice his stimulated atoms upon the bed of honor. The very words we use, that pretend to independent beauty, are nothing but the dominos that conceal till midnight the hollowness of the masquerade.

We must not be deceived by a general healthiness of disposition that preserves people, who are profoundly materialistic, in moral relations with society, and secures from them many a noble action. Their hearts are nevertheless deeply stirred with regret and vexation as scientific facts encamp before the great natural reliances, besiege and undermine them. A man will learn to confide in the unvarying operations of laws, which persist in showing, by all public and domestic circumstances, that providence is only nature's obedience. But his admiration at the spectacle of consistency, does not quiet the heart, which inherited from father and mother, and from all parents of all mankind, the feeling that exacts paternity, and claims it at the hand of law, and puts all forces at the disposal of a Person. At the very moment when his mind has plunged the world into the impassive ocean of mere sequence, and stamps upon it, waiting till it drown, there is a native revulsion at the deed. He drags it forth again, to listen if the heart yet beats. He is distracted between the inexorable facts and his equally inexorable hunger to regard himself as not a pawn of fate, but entitled to divine consideration by virtue of some moral and spiritual free-

dom, which has a casting vote, or at least an influence in
framing him. He sees a man's soul entirely disappear
under pressure upon the brain, or submit to a modification
of its qualities by removal of some portion of the cerebral
material. A youth living in Chicago, who was very dull,
and showed no tendency for anything, became a great
lover of music, and a player upon the flute, after an accident to the head, by which he lost a portion of the brain.
Can talent, then, be scooped in or out of the personality,
or is the head a kaleidoscope which need only be well
shaken to vary indefinitely its combinations? Professor
Lourdat, of Montpelier, suffered from a typhoid fever,
which destroyed the memory of five or six laborious
years, so that he was obliged to recommence his medical
studies from the beginning. What and where, then, was
the substance of his person? If his knowledge lay mi-
nutely packed in brain-cells, was the soul merely a force
that secures their normal action? The soul either shared,
or did not share, this knowledge. If it did, the total wreck
of memory is inexplicable. Death might do the same.
If it did not, the brain's function is the only person. And
there was George Nickern, of New Orleans, nearly killed
by a fall from a platform, who lay unconscious several
weeks. He recovered his health and powers of mind, ex-
cepting memory. His new memory only dates from his
recovery. Everything previous to that has been oblit-
erated, and he is forced to learn his English and German
again like a child. What relation, then, has memory to
personal identity? We read in a foreign periodical the
well-attested case of a workingman, well advanced in
years, who had a violent attack of cholera in 1865. Up to
that time he was coarse-grained, and stolid, and had manifested no spark of literary feeling or ability: but he
emerged from the crisis of his malady with a lively fancy,
and a strong capacity for literary expression; and he has
published a volume of poems. Can cholera, then, fortunately also induce collapse of poetasters, who already
lie under suspicion of living without soul?

But what is this arbitrament of change in the blood
corpuscles, and deliquescence of the body's strength,
which mounts with new spiritual expressions to the brain?
A man asks these questions with fear and wonder. He

watches nourishment as it eventuates in intellectual action, and narcotics exhale in fantasy: he traces melancholy and self-distrust to scrofulous conditions of the blood; temper and passion to hysteria; ideas of crime to chronic dyspepsia; the vices of forgotten ancestors create the bias of their posterity. He goes to hear the two-headed girl sing two parts of an air at once; and, finding that one trunk and one stomach buds, Astræa-like, into two brains, he is perplexed to decide where the real person is, or whether death itself will be able to establish two. And if the soul be, as Swedenborg affirms, in the form of a whole human frame, how can one frame be endowed with two spiritual essences? He gathers the accounts of foresight and adaptation displayed by the intelligence of animals, who seem able to invent new stratagems, to reflect upon unexpected conditions, and make them the grounds of fresh behavior; and he is incapable of assuming a difference in kind between this power of independent observation and his own, so that, if the one be purely automatic and instinctive, why, he surmises, should not the other be? The facts assail his instinct of independent personality; and he sees them springing out of all the graves upon the planet, the only things left vital enough to rise there, and to mark those pits of nothingness. But let one open near to him, and the old heart of mankind looks down through his eyes into a bottomless depth of personal continuance. He longs against, conspires against, rages against, the facts; glories in science, and yet accuses her; gives back her level and immutable look to-day, but to-morrow cannot see it for his tears.

What a country is this, that appears to smile from Atlantic to Pacific with strenuous satisfaction, as if all intelligences only cared to orient themselves through the Golden Gate, and overtake and out-time the light itself with their enlightenment! But there is not one commonwealth of the whole varied surface, over which the tracks of science are laid, that does not ache with the secret suspicion that we can only know what we perceive, and cannot touch higher than the arms will reach. Enterprise and competition blunt this instinctive disappointment, and the thin film of manners obscures it; but you may count upon it as a prevailing quality of the times to which you are to bring the disinfectant of religion.

It is the gravest part of the service that you are to render to your fellow men, to restore the primitive truths and expectations of religion to their place in the critical intelligence. Nothing that you can do against separate vices, or characteristic excesses of the people, nothing to refine the average ambition, will avail like this to reconcile the finite with the infinite. You step from this secluded place into a mental transition that will swallow you up contemptuously if you undertake to pacify and convert it by the old didactic methods. Such a serious piece of work never devolved upon the servants of ideal truth.

If you follow certain denominational modes of action, that relate to church-extension, and the concentration of parochial life, I predict that you will gain a parish, and lose your hold upon the vital exigency of the times. Not even if you run in debt for stained windows and high-priced exclusiveness, and borrow from abroad cathedral habits and perspectives, which are for us like an opera imported in a hand-organ, will you succeed in stanching the country's wound. What does the deep distrust of American intelligence care for your elaborate service, with a leviathan of an organ wallowing and tossing up sonorous phrases at one end of the decorum, while you vie with it in a chest voice at the other end, to declare that the Lord is your shepherd,—you will not want; or, "though he slay me, yet will I trust in him"? Distrust is not dissipated by the æsthetics of matins and vespers, even if you use them as a fine flourish of religiosity to introduce your faded sermon upon virtue or the miracles. And it is doubtful if, should you arrive at all the social advantages of vestries, with arrangements for unlimited tea and toast and clerical gossiping, for a united congregation, will much be done towards lifting the sublime shapes of God and immortality upon their pedestal of science. All the amiable and social feelings will hold a parish, like a club, together, provided you can also supply a pretty fair article of rhetoric, and, by manipulating the stock subjects of the pulpit, preserve the pews at their original estimate, or enhance them to the despair of would-be listeners. Will you mistake this for success? Twenty years of such a

popular ministry will not answer one of the awful questions that gnaw at the root of religion.   America is not
waiting for your fervor, volubility, or denominational
activity.   Her most dangerous and subtle intelligence,
grown sick of that, has left the pews to those for whom
texts are authorities.   She waits to hear and to confess
the retort of a faith that is as great as her intelligence; to
have you proclaim an atonement that washes the head in
the blood of the heart, and obliterates the whole discrepancy.   Will you thus bring strong men to God?   Then
you must seek out a more excellent way than any of the
sects can furnish.

The pulpit has done its best to create an impression
that science and religion occupy different domains, which
are hostile to each other.   Nature is said to be the source
of one; revelation, of the other.   As soon as the attempt
failed to harmonize the two by accommodation of old
texts to novel facts, the ban was pronounced more distinctly than ever by removing religion into a class of
emotions, a mystical inward condition, and a practical
ethical behavior.   Science was an intellectual reconstruc-
tion of nature.   Religion was Scriptural authority con-
spiring with intuitive feeling.   The next step taken by the
representatives of religion has been the fatal one; to
drive science into indifference or zealous atheism, and
religion into hatred of the logical sequence of nature.
The step was to declare that the logical sequence was
incapable of confirming the human sense of dependence
and the divine existence, and was at least neutral on the
point of the independence and immortality of persons.
Now religion need not wait for science to make the necessary advances towards a unity of all real tendencies.   Let
her take the next step.   Let her appropriate the subsidies
of science.   They are as religious as our finest emotion,
because they show the divine method and purpose by
means of all animate and inanimate things.   If they show
this, there appears a divine unity which is expressed by
means of the whole of human nature: not by one part
alone, whether called intellect or spirit, head or heart;
but by the whole human personality directly interpreting
the whole of the divine agency, in an expression which
cannot be raveled up.   The whole seamless web of a

human soul is the whole divine word, without syllables
even, of which one might be science, and one religion, but
one solid breath, flying through all atoms and functions at
one moment, to animate and retain them.

There is only an apparent discrepancy because the men
of science find the facts so absorbing. They exact the
whole intellectual patience and integrity: they crowd upon
the observer from all quarters with a pertinacity that has
not been known before. A scientific man is obliged to
renounce all other problems, and to be willing to appear
irreligious while he really is collecting the refutation of
his own apparent materialism. When this devotion is
graced by modesty, as it is so often, and the student of
nature sets to every other profession a rare example of
diligence and zeal, which nothing seems minute enough to
baffle, or grand enough to daunt, then we feel that his
reticence upon religious questions is only a graceful surrender of a task that does not belong to him. When religious men blame his neutrality, or excessive surrender
to his analysis, they ought to be reminded that the apparent discrepancy between science and religion is almost
made a real one by their own unbalanced mysticism, and
abject submission to the superstitiousness of sentiment.

But it cannot be a real one. The human mind is a unit
because it has all the laws that all the facts require. God
has made of one blood the head and the heart. They are
both floating abreast upon it, exchanging signals. The
capacity of the mind to classify and interpret all the facts
is the finite side of the divine unity. And its effort to do
this classifies religion also, strips her of many superstitious
phrases, and makes her companionable to the lowest facts
in the gradations of growth or the succession of animals.
This is the reason why the religious man must borrow
from science its mental method, in order that he may be in
a condition to furnish to science his own primitive truths
of religion. He will not care what previous conceptions
he must modify about providence, the nature of evil, the
position of man in creation, or the reality of spiritual
experiences. He will be amply recompensed for the loss
of every superfluous notion, and every word of devotional
rhetoric, by the richness of the material which science
brings to his proofs and illustrations of the Person God,

the individual man, the law of his freedom, and the continuance of his life.

You cannot become men of science, but you may learn its method, its laws of continuous development, its physical and social certainties; and you may enrich your appeals for a pure and ideal life in man and society, and for a childlike trust in a divine paternity, by spoil from every province of the earth, sea, and sky. If science has not yet exhausted God, she has not gone too far for you to follow, that you may learn his ways, and show them unto men.

For there is in man this necessity to observe, followed, step by step, and watched, by this necessity to interpret. The earth started with it in the first man; with this twofold unity of seeing the visible, and implying the invisible; of noting objects, and fitting to them a creative presence. Through all the gradations of intelligence, from the lowest barbarous condition, mankind has furnished a God to every phenomenon, a moral law to every conscience, a soul to every body. The phrasing of these primitive truths grows clearer with every accession of knowledge. Museums and explorations cannot make them obsolete. The more of God you collect, the more consistent and sublime becomes your faith. It would be very strange if the acquisition of created things should reach a point where the Creator might disappear, carrying off the legitimate hopes and laws of the soul.

The fine-grained old truths of religion have been deposited by the world's best life. Its age is theirs: but, although so many epochs and races went to make them, we use them now without a thought of their age or of the gravity of getting them well grown; like the beautiful ivory mammoth tusk, sticking six or seven feet out of the frozen ground in Alaska, which the Indians have used for generations as a hitching-post. Tribes come and go, and generations succeed each other; but we all hitch up to the solid truths which offer their convenience, embedded in the past.

This unity of science and religion is declared emphatically by the anxiety and suspicion which have been engendered in millions of minds by the discovery that laws are invariable, and that nature, instead of being exorable, is simply consistent, always, through every part of a man. How do you account for this deep dissatisfaction and unrest, if men are merely adjusted to perform sets of automatic actions, and can be put into a table of possibilities? Would a machine be disturbed if it had sense enough to discover its own inevitable operations? But men are now oppressed because the facts have gathered faster than the explanations; and when they turn for relief to religion, expecting that the counter-spell will be spoken, from her ideal world, they are met by idle assumptions of doctrine, are referred to texts, and threatened with the retributions of unbelief. At the very moment when religion's opportunity first occurs to make the finite prove the infinite which she presumes, she continues the old prescription of church-extension, Bible-worship, claims of miracles, and conventional parish-life. Men everywhere testify to the identity of science and religion by their dread lest a diversity become established. They are sick with the deferred hope of union. Their sickness is a proclamation of the health of all the facts that are pretending to unsettle them. To convince them of this by boldly taking all genuine facts out of the hands of sciolism and newspaper knowledge, and putting them to the service of ideal truth, is the task of religion.

You will find that a proper mental method is a strong ally, into whatever province of reformation and philanthropy you choose to take your truths. It is the instrument of your enthusiasm. If you love men, and long, with all of God you can contain, to liberate them from vicious indulgences, and find them moral opportunities, you must work side by side with the men who discover the conditions of health, sanity, purity, and moral accountability. Their facts and estimates will serve you better than vague pulpit homilies that turn upon the difference between vice and virtue. Social science has for its object to acquire and maintain the personal health which develops the highest amount of personal volition, and liberates it from bad births, bad education, and bad neighborhoods. Religion should rejoice to have this practical companion for her love.

How religious the whole creation becomes as science passes to and fro, touching with her wand of order the great heaps of matter, till they fall into line, and present their thought! A well-arranged series of fossils will furnish "sermons in stones" upon the direct creative presence. It is your province to take the facts out of the keeping of scepticism, which uses them to reduce God to a continuity of force. They are all ready to declare that he is a person of immediate and constant presence, of incessant thinking agency. No matter whether you incline to the theory of Darwin, that all varieties have been developed by means of varying natural conditions, in an unbroken and gradual series that offers no point for a direct creative interference; or whether, with Owen and Agassiz, you prefer to think that every epoch began with freshly created types, not derived from previous ones, and that the only development is in the underlying thought. Both of these theories presume a divine presence and a personal volition in the act of creation, as necessary to supply the line of vital thinking in Darwin's gradualism, as in the other hypothesis of successive and isolated periods. All the facts which support one or the other are God's distinct statements that he is on the spot. Science cannot be non-committal if she would. When she is the most reluctant to make confession of faith in a divine person, her investigations anticipate her reserve, and proclaim that "the invisible things of Him from the creation of the world are clearly seen, being understood by the things that are made." This act of making is independent of all theories. Force cannot make anything until it is also made, and this keeps heaven close to the exigency of each moment: otherwise a constant force could not constantly create. What a body of a Creator science is unveiling to the gaze of religion! Prick it anywhere, and you draw the blood of his presence.

I said it would be well for you to accept the mental method that has definitely broken with tradition, and is writing its own Scripture. God holds its hand, and guides the fumbling fingers through the old and new traces of his work. But your business is to use it to preserve the honor and gladness of human souls. You have a direct commission to their moral and spiritual life: they must share the moral certainty of your aspiration. They want the encouragement of your own purpose to be faith-

ful to the finest ideas. Routine would have the heart of
them if it could: they long to feel the sword of the spirit
slitting it to pieces, and giving back to God his human
pulses. What is this moral power which offers opportunity to you?

We call it the ideal, the soul's natural turn to be like
God. It was derived from that Being who never paused
during all the million years which have gone to make an
earth, never lingered in a fine reverie over any of the
epochs, never regretted anything that was made, never
recoiled from its imperfection, never despaired at its
bestiality. The divine imagination not only justified all
the strange and barbarous creations, but was in rapture
to perceive how they led on,—a polypus that could prop-
agate itself by sprouting, a worm that increased its family
by snapping to pieces, a bug that died twice to let loose a
butterfly, monstrous lizards, cold and groveling, birds
that could not fly, sloths that could hardly keep awake to
eat, reptiles whose fascinations were secreted by a poison-
bag, and myriads of venomous insects, the whole point of
whose life was to take another: these, and the noxious-
ness of all the periods before the elements learned balance
and proportion, were the successes of an ideal that mused
and planned by what road and through what shortest and
cheapest processes spiritual beauty might be gained.
Look at all the strata that are picked at by the scientific
men, as thought, kindred to the thought that planned
them, seizes the leading idea of each, and unfolds their
order. They are all coasts where the divine Being arrived. All of them mark where he burnt his ships, and
sought the exigency of victory.

We have a natural turn to imitate this action. We call
it dissatisfaction when the present palls upon us, or hurts
our sense of right: we call it aspiration, when the future
offers to redress the present. But call it what you will.
The ideal is not an impulse that merely develops us, as
trees and metals are made; not the vitality which
emanates from our collective gifts. The finest soul and
body, vegetating together in the kitchen-garden style,
could not run up to such a blossom. But when the body
plays tricks upon the soul, and the soul demurs, protests,
and rages, then the spark is struck out. Let the body

take care for its old combustible lumber that has been
accumulating ever since the earth was made.   When the
soul frets at discovering something incompatible, a difference between fact and feeling, an end put to instinct and
a beginning to resolution; or when an awkward reality
comes lumbering sideways down the current, runs against
our shells of dreams, and crushes them in, then the imagination wakes, the creative power,—it was on board, the
same that converted the mist of a nebula, into the planet:
it wakes to perform the same service for us, to take our
temperament, no matter how crude, how thin, how feebly
coherent, and roll it into an orb whose shape invents its
own path, and originates its own motion through the
heavens.   We have this good-will for the perfect, as the
human side of God's perfections; but we should not have
any ill-will for the imperfect in ourselves if we had
traveled farther away along the ideal road to a point upon
it where a prospect appears to lie on the same level as a
retrospect, and the whole view is woven of homogeneous
materials.   But what point is that?   It is God himself,
the justifier of everything that he did not think it beneath
him to create.   At present, we can only imagine that
divine impartiality, and make it one of the attributes
which vindicate God to the pitch of adorability as soon as
the mind transfers it to him.

But now the ideal is a prisoner, like those in mediæval
times, who were condemned, by a refined sentiment of
cruelty, to be wakened every fifteen minutes, day and
night, till nature sank exhausted.   Our temperament is
the jailer that is detailed to do the shaking.   But, when
the prisoner is immortal, the oftener you wake him up,
the wider open do you set his eyes, till in that width there
is liberty.

I welcome you forth to do work of awakening.   Have
no longer a box for a pulpit: but, wherever you preach,
let it be a place as large as the humanity which claims to
be real and ideal, and demands a free ministry for both
functions.   I cannot anticipate through what forms the
country will learn to be addressed; but this I know,—
that souls will not put up with phrases any longer, and
the monotone of Sunday will not charm.   Let all the
seven days rise in your message to a completed harmony.

Amiable tourists of religion delight to bring home with them a bottle from the Jordan. American rivers are rolling for the baptism of Americans: scoop up each morning fresh water, as it descends, far-traveled it may be indeed, but eager to shape new channels, and refresh a virgin soil. I commend you to the divine spirit whose lips at your ear shall bid you wake to-morrow.

ANDREW DICKSON WHITE

THE FIELD OF HISTORICAL STUDY

[Address by Andrew D. White, historian and diplomat, president
Cornell University 1867-85, appointed ambassador to Germany 1897
(born in Homer, N. Y., November 7, 1832; ———), delivered at the
opening session of the American Historical Association, as its first
president, at Saratoga, N. Y., September 9, 1884.]

GENTLEMEN:—At the founding of an association for the
advancement of historical studies in the United States it
is natural that we look over the field to see in what directions and through what channels the activity of American
historical scholars can be best directed.

In every branch of learning there are some fields into
which all scholars in all nations may enter upon equal
terms and with equal chances of success; but there are
also special fields in which each national group of scholars
works at an advantage, and in which scholars in other
nations must, as a rule, give the maximum of labor to the
minimum of result; and this is by no means least true in
the study of history.   It is evident, for example, that the
scholars of each nation have special advantages as regards
investigation in the history of their own country; having
closer access to its documents and finer appreciation of
its modes of thought, they bring themselves more easily
into the historical current flowing through their nation
than a scholar from outside generally can.   There are,
indeed, exceptions to this rule.   Such men as Ranke,
Buckle, von Sybel, Sir James Stephen, Parkman, Baird,
and Charles Kendall Adams, writing upon the history of

France; Guizot, Pauli, and Gneist, upon the general and
constitutional history of England; Motley, upon the history of Holland; Prescott, Ticknor, and Dunham, upon
the history of Spain; Robertson, Bryce, Carlyle, and Herbert Tuttle, upon the history of Germany; Haxthausen and
Wallace, upon the history of Russia; De Tocqueville,
Laboulaye, and von Holst, upon the history of the United
States, show that the general rule has many and striking
exceptions, so many exceptions indeed, as to indicate the
existence of a subordinate rule, which, simply stated, is
that an individual standing outside of the country may be
so disengaged and disentangled as to take a clearer view
of questions in which religious or patriotic prejudices are
involved than most scholars within the country are likely
to do.   Still the large rule is unquestionably that the main
work in the development of historical knowledge concerning any country must be done by the scholars of that
country.

But besides these special fields there are general fields.
These have to do with the evolution of man and society
in human events through large reaches of time and space,
—with a philosophical synthesis of human affairs, or what
may .be called the "summing up" of history.   These
fields are open to thoughtful men of all countries alike;
they can be studied with fairly equal chances of success
by men in all parts of the world where human thought is
not under some curb, and where the love of truth as truth
and faith in truth as truth predominate over allegiance
to any system: governmental, ecclesiastical, philosophical,
or scientific.

While acknowledging the great value of special investigations and contributions to historical knowledge in individual nations, it is not too much to say that the highest
effort and the noblest result toward which these special
historical investigations lead, is the philosophical synthesis
of all special results in a large, truth-loving, justice-loving
spirit.   Bearing on this point, Buckle, in a passage well
worthy of meditation, has placed observation at the foot
of the ladder, discovery next above it, and philosophical
method at the summit.   He has shown that without a true
philosophical synthesis special investigations and discoveries often lead us far from any valuable fruits, and that

such special investigations may be worse than no investigation at all.

To these general considerations as to fields may be added something as to motives of study. The scholar may indeed find his motive for any special study in curiosity, or pride, or the desire to strengthen himself in his profession, or to exalt the fame of his neighborhood or country. Out of such motives indeed good things may grow, and there may come to these growths a beautiful bloom and fruitage; but even the best of these must be special and partial. The great, deep ground out of which large historical studies may grow is the ethical ground,—the simple ethical necessity for the perfecting, first, of man as man, and, secondly, of man as a member of society; or, in other words, the necessity for the development of humanity on the one hand and society on the other. Hence it would appear that, precious as special investigations may be, most precious of all is that synthesis made by enlightened men looking over large fields, in the light of the best results of special historical research, to show us through what cycles of birth, growth, and decay various nations have passed; what laws of development may be fairly considered as ascertained, and under these what laws of religious, moral, intellectual, social, and political health or disease; what developments have been good, aiding in the evolution of that which is best in man and in society; what developments have been evil, tending to the retrogression of man and society; how various nations have stumbled and fallen into fearful errors, and by what processes they have been brought out of those errors; how much the mass of men as a whole, acting upon each other in accordance with the general laws of development in animate nature, have tended to perfect man and society; and how much certain individual minds, which have risen either as the result of thought in their time, or in spite of it,—in defiance of any law which we can formulate— have contributed toward this evolution. Here as to results we have the verification of that pithy line of Publius Syrus: "*Discipulus est prioris posterior dies.*"

This study of history, either as a whole or in large parts, is of vast value both as supplying the method and the test of special studies on the one hand, and of meeting the highest necessities of man on the other. We may indeed consider it as the trunk of which special histories and biographies are the living branches, giving to them and receiving from them growth and symmetry, drawing life from them, sending life into them.

That such a connection between general and special investigation, between critical analysis of phenomena on the one hand and synthesis of results on the other, is not a theory, but a pregnant fact, can be easily seen by a glance over the historical work going on in our own time.

Take first France. The large treatment in Bossuet's "Universal History," in Voltaire's "Essai sur les Mœurs," and in the essays of Condorcet and Turgot, was the cause and, to some extent, the result of a remarkable growth of special histories in the last century. The great philosophical treatise of Guizot upon the history of civilization in Europe, the monumental work of Professor Laurent, of Ghent, upon the history of humanity traced along the lines of international law, and the works of Daunou, Roux-Ferrand, Michelet, and Henri Martin, have been causes and results of a great new growth of special historical investigation in this century. There is no time here to dwell upon individuals, but I may at least mention the works of Thierry, Mignet, Quinet, and Lanfrey, as examples of precious special histories which would never have been written save in the light of these general philosophical histories. If it be said that Thiers is an exception to the rule, I answer that his career is but a proof of it, and that the reason why he has been the most pernicious special pleader among French historians and the greatest architect of ruin among modern French statesmen, may be found in his distinct denial of any philosophical basis of history whatever.

Take next England. We see such masterpieces of general historical work as those of Gibbon and Robertson in the last century, and Grote, Buckle, Whewell, and Lecky in this, acting powerfully both as causes and results of special histories.

Take next our own country. The works of Bancroft and Hildreth, the "History of International Law" by Henry Wheaton, fragmentary lectures of President Dew of William and Mary College, the introductory chapters of Prescott's Ferdinand and Isabella and Motley's Dutch Republic, the "History of the Intellectual Development of Europe" by Draper—warped though it is by his view of the analogy between national and individual development—and such recent works as those of Lea, Charles Kendall Adams, McMaster, Coit Tyler, Lodge, Parkman, and others, with the work now going on at Cambridge, the State Universities of Michigan and Wisconsin, Johns Hopkins and Cornell Universities, show this same law in full force.

And if we go to fields more remote, we find in Italy the great philosophical generalization of Vico working down through the writings of Sismondi, Colletta, Villari, Cantù, Bonghi, Settembrini, and a host of others. Even in Spain we find that Balmés, thoughtful as he is, having the thought and depth of a special pleader, stimulates men with the same defects in special fields.

But the greatest proof of all that these two growths of historical thought are vitally connected, is to be found in even the most rapid survey of the work going on in Germany. Of the vast number of special growths I have no time to present the slightest sketch; their thoroughness and extent are exemplified in the Monumenta Germaniæ as carried on by Waitz, Wattenbach, and their compeers. But the work in the study of general world-history, and the history of civilization has developed both as a cause and result of this special work. Of broad and philosophical treatises we have such world-histories, of different merits, as those of Leo, Schlosser, Weber, and Ranke; and, covering part of the great field but in the same general spirit, such works as those of Ranke, Mommsen, Ernst Curtius, Droysen, Giesebrecht, Gregorovius, and a multitude of others; and in histories of civilization such as those of Wachsmuth, Du Bois, Reymond, Biedermann, Carriere, Henne Am Rhyn, Kolb, Hellwald, Honegger, Grün, Lazarus, Prutz, and others,—a list extending through the whole gamut of capacity. I adduce these facts, and specially this luxuriance of growth in German general historical studies, simply to show that such general growths go with special historical study, and that however much we do and ought to do in this country as to special investigation, an indication of healthful growth will be found in general and synthetical work even though some of it be inadequate.

And here allow me to call your attention to the use of the term "investigation." There appears frequently an idea that the word can be justly applied only to search into minute material facts and documents; but is it not just as true that investigation can be made into the relations and laws of facts? So, too, regarding a phrase we constantly hear, "the advancement of knowledge." But is knowledge advanced alone by the study of minute facts and occurrences? May it not also be advanced by a study of relations and methods and of laws governing such facts and occurrences? Investigation is as truly a means to the advancement of knowledge in the hands of the philosophic historian dealing with general history, as in those of the most minute annalist dealing with some forgotten piece of diplomacy or strategy. Did it not require as much original investigation, and was not the field of knowledge as much increased, when Guizot gave us his profound and fruitful generalizations as to the laws governing and consequences flowing from national development in civilization, under the influence of one or many elements, as when Gachard discovered the facts regarding the cloister life of Charles V, or when Mr. Poole showed the connection of Manasseh Cutler with the Northwestern territorial ordinance? The two—general and special investigation—must go together. So it was in Guizot's case; so it should be in all cases.

But let us now look somewhat more closely into this matter of the investigation of historical facts, especially as to the ends sought and the qualities required. Doubtless the end sought is exact truth, and the first quality required, veracity. But then comes the question: what truth, and, veracity on what lines?

Take a case. Two men investigate the formation of one of our State constitutions. One knows little of the constitutional development of our other States, or of the nation, or of foreign countries. He gives us a plain, dry statement of the facts which he sees, which of course are mainly surface facts. He is particular to give us the dates of sessions, the names of chairmen, the heads of committees, the makers and matter of speeches. The other, of equal veracity, knows much of the development of constitutional history in our own and other nations. He, too, gives us what he sees; and therefore he makes the fundamental facts shine through the surface annals. We have simply the difference here between the history of the birth of an American commonwealth, by a keen rural lawyer—as keen, if you please, as Thiers—on the one hand, and on the other by a Story, a Cooley, or a Stubbs.

Take another case. Two men investigate the history of popular government in one of our great cities—New York, perhaps. One is a careful, painstaking annalist, and nothing more. He masters the surface facts so far as they are given by chronicles of various sorts, from Stuyvesant and Governor Dongan's charter to the overthrow of Tweed and to the supremacy of Kelly. The other is just as careful and truthful, but something more. He has studied and meditated upon other cities; he has perhaps done what Ruskin insists that every true scholar ought to do—has studied the history of the five great cities of the world; has meditated upon the growth of the commercial spirit in the Italian city republics, in the Hanseatic League, and in the great English seaports; upon the growth of city factions from the days of Claudius and Milo in Rome, through the Blues and Greens in Constantinople, the Bianchi and Neri in Florence, the Remonstrants and Counter-Remonstrants in the cities of Holland, and the New York " Halls "; upon outbursts of civic public spirit like those which produced the Parthenon at Athens, the Duomo at Florence, and the town-halls of the Netherlands; upon the good and evil tendencies of accumulated civic wealth from Crassus, Jacques Cœur, and the Medici, to Peabody, and Cooper, and Vanderbilt; upon the tendencies of a civic proletary class as typified in such examples as the Marian prescriptions in Rome, the dealings of the mobs in mediæval Laon and Liege with their bishops, the Terror and Commune of Paris, the Know-Nothing riots of Philadelphia and the Draft riots of New York. Who does not see that the latter scholar will reveal masses of important facts and relations which the other can never find?

Again, two men set out to investigate the growth of some phase of belief. Both are veracious, but one is simply minute, painstaking, limited by sectarian trammels, with little light from outside history; the other has made broad studies in comparative philology and religion. Which is likely to give us something that, even considered purely as an investigation, is of real value?

But it is not necessary to suppose cases.   Every reader of history can recall real cases of "investigation" "extending the boundaries of knowledge," showing the vast difference between the annalist and the historian.   Take one of the most recent.   Professor Ihne, in his admirable history of Rome, has made a new investigation of the story of Publius Æbutius and the panic persecution of the Bacchanalian fanatics.   Who that reads his account does not see that the most important element in his investigation comes from his general knowledge, and that he throws a powerful light into the depths of the story from his knowledge of the inmost spirit of the panic persecutions of the early Christians, of the Jews in the Middle Ages, and of the Roman Catholics in England under Charles II?

And now allow me to call attention to some subordinate indications as to method given by general history to special history.   Greatly as I admire the main drift of Mr. Herbert Spencer's argument upon historical studies, in his treatise on Education, some of his statements seem to me to require limitation.   He seems at times to confuse the study of history with the study of statistics, and thus to demand scientific proof when the nature of the material can only give moral proof.   The analogy between the study of history and of travel has justly struck many minds, and throws some side-light upon Mr. Spencer's confusion.   Let us observe this analogy in making a case.

Two young Americans go to England for a year.   One devotes himself, in strict accordance with Mr. Spencer's theory, to "descriptive sociology," which, under the rules laid down by Mr. Spencer, results in the statistical tabulation of a vast multitude of facts; the other occupies himself in getting at the thought of the time, dominant or militant, by reading the best books, by talking with the best men in every field, by noting ends and methods in work of all sorts, by studying, comparatively, various ways of solving political and social problems, by observing society in all its branches, even by listening to the current chatter and prattle, in the various social strata. Both may come back useful men; but I think that none of us will deny that, as a man, the second—the historian—will be far better developed, and as a thinker, writer, or man of affairs, far better equipped than the first—the statistician.

Mr. Spencer has much to say regarding worthless sources and worthless facts. The truth is, a fact which appears very petty may be of vast value if it be pregnant, and a fact which appears very important is worthless if it be barren. Louis XIV receiving Condé on the great staircase of Versailles was an immense fact at the time; to us, in the light of general history, it is worth little or nothing. Louis XVI calling for bread and cheese when arrested at Varennes, and declaring it the best bread and cheese he ever ate, furnishes a fact apparently worthless, but really of significance, for it reveals that easy-going helplessness which was so important a factor in the wreck of the old French monarchy,—indeed that very spirit of which Thomas Jefferson so amusingly generalized the causes and results in his letter to Governor Langdon. The fact that Rufus Choate filled this republic with his mellifluous eloquence as a special pleader and was sent to the Senate of the United States, great as it then appeared, is now, as tested by the laws of general history, of no value. On the other hand, the fact that William Lloyd Garrison was editing a petty paper in Boston, unworthy of notice as it seemed then, is now found to be one of the great facts in American history—indeed, a most instructive fact in general history.

This test applied by general history to special throws into its true light much of the cant now current regarding the worthlessness of opinion as to battles, sieges, and treaties, and the supreme worth of facts regarding the popular life.

Mr. Spencer speaks contemptuously of historical attention to battles; yet battles may be important, and a little battle may be of vast value, and a great battle of none. The little battle of Saratoga is of great importance as a turning-point in the history of mankind; the great battle of Austerlitz is of comparatively little importance, because it shows merely the result of a clash between two tem-

porary developments in European politics. Mr. Spencer
makes little of the writing of memoirs; yet the little memoir of the Baroness Riedesel throws a flood of light upon
the spirit in which this little battle of Saratoga was fought
and in which this American Colonial empire was lost by
British mercenaries and won by American yeomanry;
indeed, it throws a light into the depths of philosophic
history, for it shows the force of a love of freedom against
the service of despotism. Mr. Spencer tells us that
"familiarity with court intrigues, plots, usurpations, and
the like, and with all the personalities accompanying them,
aids very little in elucidating the causes of national progress." This is in the main just, yet somewhat too sweeping. Few subjects in modern history are more fruitful in
valuable thought than the rise, glory, and decline of the
absolute monarchy in France from Richelieu to Necker.
Every historical scholar, no matter whether he agree with
Buckle's theory or not, must acknowledge his masterly
use of this subject in conveying some of the most important moral and political lessons to our present world.
But how much less would have been Buckle's knowledge
of the inner workings of that time had there not been open
to him and to us the memoirs and diaries of St. Simon,
Dangeau, Barbier, and the like? It is very doubtful
whether the most elaborate collection of statistics would
compensate for their loss.

Mr. Spencer also pours contempt, and with much justice, over details of battles. And yet, while sympathizing
largely with his statement in this respect, a careful historian must confess that there are details of battles which
the thoughtful student may well keep in mind. For example, when at the beginning of our recent Civil War our
Northern troops yielded at Bull Run and elsewhere to the
first onset of the enemy, it was of some value to remember, in estimating the significance of such a yielding, that
in the first battles of the French Revolution with Europe
the troops afterward so successful broke more than once
in this same manner. There are those of us who can
remember how precious a knowledge of this little historical fact was to us then, and one, to my personal
knowledge, used it before large audiences to keep up the
courage of his fellow citizens in that time of peril.

Mr. Spencer asks: "Suppose that you diligently read accounts of all the battles that history mentions, how much more judicious would your vote be at the next election?" Thinking Americans of the age which most of us have reached bear an answer to this question stamped vividly in our memories. In the fearful crisis of our Civil War, there were certain histories of which battles formed a large part, that were precious. I remember at that time when at one of our greatest universities bodies of students came to my lecture-room asking: "What shall we read?" My answer was: "Read the history of Rome just after the battle of Cannæ; read Motley's history of the Dutch Republic, and especially of the siege of Leyden; read Macaulay's account of the siege of Londonderry; read Provost Stillé's pamphlet ' How a Great People Carried on a Long War.'" All of us know that at many elections, perhaps at most of them, the question is not one of knowledge but of conduct; that is, not "What ought I to do?" but "Have I the courage to do what I ought?" Sometimes historical facts which cannot be shaped into sociological tables aid us to answer either or both of these questions. The fact above referred to—that another leading nation, though its troops broke up in panic two or three times at first, carried a vast war to ultimate victory —was used at the beginning of our Civil War for the very purpose of enlightening citizens as to their duty in "voting at the next election"—used to show them that they should not vote for candidates who represented public discouragement and the tendency to make a compromise involving either disunion or the retention of slavery, forever, in the Constitution of the United States.

So, too, I recall another historical fact which was used with effect at that time to keep up the courage of our people as to voting men and means for the war, and voting for candidates determined to resist disunion and the perpetuation of slavery. It was a fact which would probably never occur to any one as fitting into a sociological table, and yet it was to the American people an important fact. It was simply that at the beginning of the great English Civil War, in the middle of the Seventeenth century, the first race of generals on the popular side—men like Manchester and Essex—failed because they could not thoroughly appreciate the questions at issue, and that success came only when men of sterner purpose were put in command. This historical fact, both in its development and results, was perfectly paralleled in our own history.

So, too, as to treaties. The Treaty of Paris after the Crimean war has but a temporary interest; the Treaty of Westphalia has been active in the development of Europe, political, intellectual, and moral, down to this hour.

So, too, as to facts apparently dried up and withered. A pamphlet by a forgotten sophist like Royer, and a speech by a contemptible demagogue like Gouy, at the beginning of the French Revolution, giving reasons for unlimited issues of paper money then, are facts which would appear in no table of descriptive sociology; and yet, when this Republic had recently to deal with the most momentous question since the Civil War,—the question of wild finance and currency inflation,—the arguments in Royer's pamphlet and Gouy's speech, and others like them, which were once used to plunge France into the abyss of bankruptcy and ruin by unlimited issues of paper money, were exhibited in our own country with decided effect, before committees at Washington, before meetings of business men in New York, and in campaign pamphlets. They were certainly facts of vast importance with reference to " a vote at the next election,"—a vote which was to decide whether this Republic should be, by similar arguments and policy, plunged into misery and disgrace.

So, too, as to facts regarding individual action; Aristotle in the apothecary shop, Plato in the grove, Erigena and Thomas Aquinas in the schools, Copernicus in his cell, Newton in the orchard, Cardinal D'Ailly writing his Imago Mundi, Grotius writing his De Jure Belli ac Pacis, Comenius writing his little Orbis Pictus Volta in his university, Watt in his workroom, Descartes turning from natural science to philosophy, Paolo Sarpi advising the Venetian Republic how to meet an interdict, and writing his history of the Council of Trent, Thomasius publishing his treatise against witchcraft in the name of a student, Beccaria writing his little book on Crimes and Punishments, Adam Smith writing his " Wealth of Nations," Kant writing his Critiques of the " Pure and Practical Reason," Beaumarchais writing his " Marriage de Figaro," Harriet Beecher Stowe writing her "Uncle Tom's Cabin," Darwin on the Beagle, Cavour meeting Napoleon III at Plombières, Bismarck meeting Frederick William IV at Venice, Lincoln taking the stump in Illinois—what facts are these!

The simple truth is that there are facts and facts. In the beginning of this century Metternich prompting the policy of Europe was supposed to be great; Stein in his bureau was thought of little account. In our own time, Napoleon III on the throne was apparently a great fact, but how much greater a fact was Pasteur in his laboratory! In England the foolish Lord John Russell, reading homilies to the Cabinets of Europe and nearly blundering into a great war with the United States, was called a statesman and seemed a controlling personage; but how small his real influence on England or the world at large compared with that of the rather forlorn Prince Consort, who, despite his birth and environment, and the limitations imposed by a sneering court and jealous people, labored so successfully for the development of art and science throughout the world, and used his influence against the war which the folly of Lord John Russell did so much to bring on.

The simple rule and test which general history and the history of civilization give to special investigation is that if close knowledge of a battle, or an intrigue, or a man is important to our knowledge of the great lines of historical evolution, then these facts are important; if not, they are not important.

To the statement, then, that history has occupied itself too much with kings and courts and conquerors, and that it should "occupy itself with the people," a true historical synthesis gives answer that history must occupy itself with men and events which signify something. The men may be saints or miscreants, popes or monks, kings or peasants, conquerors or conspirators, builders of cathedrals or weavers of verse, railway kings or day-laborers, publicists or satirists, philanthropists or demagogues, statesmen or mob orators, philosophers or phrasemongers. The event may be a poem or a constitution, a battle or a debate, a treaty or a drama, a picture or a railway, a voyage or a book, a law or an invention, the rise of a nation or the fall of a clique. Meeting our ethical necessity for historical knowledge with statistics and tabulated sociology entirely or mainly, is like meeting our want of food by the perpetual administration of concentrated essence of beef.

Again, is it possible to reduce necessary historical knowledge to such concentrated and tabulated form? There are statistics and statistics; some increase our perception of truth, some decrease it. As an example of both these facts, take a statement made in Montesquieu's "Greatness and Decline of the Romans," with Mr. Baker's excellent notes. Montesquieu shows statistically and very effectively that in the early days of Rome the ratio of soldiers to population was one to eight, whereas in Europe in Montesquieu's time it was about one to a hundred, and that this latter is the highest rate which can safely be maintained in a modern State. Mr. Baker corroborates this in a very striking manner, by showing that the number of persons serving in the armies and navies of the great modern European States remains about one to one hundred. Now, so far, these statistics increase our perception of truth. They show simply but conclusively how much more strongly the warlike feeling was cherished in Rome, when, instead of one soldier or sailor to a hundred, as in the modern States, there was one to eight.

But, on the other hand, take another statistical statement, which is, that under the Roman Empire, at the time of its greatest expansion, there was only one soldier and sailor to two hundred and sixty-six of the population, a ratio but little more than one-third as great as that in the seven great military States of Europe to-day. This statistical statement, apart from other knowledge, would inevitably lead to the conclusion that the Roman Empire had ceased to wage war; that, as compared to the great modern States of Europe, it thought little of self-defence, and needed to think little of it; whereas the fact is that Rome at that very time was perpetually at war, that war was its greatest concern,—in fact, that its statesmen thought of little else on a large scale besides war.

Again, there are material statistics and moral statistics, and to each must be assigned a proper place. The corruption and decline of Rome is one of the most important and suggestive things in human annals. This corruption and decline is as real as the existence of Rome itself. But how are we to understand it? Material statistics as to the amount of territory conquered, wealth swept into Rome after the Carthaginian and Eastern wars, agricultural populations pauperized, slaves substituted for yeomen, latifundia substituted for peasant farms, and the like, if we could obtain them, might be of use. But there are moral statistics of no less value. A poem of Lucretius, showing that thinking men had outlived the old faith, and that a great chasm had been opened between reason and religious institutions; Cicero's vacillating treatment of torture in procedure; a dialogue of Lucian, showing that the old religion had utterly broken down; a fling in Juvenal, at the hysterical superstitions arising, especially among women; a sentence in Tacitus approving the execution of four hundred slaves of Pedanius Secundus because one of them, unknown to the others, had murdered their master; the picture of a gladiatorial combat by Gérôme and Alma Tadema's picture of the prætorians dragging Claudius to the throne,—in each of these facts is included a whole column of moral statistics, which enable us to see far into the spirit of the time and the cause of that imperial decline, as columns of material statistics might not do.

Take another field—the moral deterioration of France preparatory to the Revolution. This was a fact of vast moment to Europe. Doubtless statements could be tabulated to show this deterioration, but what statistics could throw so much light into it as the simple fact that the sainted Fénelon was succeeded in the archbishopric of Cambray by the infamous Cardinal Dubois; that while the government had disgraced Fénelon, it loaded Dubois with honors; and that while the clergy had without a murmur allowed Fénelon to be crushed, they invited Dubois to preside over their National Assembly.

Take a very different subject. The wild partisan madness of England toward France which pushed on the war against the first French Republic, teaches a philosophical and practical lesson to every modern nation. What statement can be tabulated so as to show it? Yet a single caricature of Gillray, glorifying that infamous assassina-

tion by the Austrians of Bonnier and Roberjot, the French
envoys to the Congress of Rastadt, with the punning in-
scription exulting in that worst breach of international
law in modern times, tells the whole story.

Take a still more recent field. The material statistics
as to the diminution in the height of soldiers in the French
army during the later wars of Napoleon are of great value
as showing not only the fearful state of exhaustion to
which the Empire was reduced, but the price which a
nation has to pay for "glory." Look, now, at a moral
statistic showing the same thing. One of the memoir
writers tells us that when Napoleon, after throwing away
his army of over five hundred thousand men in the Moscow campaign, had hurried back to France and had entered the Tuileries almost alone, he rubbed his hands
before the fire, and simply said: "Decidedly it is more
comfortable here than in Moscow," with no further mention of the loss that France had sustained, and evidently
with no sympathy for the millions whom he had bereaved.
Here is a moral statistic to the same effect as the material
statistic just cited, and of equal value in showing the spirit
in which Napoleonism wrought, and indeed, from the
point of view of general history, the spirit which military
despotism necessarily engenders.

Again, take the history now going on among ourselves.
The future historian of the United States will, no doubt,
give especial attention to the reunion of the Northern and
Southern States as a homogeneous nation after the Civil
War. This process is going on at this moment. What
material facts that can be tabulated into a descriptive
sociology throw any light upon it? I can see none. If
you say the statistics of the votes in the Electoral College
cast at the last presidential election, my answer is that
these will certainly mislead the future historian if he is not
very careful, for they would seem to show an absolute and
complete break between North and South—a separation
greater than before the war. But are there not moral
statistics of far more real value in this case showing the
very opposite of this? I think so. Take the simple fact
that Judge Finch's poem, "The Blue and the Gray," is
recited on Decoration Day, at North and South; take the
fact that Mr. Atkinson delivered his address at the Georgia

Exposition and found most respectful audience for his very plain statements of Southern shortcomings, which, before the war, would very likely have cost him his life; take the hospitable reception of Northern military companies in the South bearing the flag against which the Southern men risked their lives with a bravery very notable in human annals;—these are types of a multitude of facts which can be arranged in no table of material statistics but which are moral indications of the greatest value.

And now as to certain limitations in the methods of investigation imposed upon us by circumstances peculiar to ourselves. I remember several years ago hearing a gentleman temporarily eminent in politics (one of Carlyle's *hommes alors celebres*) in a speech before the authorities of an American university, declare that all history must be rewritten from an American point of view. This assertion, at the time, seemed to savor of that vagueness and largeness often noted in the utterance of the American politician upon his travels, which in our vernacular, is happily named "tall talk"; but as the statement has recurred to my mind at various periods since, it seemed to me that our political friend uttered more wisely than he knew. For is it not true that we, in this Republic, called upon to help build up a new civilization with a political and social history developing before us of which the consequences for good or evil are to rank with those which have flowed from the life of Rome and the British Empire,—is it not true that, for us, the perspective of a vast deal of history is changed; that the history which, for the use of various European populations, has been written with minute attention to details, must be written for us in a larger and more philosophical way?

And is it not true that the history so rapidly developing here is throwing back a new light upon much history already developed? What legislator cannot see that the history of our American municipalities throws light upon the republics of the Middle Ages, and derives light from them? What statesman cannot understand far better the problem of the British government in Ireland in the light of our own problem in the city of New York? What classical scholar cannot better understand Cleon the leatherseller, as we laugh at the gyrations of a certain American politician now "starring it in the provinces"? What publicist cannot weigh more justly the immediate pre-revolutionary period in France as he notes a certain thin, loose humanitarianism of our day, which is making our land the paradise of murderers? What historical student cannot more correctly estimate the value of a certain happy-go-lucky optimism which sees nothing possible but good in the future, when he recalls the complacent public opinion, voiced by the Italian historian just before 1789, that henceforth peace was to reign in Europe, since great wars had become an impossibility? What student of social science cannot better estimate the most fearful anti-social evil among us by noting the sterility of marriage in the decline of Rome and in the eclipse of France?

In this sense I think that the assertion referred to as to the rewriting of history from the American point of view contains a great truth; and it is this modified view of the evolution of human affairs, of the development of man as man, and of man in society, that opens a great field for American philosophic historians, whether they shall seek to round the whole circle of human experience, or simply to present some arc of it.

The want of such work can be clearly seen on all sides. Not one of us reads the current discussions of public affairs in Congress, in the State Legislatures, or in the newspapers, who does not see that, strong and keen as many of these are, a vast deal of valuable light is shut out by ignorance of turning-points in the history of human civilization thus far. Never was this want of broad historical views in leaders of American opinion more keenly felt than now. Think of the blindness to one of the greatest things which gives renown to nations, involved in the duty levied by Congress upon works of art. Think, too, of the blindness to one of the main agencies in the destruction of every great republic thus far, shown in the neglect to pass a constitutional amendment which shall free us from the danger of *coups d'etat* at the counting of the electoral vote. Think of the cool disregard of the plainest teaching of general history involved in legislative carelessness or doctrinaire opposition to measures remedying illiteracy in our Southern States. Never was this want of broad historical views more evident in our legislation than now. In the early history of this Republic we constantly find that such men as John Adams and Thomas Jefferson, to say nothing of the lesser lights, drew very largely and effectively from their studies of human history. In the transition period such men as Calhoun, John Quincy Adams, Everett, and Webster drew a large part of their strength from this source. And in the great period through which we have recently passed the two statesmen who wrought most powerfully to shape vague hopes into great events—William Henry Seward and Charles Sumner—were the two of all American statesmen in their time who drew inspiration and strength from a knowledge of the general history of mankind. Nothing but this could have kept up Seward's faith or Sumner's purpose. The absence of this sort of light among our public men at present arises doubtless from the necessities of our material development since the Civil War, and the demand for exact arithmetical demonstration in finance rather than moral demonstration in broad questions of public policy; but as we approach the normal state of things more and more, the need of such general studies must grow stronger and stronger.

As regards the work of our American universities and colleges in the historical field, we must allow that it is wofully defective; but there are signs, especially among those institutions which are developed out of the mass of colleges into universities, of a better time coming. They must indeed yield to the current sweeping through the age. This is an epoch of historical studies. It is a matter of fact, simple and easily verified, that whereas in the last century state problems and world problems were as a rule solved by philosophy, and even historians such as Voltaire and Gibbon and Robertson were rather considered as philosophers than as historians, in this century such problems are studied most frequently in the light of history.

Still another encouraging fact is that advanced studies of every sort are more and more thrown into the historic form; the growth of the historical school in political economy is but one of many examples of this. More and more it is felt that "the proper study of mankind is man"; more and more clear becomes the idea enforced by

Draper, that the greatest problems of humanity must be approached not so much by the study of the individual man as by the study of men in general and historically. To this tendency the great universities of the old world have already conformed, and to this the institutions for advanced instruction in our own country must conform before they can take any proper rank in the higher education and be worthy to be called even the beginnings of universities.

It is largely in these institutions of learning that this work of historical study which I especially advocate— this union of close scientific analysis with a large philosophic synthesis must begin. Unquestionably the number of professors devoted to historical investigation in the German universities is the great cause of the fact that Germany has surpassed other modern nations not only in special researches, but in general historical investigations. Important researches have indeed been made outside her universities, but the great majority of them have certainly been made by university men; and this indicates the lines on which historical studies are to be best developed in our own country. Every professor of history in a university should endeavor to present some special field with thoroughness; to extend, deepen, or quicken special knowledge in that field; to lead his students to investigations in it. Doubtless of all such fields that which, as a rule, will yield the most fruit to special and original investigation by American students will be found in English and American political, social, and constitutional history. But while the professor in an American university makes special studies, he ought to be laboring toward something like a conspectus of human history,—if not of all human history, at least of some great part of it. So shall he prevent his generalizations from becoming vague, and his investigations from becoming trivial.

During a recent residence in Germany I more than once found the ablest investigators, men of world-wide rank, lamenting the relative want of this large philosophical work. Said the Rector of one of the foremost universities to me: "It saddens me to see so many of my best young men confined entirely to mere specialties and niceties. The result of all this is an excessive specialization of study which, if carried much further, will render a university impossible." To lead American students in our universities and colleges prematurely and mainly into special and original investigations is simply to fasten upon them the character of petty annalists. With such special work should go, *pari passu*, thoughtful study of great connected events.

Among many examples proving this necessity, in the university professor of large general studies in connection with the best special work, we have some especially striking in our own time. Who does not see that Professor Freeman's admirable researches into mediæval history derive perhaps the greater part of their cogency from the very wide range of his studies in time and space? Who does not feel that even when he is investigating the minutest point in what Milton compared to the " wars of kites and crows," the habit of mind engendered by this general study adds vastly to the value of his special study, enabling him to see what lies under the mere surface history here and to strike the turning-point there? So, too, with Professor Goldwin Smith. Who of us does not feel during his discussion of the simplest point, even of local Canadian history, that we are in the grasp of a man who brings to the subject a broad knowledge which enables him to flood the pettiest local event with light as the simple annalist and mere special investigator could never do? Who that has had the pleasure of hearing such professors as Ernst Curtius at Berlin or Oncken at Giessen, has not seen that the secret of strength in the German professor is not, as commonly supposed, merely in his minute investigation, but very largely in his illumination of special research by broad general study? Such are special studies when combined with general studies. But who has not seen them when not thus combined?

So, have I known a local historian devote himself to the abstruse study of such questions in the history of a country town as whether the fire-engine house was originally in the neighborhood of the village school, or of the town pump, and whether a petty official recently departed was at an early period of his life in sympathy with the Presbyterians or Methodists.

It is to be hoped then, that at the future meetings of an

Association such as we now contemplate, papers may be frequently presented giving the results not only of good special work in history and biography, work requiring keen critical analysis, but of good work in the larger field requiring a philosophical synthesis. There ought certainly to be a section or sections in American history, general and local, and perhaps in other special fields; but there ought also to be a section or sections devoted to general history, the history of civilization, and the philosophy of history. Of course, such a section will have its dangers. Just as in the section devoted to special history there will be danger of pettiness and triviality, so in that devoted to general history there will be danger of looseness and vagueness—danger of attempts to approximate Hegel's shadowy results. But these difficulties in both fields the Association must meet as they arise. Certainly a confederation like this—of historical scholars from all parts of the country, stimulating each other to new activity—ought to elicit most valuable work in both fields and to contribute powerfully to the healthful development on the one hand of man as man, and on the other to the opening up of a better political and social future for the nation at large.

None can feel this more strongly than the little band of historical scholars who, scattered through various parts of the country, far from great libraries and separate from each other, have labored during the last quarter of a century to keep alive in this country the flame of philosophical investigation of history as a means for the greater enlightenment of their country and the better development of mankind.

WOODROW WILSON

Photogravure after a photograph from life

WOODROW WILSON

THE COURSE OF AMERICAN HISTORY

[Address by Woodrow Wilson, historian, essayist, professor of jurisprudence and politics in Princeton University since 1890, elected its president June 9, 1902, and inaugurated October 25, 1902 (born in Staunton, Va., December 28, 1856; ———), delivered before the New Jersey Historical Society.]

GENTLEMEN:—In the field of history, learning should be deemed to stand among the people and in the midst of life. Its function there is not one of pride merely: to make complaisant record of deeds honorably done and plans nobly executed in the past. It has also a function of guidance: to build high places whereon to plant the clear and flaming lights of experience, that they may shine alike upon the roads already traveled and upon the paths not yet attempted. The historian is also a sort of prophet. Our memories direct us. They give us knowledge of our character, alike in its strength and in its weakness; and it is so we get our standards for endeavor,—our warnings and our gleams of hope. It is thus we learn what manner of nation we are of, and divine what manner of people we should be.

And this is not in national records merely. Local history is the ultimate substance of national history. There could be no epics were pastorals not also true,—no patriotism, were there no homes, no neighbors, no quiet round of civic duty; and I, for my part, do not wonder that scholarly men have been found not a few who, though they might have shone upon a larger field, where all eyes would have seen them win their fame, yet chose to pore all

their lives long upon the blurred and scattered records
of a country-side, where there was nothing but an old
church or an ancient village.   The history of a nation is
only the history of its villages written large.   I only marvel that these local historians have not seen more in the
stories they have sought to tell.   Surely here, in these old
hamlets that antedate the cities, in these little communities
that stand apart and yet give their young life to the nation,
is to be found the very authentic stuff of romance for the
mere looking.   There is love and courtship and eager life
and high devotion up and down all the lines of every
genealogy.   What strength, too, and bold endeavor in
the cutting down of forests to make the clearings; what
breath of hope and discovery in scaling for the first time
the nearest mountains; what longings ended or begun
upon the coming in of ships into the harbor; what pride
of earth in the rivalries of the village; what thoughts of
heaven in the quiet of the rural church!   What forces of
slow and steadfast endeavor there were in the building of
a great city upon the foundations of a hamlet: and how
the plot broadens and thickens and grows dramatic as
communities widen into States!   Here, surely, sunk deep
in the very fibre of the stuff, are the colors of the great
story of men,—the lively touches of reality and the striking
images of life.

   It must be admitted, I know, that local history can be
made deadly dull in the telling.   The men who reconstruct it seem usually to build with kiln-dried stuff,—as
if with a purpose it should last.   But that is not the fault
of the subject.   National history may be written almost
as ill, if due pains be taken to dry it out.   It is a trifle
more difficult: because merely to speak of national affairs
is to give hint of great forces and of movements blown
upon by all the airs of the wide continent.   The mere
largeness of the scale lends to the narrative a certain
dignity and spirit.   But some men will manage to be dull
though they should speak of creation.   In writing of local
history the thing is fatally easy.   For there is some neighborhood history that lacks any large significance, which is
without horizon or outlook.   There are details in the history of every community which it concerns no man to
know again when once they are past and decently buried

in the records: and these are the very details, no doubt, which it is easiest to find upon a casual search. It is easier to make out a list of county clerks than to extract the social history of the county from the records they have kept,—though it is not so important: and it is easier to make a catalogue of anything than to say what of life and purpose the catalogue stands for. This is called collecting facts "for the sake of the facts themselves"; but if I wished to do aught for the sake of the facts themselves I think I should serve them better by giving their true biographies than by merely displaying their faces.

The right and vital sort of local history is the sort which may be written with lifted eyes,—the sort which has a horizon and an outlook upon the world. Sometimes it may happen, indeed, that the annals of a neighborhood disclose some singular adventure which had its beginning and its ending there: some unwonted bit of fortune which stands unique and lonely amidst the myriad transactions of the world of affairs, and deserves to be told singly and for its own sake. But usually the significance of local history is, that it is part of a greater whole. A spot of local history is like an inn upon a highway: it is a stage upon a far journey: it is a place the national history has passed through. There mankind has stopped and lodged by the way. Local history is thus less than national history only as the part is less than the whole. The whole could not dispense with the part, would not exist without it, could not be understood unless the part also were understood. Local history is subordinate to national only in the sense in which each leaf of a book is subordinate to the volume itself. Upon no single page will the whole theme of the book be found; but each page holds a part of the theme. Even were the history of each locality exactly like the history of every other (which it cannot be), it would deserve to be written,—if only to corroborate the history of the rest, and verify it as an authentic part of the record of the race and nation. The common elements of a nation's life are the great elements of its life, the warp and woof of the fabric. They cannot be too much or too substantially verified and explicated. It is so that history is made solid and fit for use and wear.

Our national history, of course, has its own great and

spreading pattern, which can be seen in its full form and completeness only when the stuff of our national life is laid before us in broad surfaces and upon an ample scale. But the detail of the pattern, the individual threads of the great fabric, are to be found only in local history.   There is all the intricate weaving, all the delicate shading, all the nice refinement of the pattern,—gold thread mixed with fustian, fine thread laid upon coarse, shade combined with shade.   Assuredly it is this that gives to local history its life and importance.   The idea, moreover, furnishes a nice criterion of interest.   The life of some localities is, obviously, more completely and intimately a part of the national pattern than the life of other localities, which are more separate and, as it were, put upon the border of the fabric.   To come at once and very candidly to examples, the local history of the Middle States,—New York, New Jersey, and Pennsylvania,—is much more structurally a part of the characteristic life of the nation as a whole than is the history of the New England communities or of the several States and regions of the South.   I know that such a heresy will sound very rank in the ears of some: for I am speaking against accepted doctrine.   But acceptance, be it never so general, does not make a doctrine true.

Our national history has been written for the most part by New England men.   All honor to them!   Their scholarship and their characters alike have given them an honorable enrolment amongst the great names of our literary history; and no just man would say aught to detract, were it never so little, from their well-earned fame.   They have written our history, nevertheless, from but a single point of view.   From where they sit, the whole of the great development looks like an Expansion of New England.   Other elements but play along the sides of the great process by which the Puritan has worked out the development of nation and polity.   It is he who has gone out and possessed the land: the man of destiny, the type and impersonation of a chosen people.   To the Southern writer, too, the story looks much the same, if it be but followed to its culmination,—to its final storm and stress and tragedy in the great war.   It is the history of the Suppression of the South.   Spite of all her splendid contributions to the steadfast accomplishment of the great

task of building the nation; spite of the long leadership
of her statesmen in the national counsels; spite of her joint
achievements in the conquest and occupation of the West,
the South was at last turned upon on every hand, rebuked,
proscribed, defeated.   The history of the United States,
we have learned, was, from the settlement at Jamestown
to the surrender at Appomattox, a long-drawn contest for
mastery between New England and the South,—and the
end of the contest we know.   All along the parallels of
latitude ran the rivalry, in those heroical days of toil and
adventure during which population crossed the continent,
like an army advancing its encampments.   Up and down
the great river of the continent, too, and beyond, up the
slow incline of the vast steppes that lift themselves toward
the crowning towers of the Rockies,—beyond that, again,
in the gold-fields and upon the green plains of California,
the race for ascendency struggled on,—till at length there
was a final coming face to face, and the masterful folk
who had come from the loins of New England won their
consummate victory.

It is a very dramatic form for the story.   One almost
wishes it were true.   How fine a unity it would give our
epic!   But perhaps, after all, the real truth is more interesting.   The life of the nation cannot be reduced to these
so simple terms.   These two great forces, of the North
and of the South, unquestionably existed,—were unquestionably projected in their operation out upon the great
plane of the continent, there to combine or repel, as circumstances might determine.   But the people that went
out from the North were not an unmixed people; they
came from the great Middle States as well as from New
England.   Their transplantation into the West was no
more a reproduction of New England or New York or
Pennsylvania or New Jersey than Massachusetts was a
reproduction of old England, or New Netherland a reproduction of Holland.   The Southern people, too, whom
they met by the western rivers and upon the open
prairies, were transformed, as they themselves were, by
the rough fortunes of the frontier.   A mixture of peoples,
a modification of mind and habit, a new round of experiment and adjustment amidst the novel life of the baked
and untilled plain, and the far valleys with the virgin for-

ests still thick upon them: a new temper, a new spirit of adventure, a new impatience of restraint, a new license of life,—these are the characteristic notes and measures of the time when the nation spread itself at large upon the continent, and was transformed from a group of colonies into a family of States.

The passes of these eastern mountains were the arteries of the nation's life. The real breath of our growth and manhood came into our nostrils when first, like Governor Spotswood and that gallant company of Virginian gentlemen that rode with him in the far year 1716, the Knights of the Order of the Golden Horseshoe, our pioneers stood upon the ridges of the eastern hills and looked down upon those reaches of the continent where lay the untrodden paths of the westward migration. There, upon the courses of the distant rivers that gleamed before them in the sun, down the farther slopes of the hills beyond, out upon the broad fields that lay upon the fertile banks of the " Father of Waters," up the long tilt of the continent to the vast hills that looked out upon the Pacific—there were the regions in which, joining with people from every race and clime under the sun, they were to make the great compounded nation whose liberty and mighty works of peace were to cause all the world to stand at gaze. Thither were to come Frenchmen, Scandinavians, Celts, Dutch, Slavs,—men of the Latin races and of the races of the Orient, as well as men, a great host, of the first stock of the settlements: English, Scots, Scots-Irish,—like New England men, but touched with the salt of humor, hard, and yet neighborly too. For this great process of growth by grafting, of modification no less than of expansion, the colonies,—the original thirteen States,—were only preliminary studies and first experiments. But the experiments that most resembled the great methods by which we peopled the continent from side to side and knit a single polity across all its length and breadth, were surely the experiments made from the very first in the Middle States of our Atlantic seaboard.

Here from the first were mixture of population, variety of element, combination of type, as if of the nation itself in small. Here was never a simple body, a people of but a single blood and extraction, a polity and a practice brought straight from one mother land. The life of these States was from the beginning like the life of the country: they have always shown the national pattern. In New England and the South it was very different. There some of the great elements of the national life were long in preparation: but separately and with an individual distinction; without mixture,—for long almost without movement. That the elements thus separately prepared were of the greatest importance, and run everywhere like chief threads of the pattern through all our subsequent life, who can doubt? They give color and tone to every part of the figure. The very fact that they are so distinct and separately evident throughout, the very emphasis of individuality they carry with them, but proves their distinct origin. The other elements of our life, various though they be, and of the very fibre, giving toughness and consistency to the fabric, are merged in its texture, united, confused, almost indistinguishable, so thoroughly are they mixed, intertwined, interwoven, like the essential strands of the stuff itself: but these of the Puritan and the Southerner, though they run everywhere with the rest and seem upon a superficial view themselves the body of the cloth, in fact modify rather than make it.

What in fact has been the course of American history? How is it to be distinguished from European history? What features has it of its own, which give it its distinctive plan and movement? We have suffered, it is to be feared, a very serious limitation of view until recent years by having all our history written in the East. It has smacked strongly of a local flavor. It has concerned itself too exclusively with the origins and Old World derivations of our story. Our historians have made their march from the sea with their heads over shoulder, their gaze always backward upon the landing-places and homes of the first settlers. In spite of the steady immigration, with its persistent tide of foreign blood, they have chosen to speak often and to think always of our people as sprung after all from a common stock, bearing a family likeness in every branch, and following all the while old, familiar, family ways. The view is the more misleading because it is so large a part of the truth without being all of it. The common British stock did first make the country, and has

always set the pace.   There were common institutions up
and down the coast; and these had formed and hardened
for a persistent growth before the great westward migration began which was to reshape and modify every element
of our life.   The national government itself was set up and
made strong by success while yet we lingered for the most
part upon the eastern coast and feared a too distant
frontier.

But, the beginnings once safely made, change set in
apace.   Not only so: there had been slow change from
the first.   We have no frontier now, we are told,—except
a broken fragment, it may be, here and there in some barren corner of the western lands, where some inhospitable
mountain still shoulders us out, or where men are still
lacking to break the baked surface of the plains and occupy
them in the very teeth of hostile nature.   But at first it
was all frontier,—a mere strip of settlements stretched
precariously upon the sea-edge of the wilds: an untouched
continent in front of them, and behind them an unfre-
quented sea that almost never showed so much as the
momentary gleam of a sail.   Every step in the slow process of settlement was but a step of the same kind as the
first, an advance to a new frontier like the old.   For long
we lacked, it is true, that new breed of frontiersmen born
in after years beyond the mountains.   Those first frontiersmen had still a touch of the timidity of the Old World
in their blood: they lacked the frontier heart.   They were
"Pilgrims" in very fact,—exiled, not at home.   Fine
courage they had: and a steadfastness in their bold design
which it does a faint-hearted age good to look back upon.
There was no thought of drawing back.   Steadily, almost
calmly, they extended their seats.   They built homes, and
deemed it certain their children would live there after
them.   But they did not love the rough, uneasy life for its
own sake.   How long did they keep, if they could, within
sight of the sea!   The wilderness was their refuge; but
how long before it became their joy and hope!   Here was
their destiny cast; but their hearts lingered and held back.
It was only as generations passed and the work widened
about them that their thought also changed, and a new
thrill sped along their blood.   Their life had been new
and strange from their first landing in the wilderness.

Their houses, their food, their clothing, their neighborhood dealings were all such as only the frontier brings.
Insensibly they were themselves changed.   The strange
life became familiar; their adjustment to it was at length
unconscious and without effort; they had no plans which
were not inseparably a part and a product of it.   But,
until they had turned their backs once for all upon the sea;
until they saw their western borders cleared of the French;
until the mountain passes had grown familiar, and the
lands beyond the central and constant theme of their hope,
the goal and dream of their young men, they did not become an American people.

When they did, the great determining movement of our
history began.   The very visages of the people changed.
That alert movement of the eye, that openness to every
thought of enterprise or adventure, that nomadic habit
which knows no fixed home and has plans ready to be
carried any whither,—all the marks of the authentic type
of the "American" as we know him came into our life.
The crack of the whip and the song of the teamster, the
heaving chorus of boatmen poling their heavy rafts upon
the rivers, the laughter of the camp, the sound of bodies of
men in the still forests, became the characteristic notes in
our air.   A roughened race, embrowned in the sun, hardened in manner by a coarse life of change and danger,
loving the rude woods and the crack of the rifle, living to
begin something new every day, striking with the broad
and open hand, delicate in nothing but the touch of the
trigger, leaving cities in its track as if by accident rather
than design, settling again to the steady ways of a fixed
life only when it must: such was the American people
whose achievement it was to be to take possession of their
continent from end to end ere their national government
was a single century old.   The picture is a very singular
one!   Settled life and wild side by side: civilization frayed
at the edges,—taken forward in rough and ready fashion,
with a song and a swagger,—not by statesmen, but by
woodsmen and drovers, with axes and whips and rifles in
their hands, clad in buckskin, like huntsmen.

It has been said that we have here repeated some of the
first processes of history; that the life and methods of our
frontiersmen take us back to the fortunes and hopes of

the men who crossed Europe when her forests, too, were
still thick upon her.   But the difference is really very fundamental, and much more worthy of remark than the likeness.   Those shadowy masses of men whom we see moving upon the face of the earth in the far-away, questionable days when states were forming: even those stalwart
figures we see so well as they emerge from the deep forests
of Germany, to displace the Roman in all his western
provinces and set up the states we know and marvel upon
at this day, show us men working their new work at their
own level.   They do not turn back a long cycle of years
from the old and settled States, the ordered cities, the tilled
fields, and the elaborated governments of an ancient civilization, to begin as it were once more at the beginning.
They carry alike their homes and their States with them
in the camp and upon the ordered march of the host.
They are men of the forest, or else men hardened always
to take the sea in open boats.   They live no more roughly
in the new lands than in the old.   The world has been
frontier for them from the first.   They may go forward
with their life in these new seats from where they left off
in the old.   How different the circumstances of our first
settlement and the building of new States on this side the
sea!   Englishmen, bred in law and ordered government
ever since the Norman lawyers were followed a long five
hundred years ago across the narrow seas by those masterful administrators of the strong Plantagenet race, leave
an ancient realm and come into a wilderness where States
have never been; leave a land of art and letters, which
saw but yesterday "the spacious times of great Elizabeth," where Shakespeare still lives in the gracious leisure
of his closing days at Stratford, where cities teem with
trade and men go bravely dight in cloth of gold, and turn
back six centuries,—nay, a thousand years and more,—
to the first work of building States in a wilderness!   They
bring the steadied habits and sobered thoughts of an
ancient realm into the wild air of an untouched continent.
The weary stretches of a vast sea lie, like a full thousand
years of time, between them and the life in which till now
all their thought was bred.   Here they stand, as it were,
with all their tools left behind, centuries struck out of
their reckoning, driven back upon the long dormant in-

stincts and forgotten craft of their race, not used this long age. Look how singular a thing: the work of a primitive race, the thought of a civilized! Hence the strange, almost grotesque groupings of thought and affairs in that first day of our history. Subtle politicians speak the phrases and practice the arts of intricate diplomacy from council chambers placed within log-huts within a clearing. Men in ruffs and lace and polished shoe-buckles thread the lonely glades of primeval forests. The microscopical distinctions of the schools, the thin notes of a metaphysical theology are woven in and out through the labyrinths of grave sermons that run hours long upon the still air of the wilderness. Belief in dim refinements of dogma is made the test for man or woman who seeks admission to a company of pioneers. When went there by an age since the great flood when so singular a thing was seen as this: thousands of civilized men suddenly rusticated and bade to do the work of primitive peoples,—Europe frontiered!

Of course there was a deep change wrought, if not in these men, at any rate in their children; and every generation saw the change deepen. It must seem to every thoughtful man a notable thing how, while the change was wrought, the simples of things complex were revealed in the clear air of the New World: how all accidentals seemed to fall away from the structure of government, and the simple first principles were laid bare that abide always; how social distinctions were stripped off, shown to be the mere cloaks and masks they were, and every man brought once again to a clear realization of his actual relations to his fellows! It was as if trained and sophisticated men had been rid of a sudden of their sophistication and of all the theory of their life, and left with nothing but their discipline of faculty, a schooled and sobered instinct. And the fact that we kept always, for close upon three hundred years, a like element in our life, a frontier people always in our van, is, so far, the central and determining fact of our national history. "East" and "West," an ever-changing line, but an unvarying experience and a constant leaven of change working always within the body of our folk. Our political, our economic, our social life has felt this potent influence from the wild border all our history through. The "West" is the great word of our

history. The "Westerner" has been the type and master
of our American life. Now at length, as I have said, we
have lost our frontier: our front lies almost unbroken
along all the great coast-line of the western sea. The
Westerner, in some day soon to come, will pass out of our
life, as he so long ago passed out of the life of the Old
World. Then a new epoch will open for us. Perhaps it
has opened already. Slowly we shall grow old, compact
our people, study the delicate adjustments of an intricate
society, and ponder the niceties, as we have hitherto pon-
dered the bulks and structural framework, of government.
Have we not, indeed, already come to these things? But
the past we know. We can "see it steady and see it
whole"; and its central movement and motive are gross
and obvious to the eye.

Till the first century of the Constitution is rounded out
we stand all the while in the presence of that stupendous
westward movement which has filled the continent: so
vast, so various, at times so tragical, so swept by passion.
Through all the long time there has been a line of rude
settlements along our front wherein the same tests of
power and of institutions were still being made that were
made first upon the sloping banks of the rivers of old
Virginia and within the long sweep of the Bay of Massachusetts. The new life of the West has reacted all the
while—who shall say how powerfully?—upon the older
life of the East; and yet the East has molded the West
as if she sent forward to it through every decade of the
long process the chosen impulses and suggestions of history. The West has taken strength, thought, training,
selected aptitudes out of the old treasures of the East,—
as if out of a new Orient; while the East has itself been
kept fresh, vital, alert, originative by the West, her blood
quickened all the while, her youth through every age renewed. Who can say in a word, in a sentence, in a volume, what destinies have been variously wrought, with
what new examples of growth and energy, while, upon this
unexampled scale, community has passed beyond community across the vast reaches of this great continent!

The great process is the more significant because it has
been distinctively a national process. Until the Union
was formed and we had consciously set out upon a separate

national career, we moved but timidly across the nearer hills. Our most remote settlements lay upon the rivers and in the open glades of Tennessee and Kentucky. It was in the years that immediately succeeded the war of 1812 that the movement into the West began to be a mighty migration. Till then our eyes had been more often in the East than in the West. Not only were foreign questions to be settled and our standing among the nations to be made good, but we still remained acutely conscious and deliberately conservative of our Old World connections. For all we were so new a people and lived so simple and separate a life, we had still the sobriety and the circumspect fashions of action that belong to an old society. We were, in government and manners, but a disconnected part of the world beyond the seas. Its thought and habit still set us our standards of speech and action. And this, not because of imitation, but because of actual and long-abiding political and social connection with the mother country. Our statesmen,—strike but the names of Samuel Adams and Patrick Henry from the list, together with all like untutored spirits, who stood for the new, unreverencing ardor of a young democracy,—our statesmen were such men as might have taken their places in the House of Commons or in the Cabinet at home as naturally and with as easy an adjustment to their place and task as in the Continental Congress or in the immortal Constitutional Convention. Think of the stately ways and the grand air and the authoritative social understandings of the generation that set the new government afoot,—the generation of Washington and John Adams. Think, too, of the conservative tradition that guided all the early history of that government: that early line of gentlemen Presidents: that steady "cabinet succession to the Presidency" which came at length to seem almost like an oligarchy to the impatient men who were shut out from it. The line ended, with a sort of chill, in stiff John Quincy Adams, too cold a man to be a people's prince after the old order of Presidents; and the year 1829, which saw Jackson come in, saw the old order go out.

The date is significant. Since the war of 1812, undertaken as if to set us free to move westward, seven States had been admitted to the Union: and the whole number

of States was advanced to twenty-four. Eleven new
States had come into partnership with the old thirteen.
The voice of the West rang through all our counsels; and,
in Jackson, the new partners took possession of the Government. It is worth while to remember how men stood
amazed at the change: how startled, chagrined, dismayed
the conservative States of the East were at the revolution
they saw effected, the riot of change they saw set in; and
no man who has once read the singular story can forget
how the eight years Jackson reigned saw the Government,
and politics themselves, transformed. For long,—the story
being written in the regions where the shock and surprise
of the change was greatest,—the period of this momentous
revolution was spoken of amongst us as a period of degeneration, the birth-time of a deep and permanent demoralization in our politics. But we see it differently now.
Whether we have any taste or stomach for that rough age
or not, however much we may wish that the old order
might have stood, the generation of Madison and Adams
have been prolonged, and the good tradition of the early
days handed on unbroken and unsullied, we now know
that what the nation underwent in that day of change was
not degeneration, great and perilous as were the errors of
the time, but regeneration. The old order was changed,
once and for all. A new nation stepped, with a touch
of swagger, upon the stage,—a nation which had broken
alike with the traditions and with the wisely wrought experience of the Old World, and which, with all the haste
and rashness of youth, was minded to work out a separate
policy and destiny of its own. It was a day of hazards,
but there was nothing sinister at the heart of the new
plan. It was a wasteful experiment, to fling out, without
wise guides, upon untried ways; but an abounding continent afforded enough and to spare even for the wasteful. It was sure to be so with a nation that came out of
the secluded vales of a virgin continent. It was the bold
frontier voice of the West sounding in affairs. The timid
shivered, but the robust waxed strong and rejoiced, in the
tonic air of the new day.

It was then we swung out into the main paths of our
history. The new voices that called us were first silvery,
like the voice of Henry Clay, and spoke old familiar words

of eloquence.   The first spokesmen of the West even tried
to con the classics, and spoke incongruously in the phrases
of politics long dead and gone to dust, as Benton did.
But presently the tone changed, and it was the truculent
and masterful accents of the real frontiersman that rang
dominant above the rest, harsh, impatient, and with an
evident dash of temper.   The East slowly accustomed
itself to the change; caught the movement, though it
grumbled and even trembled at the pace; and managed
most of the time to keep in the running.   But it was
always henceforth to be the West that set the pace.
There is no mistaking the questions that have ruled our
spirits as a nation during the present century.   The public
land question, the tariff question, and the question of
slavery,—these dominate from first to last.   It was the
West that made each one of these the question that it
was.   Without the free lands to which every man who
chose might go, there would not have been that easy
prosperity of life and that high standard of abundance
which seemed to render it necessary that, if we were to
have manufactures and a diversified industry at all, we
should foster new undertakings by a system of protection
which would make the profits of the factory as certain and
as abundant as the profits of the farm.   It was the constant movement of the population, the constant march of
wagon-trains into the West, that made it so cardinal a
matter of policy whether the great national domain should
be free land or not: and that was the land question.   It
was the settlement of the West that transformed slavery
from an accepted institution into passionate matter of
controversy.

Slavery within the States of the Union stood sufficiently
protected by every solemn sanction the Constitution could
afford.   No man could touch it there, think, or hope, or
purpose what he might.   But where new States were to
be made it was not so.   There at every step choice must
be made: slavery or no slavery?—a new choice for every
new State: a fresh act of origination to go with every
fresh act of organization.   Had there been no Territories,
there could have been no slavery question, except by
revolution and contempt of fundamental law.   But with
a continent to be peopled, the choice thrust itself insist-

ently forward at every step and upon every hand. This was the slavery question: not what should be done to reverse the past, but what should be done to redeem the future. It was so men of that day saw it,—and so also must historians see it. We must not mistake the pro- gramme of the Anti-Slavery Society for the platform of the Republican party, or forget that the very war itself was begun ere any purpose of abolition took shape amongst those who were statesmen and in authority. It was a question, not of freeing men, but of preserving a Free Soil. Kansas showed us what the problem was, not South Carolina: and it was the Supreme Court, not the slave-owners, who formulated the matter for our thought and purpose.

And so, upon every hand and throughout every national question, was the commerce between East and West made up: that commerce and exchange of ideas, inclinations, purposes, and principles which has constituted the moving force of our life as a nation. Men illustrate the operation of these singular forces better than questions can: and no man illustrates it better than Abraham Lincoln.—

> " Great captains with their guns and drums
> Disturb our judgment for the hour;
> But at last silence comes:
> These all are gone, and, standing like a tower,
> Our children shall behold his fame,
> The kindly-earnest, brave, foreseeing man,
> Sagacious, patient, dreading praise not blame,
> New birth of our new soil, the first American."

It is a poet's verdict; but it rings in the authentic tone of the seer. It must be also the verdict of history. He would be a rash man who should say he understood Abraham Lincoln. No doubt natures deep as his, and various almost to the point of self-contradiction, can be sounded only by the judgment of men of a like sort,—if any such there be. But some things we all may see and judge concerning him. You have in him the type and flower of our growth. It is as if Nature had made a typical American, and then had added with liberal hand the royal quality of genius, to show us what the type could be. Lincoln owed nothing to his birth, everything

to his growth: had no training save what he gave himself;
no nurture, but only a wild and native strength. His life
was his schooling, and every day of it gave to his character
a new touch of development. His manhood not only, but
his perception also, expanded with his life. His eyes, as
they looked more and more abroad, beheld the national
life, and comprehended it: and the lad who had been so
rough-cut a provincial became, when grown to manhood,
the one leader in all the nation who held the whole people
singly in his heart:—held even the Southern people there,
and would have won them back. And so we have in him
what we must call the perfect development of native
strength, the rounding out and nationalization of the
provincial. Andrew Jackson was a type, not of the nation,
but of the West. For all the tenderness there was in the
stormy heart of the masterful man, and stanch and simple
loyalty to all who loved him, he learned nothing in the
East; kept always the flavor of the rough school in which
he had been bred; was never more than a frontier soldier
and gentleman. Lincoln differed from Jackson by all the
length of his unmatched capacity to learn. Jackson could
understand only men of his own kind; Lincoln could understand men of all sorts and from every region of the
land: seemed himself, indeed, to be all men by turns, as
mood succeeded mood in his strange nature. He never
ceased to stand, in his bony angles, the express image of
the ungainly frontiersman. His mind never lost the vein
of coarseness that had marked him grossly when a youth.
And yet how he grew and strengthened in the real stuff of
dignity and greatness: how nobly he could bear himself
without the aid of grace! He kept always the shrewd and
seeing eye of the woodsman and the hunter, and the
flavor of wild life never left him: and yet how easily his
view widened to great affairs; how surely he perceived the
value and the significance of whatever touched him and
made him neighbor to itself!

Lincoln's marvelous capacity to extend his comprehension to the measure of what he had in hand is the one
distinguishing mark of the man: and to study the development of that capacity in him is little less than to study,
where it is as it were perfectly registered, the national life
itself. This boy lived his youth in Illinois when it was a

frontier State. The youth of the State was coincident
with his own: and man and State kept equal pace in their
striding advance to maturity. The frontier population
was an intensely political population. It felt to the quick
the throb of the nation's life,—for the nation's life ran
through it, going its eager way to the westward. The
West was not separate from the East. Its communities
were every day receiving fresh members from the East,
and the fresh impulse of direct suggestion. Their blood
flowed to them straight from the warmest veins of the
older communities. More than that, elements which were
separated in the East were mingled in the West: which
displayed to the eye as it were a sort of epitome of the
most active and permanent forces of the national life. In
such communities as these Lincoln mixed daily from the
first with men of every sort and from every quarter of
the country. With them he discussed neighborhood
politics, the politics of the State, the politics of the nation,
—and his mind became traveled as he talked. How
plainly amongst such neighbors, there in Illinois, must it
have become evident that national questions were center-
ing more and more in the West as the years went by:
coming as it were to meet them. Lincoln went twice
down the Mississippi, upon the slow rafts that carried
wares to its mouth, and saw with his own eyes, so used
to look directly and point-blank upon men and affairs,
characteristic regions of the South. He worked his way
slowly and sagaciously, with that larger sort of sagacity
which so marked him all his life, into the active business
of State politics; sat twice in the State legislature, and
then for a term in Congress,—his sensitive and seeing
mind open all the while to every turn of fortune and every
touch of nature in the moving affairs he looked upon. All
the while, too, he continued to canvass, piece by piece,
every item of politics, as of old, with his neighbors,
familiarly around the stove, or upon the corners of the
street, or more formally upon the stump; and kept always
in direct contact with the ordinary views of ordinary men.
Meanwhile he read, as nobody else around him read, and
sought to gain a complete mastery over speech, with the
conscious purpose to prevail in its use; derived zest from
the curious study of mathematical proof, and amusement

as well as strength from the practice of clean and naked statements of truth. It was all irregularly done, but strenuously, with the same instinct throughout, and with a steady access of facility and power. There was no sudden leap for this man, any more than for other men, from crudeness to finished power, from an understanding of the people of Illinois to an understanding of the people of the United States. And thus he came at last, with infinite pains and a wonder of endurance, to his great national task with a self-trained capacity which no man could match, and made upon a scale as liberal as the life of the people. You could not then set this athlete a pace in learning or in perceiving that was too hard for him. He knew the people and their life as no other man did or could: and now stands in his place singular in all the annals of mankind, the "brave, sagacious, foreseeing, patient man" of the people, "new birth of our new soil, the first American."

We have here a national man presiding over sectional men. Lincoln understood the East better than the East understood him or the people from whom he sprung: and this is every way a very noteworthy circumstance. For my part, I read a lesson in the singular career of this great man. Is it possible the East remains sectional while the West broadens to a wider view?—

> "Be strong-backed, brown-handed, upright as your pines;
>   By the scale of a hemisphere shape your designs,"

is an inspiring programme for the woodsman and the pioneer; but how are you to be brown-handed in a city office? What if you never see the upright pines? How are you to have so big a purpose on so small a part of the hemisphere? As it has grown old, unquestionably, the East has grown sectional. There is no suggestion of the prairie in its city streets, or of the embrowned ranchman and farmer in its well-dressed men. Its ports teem with shipping from Europe and the Indies. Its newspapers run upon the themes of an Old World. It hears of the great plains of the continent as of foreign parts, which it may never think to see except from a car window. Its life is self-centered and selfish. The West, save where special interests center (as in those pockets of silver where men's eyes catch as it were an eager gleam from the very ore itself): the West is in less danger of sectionalization. Who shall say in that wide country where one region ends and another begins, or, in that free and changing society, where one class ends and another begins?

This, surely, is the moral of our history. The East has spent and been spent for the West: has given forth her energy, her young men and her substance, for the new regions that have been a-making all the century through. But has she learned as much as she has taught, or taken as much as she has given? Look what it is that has now at last taken place. The westward march has stopped, upon the final slopes of the Pacific; and now the plot thickens. Populations turn upon their old paths, fill in the spaces they passed by neglected in their first journey in search of a land of promise; settle to a life such as the East knows as well as the West,—nay, much better. With the change, the pause, the settlement, our people draw into closer groups, stand face to face, to know each other and be known: and the time has come for the East to learn in her turn; to broaden her understanding of political and economic conditions to the scale of a hemisphere, as her own poet bade. Let us be sure that we get the national temperament; send our minds abroad upon the continent, become neighbors to all the people that live upon it, and lovers of them all, as Lincoln was.

Read but your history aright, and you shall not find the task too hard. Your own local history, look but deep enough, tells the tale you must take to heart. Here upon our own seaboard, as truly as ever in the West, was once a national frontier, with an elder East beyond the seas. Here, too, various peoples combined, and elements separated elsewhere effected a tolerant and wholesome mixture. Here, too, the national stream flowed full and strong, bearing a thousand things upon its currents. Let us resume and keep the vision of that time; know ourselves, our neighbors, our destiny, with lifted and open eyes; see our history truly, in its great proportions; be ourselves liberal as the great principles we profess; and so be the people who might have again the heroic adventures and do again the heroic work of the past. 'Tis thus we shall renew our youth and secure our age against decay.

ROBERT CHARLES WINTHROP

THE DEATH OF JOHN C. CALHOUN

[Address by Robert Charles Winthrop, statesman and orator (born in Boston, May 12, 1809; died there, November 17, 1894), delivered in the House of Representatives, Washington, April 1, 1850, on the announcement of Mr. Calhoun's death.]

I am not unaware, Mr. Speaker, that the voice of New England has already been heard to-day, in its most authentic and most impressive tones, in the other wing of the Capitol. But it has been suggested to me, and the suggestion has met with the promptest assent from my own heart, that here, also, that voice should not be altogether mute on this occasion.

The distinguished person, whose death has been announced to us in the resolutions of the Senate, belongs not, indeed, to us. It is not ours to pronounce his eulogy. It is not ours, certainly, to appropriate his fame. But it is ours to bear witness to his character, to do justice to his virtue, to unite in paying honor to his memory, and to offer our heartfelt sympathies, as I now do, to those who have been called to sustain so great a bereavement.

We have been told, sir, by more than one adventurous navigator, that it was worth all the privations and perils of a protracted voyage beyond the line, to obtain even a passing view of the Southern Cross,—that great constellation of the Southern hemisphere. We can imagine, then, what would be the emotions of those who have always enjoyed the light of that magnificent luminary, and who have taken their daily and their nightly direction from its refulgent rays, if it were suddenly blotted out from the sky.

Such, sir, and so deep, I can conceive to be the emotions at this hour, of not a few of the honored friends and associates whom I see around me. Indeed, no one who has been ever so distant an observer of the course of public affairs for a quarter of a century past can fail to realize that a star of the first magnitude has been struck from our political firmament. Let us hope, sir, that it has only been transferred to a higher and purer sphere, where it may shine on with undimmed brilliancy forever!

Mr. Speaker, it is for others to enter into the details of Mr. Calhoun's life and services. It is for others to illustrate and to vindicate his peculiar opinions and principles. It is for me to speak of him only as he was known to the country at large, and to all, without distinction of party, who have represented the country of late years, in either branch of the National Councils.

And speaking of him thus, sir, I cannot hesitate to say, that, among what may be called the second generation of American statesmen since the adoption of the Federal Constitution, there has been no man of a more marked character, of more pronounced qualities, or of a wider and more deserved distinction.

The mere length and variety of his public services, in almost every branch of the National Government, running through a continuous period of almost forty years,— as a member of this House, as Secretary of War, as Vice-President of the United States, as Secretary of State, and as a Senator from his own adored and adoring South Carolina,—would alone have secured him a conspicuous and permanent place upon our public records.

But he has left better titles to remembrance than any which mere office can bestow. There was an unsullied purity in his private life; there was an inflexible integrity in his public conduct; there was an indescribable fascination in his familiar conversation; there was a condensed energy in his formal discourse; there was a quickness of perception, a vigor of deduction, a directness and a devotedness of purpose, in all that he said, or wrote, or did; there was a Roman dignity in his whole Senatorial deportment; which, together, made up a character, which cannot fail to be contemplated and admired to the latest posterity.

I have said, sir, that New England can appropriate no

part of his fame.   But we may be permitted to remember, that it was in our schools of learning and of law that he was trained up for the great contests which awaited him in the forum or the Senate chamber.   Nor can we forget how long and how intimately he was associated, in the Executive or Legislative branches of the Government, with more than one of our own most cherished statesmen.

The loss of such a man, sir, creates a sensible gap in the public councils.   To the State which he represented, and the section of country with which he was so peculiarly identified, no stranger tongue may venture to attempt words of adequate consolation.   But let us hope that the event may not be without a wholesome and healing influence upon the troubles of the times.   Let us heed the voice, which comes to us all, both as individuals and as public officers, in so solemn and signal a providence of God.   Let us remember, that, whatever happens to the Republic, we must die!   Let us reflect how vain are the personal strifes and partisan contests in which we daily engage, in view of the great account which we may so soon be called on to render!   Well may we exclaim, as Cicero exclaimed, in considering the death of Crassus: "*O fal lacem hominum spem, fragilem que fortunam, et inanes nostras contentiones!*"

Finally, sir, let us find fresh bonds of brotherhood and of union in the cherished memories of those who have gone before us; and let us resolve that, in so far as in us lies, the day shall never come, when New England men may not speak of the great names of the South, whether among the dead or the living, as of Americans and fellow countrymen!

THE DEATH OF PRESIDENT TAYLOR

[Address by Robert Charles Winthrop, delivered in the House of Representatives, Washington, D. C., July 10, 1850, on the announcement of the death of General Taylor.]

It would not be easily excused, Mr. Speaker, by those whom I represent in this Hall, if there were no Massachusetts voice to respond to the eulogy which has been pronounced by Louisiana upon her illustrious and lamented son.   Indeed, neither my personal feelings nor my political relations, either to the living or to the dead, would permit me to remain altogether silent on this occasion.   And yet, sir, I confess, I know not how to say anything satisfactory to myself, or suitable to the circumstances of the hour.

The event which has just been officially announced, has come upon us so suddenly—has so overwhelmed us with mingled emotions of surprise and sadness—that all ordinary forms of expression seem to lose their significance, and one would fain bow his head to the blow in silence, until its first shock has in some degree passed away.

Certainly, sir, no one can fail to realize that a most momentous and mysterious Providence has been manifested in our midst.   At a moment when, more than almost ever before in our history, the destinies of our country seemed, to all human sight, to be inseparably associated with the character and conduct of its Chief Executive Magistrate, that Magistrate has been summoned from his post, by the only messenger whose mandates he might not have defied, and has been withdrawn forever from the sphere of human existence!

There are those of us, I need not say, sir, who had looked to him with affection and reverence as our chosen leader and guide in the difficulties and perplexities by which we are surrounded.   There are those of us, who had relied confidently on him, as upon no other man, to uphold the Constitution and maintain the Union of the country in that future, upon which " shadows, clouds, and darkness " may well be said to rest.   And, as we now behold him, borne away by the hand of God from our sight, in the very hour of peril, we can hardly repress the exclamation, which was applied to the departing prophet of old: "My father, my father! the chariot of Israel and the horsemen thereof."

Let me not even seem to imply, however, that the death of General Taylor is anything less than a national loss. There may be, and we know there is, in this event, a privileged and pre-eminent grief for his immediate family and relatives, to which we can only offer the assurance of our heartfelt sympathy. There is, too, a peculiar sorrow for his political friends and supporters, which we would not affect to conceal. But the whole people of the United States will feel, and will bear witness, when they receive these melancholy tidings, that they have all been called to sustain a most afflicting national bereavement.

I hazard nothing, sir, in saying, that the roll of our Chief Magistrates, since 1789, illustrious as it is, presents the name of no man who has enjoyed a higher reputation with his contemporaries, or who will enjoy a higher reputation with posterity, than Zachary Taylor, for some of the best and noblest qualities which adorn our nature.

His indomitable courage, his unimpeachable honesty, his Spartan simplicity and sagacity, his frankness, kindness, moderation, and magnanimity, his fidelity to his friends, his generosity and humanity to his enemies, the purity of his private life, the patriotism of his public principles, will never cease to be cherished in the grateful remembrance of all just men and all true-hearted Americans.

As a Soldier and a General, his fame is associated with some of the proudest and most thrilling scenes of our military history. He may be literally said to have conquered every enemy he has met save only that last enemy, to which we must all, in turn, surrender.

As a Civilian and Statesman, during the brief period in which he has been permitted to enjoy the transcendent honors which a grateful country had awarded him, he has given proof of a devotion to duty, of an attachment to the Constitution and the Union, of a patriotic determination to maintain the peace of our country, which no trials or temptations could shake. He has borne his faculties meekly but firmly. He has been "clear in his great office." He has known no local partialities or prejudices, but has proved himself capable of embracing his whole country, in the comprehensive affections and regards of a large and generous heart.

But he has fallen almost at the threshold of his civil career and at a moment when some of us were looking to him to render services to the country, which we had thought no other man could perform. Certainly, sir, he has died too soon for everybody but himself. We can hardly find it in our hearts to repine that the good old man has gone to his rest. We would not disturb the repose in which the brave old soldier sleeps. His part in life had been long and faithfully performed. In his own last words, " he had always done his duty, and he was not afraid to die." But our regrets for ourselves and for our country are deep, strong, and unfeigned. " He should have died hereafter."

Sir, it was a fit and beautiful circumstance in the close of such a career, that his last official appearance was at the celebration of the birthday of our National Independence, and more especially, that his last public act was an act of homage to the memory of him, whose example he had ever revered and followed, and who, as he himself so well said, "was, by so many titles, the Father of his Country."

And now, Mr. Speaker, let us hope that this event may teach us all how vain is our reliance upon any arm of flesh. Let us hope that it may impress us with a solemn sense of our national as well as individual dependence on a higher than human Power. Let us remember that " the Lord is king, be the people never so impatient! that He sitteth between the cherubim, be the earth never so unquiet." Let us, in language which is now hallowed to us all, as having been the closing and crowning sentiment of the brief but admirable Inaugural Address with which this illustrious Patriot opened his Presidential term, and which it is my privilege to read at this moment from the very copy from which it was originally read by himself to the American people, on the fourth day of March, 1849,— " Let us," in language in which "he, being dead, yet speaketh "—" let us invoke a continuance of the same

Protecting Care which has led us from small beginnings to the eminence we this day occupy; and let us seek to deserve that continuance by prudence and moderation in our councils; by well-directed attempts to assuage the bitterness which too often marks unavoidable differences of opinion; by the promulgation and practice of just and liberal principles; and by an enlarged patriotism, which shall acknowledge no limits but those of our own wide-spread Republic."

EMILE ZOLA

APPEAL FOR DREYFUS

[Address by Emile Zola, novelist (born in Paris, April 2, 1840;
———), delivered to the jury at his trial for libel in connection with
the Dreyfus case, Paris, February 21, 1898.]

In the Chamber at the sitting of January 22, M. Meline,
the Prime Minister declared, amid the frantic applause of
his complaisant majority, that he had confidence in the
twelve citizens to whose hands he intrusted the defense
of the army. It was of you, gentlemen, that he spoke.
And just as General Billot dictated its decision to the
court martial intrusted with the acquittal of Major Esterhazy, by appealing from the tribune for respect for the
chose jugée, so likewise M. Meline wished to give you the
order to condemn me out of respect for the army which
he accuses me of having insulted!

I denounce to the conscience of honest men this pressure brought to bear by the constituted authorities upon
the justice of the country. These are abominable political
manœuvres, which dishonor a free nation. We shall see,
gentlemen, whether you will obey.

But it is not true that I am here in your presence by the
will of M. Meline. He yielded to the necessity of prose-
cuting me only in great trouble, in terror of the new step
which the advancing truth was about to take. This everybody knew. If I am before you, it is because I wished it.
I alone decided that this obscure, this abominable affair,
should be brought before your jurisdiction, and it is I
alone of my free will who chose you,—you, the loftiest, the
most direct emanation of French justice,—in order that
France might at last know all, and give her opinion. My

act had no other object, and my person is of no account. I have sacrificed it, in order to place in your hands not only the honor of the army, but the imperiled honor of the nation.

It appears that I was cherishing a dream in wishing to offer you all the proofs: considering you to be the sole worthy, the sole competent judge. They have begun by depriving you with the left hand of what they seemed to give you with the right. They pretended, indeed, to accept your jurisdiction, but if they had confidence in you to avenge the members of the court martial, there were still other officers who remained superior even to your jurisdiction. Let who can understand. It is absurdity doubled with hypocrisy, and it is abundantly clear that they dreaded your good sense,—that they dared not run the risk of letting us tell all and of letting you judge the whole matter. They pretend that they wished to limit the scandal. What do you think of this scandal? Of my act, which consisted in bringing the matter before you,— in wishing the people, incarnate in you, to be the judge? They pretend also that they could not accept a revision in disguise, thus confessing that in reality they have but one dread, that of your sovereign control. The law has in you its entire representation, and it is this law of the people elect that I have wished for,—this law which, as a good citizen, I hold in profound respect, and not the suspicious procedure whereby they hoped to make you a derision.

I am thus excused, gentlemen, for having brought you here from your private affairs without being able to inundate you with the full flood of light of which I dreamed. The light, the whole light,—this was my sole, my passionate desire! And this trial has just proved it. We have had to fight—step by step—against an extraordinarily obstinate desire for darkness. A battle has been necessary to obtain every atom of truth. Everything has been refused us. Our witnesses have been terrorized in the hope of preventing us from proving our point. And it is on your behalf alone that we have fought, that this proof might be put before you in its entirety, so that you might give your opinion without remorse in your consciences. I am certain, therefore, that you will give us credit for our efforts, and that, moreover, sufficient light has been thrown upon the affair.

You have heard the witnesses; you are about to hear my counsel, who will tell you the true story: the story that maddens everybody and which no one knows. I am, therefore, at my ease. You have the truth at last, and it will do its work. M. Meline thought to dictate your decision by intrusting to you the honor of the army. And it is in the name of the honor of the army that I too appeal to your justice.

I give M. Meline the most direct contradiction. Never have I insulted the army. I spoke, on the contrary, of my sympathy, my respect for the nation in arms, for our dear soldiers of France, who would rise at the first menace to defend the soil of France. And it is just as false that I attacked the chiefs, the generals who would lead them to victory. If certain persons at the War Office have compromised the army itself by their acts, is it to insult the whole army to say so? Is it not rather to act as a good citizen to separate it from all that compromises it, to give the alarm, so that the blunders which alone have been the cause of our defeat shall not occur again, and shall not lead us to fresh disaster.

I am not defending myself, moreover. I leave history to judge my act, which was a necessary one; but I affirm that the army is dishonored when gendarmes are allowed to embrace Major Esterhazy after the abominable letters written by him. I affirm that that valiant army is insulted daily by the bandits who, on the plea of defending it, sully it by their degrading championship,—who trail in the mud all that France still honors as good and great. I affirm that those who dishonor that great national army are those who mingle cries of "Vive l'armee!" with those of "A bas les juifs!" and "Vive Esterhazy!" Grand Dieu! the people of St. Louis, of Bayard, of Condé, and of Hoche: the people which counts a hundred great victories, the people of the great wars of the Republic and the Empire, the people whose power, grace, and generosity have dazzled the world, crying "Vive Esterhazy!" It is a shame the stain of which our efforts on behalf of truth and justice can alone wash off!

You know the legend which has grown up: Dreyfus was

condemned justly and legally by seven infallible officers, whom it is impossible even to suspect of a blunder without insulting the whole army. Dreyfus expiates in merited torments his abominable crime. And, as he is a Jew, a Jewish syndicate is formed, an international *sans patrie* syndicate, disposing of hundreds of millions, the object of which is to save the traitor at any price, even by the most shameless intrigues. And thereupon this syndicate began to heap crime on crime: buying consciences, casting France into a disastrous agitation, resolved on selling her to the enemy, willing even to drive all Europe into a general war rather than renounce its terrible plan.

It is very simple, nay childish, if not imbecile. But it is with this poisoned bread that the unclean Press has been nourishing our poor people now for some months. And it is not surprising if we are witnessing a dangerous crisis; for when folly and lies are thus sown broadcast, you necessarily reap insanity.

Gentlemen, I would not insult you by supposing that you have yourselves been duped by this nursery tale. I know you; I know who you are. You are the heart and the reason of Paris, of my great Paris: where I was born, which I love with an infinite tenderness, which I have been studying and writing of now for forty years. And I know likewise what is now passing in your brains; for, before coming to sit here as defendant, I sat there on the bench where you are now. You represent there the average opinion; you try to illustrate prudence and justice in the mass. Soon I shall be in thought with you in the room where you deliberate, and I am convinced that your effort will be to safeguard your interests as citizens, which are, of course, the interests of the whole nation. You may make a mistake, but you will do so in the thought that while securing your own weal you are securing the weal of all.

I see you at your homes at evening under the lamp; I hear you talk with your friends; I accompany you into your factories and shops. You are all workers—some tradesmen, others manufacturers, some exercising liberal professions. And your very legitimate anxiety is the deplorable state into which business has fallen. Everywhere the present crisis threatens to become a disaster. The

receipts fall off; transactions become more and more difficult. So that the idea which you have brought here, the
thought which I read in your countenances, is that there
has been enough of this and that it must be ended. You
have not gone the length of saying, like many: " What
matters it that an innocent man is at the Ile du Diable?
Is the interest of a single man worth this disturbing a
great country? " But you say, nevertheless, that the agitation which we are raising, we who hunger for truth and
justice, costs too dear! And if you condemn me, gentlemen, it is that thought which will be at the bottom of
your verdict. You desire tranquillity for your homes, you
wish for the revival of business, and you may think that
by punishing me you will stop a campaign which is injurious to the interests of France.

Well, gentlemen, if that is your idea, you are entirely
mistaken. Do me the honor of believing that I am not
defending my liberty. By punishing me you would only
magnify me. Whoever suffers for truth and justice becomes august and sacred. Look at me. Have I the look
of a hireling, of a liar, and a traitor? Why should I be
playing a part? I have behind me neither political ambition nor sectarian passion. I am a free writer, who has
given his life to labor; who to-morrow will reenter the
ranks and resume his suspended task. And how stupid
are those who call me an Italian;—me, born of a French
mother, brought up by grandparents in the Beauce, peasants of that vigorous soil; me, who lost my father at seven
years of age, who did not go to Italy till I was fifty-four.
And yet, I am proud that my father was from Venice,—
the resplendent city whose ancient glory sings in all
memories. And even if I were not French, would not the
forty volumes in the French language, which I have sent
by millions of copies throughout the world, suffice to
make me a Frenchman?

So I do not defend myself. But what a blunder would
be yours if you were convinced that by striking me you
would reestablish order in our unfortunate country! Do
you not understand now that what the nation is dying of
is the obscurity in which there is such an obstinate determination to leave it? The blunders of those in authority
are being heaped upon those of others; one lie necessitates

another, so that the mass is becoming formidable. A judicial blunder was committed, and then to hide it a fresh crime against good sense and equity has had daily to be committed! The condemnation of an innocent man has involved the acquittal of a guilty man, and now to-day you are asked in turn to condemn me because I gave utterance to my pain on beholding our country embarked on this terrible course. Condemn me, then! But it will be one more fault added to the others—a fault the burden of which you will bear in history. And my condemnation, instead of restoring the peace for which you long, and which we all of us desire, will be only a fresh seed of passion and disorder. The cup, I tell you, is full; do not make it run over!

Why do you not exactly estimate the terrible crisis through which the country is passing? They say that we are the authors of the scandal, that it is lovers of truth and justice who are leading the nation astray, and urging it to riot. Really this is a mockery! To speak only of General Billot—was he not warned eighteen months ago? Did not Colonel Picquart insist that he should take in hand the matter of revision, if he did not wish the storm to burst and overturn everything? Did not M. Scheurer-Kestner, with tears in his eyes, beg him to think of France, and save her from such a catastrophe? No! our desire has been to facilitate everything, to allay everything: and if the country is now in trouble, the responsibility lies with the power, which, to cover the guilty, and in the further-ance of political interests, has denied everything, hoping to be strong enough to prevent the truth from being shed. It has manœuvred in behalf of darkness, and it alone is responsible for the present distraction of conscience!

The Dreyfus case! ah, gentlemen, that has now become a very small affair. It is lost and far-away in view of the terrifying questions to which it has given rise. There is no longer any Dreyfus case. The question now is whether France is still the France of the rights of man, the France that gave freedom to the world, and that ought to give it justice. Are we still the most noble, the most fraternal, the most generous nation? Shall we preserve our repu-tation in Europe for equity and humanity? Are not all the victories that we have won called in question? Open your eyes, and understand that, to be in such confusion, the French soul must have been stirred to its depths in face of a terrible danger. A nation cannot be thus upset without imperiling its moral existence. This is an exceptionally serious hour; the safety of the nation is at stake.

And when you shall have understood that, gentlemen, you will feel that but one remedy is possible,—to tell the truth, to do justice. Anything that keeps back the light, anything that adds darkness to darkness, will only prolong and aggravate the crisis. The rôle of good citizens, of those who feel it to be imperatively necessary to put an end to this matter, is to demand broad daylight. There are already many who think so. The men of literature, philosophy, and science are rising on every hand in the name of intelligence and reason. And I do not speak of the foreigner, of the shudder that has run through all Europe. Yet the foreigner is not necessarily the enemy. Let us not speak of the nations that may be our adversaries to-morrow. Great Russia, our ally, little and generous Holland; all the sympathetic peoples of the north; those lands of the French tongue, Switzerland and Belgium,—why are men's hearts so full, so overflowing with fraternal suffering? Do you dream then of a France isolated in the world? When you cross the frontier, do you wish them to forget your traditional renown for equity and humanity?

Alas! gentlemen, like so many others, you expect the thunderbolt to descend from heaven in proof of the innocence of Dreyfus. Truth does not come thus. It requires research and knowledge. We know well where the truth is, or where it might be found. But we dream of that only in the recesses of our souls, and we feel patriotic anguish lest we expose ourselves to the danger of having this proof some day cast in our face after having involved the honor of the army in a falsehood. I wish also to declare positively that, though, in the official notice of our list of witnesses we included certain ambassadors, we had decided in advance not to call them. Our boldness has provoked smiles. But I do not think that there was any real smiling in our foreign office, for there they must have understood! We intended to say to those who know the whole truth that we also know it. This truth is gossiped about at the embassies: to-morrow it will be known to all; and, if it is now impossible for us to seek it where it is concealed by official red tape, the Government which is not ignorant,—the Government which is convinced—as we are—of the innocence of Dreyfus, will be able, whenever it likes and without risk, to find witnesses who will demonstrate everything.

Dreyfus is innocent. I swear it! I stake my life on it —my honor! At this solemn moment, in the presence of this tribunal, which is the representative of human justice: before you, gentlemen, who are the very incarnation of the country, before the whole of France, before the whole world, I swear that Dreyfus is innocent. By my forty years of work, by the authority that this toil may have given me, I swear that Dreyfus is innocent. By the name I have made for myself, by my works which have helped for the expansion of French literature, I swear that Dreyfus is innocent. May all that melt away, may my works perish, if Dreyfus be not innocent! He is innocent. All seems against me—the two Chambers, the civil authority, the most widely-circulated journals, the public opinion which they have poisoned. And I have for me only the ideal,—an ideal of truth and justice. But I am quite calm; I shall conquer. I was determined that my country should not remain the victim of lies and injustice. I may be condemned here. The day will come when France will thank me for having helped to save her honor.